Frontispiece. Mujū Ichien (1226–1312), statue of Japanese cypress, 79.4 cm. high, late Kamakura. (Chōboji, Important Cultural Property.) *Photo by Chūnichi Shimbun.*

SUNY Series in Buddhist Studies
Kenneth Inada, Editor

Sand and Pebbles

(Shasekishū)

The Tales of Mujū Ichien, A Voice for Pluralism in Kamakura Buddhism

Robert E. Morrell

State University of New York Press

For Sachiko and Audrey

Published by
State University of New York Press, Albany

©1985 State University of New York

All rights reserved

Printed in the United States of America

For information, address State University of New York
Press, State University Plaza, Albany, N.Y., 12246

Library of Congress Cataloging in Publication Data

Mujū Ichien, 1227-1312.
    Sand and Pebbles (Shasekishū).
    (SUNY series in Buddhist studies)
    Translation of: Shasekishū.
    Bibliography: p. 343
    Includes index.
    1. Legends, Buddhist—Japan.   2. Tales—Japan.
3. Buddhism—Folklore.   I. Morrell, Robert E.
II. Title.   III. Series.
BQ5810.M8413   1985   895.6'32   84-16348
ISBN 0-88706-059-5
ISBN 0-88706-060-9 (pbk.)

Contents

List of Illustrations   vii

Preface   ix

Acknowledgments   xiii

Abbreviations   xvii

Chronology   xix

Introduction   1

Part I. Mujū Ichien (1226–1312)
    "No Fixed Abode": 1226–1261   13
    Chōboji: 1262–1312   35
    Mujū's World of Ideas   57

Part II. Sand and Pebbles (Shasekishū)
    Translations and Summaries   69

Part III. Casual Digressions (Zōtanshū)
    Selected Translations   273

Appendices
    A. Two Tokugawa Biographers: Kenryō and Tainin   283
    B. Mujū's Doctrinal Affiliations   287
    C. Mujū and the Esotericism of the Sambōin School 289
    D. Yamada Family Genealogy   291

Notes   293

Glossary of Selected Terms   331

Glossary of Selected Characters   339

Selected Bibliography   343

General Bibliography   347

Index   360

List of Illustrations

Frontispiece. Mujū Ichien (1226–1312)

Figure 1. Verse from Hui-neng's *Platform Sutra* in Mujū's
   calligraphy   28

Figure 2. Record of a Dream (*Musō no koto*)   38

Figure 3. Deed of Transfer (*Yuzurijō*) by which Mujū ceded the
   Chōboji to Muō in 1305   53

Figure 4. Map of Miya (Nagoya) showing the Relationship
   of Atsuta Shrine, Chōboji, Rengeji, and Tainin's Kōshōji   67

Figure 5. Woodblocks of the Jōkyō (1686) edition of the
   Shasekishū   72

Figure 6. Chōboji and Environs. From the *Owari meisho zue*
   (Illustrated Gazetteer of Owari Province), Latter Series,
   1880   270–271

Figure 7. Chōboji today   281

Preface

Mujū Ichien (1226–1312) was a teller of tales (*setsuwa*) and a writer of vernacular tracts (*kana hōgo*). His kind of literature is less familiar to us than that of the Heian courtier, the Kamakura warrior, or the Edo merchant, whose lives have been relatively well-documented by Western scholars. In our day the medieval monk, of the East or of the West, does not inspire easy rapport, either because of his austerity or his moralizing. But his acquaintance can often be rewarding, if we would take the time to enter empathetically into the thoughts and feelings of such a person who was deeply conscious of our common human concerns. It may take some time to adjust to his vocabulary and to his style of thought, but the effort will bring us not merely to a better understanding of an obscure Buddhist monk, but of ourselves as well.

The *Collection of Sand and Pebbles* (Shasekishū, 1279–1283), Mujū's major writing, was completed shortly after the second Mongol Invasion (about which he makes no comment). A little more than a century earlier Hōnen had initiated the popular movements of Pure Land Buddhism which were to engulf the traditional sects of Nara and Heian. Eisai and his successors had laid the foundations of Japanese Zen, and Nichiren had just recently advocated the invocation of the name of the *Lotus Sutra*. Rather late in life Mujū came under the influence of Rinzai's Enni Ben'en, sharing with him the belief that the new Zen practices were compatible with Shingon, Tendai, and the older schools of Nara Buddhism. In an age of increasing parochialism, Mujū stoutly defended the traditional Mahāyāna principle of "skillful means" (*hōben*) and had a sympathetic interest in every variety of thought and practice.

Mujū saw himself basically as a moralist, but later generations have been more interested in him as a storyteller — a storyteller with a message, no doubt, but still a storyteller. Modern literary scholars have little interest in his doctrinal theorizing. His current reputation rests mainly on the insights which he provides us into the everyday life of Kamakura Japan, often presented with a sense of humor which survives the differences of time and place. But in the end we cannot casually dismiss the underlying ideological assumptions of any writer without, in effect, imposing our own upon him. Mujū's world of ideas was rich in Buddhist lore and allusion, and we cannot enter that world without patience and a willingness to meet him on his own terms.

Most of what we know of Mujū's life must be gleaned from his own writings, especially the *Casual Digressions* (Zōtanshū, 1305) which he composed late in life. Sometimes we wish that we knew more of the external particulars, but Mujū's real biography is to be found in his sequence of thoughts, to which a close translation does little violence. The language may differ, but the pattern of interconnected ideas remains the same. Mujū reveals himself in his writings as an individual with his own distinctive presence. His voice may not be as elegant as Murasaki's nor as worldly-wise as Saikaku's; but it is a witty and intelligent voice, commenting in the vernacular and from first-hand experience, on one of the most intriguing moments of Japanese religious history, the early period of Kamakura Buddhism.

I have occasionally been surprised by readers who feel that I am too critical of Mujū in reconstructing his biography from the fragments which remain to us. So perhaps I should explain that my goal has been to create a balanced portrait, following Othello's ever-pertinent advice: "Speak of me as I am; nothing extenuate, nor set down aught in malice." Mujū's foibles, which he freely admits, help us to see him as a human being, a basically honest man with a sense of purpose, but with a realization of his own limitations and life's absurdities. We do not need another icon. The Kamakura period already provides us with more than enough of these; but they are too remote, and in the end, not really credible.

My rendering of the *Shasekishū* is part translation and part summary. To have provided detailed, footnoted translations of every argument and every citation would have added substantially to the size of this book, without a corresponding benefit to the reader. A friend once remarked that Mujū was badly in need of an editor. And the reason is not hard to locate: our moralist is not content to explain an issue from a single sectarian position. His syncretic stance requires that he show how it is supported from every possible point of view. But the details of this will interest only a few specialists in religious history, and they can be expected to check the original for themselves.

On the other hand, a sense of the book as a whole will concern most readers, and so editorial cuts must be made with care. I decided to solve the problem by alternating translations with summaries (indicated by italic type) and following the sequence of items just as they appear in the original. I begin with a literal translation of the Preface and the ten chapters of Book One, perhaps the most coherent of the *Shasekishū*'s ten books. Subsequently, the anecdotal material which was more developed, which appeared to have greater appeal as literature, or which was more influential on later readers and writers was selected for translation, with summaries provided for the rest and for the moralistic elaboration. But here, too, I felt that I should show the direction of the argument and provide at least the names of the scriptural sources cited in support of Mujū's thought. Then in Part III I have included a few selected translations from the *Casual Digressions.*

The reader will notice that I have tried to give an English equivalent in the translations and summaries for virtually every work cited. My reason is simple: the *names* of these scriptures *meant* something to Mujū and his contemporaries, and they should mean something to the reader of a translation. If the specialist cannot immediately guess the original from my English equivalent, he can quickly find it cross-listed in the index. We are still in the process of developing a standardized vocabulary for Buddhism in English, and it will take time. While "*Lotus Sutra*" is a concise, universally-understood equivalent for *Myōhōrengekyō* (or *Hokkekyō*; *Saddharmapuṇḍarīka-sūtra*), we are not so fortunate elsewhere. In general I have adopted English equivalents which others have proposed whenever it seemed that this would become the accepted term. But at times I have had to choose between alternatives whose merits could be argued either way. Shall we, for example, refer to the *Kegonkyō (Avataṃsaka-sūtra)* as the "Flower Ornament Scripture" (Cleary), or simply as the "Garland Sutra" (McCullough)? (Perhaps hoping that eventually we will all recognize "Garland" as easily as "Lotus," I have opted for the shorter equivalent.) With still other titles I have had to come up with my own translation.

Similarly, in the notes I have attached the T. *(Taishō Shinshū Daizōkyō)* number to Buddhist writings, not to be pedantic, but to encourage more precision through the use of this widely-accepted system of identification. (Again the *Kegonkyō* provides a good example: a writer might refer to any of three translations into Chinese; see note 14.)

Acknowledgments

My sincere thanks go to all who have directly or indirectly contributed to the appearance of this book. "I am a part of all that I have met," so I can here single out for special mention only a handful of the many who have been a positive influence. I must begin, of course, with my families both in the United States and in Japan, without whose long-term reinforcement no project at all would have been possible.

During my formative academic years I was fortunate to have been inspired by Miyamoto Shōson, Hori Ichirō, Murano Senchū, Sekiguchi Shindai, and T.R.V. Murti. Then, already some decades ago, Edward G. Seidensticker introduced me to Mujū at Stanford University. Robert H. Brower not only directed my first halting steps through the *Shasekishū* but perseveringly saw me through the dissertation. At the Stanford Center in Tokyo, William H. McCullough was a most helpful adviser.

Among those who continued to support my research at Washington University in St. Louis, were my colleagues Stanley Spector, J. Thomas Rimer and Robert H. Hegel. The university Graduate School helped me with Summer Research Grants, a semester's released time from teaching, and funds for miscellaneous expenses. The East Asian and Olin Libraries have been an invaluable resource. Debra Jones typed up the final manuscript. Deborah Moellering redrew the map of Miya.

In 1970 Roy E. Teele accepted translations from the *Shasekishū* for publication in *Literature East & West*. In 1971 a Fulbright-Hays Faculty Research/Study Award permitted me to spend six months in Japan, where Sakakura Atsuyoshi of Kyoto University gave me invaluable guidance. Subsequently, *Monumenta Nipponica* published my translation of Book One of the *Shasekishū*, and, some years later, Mujū's *Tsuma kagami*. Its editor, Michael Cooper, was most helpful.

As my manuscript began to take shape over the years, I was warmly encouraged by Kawabe Ryōsuke, the present abbot of

xiii

Mujū's Chōboji; and by the late Watanabe Tsunaya of Niigata University, the preeminent authority on the *Shasekishū*.

Now as my plans for a book on Mujū are about to be realized, I am fortunate to enjoy the help and cooperation of the staff of the State University of New York Press, including Kenneth Inada, William D. Eastman, Michele Martin, and Judith Block.

But certainly I owe a special debt of gratitude to my wife Sachiko, who has collaborated with me on this project over the years, answering my questions, providing direction, and accompanying me every step of the way back to Mujū's Kamakura.

In reprinting material from other sources, I have made every reasonable effort to observe the guidelines of fair use. Acknowledgment is made to the publishers and authors of the following books for permission to quote material or for advising me that the work is now in the public domain:

Yoshito S. Hakeda, *The Awakening of Faith*. New York & London: Copyright © 1967 by Columbia University Press.

Martin Colcutt, *Five Mountains: The Rinzai Zen Monastic Institution in Medieval Japan*. Cambridge and London: Copyright ©1981 by The President and Fellows of Harvard College.

Delmer M. Brown and Ichirō Ishida, *The Future and the Past: A translation and study of the Gukanshō, an interpretative history of Japan written in 1219*. Berkeley, Los Angeles and London: Copyright © 1979 by the Regents of the University of California.

Fung Yu-Lan, *A History of Chinese Philosophy*, Vol. II, translated by Derk Bodde. Princeton: Princeton University Press, 1953.

Burton Watson, tr. *Hsün Tsu*. New York and London: Copyright © 1963 by Columbia University Press.

Earl Miner, *Japanese Poetic Diaries*. Berkeley and Los Angeles: Copyright © 1969 by The Regents of the University of California.

Yoshito S. Hakeda, *Kūkai: Major Works*. New York and London: Copyright © 1972 by Columbia University Press.

Minoru Kiyota, *Shingon Buddhism: Theory and Practice*. Los Angeles-Tokyo: Copyright © 1978 by Buddhist Books International.

Marian Ury, *Tales of Times Now Past: Sixty-Two Stories from a Medieval Japanese Collection*. Berkeley, Los Angeles and London: Copyright © by the Regents of the University of California.

Hajime Nakamura, *Ways of Thinking of Eastern Peoples: India, China, Tibet, Japan*. Honolulu: The University Press of Hawaii. Copyright © 1964 by East-West Center Press.

Abbreviations

CD; Casual Digressions	Mujū's *Zōtanshū* (Collection of Casual Digressions, 1305). Translations based on Yamada and Miki, *Zōtanshū* (See Selected Bibliography.)
S&P; Sand and Pebbles	Mujū's *Shasekishū* (Collection of Sand and Pebbles, 1279–83). Translation based on Watanabe, *Shasekishū*, unless otherwise indicated.
Mirror	Mujū's *Tsuma kagami* (Mirror for Women, 1300). Translation based Miyasaka, ed. *Kana hōgoshū*.
Sketch	Kenryō's *Mujū Kokushi ryakuengi* (Biographical Sketch of Mujū Kokushi). See Appendix A.
Kigasaki	Kenryō's *Kigasaki ryakuengi* (Short History of Kigasaki), subsection of the *Sketch*.
Traces	Tainin's *Mujū Kokushi dōshakukō* (Religious Traces of National Teacher Mujū). See Appendix A.
T.	*Taishō shinshū daizōkyō* (Newly Revised Tripitaka of the Taishō Era), eds. Takakusu Junjirō, et al. Numbering through vol. 55 in Demieville, et al., eds. *Hōbōgirin: Fascicule Annexe.*

Chronology

949 B.C.	Death of Śākyamuni, the historic Buddha, according to traditional Sino-Japanese calculations (see 1052 A.D.).
406 A.D.	Kumārajīva translates *Lotus Sutra* into Chinese.
552 (538)	Traditional date for the introduction of Buddhism to Japan (*Nihon shoki*).
573–621	Prince Shōtoku, patron of Japanese Buddhism.
638–713	Hui-neng (J. Enō), sixth patriarch of Chinese Ch'an (Zen).

Nara Period 710–784

788	Saichō (Dengyō Daishi, 767–822) founds Tendai Enryakuji on Mt. Hiei.

Heian Period 794–1185

817	Kūkai (Kōbō Daishi, 774–835) founds Shingon Kongōbuji on Mt. Kōya.
985	*The Essentials of Salvation* (Ōjōyōshū) by the Tendai Amidist, Genshin (Eshin, 942–1017).
ca. 1001–15	Murasaki Shikibu: *The Tale of Genji* (Genji monogatari).
1052	First year of the Period of the Decline of the Law (*mappō*), beginning two millennia after the death of Śākyamuni.
1173–1232	Myōe (Kōben), Kegon reformer.
1175	Hōnen (Genkū, 1133–1212) founds Pure Land Sect (Jōdoshū), advocating exclusive practice of the invocation to Amida.

1179	Momooji, later renamed Chōboji, built by Yamada Shigetada (1165–1221).
1185	Final defeat of the Taira (Heike) clan by the Minamoto (Genji) at the Battle of Dan-no-Ura.
1189	Minamoto Yoshitsune (b. 1159) slain with Benkei at Koromo River.
1191	Myōan Eisai (1141–1215) returns to Japan with Lin-chi (Rinzai) Zen (Huang-lung line) and tea.

Kamakura Period 1192–1333

1192	Minamoto Yoritomo (1147–1199) establishes military government (*shōgunate*) at Kamakura.
1200	Kajiwara Kagetoki (Mujū's relation) slain with son Kagesue; Eisai founds Jufukuji, first Zen temple in Kamakura.
ca. 1190–1242	*Tales Gleaned at Uji* (Ujishūi monogatari), *setsuwa* collection.
1206	Teika, et al.: *New Collection of Ancient and Modern Times* (Shinkokinshū), eighth Imperial Anthology of *waka* poetry.
1212	Kamo no Chōmei (1153–1216): *An Account of My Hut* (Hōjōki).
1219	Jien (1155–1225): *Miscellany of Ignorant Views* (Gukanshō).
1221	Jōkyū War. Yamada Shigetada perishes; Akinaga miraculously saved.
1224	Shinran (1173–1262) composes *Teaching, Practice, Faith, Attainment* (Kyōgyōshin-shō); founds True Pure Land Sect (Jōdo Shinshū).
1226	Mujū Ichien (d. 1312) born in Kamakura.
1227	Dōgen Kigen (1200–1253), founder of Sōtō Zen, returns from China, composes *General Teaching for Meditation* (Fukan zazengi).
1241	Enni Ben'en (1202–1280) returns from China with Yang-ch'i transmission of Lin-chi (Rinzai) Zen.

1243	Mujū (age 18) takes tonsure at Hōonji in Hitachi province.
1245	Mujū becomes abbot of Hōonji.
1246	Dōgen builds Eiheiji in Echizen province.
1252	*Tales to Illustrate Ten Maxims* (Jikkinshō), *setsuwa* collection.
1253	Nichiren (1222–1282) founds Lotus Sect (Hokkeshū), advocating utterance of the title (*daimoku*) of the *Lotus Sutra*. Mujū leaves Hōonji.
1254	Tachibana Narisue: *Things Heard from Past and Present* (Kokonchomonjū), *setsuwa* collection.
1260	Mujū (35) practices *zazen* at Jufukuji, stops because of beriberi.
1262	Eizon (1201–1290), founder of Esoteric Disciplinary Sect, visits Chōboji; later in the year Mujū becomes "founder" (*kaizan*) of the reconstructed temple, formerly Momooji (see 1179).
1266	*Mirror of the East* (Azuma kagami), military government history.
1274	First Mongol Invasion; Ippen (1239–1289) founds Ji Sect of Pure Land Buddhism.
1277	Abutsu travels to Kamakura; incidents recounted in *Diary of the Waning Moon* (Isayoi nikki, 1280).
1279–83	*Collection of Sand and Pebbles* (Shasekishū) begun, set aside, completed; later revisions.
1281	Second Mongol Invasion.
1299	*Collection of Sacred Assets* (Shōzaishū) completed; revised 1308.
1300	*The Mirror for Women* (Tsuma kagami).
1305	Mujū completes *Casual Digressions* (Zōtanshū), cedes Chōboji to Muō.
1312	Mujū (b. 1226) dies at Chōboji. Kyōgoku Tamekane compiles *Collection of Jeweled Leaves* (Gyokuyōshū), *waka* anthology.
1322	Kokan Shiren (1278–1346) compiles the *Genkō Era's History of Buddhism* (Genkō shakusho).

1333	Fall of Kamakura to Nitta Yoshisada (1301–1338).

Ashikaga (Muromachi) Period 1336–1568

1463	Shinkei (1406–1475): *Whisperings* (Sasamegoto).
1546	Emperor Gonara awards Mujū posthumous title, Daien Kokushi.
1597	Monk Bonshun (1553–1632) copies unabbreviated *Shasekishū*.

Tokugawa Period 1603–1868

1707	Kenryō's *Biographical Sketch of Mujū Kokushi* (Mujū Kokushi ryakuengi).
1769	Tainin's *Religious Traces of National Teacher Mujū* (Mujū Kokushi dōshakukō).

Introduction

No one in Kamakura Japan doubted that the times were bad and getting worse. The scriptures were in agreement on this point, although there might be differences of opinion about the specifics. It was commonly known that after the death of Śākyamuni, for a fixed period of a thousand years human beings would have the ability to understand the teaching, to perform the required practices, and to reap the fruits of enlightenment. This was the Period of the True Law. Then ensued the Period of the Imitation Law, also for an interval of a millennium. People still had the capacity to understand the teaching and perform the practices, but there was no attainment of enlightenment. The human condition continued to deteriorate. And finally, during the Latter Days of the Law (*mappō*), a period which all agreed would last for ten thousand years, only conceptual understanding of the Law would remain. Even this would gradually wither away until the advent of the Buddha Maitreya would again set the cycle in motion.

Within this broad tripartite framework some ameliorization was possible through such agencies as the ancestral native gods (*kami*). But in the end, only the rate of decline could be changed, not the direction. The idea had not been unknown in India, China and Heian Japan, but it came into its own in the climate of social deterioration and armed conflict which culminated in the defeat of the Taira clan in the straits at Dannoura in 1185, the eclipse of the emperor and his court, and the establishment of the military government at Kamakura in 1192. Late in the Heian period the prevailing opinion was that the year Eishō 7 (A.D. 1052) marked the beginning of the Latter Days of the Law, two millennia having then elapsed since the demise of Śākyamuni (in B.C. 949, according to the present Western calendar). Its analogue, but not its parallel, is found in several varieties of Western millenarianism which postulated the coming of a savior who would establish a kingdom of righteousness on earth. Latter Day thought, by contrast, saw a long

1

period of personal and social decline in a cyclical process of history each phase of which began with the appearance of a new Buddha to preach the Law yet another time.[1]

In a musical comparison, Latter Day thought would be the recurring ground bass in the institutional and conceptual chaconne that was the new Kamakura Buddhism. Whatever the variations in the currents of Pure Land Buddhism, of the Zen newly-imported from China, or of the old sects which were to be renewed (Myōe's Kegon, Jōkei's Hossō, Eizon's Esoteric Disciplinary Sect, or Nichiren's Lotus Sect) — all were conditioned by the underlying theme, in a minor key, that human institutions were in decline and that human abilities had badly deteriorated and would get worse. The theme dictated that the variations be simple, and that the elaborate embellishments of the earlier Tendai, Shingon, and Kegon sects be eschewed as not appropriate to the current mood of debility. Seven centuries later we may idly speculate whether or not another kind of theme might have provided the leaders of the new Buddhism with greater freedom of invention; perhaps in the history of ideas it is possible and useful to make a judgment on the value of a pervasive idea of another time and another place, even while ad- mitting that any such judgment inevitably involves our own priorities and biases. Be that as it may, Latter Day thought was the ground of a magnificent chaconne whose figures and harmonies still reverberate down to the present day. Mujū Ichien knew the theme well, and its variations appear throughout his writings.

The effect of Latter Day thought was not limited to religious deliberations; or perhaps it would be better to say that such deliberations cannot neatly be divorced from other human ac- tivities. The Decline of the Law was seen as the major, but not the sole, impetus in the unfolding of human affairs according to the monumental interpretive history, *Miscellany of Ignorant Views* (Gukanshō, 1219), composed by the Tendai archabbot Jien (Ji- chin, 1155-1225), seven years before Mujū was born. Latter Day thought influenced not only the content of the work but its style as well. If one wished to communicate with people, he must write at their level of understanding, and this meant to write in Japanese in- stead of the more prestigious Chinese. "I do so in order to make it possible for the reader to comprehend the changing conditions of the world . . . In these final reigns no one understands anything. Everyone is like a 'Dog watching the stars [without knowing what he sees].'"[2]

This was also the rationale of the vernacular tract (*kana hōgo*), which virtually began with the Kamakura renovations. In addition to the formal doctrinal tracts (*hōgo*) which continued to be written in Chinese without concessions to human frailty, a new genre emerged as an accommodation to those of inferior capacity, priests as well as laymen. Mujū's *Collection of Sacred Assets* (1299) and his *Mirror for Women* (1300) are both examples of this literary form, distinguished from the genre of Buddhist tale literature (*bukkyō setsuwa*)[3] largely by its higher ratio of homily to anecdote. But the line between the two forms is fine; and both *Sand and Pebbles* and *Casual Digressions* might appear under either rubric. These varieties of popular religious indoctrination were influential on the growth of vernacular literature, as were translations of the Bible into the national languages of the West. Since the Japanese had to read the sutras and important commentaries in Chinese, there being few translations into the vernacular until modern times, these kinds of popular writings served as a bridge between them and the untutored understanding.

A view of history which organized human activities into two periods of a thousand years, and a third period which was a multiple of a thousand, could easily have provided Mujū and his contemporaries with a sense of their place in world affairs not unlike our own in the last decades of the twentieth-century West. Just as our framework consists of several intervals of a thousand years subdivided into centuries before and after the birth of Christ, so also could the medieval Japanese have located all human events, in whatever country, on a common reference line in time starting with the death of the historical Buddha in B.C. 949. Then, just as we see the Battles of Hastings and Dannoura as occurring in A.D. 1066 and A.D. 1185, respectively, Mujū might have used the dates B.E. 2015 and B.E. 2134. And the colophon to *Sand and Pebbles* would have read: "The time is mid-autumn in the year 2232 of the Buddhist Era" (A.D. 1283).

In fact, the colophon says: "The time is mid-autumn in the sixth year of Kōan." A sense of events as occurring within the framework of millennia had some meaning for the medieval Japanese within the special area of Buddhist religious thought, but as a feature of the prevailing shared sense of time it was clearly secondary to the view of events as taking place in one of a sequence of short periods (each with its own "reign name") during the role of a particular sovereign. To have a sense of time on a grand scale would thus require that an individual memorize the succession of emperors as well as the order and length of the reign names. The result of such complexity was to blur the sense of time and of a particular event in its relationship to others. Mujū and his contemporaries commonly referred to events as happening "recently," or "in antiquity," or perhaps, "during the Kōchō era" (*S&P* 1:1). To have a sense of the world as they experienced it is temporarily to set aside our familiar thought patterns — in other contexts as well — and to try to view events as taking place in some more-or-less determinate time in the past. Residents of the United States might approximate this sense by thinking of events as taking place during the term of office of their presidents. (Citizens of other countries can easily conjure up a comparable framework appropriate to their own political conditions.) Thus, in Pierce 1 (i.e., the first year of the administration of Franklin Pierce), the American squadron under Commodore Perry entered Edo Bay; in Polk 4, Marx and Engels issued the Communist Manifesto; and in Hoover 3, Maurice Ravel wrote his Piano Concerto for the Left Hand. A cumbersome system, no doubt, but one that would promote an awareness of presidential succession; and then it would be reasonably workable. (For the reader whose awareness is not sufficiently raised, the years in question are 1853, 1848, and 1931!)

Another comparison may help us to empathize with Mujū's perception of his relationship to the far-reaching theoretical and social changes of thirteenth-century Japan, even while we must be aware of the many imponderable factors which impinge on different people's *sense* of time. In Kamakura Japan, for example, a shorter average lifespan and the relatively paucity of images of the past (books, films, photographs, recordings, etc.) should have contributed to a greater sense of distance in time between events; but one could also argue cogently that keeping fewer images in one's mental focus, and proportionately more of earlier people and events, would tend to an easier identification with the past, and thus narrow the sense of distance in time.

In any case, Mujū completed his first and most significant work, *Sand and Pebbles*, in 1283 — seven centuries to the very decade in which this is being written. When we look backwards in time from the 1980s over the significant ideological events of the twentieth century, we see — with a greater or less sense of distance — a number of landmarks; and as we get closer to our own day, their relative importance becomes arguable. Like Mujū, we are too close to the events of our own time to assess them with the clarity of future hindsight.

The military government established by Minamoto Yoritomo in

Kenkyū 3 (or 1192, if the reader prefers) set the rules and boundaries of Mujū's social and political world, a world divorced, or at least separated, from the refinements idealized in Lady Murasaki's eleventh century classic, the *Tale of Genji*. Its ideals were more austere and somber, popular religious movements proliferated, and the warrior replaced the courtier as the trend setter. But in spite of the Byzantine intrigues that marked its initial phases, the Minamoto/Hōjō regime did provide the country with more than a century of peace and efficient government, more-or-less. By the time *Sand and Pebbles* was completed in the late thirteenth century, Yoritomo and his crowd would have seemed to Mujū as remote as we in the final decades of the twentieth century perceive, say, the Spanish-American War (1898) or the Dreyfus vindication (1899).

Politics held little interest for Mujū, and need not detain us here. I would only remind the reader that shortly after Yoritomo's death in 1199, a series of Hōjō regents replaced the Minamoto as the real power in Kamakura, although the shogun might be one of Yoritomo's own sons (Yoriie, Sanetomo), or later, an imperial prince from the capital. The emperor continued as nominal head of the state, and it was the tension between the Kyoto court and the Kamakura military establishment that climaxed in the major internal military action of the thirteenth century. The Jōkyū War of 1221 was an abortive attempt by Emperor Gotoba to reassert his authority against the military power in Kamakura; he was head of the country in name only, although with still more control of affairs than was to be enjoyed by emperors in later centuries after rule by a shogun under the guise of protecting the throne had become a familiar and accepted government arrangement. (In the following century Emperor Godaigo's resistance would be the last serious attempt to re-establish the supremacy of the court until the Meiji Restoration of 1868.)

Several patrons of Mujū's Chōboji, members of the Yamada clan, sided with the ill-fated imperial cause; and thus the conflict—as far back in time from Mujū as World War I is from us—loomed larger in this thought than either the Taira-Minamoto war a few decades earlier, or the Mongol invasions (1274, 1281) which took place during, or shortly before, the time he was writing *Sand and Pebbles*. Unlike the historian Jien, Mujū did not take sides politically. The second Hōjō regent, Yoshitoki (in office 1205-1224) is mentioned dispassionately in the account of Yamada Akinaga (*S&P* 2:4) as ordering his execution. His successor, Yasutoki (in office 1224-1242), moreover, is eulogized in several anecdotes and described as "one who made the troubles of the people his own troubles, being father and mother to the masses" (*S&P* 3:2). Yet this was the man who led the Kamakura troops against Gotoba in the conflict in which Yamada Shigetada, "in all respects a gentleman," perished with his son, and in which Akinaga was seriously injured. And the fifth Hōjō regent, Tokiyori (in office 1246-1256), whom Mujū also mentions favorably (*S&P* 9:7, *CD* 3:5), may have made a substantial contribution to Chōboji's restoration in 1262.

Mujū's religious world was dominated by the Tendai sect which had been established four centuries earlier at the Enryakuji on Mount Hiei by Saichō (Dengyō Daishi, 767-822). Throughout the Heian period this monastic center, situated in the nearby mountains northeast of Kyoto, had become enmeshed in secular power struggles. Its political machinations, which included even the use of military force to press its demands, eventually led to the complete destruction of the complex on Mount Hiei and the slaughter of its monks by Nobunaga in 1571. But in Mujū's day Tendai was still the secure center of the Buddhist establishment, providing the ground rules, the vocabulary, and the schedule of issues by which the game was to be played. Four centuries earlier it had been the revolutionary party, forced to define itself in terms of the issues raised by the Nara establishment. The heirs of every revolution become the new orthodoxy. Today we see Kamakura Buddhism largely through the eyes of the heirs of the reformers, now become the establishment. The popular movements did in time replace Heian Tendai and Shingon, but we must remind ourselves that this did not take place overnight. In Mujū's day the concerns, issues, and scriptures of Tendai were given.

Tendai's basic scripture was the *Lotus Sutra*,[4] which states that the Eternal Buddha employs a variety of provisional teachings, accommodations (*hōben*) to human needs and biases. "Truth" was not a term confined to the operations of logic, or to the correspondence between statement and fact. Religious "truth" is a matter of immediate experience ultimately beyond the grasp of all conceptual formulations. These might be more or less helpful (but they could also be a hindrance) in bringing us to the threshhold of this Awareness; and their relative usefulness to the devotee to attain this goal was their "empirical verification." Doctrinal variety was not only possible but inevitable. Dogmatic exclusiveness was a fundamental error and became the common issue of the Tendai establishment against the new sects which arose in the Kamakura era. Tendai did not deny that the new methods — or, rather, the new emphases — would lead the devotee to Enlightenment; it only objected to the claims that a specific method was the *only* road to salvation. Curiously, it was not the establishment which opposed its entrenched dogma against new interpretations of scripture; rather, it was the establishment which defended the possibility of innovative plurality against the single-minded dogmatists.

The concepts and literary images of the *Lotus Sutra* pervaded the thought of Hcian and Kamakuia Japan; and many of the important rituals, such as the "Eight Expoundings of the Lotus" (*hokke hakkō*),[5] originate with this scripture. Specific Buddhist themes appear fairly late in the imperial anthologies of *waka* poetry, the *Later Collections of Gleanings* (Goshūishū, 1086) being the first to introduce a group of poems under the special heading of "Poems on the Teaching of Śākyamuni" (*shakkyōka*).[6] Of the nineteen poems included in this collection, well over half refer either directly to the parables or doctrines of the *Lotus Sutra*, or to Tendai-associated ideas or scriptures, such as the *Nirvana Sutra*.[7] The influence of the *Lotus Sutra* on Heian life and thought can hardly be exaggerated. During the Kamakura period it gradually had to share its popularity with the scriptures of the Zen and Pure Land movements. But for Mujū and his contemporaries it was still a work of enormous authority.

The doctrine of accommodation permitted Tendai a wide diversity of doctrine and practice, and Tendai provided the theoretical framework within which each of the emerging sects defined itself. Not only did the leaders of the new movements — Hōnen, Shinran, Nichiren, Eisai, Dōgen, Enni — all begin their careers either on Mt. Hiei or at Miidera (Onjōji), but the Tendai synthesis contained within itself the seeds of their religious emphasis: a program for meditation, devotion to Amida, and reliance on the *Lotus Sutra* — all held together by the doctrine of Accommodation. It was necessary for Hōnen and Shinran to demonstrate that their new Pure Land movement was an improvement on the Amidism promoted by Tendai's Genshin (942–1017) in his *Essentials of Salvation*.[8] Nichiren was to show that he had taken from the complexities of Tendai all that was useful for the degenerate times in which he lived, simple faith in the *Lotus Sutra*. And the proponents of Zen were to reassert their methods of meditation in full awareness of those elaborated in the *Great Cessation and Insight*[9] (an issue that their Chinese predecessors had resolved centuries earlier), and also to decide whether they would accommodate or reject other practices.

As opposed to those practices which are conceptually-based — preaching, the reading of scriptures, philosophical argument, etc. — Mahāyāna Buddhism recognizes non-discursive "esoteric" practices as means to religious realization. Since the goal of all religious practice ultimately eludes human reasoning, so that, in the familiar phrase, even the sutras and other sacred *conceptual* teachings of Buddhism are no more than "fingers pointing at the moon,"[10] sometimes useful as crude guides to direct our attention but essentially incapable of grasping Reality, esoteric practices provide us with a viable option. One might also employ non-discursive "fingers": visual representations (*maṇḍalas*), mystic phrases (*mantras, dhāraṇī*), and physical gestures (*mudrās*; "body language") as means to realize the ineffable. In Heian Buddhism, the Shingon sect of Kūkai (Kōbō Daishi, 774-835) was the preeminent exponent of these methods, although eclectic Tendai also had its esoteric component. Mujū uses the term *shingon* ("True Words", i.e., *mantras*) to indicate esoteric practices in general, not just the Shingon Sect. And throughout his works, and particularly toward the end of his life, he defends these methods associated with the older forms of Buddhism against the neglect, and even open hostility, by the new movements in Kamakura Buddhism.

Even older than Tendai and Shingon were the so-called "Six Nara Sects" — Kusha, Jōjitsu, Ritsu, Sanron, Hossō and Kegon — whose doctrinal positions were also to be recognized under the umbrella of Accommodation. Several of these had never existed as independent sects in Japan, but survived as special areas of study within the larger institutions. The others — Hossō, Ritsu, and Kegon — continued to have major roles in the religious politics of the day. References to all six are sprinkled throughout Mujū's writings.

At the Gangōji in Nara in 625 a Korean monk named Hyegwan (J. Ekan) introduced Sanron, a sect based on "Three Treatises" of Nāgārjuna's Mādhyamika school; the Jōjitsu, supporting the viewpoint of the *Completion of Truth*,[11] was a subdivision of Sanron, which also never existed administratively as a distinct sect but whose theories were studied at Tōdaiji and other large centers of learning. The Kusha, maintaining the views of Vasubandhu's early *Treasury of Analyses*[12], was brought to Japan in 658. Important philosophically because it defined the Sarvāstivādin position of radical pluralism, the school was absorbed by the Hossō sect in 793.

Hossō, with its headquarters at the Fujiwara-supported Kōfukuji in Nara, was the idealist school of the mature Vasubandhu (ca. 420-500) by way of Hsüan-tsang (600-664). It was introduced to Japan in 654, also at the Gangōji, and continued to play a limited but influential role throughout the history of Japanese Buddhism. Among its adherents were the legendary Gyōgi Bosatsu, the infamous Dōkyō (d. 772), who almost usurped the throne with the help of Empress Shōtoku, and the early Kamakura scholar Jōkei (Gedatsubō, 1155–1213).

The Ritsu (Disciplinary) sect was founded by the Chinese monk Chien chcn (Ganjin, 687–763), with headquarters at Tōshōdaiji in Nara. As its name implies, the contribution of the Disciplinary sect to Japanese Buddhism was its emphasis on the correct observance of monastic regulations, including proper ordination procedures. Eizon (1201–1290),[13] who established the Esoteric Disciplinary (Shingon Ritsu) sect at Saidaiji in Nara, has left an account of his visit to Chōboji in 1262, shortly before Mujū assumed responsibility for the temple. Mujū appears to have been somehow involved in Eizon's movement, but the details are unclear.

The last of the Six Nara Sects, Kegon, based on the teaching of the *Garland Sutra*,[14] came into being with the dedication of the great Tōdaiji temple in Nara by Emperor Shōmu in 752. The Kegon doctrine of "Interdependent Origination" (*hokkai engi*) has always been admired by Buddhist thinkers, but Kegon as a sect never had widespread support. Mujū shared the high regard which the religious and secular leaders of the age had for priest Myōe (1173–1232), who tried to rejuvenate the sect early in the Kamakura period.

For Mujū such doctrinal diversity was an expression of the Buddha's compassion. Each method had its special purpose, and all were approaches to the same experiential Truth which in the end transcended every particular formulation. Some might be more or less useful, but all were possible. And the new movements of his age were entirely compatible with the tolerant Mahāyāna attitude toward the word games of philosophy and myth-making of religion.

Mujū's inability to recognize the revolutionary impact of the religious movements of his age largely stems from his inability to read the future. He could hardly have foreseen the powerful influence of the new Zen movement on the literature and arts of the Ashikaga period, an influence in which the Shōichi School of his mentor, Enni Ben'en of the Tōfukuji, generously participated. Nor could he have foreseen that the powerful sects of Nara and Heian would be overwhelmed by the new movements of Pure Land, Zen, and Nichiren, which began merely as emphases within the older traditions. But, lacking that vision, neither could he be tempted to interpret, weigh, and evaluate the religious events of his age in the light of their effect decades or centuries in the future. For us, seven centuries later, our "objective" perspective is both a tool and a danger. To know Kamakura Buddhism as its participants knew it is another kind of understanding, harder to manage systematically, but surely no less valuable, than an understanding shaped by predilections and biases of later ages. Mujū did not realize that Myōe, Jōkei, Eizon and Ninshō were only supporting characters in the drama in which he also was a player; to him they seemed to have major roles. Nor did he realize that Tendai, Shingon, and the Six Nara Sects were the heavies of the piece. The critic, dramatic or historical, who stands outside the play has something of value to say; but might not the players also be worth listening to? And we can hear them only by listening to what they themselves say, not what others say about them, with a conscious effort to put aside our preconceptions.

Part I.
Mujū Ichien (1226–1312)

"No Fixed Abode": 1226-1261

Our story does not begin at the beginning—a paradox that would have delighted Mujū. "Only by beginning at the end," we can hear him say, "do we begin at the beginning." We must begin our account by taking note of the fact that most of what we know about Mujū's long life—long even by today's standards, not to mention those of Kamakura Japan—is to be gleaned from scattered reminiscences in his *Casual Digressions* of 1305. He was then in his eightieth year, and the details of his early life are refracted through the prism of nostalgia:

> This foolish old man was born at the hour of the Hare (around 6 a.m.) on the twenty-eighth day of the twelfth month of Karoku 2 (1226). In my father's dream appeared a man who foretold that a baby born in the town that night would be blessed with good fortune. (*CD* 3:5)

Like the utterances of the Delphic oracle, this prophecy was ambiguous enough to permit the hearer wide latitude of interpretation; and the oracle was safe from contradiction by such a lover of paradox as Mujū, for whom losing was winning. But of this, more later. What concerns us at present is that even in recording the moment of his birth, Mujū speaks of a "foolish old man" coming into the world. We are tempted to imagine the infant being delivered into a monastic robe, and being capped with an abbot's biretta. Recognizing the danger, we should make a special effort to seek out the youthful Mujū, who, after all, was once as young as anyone ever is. At the same time, I would like our story to be as autobiographical as possible, frequently citing statements of the old monk himself.

The climax of military events at Dannoura, its antecedents during the prior half-century and its immediate consequences, are related in the great military epic, *The Tale of the Heike* (Heike monogatari), whose episodes have been retold through successive

13

generations with adaptations by the Nō and Kabuki theaters, and other popular literary forms. The successful general of the Minamoto forces, Yoshitsune (1159–1189) in time became the outstanding literary hero of these times, the model of the "failed hero."[15] He became celebrated in legend, there being hardly a Japanese today who does not know of his cavalry charge down the precipice at Ichinotani, the exploits with his faithful retainer Benkei, the falling out with his brother Yoritomo (who later founded the Kamakura shogunate in 1192), and his eventual annihilation at the battle of Koromo River.

The person largely responsible for the tension between Yoshitsune and Yoritomo was a subordinate Genji general, Kajiwara Kagetoki, who, after a series of confrontations with Yoshitsune, maligned him to his brother. This treachery led to Yoshitsune's eventual destruction at Koromo River in Hiraizumi, which the poet Bashō visited five centuries later to compose his haiku on the summer grasses being all that is left of old warriors' dreams.[16] Kagetoki became a member of the inner circle of the military government established by Yoritomo in Kamakura in 1192, but he was a continuing annoyance to his colleagues, who did away with him in 1200.

All of which is germane to our story because Mujū was a Kajiwara. On this point all of our biographical sources agree, although most differ on the precise relationship between Mujū and Kagetoki. Some say he was Kagetoki's third son, or his uncle—both relationships chronologically impossible; others state that he was a nephew, a distant descendant, or simply a member of the Kajiwara family in Kamakura. Mujū himself obliquely confirms his relationship in this ill-fated family, but he does not solve the genealogical puzzle for us. He does tell us that the decline in his family fortunes had a strong influence on his decision to take religious orders.

> Although my ancestor [Kajiwara Kagetoki?] served well as a favored retainer in the house of the Captain of the Palace Guards of the Right [i.e., Minamoto Yoritomo], his good fortune became exhausted and he came to an untimely end. There was no one to follow after him.
>
> In my thirteenth year I lived in monastic quarters in Kamakura [as a page at Jufukuji?]. At fifteen I went to the house of my aunt [Kagetoki's daughter?] in Shimozuke. In my sixteenth year I was cared for by close relatives in Hitachi, and at eighteen I became a priest . . . (CD 3:5) This poor monk, born into a military family, would have followed in its footsteps but for my ancestor's untimely end. Being an orphan with none to depend on, I quite naturally entered the monastic life. To have met and established karmic af-

finities with the famous scholars of the day and patriarchs of the Zen teaching is solely the result of my family's destitution.

When I consider the matter carefully, I come to the conclusion that my not succeeding to the profession of my military family and my having become destitute were the reward of good acts through many lives. As Lao Tzu has said: "Misery is that from which happiness arises."[17] An untimely end was the cause for my entering the religious life. Being the last leaf on the tree of a family involved in such worldly delusion has been cause and condition for me to become enlightened. Thus, having been deluded is the starting point for becoming enlightened.

Mayoi koso	So delusion
Satori narikere	Has become enlightenment!
Mayowazu wa	Had I not wandered unaware,
Nani yorite ka	How would enlightenment
Satori hirakan	Have opened itself to me?

Those who stumble and fall to the ground also arise by virtue of the support which the ground provides.[18] When one who is deluded through intellection becomes enlightened with respect to that intellection, he is Buddha. (*CD* 1:1)

Mujū is tantalizingly vague. But, after all, he is writing about events which had occurred a century earlier, events of which he had forgotten many of the particulars and probably lost all interest. At Kagetoki's death the family estate had been confiscated, and a nephew or grandson would hardly care to dwell on the decline of the clan's status and prosperity. But we do know a few facts from which to speculate about Mujū's early life and connections.

Eisai (1141-1215) had returned to Japan in 1191 with the first transmission of Rinzai Zen, founding the Shōfukuji in Kyūshū that same year. The first Zen temple in Kamakura was Jufukuji,[19] established in 1200 as a memorial to Yoritomo (d. 1199) by his widow, Masako, who appointed Eisai its abbot. (The graves of Masako and the shogun-poet, Sanetomo, are in the temple grounds.) Eisai began building Kenninji, the center of his teaching in Kyoto, in 1202, the main construction being completed in 1205.

Mujū tells us that Kagetoki's widow, the nun Kano, was in great distress over the loss of her husband and went to Eisai for counsel. Kano had been given a large manor, possibly on the occasion of a memorial service held by Sanetomo (1192-1219) in 1209 at the Hokkedō (Lotus Hall) in Kamakura for Kagetoki and other members of the Kajiwara family who had perished.[20] At Eisai's urg-

ing, Kano donated funds to construct the pagoda at Kenninji.
Mujū's Tokugawa biographer, Tainin, states that in his thirteenth
year (1238) Mujū served as a page at Jufukuji; and it may well be
that this came about through connections between the Kajiwara
family and Eisai's successors.

In his eighteenth year (1243) Mujū took the tonsure at Hōonji
in Hitachi Province, northeast of Kamakura. A mere two years later
his teacher put him in charge of the temple, where he remained until 1253. We do not know why the young inexperienced monk was
given this responsibility, but it is reasonable to suppose that the Kajiwara connection may have again played a part. Certainly Mujū
showed no flair for administration, and his management of the temple was evidently a disaster. A full half-century later the old monk
recalled the events of those days with painful clarity.

> I declined three times, being unsuited to worldly affairs. But cir-
> cumstances were such that the temple was transferred. My teacher
> gave me detailed instructions on practical matters, planning and
> helping me out with everything. I did not even know the number of
> the few implements that were there, and I could not distinguish be-
> tween what belonged to me and what belonged to others. Being un-
> suited to the job, things did not go well. (CD 3:5)

Tainin's *Traces* suggests that the teacher who transferred
Hōonji to Mujū was one Enkō Kyōōbō, a scholar from Miidera, the
great Tendai center down the mountain from Hieizan. In spite of
Mujū's remarks about having received "detailed instructions on
practical matters," the transfer may well have been a case of the
blind leading the blind. Two anecdotes in *Sand and Pebbles* (5A:7),
completed some three decades later, ridicule Enkō as completely
detached from the realities of life. Whether or not this Enkō was abbot of Hōonji, Mujū did study with the Tendai cleric (*CD* 3:5).
These short sketches which wickedly caricature the teacher of his
youth reveal an unsympathetic streak in Mujū's character which
may partly account for his own alienation from friends and disciples
in later life.

We know nothing else about Mujū's decade at Hōonji except
that finally he decided to leave.

> When I was in my twenty-seventh year [1252], I converted Hōonji
> into a temple where the regulations were observed (*ritsuin*). At
> twenty-eight, I became a monk without any temple affiliations
> (*tonsei*);[21] and when, after studying the regulations for priestly

behavior for six or seven years I then decided to pursue the practice of meditation, in my thirty-fifth year [1260] while staying at Jufukuji, I listened to Higan Chōro[22] lecture on the *Explanation of Mahāyāna*[23] and on the *Sutra of Perfect Enlightenment.*[24] (I had heard him speak before on the *Explanation* [at Chōrakuji][25] in Serada in my twenty-seventh year.) I practiced zazen but within a year gave it up; being sick with beriberi, I could not achieve zen awareness. (*CD* 3:5)

Is Mujū merely telling us that before leaving Hōonji he set up new guidelines for behavior at the temple? Or does he imply a sectarian realignment, perhaps with Eizon's Esoteric Disciplinary sect, with which he had later dealings? Whatever the facts may be, we do know that Mujū had a lifelong concern about proper monastic discipline.

Ordinary people in this degenerate age shave their heads and dye their robes, but they do not practice the Buddhist austerities. Those who casually learn the doctrines treat the Buddha's Law as a game; and because the Law is really a means to ferry people across this material life, it becomes a source of deceit and perplexity. This is an unspeakably wretched business.[26]

Laxity in the observance of the regulations by the clergy was a recurring problem in Japanese Buddhism. Shortly after Ganjin founded the Disciplinary sect, permission for a special Mahāyāna ordination platform on Mt. Hiei became a major issue between the Nara establishment and the new Tendai sect advocated by Saichō. Toward the end of the Heian period the widespread view that the Latter Days of the Law had arrived made many resigned to a lax clergy. But not everyone, as we can see from the emergence of the Esoteric Disciplinary sect, which, as its name suggests, advocated the strict observance of the discipline (*vinaya*) together with the practice of esoteric rituals. To underline its attempt to return to fundamentals, it took as its main object of worship the historical founder of Buddhism, Śākyamuni, and observed the post-noon fast. Mujū's relationship with Eizon is unclear, but they shared many common ideals. In a lighter vein, Mujū's criticism of the relaxed standards of his time is reflected in an anecdote about Zōsō Rōyo's predecessor at Chōrakuji (see Appendix B).

Once when the Preceptor Eichō, founder of Serada Chōrakuji on Nitta Manor in Kōzuke Province, was speaking to a large group of people at a meeting to expound the precepts, he lamented the current decline in the observance of the regulations.

"Although monks today talk of receiving the precepts, they do not know what it means to observe them. While half-heartedly calling themselves priests, taking alms, and performing services, it is a strange breed of priest which abounds throughout the country, bringing disgrace to the disciples of the Buddha. Some have families and others bear arms, or go hunting and fishing. In these wretched latter days there are those who do not even know the meaning of the word 'repentance.'

I see one from where I am sitting. I look and ask myself if he is a layman—but he wears a priest's scarf. He is neither adult, child, priest nor menial. He isn't even shit, but something like diarrhea!"

Because his remarks were directed at a fierce mountain ascetic who was present, some of the monks feared that he might be made to pay for them. But since he did not speak out of spite but out of compassion, they brought forth a sympathetic response. The mountain ascetic repented and abandoned his worldly ways. (S&P 6:9)

To follow Mujū through his sectarian adventures is to experience the conscious acceptance of diversity which is basic to the man's thought and character. Each encounter was not merely a stage to be passed and left behind in relentless pursuit of some final, true, ideological position; rather, each was a moment carefully accommodated into a pluralistic world view whose diversity was not only possible, but doctrinally inevitable. References to every variety of teaching and to individuals representing these positions are scattered throughout his works, including even the minor sects of Nara Buddhism and excluding only those whose intransigence violated the spirit of Accommodation.

It is inconceivable that Mujū was unaware of the three great charismatic leaders of Kamakura Buddhism: Shinran (1173-1262), Hōnen's disciple in the Pure Land movement; Dōgen, foremost Japanese Zen philosopher and founder of Sōtō; and Nichiren (1222-1283), fiery advocate of the *Lotus Sutra* and founder of the sect which today bears his name. All were flamboyant individuals who did not shrink from public controversy and who had already lived out their careers by the time *Sand and Pebbles* was completed in 1283. And yet they appear nowhere in its pages, at least not by name. The reason for Mujū's silence is surely because all three reformers, however greatly they differed in their religious programs, shared a common attitude: the rejection of the doctrine of "skillful means", which Mujū never tires of defending.[27] The fervor of the

zealot or fanatic in any society is all too easily reinforced by the belief
that he alone has the truth. History can provide us with many examples of single-minded individuals who were adequately motivated
to great actions because the truth as they knew it worked for *them*,
without denying that others might have equally effective rationaliza-
tions of the human condition. It helps when a system of belief—such
as the Mahāyāna—explicitly defends the need for diversity. But over
all, the tolerant individual tends to be the exception rather than the
rule.

Mujū was such an exception. He is intolerant only of intolerance (and was himself aware of, and intrigued by, the paradox
of the position). He criticizes those who are lax in the performance
of their chosen religious activities, whatever they may be, only in the
abstract; he does not name individuals because appearances can
deceive. "In general it is difficult to recognize a sage's blessedness or
sinfulness through his observance or transgression of the Law, for it
is not easy to fathom his motivation."[28] Judge not but look to your
own faults. Mujū tells us that he is careful not to criticize others by
name. (The anecdote about his teacher Enkō was evidently an exception.) In relating an embarrassing episode Mujū often says that
although he knew the names of the people involved, he hesitated to
make them known for fear of causing discomfort. A young girl in
Kamakura died of unrequited love for a page in a monastery and
her cremated remains changed into small snakes (*S&P* 7:2); or a nun
held a Shingon service at which the preacher's remarks got out of
hand (*S&P* 6:1, translated below). In both cases Mujū withheld the
names of those involved in order to avoid making trouble for the
relatives.

And to criticize another's choice of religious practice was an
even more serious matter; for this was to criticize the Buddhist
teaching in one of its manifold forms. Dōgen is remembered for
likening the chanting of the name of Amida Buddha by Pure Land
devotees to the day and night croaking of frogs in spring rice pad-
dies.[29] Nichiren's attacks against other sects are summarized in the
statement: "Nembutsu followers will fall into the Avīci hell, Zen
followers are devils, Shingon will destroy the nation, the Ritsu are
enemies of the state, Tendai is an outdated calendar."[30] And some
proponents of the Pure Land movements aggressively rejected the
Lotus Sutra and all other methods in their total reliance on recitation of the name of Amida Buddha. But for Mujū:

There is not just one method for entering the Way, the causes and
conditions for enlightenment being many. Once a person

understands their general significance, he will see that the purport of
the various teachings does not vary. And when he puts them into
practice, he will find that the goal of the myriad religious exercises is
the same. (*S&P* Preface) . . . When a man who practices one version
of the Way of the Buddha vilifies another because it differs from his
own sect, he cannot avoid the sin of slandering the Law. It has been
said that a man who slanders the methods of another out of attachment to his own beliefs will surely suffer the pains of hell even though
he observes the commandments.[31]

Such an attitude partly reflects his Tendai upbringing, but the
decision to accept or to oppose its doctrine of Accommodation was
also a matter of personal temperament. In allying himself later in
life with the eclectic Enni, Mujū made a similar choice.

He does not tell us where and with whom he studied the *Lotus
Sutra*, a work that figures prominently in his writings, because the
scripture was common knowledge. Hōonji has disappeared without
a trace, but we can reasonably assume that it was affiliated with
Tendai, and that Mujū's early training centered on the literature of
that sect. He tells us that he read three Tendai-related works while,
or shortly after, he was living at Hōonji.

> In my youth I studied parts of the *Commentary on the Treasury of
> Analyses of the Law*[32] with Bridge-of-the-Law Enkō Kyōōbō of
> Miidera. In my twentieth year I heard the *Profound Meaning of the
> Lotus Sutra*[33] from the Venerable Hosshimbō; and, at twenty-nine,
> the *Great Cessation and Insight* from Jitsudōbō.[34] (*CD* 3:5)

After leaving Hōonji in 1253, Mujū spent the following eight
years in travel and study. Travel has always been part of a way of life
in Japan, not merely a passage from one place to another; and
Japanese literature of every period reflects this preoccupation.[35]
With some—Saigyō and the haiku poet Bashō—it was elevated to
the status of a kind of religious exercise. Man's life is a journey, a
series of episodes with no place to abide. "Non-abiding"—*mujū*—is
a recurring message of the sutras: "Awaken the mind without fixing
it anywhere," says the *Diamond Sutra*. In the *Traces*, Tainin quotes
Gidō Shūshin (1325–1388), an outstanding figure in the Zen "Five
Mountains" literary movement, on "Non-Abiding":

> All things are rooted in the One Mind, and the One Mind is rooted
> in non-abiding. Because of non-abiding, things do not maintain any
> self-nature; and because they have no self-nature, it is we who create
> the six ordinary stages of rebirth in accordance with our karma . . .[36]

That is, according to the Buddhist idealism conspicuous in Zen thought, "there is nothing either good or bad [—nor any other phenomenal thing, for that matter—], but thinking makes it so," according to the karmic predisposition of our thought processes.

With Tainin we may wonder if any such considerations were present to Mujū in his choice of his name. But certainly the ideal of the unfettered spirit, the man who abandons the world (*tonsei*), was part of Mujū's world view as a Buddhist, but also as a man who wished to avoid administrative responsibilities. Although "non-abiding" refers primarily to the goal of an undifferentiated state of awareness, temporal non-abiding, i.e., travel, was an appropriate metaphor. In summing up the blessings of a lifetime, the elderly Mujū refers to his travels, many of which took place just after he left Hōonji.

> During a long life in the pursuit of learning, I have freely paid homage at various famous places in the capital and throughout the provinces, at holy temples and sacred shrines: the complex on Mount Hiei, the Seven Great Temples of the Southern Capital [i.e., Tōdaiji, Kōfukuji, Gangōji, Daianji, Yakushiji, Saidaiji, and Hōryūji in Nara], especially the Great Buddha which is known as the greatest in all the world;[37] Kumano, the most spiritual area of Japan; Zenkōji, where the image is thought to be like the living Buddha; Mt. Kōya, where the Great Teacher [Kūkai] entered into final meditation; the Shitennōji, where Buddhism was first propagated, founded by Prince Shōtoku; the Tachibanadera, where he was born, and the sanctuary of the Hōryūji, which he built. When I recall this world in which I have been born, I must say that the experience of visiting these places has been my great good fortune. (*CD* 3:5)

Mujū has told us that after leaving Hōonji he studied the "regulations for priestly behavior (*ritsugaku*) for six or seven years." The most likely location for this would have been Eizon's Saidaiji in Nara, where he would also have had opportunity to visit the Seven Great Temples and Mount Bodai. However, had he stayed there for any length of time, Mujū surely would have figured prominently in the account of Eizon's visit to Chōboji in 1262, which we will presently examine. The context of the following statement by Mujū is ambiguous, but it may refer to a visit to Mount Bodai in 1254.

> . . . At Mt. Bodai[38] I heard something of the principles of the Hossō sect; but I was unable to plumb the significance of any sect thoroughly. Only the basic principles passed through my ears . . . (*CD* 3:5)

Elsewhere in his writings Mujū refers to the Kegon prelates, Shunjō and Myōe, to the Sanron scholars Chikō and Raikō, to "two Kusha scholars living at Miidera," and to Hossō doctrine — among other items related to Nara Buddhism. But he is impatient with the Nara sects' — and Tendai's — tendency to cultivate theory without practice.

The Great Teachers Dengyō [Saichō 767-822], Kōbō [Kūkai, 774-835], Jikaku [Ennin, 792-862], and Chishō [Enchin, 814-891] brought the teachings of Shingon to our country because we have an affinity for it. Japan is a country which has had an affinity for Tendai, Shingon and the *nembutsu.* Hossō, Sanron, and Kegon are merely studied in Nara and have not been propagated throughout the provinces. The Ritsu and Zen sects have not been remiss in propagating their ideas, but until now results have been few. However, perhaps it is the skillful design (*hōben*) of the Great Sage that Ritsu and Zen will be widespread in the world today. In these times they are being established and promoting practice. Perhaps the time has arrived for them to be popular. Although there are many Tendai and Hossō scholars, in these Latter Days people practice *zazen*, those being few who employ the reflective techniques (*kannen*) of Mind Only, or the Perfect and Sudden (*endon*) methods of Tendai. The scholars merely argue points of doctrine, quarrel over what is provisional or absolute in a sect, and decide what is shallow or profound in a teaching. (*S&P* 10B:3)

It was dissatisfaction with the arid word-games of the older traditions which finally led him to Enni, who combined broad doctrinal interest with a living practice of meditation.

In 1241 Enni Ben'en (Shōichi Kokushi, 1202-80)[39] returned from China after receiving the seal of approval from Wu-chun Shih-fan (1177-1249) of the Yang-ch'i school of Lin-chi (Rinzai) Zen. Unlike some of his abrasive contemporaries, Enni built a good relationship with the court in Kyoto, the military government in Kamakura, and the Buddhist establishment. The center of his teaching was the great Tōfukuji monastery in Kyoto, on which the Regent Kujō Michiie (1193-1252) had begun construction already in 1235. Enni was appointed its first abbot two decades later and shaped it into a powerful center of the Five Mountains (*gosan*)[40] movement of Rinzai Zen in Japan. Mujū is counted as a member of his Shōichi-ha.

Both Eisai and Enni began their religious training in Tendai, and both advocated a syncretic Zen which allowed the concurrent practice of other methods. Historians analyzing the movement with the perspective of a much later age, sometimes describe Eisai's Zen as a reluctant compromise with the Tendai, Shingon, and Nara establishment. (Hōnen's Pure Land teaching is similarly viewed as the best that could be done to anticipate Shinran's teaching of exclusive reliance on Amida.) Eisai's Zen is seen as adulterated with esoteric and other regressive elements, eventually to be superseded by the "pure" or "true" Zen of a Lan-chi (Rankei, 1213–1278), founder of Kenchōji, or a Dōgen (1200–1253), the outstanding philosopher of the movement, once Zen was politically strong enough to hold its own against the reactionary forces of Nara and Heian Buddhism.

Such a characterization would certainly have been rejected by Mujū, if not also by Eisai, Eichō, Enni and others for whom admission of a variety of religious methods in addition to Zen was simply an affirmation of a central principle of Mahāyāna Buddhism, the doctrine of Accommodation (Skillful Means, Expediency, hōben), according to which the Buddha prescribes the cure to each depending on his specific malady. To reject this variety in the interest of a "pure" or "true" Zen would not be doctrinally sound even if politically feasible.

> The movement of Eisai, the late Hongan Sōjō of Kenninji, does not discriminate among the various spiritual methods. Teaching observance of the regulations and supporting proper behavior, it cherishes Tendai, Shingon and Zen all at the same time. It also encourages the practice of calling on the name of Amida (nembutsu) . . .
>
> The conduct of the bodhisattva adapts to the times, without standing on form. Eisai founded Shōfukuji in Kyūshū, Kenninji in Kyoto, and Jufukuji in the eastern regions to be the first Zen institutions in the country. Without opposing the customs of the region into which he went, he adapted to the Ritsu, Tendai and Shingon and other methods; nor did he make a fetish of Chinese ways. Was this simply because he was biding his time? Eisai was a man of profound understanding. His method was outwardly Shingon but inwardly it was Zen. . . . (S&P 10B:3)

Among many books and artifacts with which Enni returned from China was the *Mirror of Sectarian Differences*,[41] on which he frequently lectured. It is a lengthy compilation of scriptural citations and arguments to demonstrate similarities and differences between meditation-centered Ch'an and the doctrinal sects. The nonconceptual One Mind of Ch'an, the Buddha Mind, reflects as a mirror the conceptual expediencies of T'ien T'ai (Tendai), Hua Yen

(Kegon), and the rest. Its author was Yung-ming Yen-shou (Yōmyō Enju, 904–975),[42] noted in his day for advocating the harmonization of Ch'an meditation with the Pure Land calling on the name of Amida Buddha. The Fa-yen (Hōgen) school of Ch'an to which he belonged died out in the middle of the Sung period, but the work evidently was transmitted through the Lin-chi (Rinzai) sect to reach Enni by way of his Chinese teacher, Wu-chun Shih-fan. Among the voluminous writings available to Enni and Mujū, it is not surprising that they should have paid special attention to the *Mirror of Sectarian Differences*, given their doctrinal leanings. We can see in their choice another indication that their own spirit of doctrinal accommodation was motivated by internal considerations rather than the external pressures of the religious establishment.

Moreover, in the epilogue to *Sand and Pebbles*, Mujū says that in his "thatched mountain hermitage [Chōboji] out in the country, I have had only my own heart and mind to rely upon, for I am without books. . . . The citations from literary works and the names of men of old are, I think, correct; but there may be many inadvertent errors." An examination of Mujū's writings reveals that many citations, rather than following the wording of the original, appear as they are found in the *Mirror of Sectarian Differences*, the *Commentary on the Great Wisdom Sutra*,[43] and the *Great Cessation and Insight*.

In addition to being able to relate to Enni's brand of eclectic Zen, Mujū was highly impressed by the force of the man's character. His writings do not tell us as much as we would like, or expect, about Enni; but they clearly show that Mujū found in him a teacher whom he could sincerely respect and follow. Mujū has already told us that he began Zen meditation at Jufukuji in 1260.

I attended lectures on Buddhism by the late Priest Shōichi [i.e., Enni] of Tōfukuji and heard what he had to say. Although I did not completely grasp the significance of that which I heard with sincere gratitude covering the essentials of the overt and esoteric, as well as the Zen, teachings, I feel honored to have immersed myself in the essentials of the doctrines as far as my understanding would reach. My only regret is that I met this priest in the evening of his life, and I was not long under his guidance.[44] Nevertheless, I received his kind counsel on the essentials of the Buddha's teaching.

Once when he was traveling down to the Kantō, I prepared a repast for him at one of the stops along the Eastern Sea Route. Had his been the disposition of an ordinary person, he would simply had acknowledged the offering and remarked "Very good!" But what he said was: "Why did you make such preparations? You should not have done this. Truly is it said that the incipient bodhisattva is diverted by worldly things, they destroy the bud of the Dharma."... and nothing more. These words sunk into my heart and rang in my ears . . . (*S&P* 3:8; *Traces*)

These remarks from the early chapters of *Sand and Pebbles* were written around 1280. A quarter of a century later in *Casual Digressions* Mujū repeats this sentiment in somewhat more detail:

Subsequently, when [in 1261] I visited the founder of Tōfukuji, I was successively initiated into the Tendai Valley School's Dual Ritual,[45] and the Secret Initiation Ritual.[46] Among the works I heard discussed were the *Commentary on the Great Sun Sutra*,[47] *Yung Chia's Collection*,[48] the *Aspiration to Enlightenment*,[49] and the *Record of Essentials*.[50] By nature I am neither meticulous nor bright, and having begun my studies late in life, I have been unable to plumb the significance of any sect thoroughly; I have just heard about their general ideas. The general principles of the overt, esoteric, and Zen teachings are inscribed in my heart and perfume my "store consciousness" (*shikizō*). And I owe this all to the graciousness of the founder [Enni]. On stopping to peruse the *Mirror of Sectarian Differences*, I found that Enni's behavior was in accord with that work. I have thought about this from various angles. (*CD* 3:5)

The date of the encounter during Enni's trip to Kamakura is hard to determine, although the *Chronological Record of Shōichi Kokushi, founder of Tōfukuji*[51] puts it at 1254, the year after Mujū left Hōonji. The entry speaks of Enni's "disciple Ichien, who lived at Kigasaki in Owari Province"; but Mujū would not be there for seven or eight years.

Biographer Kenryō tells us that he received Enni's Seal of Approval (*koka*) during his visit in 1261. It is also Kenryō who assures us that in 1281 Mujū thrice turned down a request from Emperor Gouda to succeed Enni as abbot of Tōfukuji, giving as his reason that "although he was grateful for the honor, his monthly visits to Atsuta Shrine to supervise the meditation made it difficult for him to leave Kigasaki". But given Mujū's own statement that he was forced to discontinue his *zazen* practice within less than a year without realizing his objective, we can probably discount both of Kenryō's claims.[52]

In spite of the fact that Mujū was a dedicated traveler in an age when this required considerable physical stamina, and in spite of his remarkable longevity, the beriberi which he developed at Jufukuji plagued him for the rest of his life. Beriberi is a disease which begins by causing weakness in the musclcs of the legs, a serious obstacle for a person sitting in meditation. It is often associated with the consumption of polished rice, from which thiamine is removed during milling; but one would expect Jufukuji to be serving a spartan fare of rough rice and a few vegetables, especially under the watchful eyes of Enni and the temple's patron, Hōjō Tokiyori.

Mujū makes almost no other reference to Enni in his writings. But in the final chapter of *Sand and Pebbles*, completed within three years of the event, he briefly takes note of Enni's death at Tōfukuji in 1280.

> The Elder of Tōfukuji, priest Shōichi, died on the seventeenth day of the tenth month of Kōan 3. He had been ill for some time since the early summer, and, being unable to carry on his normal routine, was cared for in a detached building on the temple grounds. On the fifteenth day of the tenth month, he announced that he would go up to the Dharma Hall to lecture and then to pass away; but his disciples would not permit it. Then on the seventeenth day he told his attendants to call the monks together and to beat the drum in the Dharma Hall to announce his death. Seated on a chair, he wrote his verse of departure from the world and expired. In the capital, priest and layman and those of high and low station assembled in droves to pray for three days. After this Shōichi was placed in a coffin still seated on his chair. This happened just recently, so I will not record the details. The death verse said:
>
> > Seventy-nine years of Skillful Means
> > To benefit sentient beings;
> > We desire to know the Ultimate as it is,
> > But this is transmitted by no Buddha or Patriarch.
> > Kōan 3, 10/17
> > > The Elder of Tōfuku
> > > Take care.

The final chapter of *Sand and Pebbles* (10B:3) is devoted to the last days and moments of those whom Mujū believed died in a manner which confirmed their religious attainments, especially among "the followers of the Kenninji". He also mentions Eisai, his disciple Eichō (d. 1247) of Chōrakuji, Eichō's successor Zōsō Rōyo (1193–1276), the Chinese monk Lan-chi (Rankei Dōryū, 1213–1278), first abbot of Kenchōji, and several others of less importance to our story (see Appendix B: Mujū's Religious Affiliations). Conspicuously absent is the greatest Zen leader of the age, Dōgen Kigen (1200–1253), who would qualify for inclusion as a disciple Myōzen (1184–1225), second abbot of Kenninji, before traveling to China and then returning to establish the Sōtō sect of Zen. When Dōgen left Kyoto for Echizen in 1243 after submitting a petition to the court which angered the religious establishment, his principal Zen rival was Enni. In Echizen, Dōgen built the temple which, in 1246, he named Eiheiji.

However modest his own attainment in Zen practice may have been, Mujū considered himself a disciple of Enni; and Chōboji, where he lived from 1262 until his death, became a branch temple of Tōfukuji. Like Enni, he never doubted the value of doctrinal Accommodation, while choosing to affiliate himself with the new movement of Rinzai Zen. We do not know if Mujū attempted to practice *zazen* in his later years. But the *Deed of Transfer* does say of his successor, Muō, that "his learning is not extensive, but he has been engaged in Zen practice for years" — under Mujū guidance?

One of the few fragments in Mujū's hand which still survive is a signed calligraphic paper, now mounted on a scroll, of the famous verse by Hui-neng (638–713), the sixth Chinese patriarch of Ch'an (see Figure 1):

> Originally there was no *Bodhi*-tree
> Nor was there any mirror.
> Since originally there was nothing,
> Whereon can the dust fall?

> Written by Mujū (Seal)

The verse is the celebrated reply by Hui-neng (Enō, 638–713) to the poem of his rival for the Ch'an succession, Shen-hsui (Jinshū, 605–706):

> The body is like unto the *Bodhi*-tree
> And the mind to a mirror bright.
> Carefully we cleanse them hour by hour
> Lest dust should fall upon them.

Mujū's version has the emended, and more famous, third line: "Since originally there was nothing," instead of the presumably original line found in the Tun-huang manuscript: "Buddha nature is always clean and pure."[53]

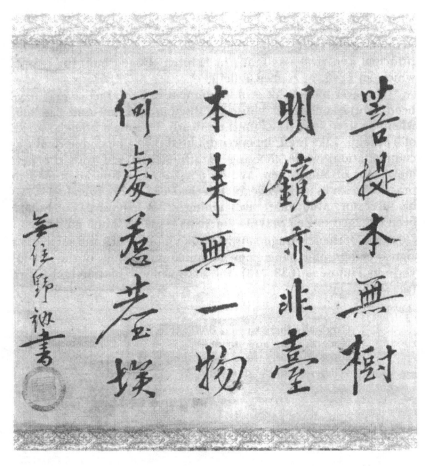

Figure 1. Verse from Hui-neng's *Platform Sutra* in Mujū's calligraphy. (Chōboji, Important Cultural Property.) *Photo by Andō Naotarō.*

So far our investigation has considered only Mujū's acceptance of ideological differences within Buddhism. In his works we find the same attitude extended to Shintō, Confucianism, and Taoism, but we can relate this to no biographical events. We do not know, for example, when he might have read the Taoist *Way and Its Power*[54] and the *Chuang-tzu*,[55] or the Confucian *Analects*,[56] all cited in *Sand and Pebbles*. One of Mujū's favorite stories is that of Pei Sou,[57] who never smiled because he knew that worldly good fortune produced its opposite, and bad fortune produced good. Having had the misfortune to lose a horse, he obtained a better one. This blessing proved to be the reverse when his son fell off and broke his elbow — which misfortune in turn was a blessing by excusing the son from military service in which his more "fortunate" friends perished. Mujū sometimes alludes to this paradox in human experience through the metaphor of the two sisters, Kudoku, Goddess of Virtue, and Kokuan, Goddess of Darkness. While Kudoku brings happiness and good fortune, Kokuan brings misfortune and calamity. But both are inseparable, and we can avoid pain only by expelling them both. There is no life without death, no meeting without parting. Like Pei Sou, we are to face the ups and downs of life with equanimity.[58] And so, Mujū concludes, to have had the good fortune of meeting with "the famous scholars of the day and patriarchs of the Zen teaching is solely the result of my family's destitution."

After meeting with Enni at Jufukuji in 1260 and at Tōfukuji the following year, Mujū again visited Nara.

> In my thirty-sixth year (1261) I climbed Mount Bodai wishing to study Shingon. There the essentials of Tōji's Sambōin school[59] were formally transmitted to me. (*CD* 3:5)

Kenryō says that his predecessor was lecturing on Zen in Echizen when he was approached by the Atsuta Deity, Kitayū, who wished to become his disciple. If there is any historical basis for this claim, the most probable time for the encounter would be between the time Mujū left Mount Bodai and his arrival at Chōboji. It was a most eventful period in his life.

Early in the second month of 1262, Eizon, founder of the Esoteric Disciplinary sect, left Nara's Saidaiji for a trip to Kamakura, accompanied by five disciples. His most illustrious follower, Ninshō,[60] was not in the party, having some years earlier received permission from Eizon to propagate the new teachings in the eastern provinces. In 1252, he was at Mimuraji in Hitachi Province, and in 1259 began working on Gokurakuji in Kamakura, which became his center as leader of the Kamakura religious establishment.

Shōkai, one of the five disciples who accompanied Eizon, has left us a short record of this trip, *Back and Forth to the Kantō Region*,[61] in which he describes a detour to a small country temple in Owari Province, a short distance from Atsuta Shrine. The temple had originally been called Momooji, and this is the first time in

historical records that it is referred to as Chōboji. Mujū had come to
stay at the temple sometime after leaving Enni, and its administration would pass into his hands shortly after Eizon's departure. In
Shōkai's account we may catch a glimpse of Mujū and his future
patron, Dōen.

On the sixth day of the second month, while passing through
Ōmi Province, Eizon and his group stopped for tea at the
Moriyama[62] post station, arriving at Kagami by evening. The
record's frequent mention of tea stops should not conjure up a party
of loose monks dallying along the stations of the Tōkaidō as depicted
in Hiroshige's colorful prints five centuries later. The strict regulations of the Shingon Ritsu sect permitted only one daily meal—the
record refers to the post-noon fast (jōsai)—and the evening "tea"
was just that, and considered to be medicine. Although the Zen
pioneer Eisai did not introduce tea in Japan, he did promote its use
after returning from China with seeds, and then composed a tract,
Drink Tea and Prolong Life,[63] extolling its medicinal properties.
Eizon's lectures at Chōboji during the supper hour were probably
accompanied by the drinking of tea, but no substantial meal. In any
case, the six monks followed the well-traveled route taken by the
nun Abutsu fifteen years later,[64] except that at Orido they veered
north off the highway toward Chōboji while Abutsu continued on to
the Atsuta Shrine.

The morning of the seventh day in the second month of 1262.
Received a letter from priest Dōkyō who was at Mimuraji in Hitachi
Province, asking us to stop for two or three days at Chōboji in Owari
Province where there were more than thirty novices who wished to be
initiated into the discipline, and where we should correctly prescribe
the mystic boundaries of spiritual protection within the monastery.
We had lunch at Gamōno in the same province, tea at the Aichi
River station, and we stopped for the night at Ono.

On the eighth day we had lunch at Samegai in the same province,
took tea at Kashiwabara in Mino Province; then, passing beyond
Fuwa Barrier, we arrived at Tarumi.

On the ninth day we had lunch at Kasanui, where there is now a
stage on the east bank of Kuize River. We had tea on the west bank
of Sunomata River in Owari Province where two monks from Chōboji came to meet us. We crossed the river by boat, and, after having
traversed the floating bridge at Ashika River, we arrived at Kuroda.

On the tenth day we had lunch at Orido in the same province.
Several horses had been sent by Chōboji to transport us, but since

there were none among us either ailing or all that distinguished, and since there were not sufficient horses for each to ride one, we sent them back. From here we could not follow the mainroad; heading north, we proceeded on to Chōboji. Although it rained along the way, this did not impede us, and by night we arrived at Chōboji. The monks at the temple provided us with a bath. Even before this first night, Shōhen had made arrangements with the monks for our ablutions.

The resident monks had earlier entreated Jōshun that we stay for a while so that they might receive instruction, and that we might guide those in whom the desire for enlightenment had lately arisen. Their request was so earnest that Jōshun relayed it to the Master, who was also informed that more than thirty people were involved. Rōen [= Dōen?], head of the temple (son of Yamada Jirō, called Jijū Ajari, the "Chamberlain Teacher"), transmitted his teacher's legacy, administering the land and the temple. The land holdings were extensive and the assets many.

Perhaps it was by virtue of some karmic affinity that one or two monks residing at the temple had stopped at Saidaiji one summer to observe the monks' practice and to hear the principles of the Buddha's teaching. On returning to their own temple, they told Rōen in general terms what the practice was like at Saidaiji. Rōen was immediately inspired by their report. Proceeding in the light of their description, he enlarged the compound into a temple where a great many monks could take refuge, using his assets to provide for them. When he had thus made arrangements, more than thirty came to reside here with a common purpose, having rejected material possessions and that to which they were attached. They wear the monk's robe and observe the post-noon fast (*jōsai*). When the Master heard of these things, he was deeply moved.

On the morning of the eleventh day the monks residing at the temple, more than thirty in number, came in single file to pay their respects to the Master. After repeatedly being asked for instruction, he promised to lecture on the Ten Major Commandments of the *Net of Brahma Sutra*[65] from that day until the fifteenth. During the supper hour he lectured on the sutra at the temple's Śākyamuni Hall. The audience of priests and laymen was moved to tears of gratitude.

During the supper hour on the twelfth day when he lectured on the sutra, the Śākyamuni Hall could not accommodate all the men and women, rich and poor, who assembled to hear him. From that day on he lectured at the Main Hall.

On the thirteenth day he lectured to a large audience during the supper hour. At the Hour of the Dog [about 8 p.m.] in the private oratory in his quarters he established the mystic boundaries [for an altar].[66]

On the morning of the fourteenth he conducted a Repentance Meeting based on the Four Groups [of regulations][67] in the Main Hall, his disciple Shōhen interpreting the regulations. Following this, he exhorted the monks individually to observe the discipline. During the supper hour Eizon lectured on the sutra, and that night the thirty resident monks and an assembly of 197 laymen took the Bodhisattva Vows.[68]

On the morning of the fifteenth Eizon removed the mystic boundary within the oratory, extending it to other areas throughout the temple compound. After the noon repast he held an Expounding of the Nirvana Sutra (*Nehankō*) to an audience which overflowed the Main Hall so that it was difficult to hear him. He then conducted a Net of Brahma Repentance Meeting (*Bommō fusatsu*) in a lane outside the building with the Master explaining the regulations, with forty-nine attending priests and a crowd of 3,077 people who wished to establish karmic affinities with him. That night in the Main Hall he conducted a Relic Venerating Ceremony (*sharikō*), after which the lay priest Yamada Jirō, Rōen's father [Akinaga], presented him with a robe. Then the party moved on, stopping at the Maejima stage in Suruga Province . . .

Could Eizon ever have imagined that his record of stopping at an obscure country temple would be pored over centuries later in lands far beyond remotest India, he might have provided us with a mass of careful details about Chōboji. But we must be grateful for the sketch that has survived, with Mujū himself somewhere in the shadows.

The record does raise questions. Eizon's "Rōen" is presumably Mujū's "Dōen", the names being sufficiently homophonous for Eizon — actually the scribe Shōkai — to have misunderstood. Other temple records belonging to Saidaiji refer to several individuals called Dōen, Dōgyō (Mujū's personal name), and "a man from Hitachi Province" (possibly Mujū). In spite of ambiguities, there was evidently a close connection between Mujū, Chōboji, and Saidaiji. The "one or two monks residing at the temple who had stopped at Saidaiji one summer to observe the monks' practice" could well have been Mujū and his immediate predecessor, the Disciplinary sect monk mentioned in the "Record of a Dream," Mujū's fragmentary account of events leading to his becoming abbot of Chōboji. And Dōen's predilection for disciplinary practices might explain the temple's transfer first to one and then the other. But where is priest

Jōgan, from whom Mujū says he received the temple? And why is Dōen so prominent? Whatever the answers to these questions, we do see Chōboji as an active religious center with a substantial following of monks and laymen: people are being ordained, lecturing, sending out horses, eating, and taking baths. We do not get this sense from the old monk's writings; there we see a solitary individual recording the isolated anecdotes and reminiscences of many years and many places.

Mujū could not have realized it at the time, but he had come to Chōboji to stay. The year was 1262.[69] Enni's disciple Mukan Fumon (1212-1291) was returning from China and would eventually become first abbot of Nanzenji in Kyoto. And toward the end of the year Shinran Shōnin, the great Pure Land leader, died at the age of ninety.

Chōbōji: 1262-1312

The commercial and industrial city which has been known as Nagoya only since the Tokugawa period (1603-1868) was quite a different place in Mujū's day. The center of attention then was the great Atsuta Shrine,[70] a Shintō sanctuary second in importance only to the shrine at Ise dedicated to the Sun Goddess, Amaterasu — its only competitor being the ancient shrine at Izumo associated with the Wind God, Susa-no-o, and his descendant, the Great Land-Ruler Deity, Ō-kuni-nushi. Atsuta was important because it housed the Heavenly Grass-Mowing Sword, one of the Three Imperial Regalia, the others being the Mirror and the Jewel. According to the most ancient legends, the Heavenly Grass-Mowing Sword had been discovered in a tail of the eight-tailed dragon slain by the Wind God, who presented it to his sister, the Sun Goddess. Later this same sword was used by the semi-legendary hero, Yamato Takeru (4th cen. A.D.)[71] against the hairy Emishi; but he made the mistake of not having the invincible sword with him during his final encounter with a mountain god. After his death his wife, Princess Miyasu of Owari Province, erected a shrine in which to venerate the divine sword, this being the origin of Atsuta Jingū.

Atsuta was a regular stop on the major artery, the Eastern Sea Road (Tōkaidō) connecting Miyako, the capital (i.e., Kyoto), with the eastern regions. In Mujū's day the traffic was mainly between the capital and Kamakura, site of the Minamoto-Hōjō military establishment since 1192; after 1600 the eastern terminus was Edo (later Tokyo), where the Tokugawas also ruled in the name of the emperor. But whatever the century, Atsuta, or simply "The Shrine" (Miya), was a major stop along the way (see Figure 4). Two travel diaries written in the first half of the thirteenth century, the *Sea Route Journal* and the *Journal of a Trip to the Eastern Barrier*,[72] describe passing through Atsuta. So also does the famous *Diary of the Waning Moon* by the nun Abutsu, who traveled to Kamakura in 1277 for redress from the military authorities. She speaks of visiting Atsuta Shrine, "since it was not out of our way,"[73] on the twentieth day of the tenth month. But none of our three travelers had any

35

reason to go an hour out of their way to visit Chōboji. In trying to visualize Mujū's neighborhood, we must strip away the steel and concrete of modern commercial Nagoya, replacing them with trees, cultivated fields, and dirt roads between temples, shrines, and other centers of interest. Even the famous castle is not ancient enough for our visual re-creation, having been built only in the early seventeenth century. Most of the activity was to the south and southeast of Chōboji, with a route to the northeast leading through the Kiso region to Zenkōji, the modern city of Nagano. When Mujū speaks of being a rustic living in a country temple, he is only slightly exaggerating. Chōboji was within easy walking distance of both Atsuta Shrine and stages along the Eastern Sea Road, but far enough away to be isolated from the throngs and the traffic.

As we might expect, the fortunes of Chōboji were closely tied to Atsuta Shrine. From the first to the seventh day of the first month in 1179, lightning was seen flashing between Atsuta and Kigasaki, the site where Chōboji would be built. The lord of the district, Yamada Jirō Shigetada (1165–1221), was informed in a dream that after a hundred years Kigasaki would be a flourishing center for the propagation of Buddhism, and that he was to construct a temple there. Mujū says of Shigetada, who later supported Emperor Gotoba in the Jōkyū War, that he was

> . . . skillful in the Way of Bow and Arrow. Being highminded and a man of dignity, he also had a gentle disposition and was aware of the people's sufferings. In all respects he was a gentleman. (*S&P* 9:4; *Traces*)

The temple constructed by Shigetada was formally named Momooji and was affiliated with Tendai. But because of its dedication, it acquired the nickname Chōboji, the "Temple for the Eternal [Life] of the Mother [of Yamada Shigetada]." This became its official designation when Mujū took charge as abbot.[74]

While events of far-reaching national importance were taking place, the Momooji continued its day-to-day operations without any particular distinction. We know the names of the abbots who preceded Mujū, and very little else about them. Perhaps they had decided that there was nothing for them to do until the hundred year prophecy was to be realized. In any case, Mujū came to live at Momooji in 1261, a decade and a half short of the century mark, at the behest of the Atsuta Deity. He was thirty-five years of age. Shortly thereafter the temple buildings burned to the ground but were soon restored.

At that time the Echigo lay-priest Dōen, son of Yamada Akinaga, became Mujū's disciple, together with his wife. They built the Buddha Hall, monks quarters, abbot's residence, and other buildings, donating to the temple their entire worldly possessions of land and household goods. (*Kigasaki*)

Dōen's father, Akinaga (1181–1266), was Shigetada's brother (see App. D: Yamada Family Genealogy). He had also been involved in the Jōkyū fighting but escaped beheading through the intercession of the bodhisattva Yakushi, according to Mujū, who was told of the incident by "the lay priest who had been his adopted son." The data is fragmentary, but it is at least clear that the Yamada family had a continuing interest in Chōboji during its early years. It is also likely that Muō, Mujū's successor to the temple, was the great-grandson of its founder, Shigetada.

The military dictator, Hōjō Tokiyori, of whom Mujū speaks well, is said to have constructed the Main Gate to the temple and to have donated land for its support (*Kigasaki*). The Momooji was rebuilt as a small building within the temple precincts, and from this time forward the complex was officially known as Ryōjusen ("Numinous Eagle Mount") Chōboji. Ryōjusen is a modest "mountain," the temple being on somewhat higher ground than the surrounding neighborhood. Its name is borrowed from the site where the *Lotus Sutra* was proclaimed: Gṛdhrakūta, "Mount of the Numinous Eagle." Kigasaki Ryōjusen Chōboji, located at Yadamachi, Higashi-ku, in Nagoya, continues to thrive today as a Rinzai temple. Rebuilt in 1682, none of its structures date from the Kamakura period although several documents and a wooden sculpture of Mujū survive.

When Mujū first arrived at Momooji, its abbot was a certain Jōgan Shōnin (or simply, Jōgambō) who was anxious to transfer responsibility for the temple to other hands. It seems that even before the fire he had appointed as his successor a monk associated with Eizon's Saidaiji, who stayed only briefly. This could account both for the fact that Mujū saw himself as immediately succeeding Jōgan, and for the fact that Jōgan does not appear in the record of Eizon's visit.

Mujū had a dream, recorded in a surviving fragment in his own hand (*Musō no koto*; Fig. 2), which he later interpreted as sanction for the transfer of Momooji from Jōgan. In this "Record of a Dream" he tells of seeing the first abbot of Momooji, the Venerable Kanshō, reciting the *Lotus Sutra* for the edification of the Shintō deity Hachiman. This deity was associated with the Yamada manor and

Figure 2. Record of a Dream (*Musō no koto*). Fragment in Mujū's hand describing his receipt of the Chōboji from Jōgambō in 1262. (Chōboji, Important Cultural Property.) *Photo by Kawabe Ryōsuke.*

appeared to Mujū in Shintō garb, although he is referred to as a "Great Bodhisattva," a Buddhist title. The *Lotus Sutra* is not an esoteric text, of course, but it is the basic scripture of Tendai, which incorporated esoteric practices. Here is Mujū's account:

A year after I came to the temple, the administration of Momooji was handed over to a priest [of the Esoteric Disciplinary Sect] who did not accept the esoteric practices. This was completely at variance with the ideas of the late Jōgan Shōnin, and he himself was preparing to leave the temple.

One night in a dream I saw a man wearing a pure white robe and tall headgear, looking not at all like a monk and seated elegantly in the abbot's quarters. Also with a diligent air, another sat facing a copy of the *Lotus*, while holding a long string of rosary beads in his hands and chanting the sutra quietly.

In my dream I wondered if this was the Venerable Kanshō; and if it was the god Hachiman Daibosatsu who worshipped at this Buddhist service. The following morning when I awoke, I found that the new abbot, angered by some minor incident, had left the temple. Was it because he considered the esoteric practices evil? Or did Hachiman arrange for his departure? In the light of all this, I have practiced the esoteric rituals with diligence.[75]

Mujū took charge of Momooji, as he had assumed responsibility for Hōonji sixteen years earlier, without the gradual preparation during years of apprenticeship that would have guaranteed a smooth transition. The beginnings were promising, but the results were as before. The responsibilities of a rural temple, whether it be the Tendai Hōonji or the Zen Chōboji, differed from those of the great establishments in Kyoto or Kamakura. The Zen pioneers had introduced a monastic regimen based on Sung Chinese models that was unique in its time.

The Zen monastery and its lifestyle are today so accepted as Japanese that it is difficult to realize how exotic the new Zen monasteries must have seemed in the thirteenth century. Not only were monastery buildings different in style, disposition, and furnishing from anything existing in Japan; the robes of Zen monks, their manner of walking and bowing, their etiquette before and after eating, bathing, and even defecating were also distinctive.[76]

However, the meditation-centered programs at Eisai's Jufukuji or Enni's Tōfukuji differed radically from the community-oriented activities at rural Chōboji, activities which have probably changed little over the centuries. Although Mujū does not provide us with a detailed job description, we can easily sketch a composite of the details of his daily routine and responsibilities. He is acutely aware of his responsibility to provide adequate services to those who support him, some of his harshest criticism being directed at those who are mere parasites, or who cause inconvenience to others even in a good cause. He is generally tolerant of human foibles, but not of exploitation.

Basically, Chōboji was a rural community center, and Mujū's responsibilities were to pray for the living, to visit the sick, and to bury the dead. Since his own practice of *zazen* was severely limited by chronic beriberi, it is possible that he did not feel qualified to supervise a meditation program for his own disciples. Mujū frequently mentions that Chōboji was a temple where the regulations were observed (perhaps referring to the post-noon fast, and possibly also to new Zen rules adopted from Enni), and that he had been faithful to the practice of esoteric rites. We also know that Mujū wrote and traveled. The *Sketch* discusses his close association with Atsuta Shrine and shows him puttering around the temple complex planting trees and lotuses, lugging in bushels of consecrated soil from distant Mt. Kōya, and rearranging the mortuary tablets, etc. — which may tell us more about Kenryō than Mujū. Still, the description is consistent with the personality that emerges from Mujū's writings. The old monk never married. Although at the time marriage for the clergy was gradually being accepted in the Pure Land and Nichiren movements, the Zen sects insisted on monastic celibacy until the Meiji period. However, Mujū considers the pros and cons of the arrangement in a sequence of humorous anecdotes in *Sand and Pebbles* (4:3–4:6).

Shortly after becoming abbot, Mujū made a trip to the shrine of the Sun Goddess at Ise, "during the Kōchō era 1261-64" (*S&P* 1:1); and this inspired him to take up his writing brush. Mujū was a late bloomer. There are no indications that he wrote anything before beginning his first, and most famous, composition: the *Collection of Sand and Pebbles*. Begun in 1279, when Mujū was already past fifty, the work proceeds systematically and with restraint, as befits a debut. After a short preface in which he proposes to extract the gold and jewels of the Buddha's teachings from the sand and pebbles of ordinary events, Mujū mentions the pilgrimage which he made to the great shrine, and then explains that the outward manifestations of Shintō are accommodations made by the buddhas and bodhisattvas to meet the specific needs of the people of Japan. The ten chapters of the first of ten books of the collection (translated here in their entirety) are variations on the theme of "skillful means," accommodation, the focus of Mujū's religious thought. These first tentative chapters are carefully organized, but contain only a glimmer of the sense of humor for which *Sand and Pebbles* was to become noted: the story of the monk who prayed for better lodgings, only to be moved from the East Pagoda's Northern Valley on Mount Hiei to the West Pagoda's Southern Valley (1:7). As he gradually warms to his task, the work becomes more diffuse (especially chapters 6-10) and Mujū often concentrates on the anecdote rather than the moral which it is supposed to illustrate. By the latter half of Book Five, he is discussing poetry, which, however, is defended on religious grounds; and in the first half of Book Six, he includes a set of bawdy anecdotes which were subsequently excised by the author as he revised the work in his later years, resulting in the "abbreviated" family of texts. The first draft of *Sand and Pebbles*, the source of the "unabbreviated" texts, was completed in the autumn of 1283. Then "his disciple Mujin Dōshō took the manuscript to be copied at Kyoto's Saihōji. This work has been popular up to the present day and has circulated widely. There has never been anyone — priest, layman, noble or commoner — who has not thought well of it." (*Traces*) Affiliated with the Rinzai Zen sect, Saihōji in west Kyoto is famous today for its garden designed by Musō Kokushi (1275-1351); hence its popular name, Kokedera ("Moss Temple"). The temple claims to have been founded by Gyōgi Bosatsu and had an impressive history even by Mujū's day.

    Sand and Pebbles, both as a literary and as a social document, is Mujū's major claim to our attention today. Although it is one of the last examples of the *setsuwa* genre, it is not merely a reworking of older materials. In the Epilogue we are told that . . .

> There is an abundance of old stories, but it seems that people do not write about things which have happened recently. . . . So I have written down, just as I have happened to recollect them, various anecdotes from here and there, things which happened in China and Japan, and tales from both ancient and modern times.

    Mujū frequently tells us that he either witnessed an event himself, or that he had it on unimpeachable authority. The result is a collection of vignettes mostly of ordinary life, a view of medieval Japan which we do not find in the better-known literature of the military class and of the court. For a well-rounded picture of those times, we must look to the neglected genres of Tale Literature and the Vernacular Tracts. Here we can catch a glimpse of everyday Japan, a world apart from the Japan of court intrigues, military prowess, and refined sensibilities. The ore of these neglected genres often seems too poor to be refined; but it contains elements not found elsewhere. The content of *Sand and Pebbles* owes little to such *setsuwa* collections as *Tales of Times Now Past* (ca. 1120) and *Tales Gleaned at Uji* (ca. 1190-1242),[77] but its style also differs considerably. These earlier collections have their story to tell, and then they may append a moral. *Sand and Pebbles* tends to subordinate the story to the moral.

There are no serious doubts that Mujū is the author of *Sand and Pebbles,* its authenticity being confirmed by internal and external cosiderations. For most *setsuwa* collections it is difficult to determine either the author or the date, and the important link to a specific historical and social situation is broken. Mujū's fairly extensive literary production permits us to explore in some depth the mental furnishings of an intelligent, pedantic cleric of average social position and with a saving sense of humor. His ideas are a mixture of old and new, as were the times in which he lived. The emphases, the repetition of certain themes, the choice of examples and scriptural citations, all contribute to a coherent intellectual portrait of a man who was in touch with popular Buddhism on the ground level, while at the same time being unusually knowledgeable about the various sectarian positions of his age. As pieces of a composite portrait the lesser literary productions of his old age now have a value that they would not have as anonymous works. Moreover, great personages are soon turned into icons by admiring hagiographers. But Mujū has enough failings to make him all too human, and he himself is aware of them. Few personages from earlier Japan lend themselves so well to sympathetic reconstruction. It is difficult to imagine many of Mujū's exalted contemporaries, for example, taking a drink to relieve the discomfort of beriberi.

One wonders what Mujū's younger contemporary, Marco Polo (ca. 1254-1324), and medieval Europe, would have made of *Sand and Pebbles.* Marco had been received by Kublai Khan in 1275; and, had the Mongols been successful in their two attempts to invade Japan, he might well have been dispatched on a mission to that distant chain of islands, as he had been to other remote regions. When he returned to Venice in 1295, he might have carried a copy of the new manuscript in his luggage—idle speculation, of course, but helpful in seeing Japan in relation to contemporary Western affairs.

Mujū was fifty-three when he began to write the draft of *Sand and Pebbles,* already seeing himself as an old man, although he still had a third of a century before him.

At a time when he should be aware of the things of impermanence which thought-by-thought obstruct his apprehension of Reality, and when he should be concerned over his step-by-step approach to the nether world, piling up provisions for the long journey to the subterranean regions and preparing the boat to carry him over the deep currents of the troubled seas of life, this old priest is writing down incidents that strike his fancy, and recording frivolous worldly anecdotes.

These writings and the daily affairs of temple management now engaged his attention. We know little of his relationships with his parishioners, except that they continued to decline. One positive insight into his stewardship, if we are to believe the Tokugawa biographers, was his role in originating Owari Manzai, a folk performance to celebrate the New Year which survives even today as a local custom in the Chita Region, on a small peninsula just south of Nagoya.

There was a man called Yūsuke who had two children, an elder son called Arimasa, and a younger, Tokuwaka. Both father and sons made a living sweeping gardens and doing odd jobs (Sketch) . . . Sometime during the Shōō Period (1288-1292) Mujū composed a singing performance to celebrate the festivities of the New Year, calling it Manzaigaku. He gave it to Tokuwaka to perform, taking it from door to door. By now the practice has become widespread. The words of the performance are for the most part taken from the Lotus Sutra. Mujū's intention is said to have been to utilize "wild words and specious phrases" (kyōgen kigo) as cause for praising the Buddha-Vehicle, and as condition for turning the Wheel of the Law. (Traces)[78]

During the last two decades of the thirteenth century and the first decade of the fourteenth, Mujū occupied himself with his writings, both new works and the revisions we spoke of earlier. He mentions at the very end of Casual Digressions that some years earlier he had compiled a number of items that appealed to him during his illness, and that when he circulated them as Sand and Pebbles without revisions, the response was mixed. So Mujū continued to revise the work for the next quarter century, with the result that it subsequently appeared in two significantly different versions: an "unabbreviated text", presumably the original of 1283; and an "abbreviated text", which had been worked on as late as 1308. Not only were some items deleted and others added to the "abbreviated text", but separate anecdotes and entire chapters were rearranged into different books of the collection. And since both versions are still current in a variety of Tokugawa and modern print-ings, confusion often results. The current standard edition (Watanabe's *Shasekishū*) is unabbreviated; but the most widely cir-culated versions since the early Tokugawa period have been ab-breviated. The general reader need only remember that there are two main families of *Sand and Pebbles* texts, and that he should be cautious when checking citations.[79]

Mujū's other three works never enjoyed the popularity of *Sand and Pebbles*. The next to be composed was the *Collection of Sacred Assets* (Shōzaishū), a doctrinal tract in three books begun at Chōboji in 1299 and revised in 1308 at Rengeji, a nearby temple which Mujū often visited in his late years.

> Although sick and uncomfortable in this mid-winter, I wiped these tired old eyes and drove my failing mind for several days from a deep hope that this work would circulate widely, finally copying one volume in its present form.
> Kongō Busshi (son of the Diamond Buddha)
> in the tradition of Tōji Temple, Dōgyō,
> at the worldly age of eighty-three,
> sixty-six years a monk.
> Signed Ichien, my residence name;
> and Mujū, my religious name.[80]

Sacred Assets is similar in style and content to the *Mirror for Women* (Tsuma kagami), a vernacular tract traditionally believed to have been completed in 1300, when Mujū was in his seventy-fifth year.[81] Whether or not it was actually written by Mujū, the *Mirror* does provide a convenient synopsis of the moral concerns pervading his writings; and it is easy to see why he has been credited with the work. We should be diligent in religious practice, fortunate in hav-ing attained birth in human form and in having encountered the Law of the Buddha; for the law of karma is inexorable and today's folly surely leads to tomorrow's suffering. But while the wise observe the precepts, they are not taken in by the ambiguity of appearances. And "the mass of men sink or float in the sea of birth-and-death in accordance with their state of mind." Aware of the evanescence of life, we should lay up treasures where the moth and rust do not con-sume, developing evenmindedness toward both the joys and the ills of worldly life. Among the methods which we might employ in this degenerate age are Zen, devotion to Amida, but also the esoteric

and other practices of an earlier day. "Inasmuch as natural dispositions are not all identical, the teaching has a myriad differences."
We should take guidance where we find it, being careful not to
disparage the methods of others.

A curious feature of the *Mirror for Women* is that Mujū is more
than halfway through the work before he first addresses the question
of right behavior as it specifically applies to women. It is as if he
were continuing *Collection of Sacred Assets*, and belatedly decided
to give his new composition a particular emphasis. The main theme
of the *Mirror* is that life for all human beings is transient, and that
we should strive diligently for our salvation. In the course of the
tract Mujū quotes Tao-hsüan,[82] patriarch of the Chinese
Disciplinary Sect, on "the seven grave vices of women", following
this with several anecdotes about women before returning to themes
of general religious practice. There may be "many serious instances
of the sins of women", but "there is no time to discuss them in
detail."

Quite apart from Mujū's personal choice of topics to discuss or
to ignore is the fact that Buddhist ethics is basically asexual and,
indeed, is not even confined to human kind. Specific rules inevitably reflect the biases of the societies to which the ideal is
adapted, an ideal of enlightenment for all sentient beings without
regard to sex or even species. In male-dominated societies one would
expect to see this adaptation reflect anti-feminist attitudes, but we
must be careful to distinguish the essential from the peripheral.
While social relationships are the basis of Confucian ethics, they are
of little interest, and indeed often a hindrance, to one whose goal is
liberation from conceptual, including social, restraints. As Mujū
remarks in the *Mirror*, "It is characteristic of death that it varies for
neither warrior nor slave." Instead of telling women to obey their
husbands—see, for example, the notorious *Greater Learning for
Women*, ascribed to Kaibara Ekiken[83]—Mujū tells them to avoid
envy. But this admonition applies equally to all creatures. The basic
fault is attachment that hinders us from realizing enlightenment;
and sensuality, envy, and delusion are only so many facets of it. The
social implications of behavior are not Mujū's concern.

The *Mirror for Women* is similar in style to *Sand and Pebbles*
in its doctrinal diversity, in the rather terse treatment of the anecdotes which illustrate a moral, and even in an occasional flash of the
humor for which Mujū is noted. But on the whole the *Mirror* is a
staid piece of writing by a man in his mid-seventies residing at a
small country temple where he found it increasingly difficult to get

along with his disciples and friends. Nevertheless, when we recall the humorous incidents recorded in *Sand and Pebbles*, we are not surprised to find in the *Mirror* the story of Ciñcā, who feigned pregnancy by hanging a bowl under her dress, or Yajñadattā, who thought that she had lost her head, or of the venal priest who turned into a cow.

Nowhere does Mujū describe the circumstances of the composition of the *Mirror*, but in the concluding paragraph he does give an explanation of its title: ". . . should a woman make these precepts her constant companion [as she would a mirror], she will show herself to be a person of sensibility, a follower of the Way. And so I give this work the title, *Mirror for Women*." But why should he use the character for *tsuma* (literally, "wife") in the title rather than, say, the character for *onna* ("woman")? To the extent that the tract is directed to women at all, it is not directed to them in their roles as wives. Given Mujū's penchant for wordplay, it is possible that "*Tsuma kagami*" may have been suggested by the title of the famous chronicle of the Kamakura military establishment, *Azuma kagami*,[84] Mirror of the East, whose text was largely completed by 1270 and may well have been known to Mujū. The characters for *azuma* (*a-tsuma*, literally, "my wife") may be used as rebus symbols, or *ateji*, for the word pronounced *azuma*, meaning "east" — thus, *Azumi kagami*, "Mirror of the East". By simply omitting the first character, we have the title of Mujū's discourse. The probability of wordplay is reinforced by the fact that the folk etymology of *azuma* is associated with Yamato Takeru, after whom the Heavenly Grass-Mowing Sword was deposited at Nagoya's Atsuta Shrine.

> Therefore, when he ascended to the summit of Usuhi and looked down towards the southeast, he sighed three times, and said, 'Alas! my wife!' Therefore the provinces east of the mountains were given the name Azuma.[85]

The role of women in the establishment of Chōboji may have had an indirect influence on Mujū's concern for women's salvation. As we saw earlier, the temple was originally established by Yamada Shigetada in 1179 as a memorial to his mother. Shigetada and his son Shigetsugu both perished in the Jōkyū War in 1221; and Shigetsugu's wife Sukeko (1182-1249) may have been the grandmother of Mujū's successor, Muō. In addition, the lay priest Dōen *and his wife* are said to have rebuilt Chōboji after a fire in 1262, and to have become Mujū's disciples. (Dōen was the son of Shigetada's brother, Akinaga; see Appendix D: Yamada Family Geneology). It is not unlikely that Shigetada's mother, Sukeko, and Dōen's wife, all of whom were prominent in the fortunes of Chōboji, and thus of Mujū himself, were in his thoughts when he composed the *Mirror for Women*. In 1300, Mujū was given to the nostalgia and reminiscence of old age, traits seen conspicuously in *Casual Digressions* a few years later. Perhaps Mujū wrote the *Mirror for Women* with some sense of paying back old debts. But whatever the circumstances of its composition, it provides us with a concise sketch of Mujū the moralist.

Mujū's final composition was *Casual Digressions*, begun at Rengeji in 1304 and completed at Chōboji the following year. Like *Sand and Pebbles*, it is a *setsuwa* collection in ten books, although only about seven-tenths the length of that work. The writing style employs more Chinese constructions, and its content tends toward the doctrinal tract. *Casual Digressions* is particularly valuable for what Mujū tells us about himself, as we have seen in these introductory chapters. Mujū also explains why he decided to write the work.

> I composed the *Collection of Casual Digressions* at the request of certain colleagues, following my hand where it led. There seem to be many stylistic faults, with one thing piled upon another. This life of eight decades has left only the time from morning to evening, and the end is only a breath away. If my colleagues, perusing this after my death and thinking that it were just as if I was talking to them, follow my dying admonitions, then they would repay a part of their filial obligations as disciples.

> I call this work *Casual Digressions* but I have included much Buddhist doctrine. It is difficult to distinguish right from wrong. But if a man of understanding peruses this, he may delete what is not good and add what is. The work can be utilized as cause and condition (*in'en*) for instructing beginners. Used properly, it converts the error of "wild words and specious phrases" (*kyōgen kigo*) into a cause (*in*) for praising the vehicle of the Buddha, and a condition (*en*) for turning the Wheel of the Law. . . .(*CD* 8:5)[86]

Toward the end of *Casual Digressions* (1305) Mujū again speaks of writing during illness, now in his evening years when this might be expected. His beriberi apparently was a chronic condition throughout his life; and, from about age forty, he found that a little *sake* now and then eased his discomfort, although he was ambivalent about calling drink by the euphemism, "medicine."

> Some years ago when I was staying in the monastic quarters of a friend, he asked me if I would care to have any "medicine" (*kusuri*).

"I drink because I am a sick man, but it's still wrong, " I replied.
"Why should I lie about it by calling *sake* 'medicine'?" Pleased by my
response, he offered me spirits unobtrusively.

When I related this incident to a fellow priest who observed the
strict regulations, he commended me. Certainly I was not praised
because my behavior was good, but rather because I was aware of the
regulations.

A sick person may drink *sake.* In the regulations[87] appears the
passage: "If a doctor prescribes liquor to relieve illness, it may be
taken at will." In the Mahāyāna a little *sake* and many medicines are
prescribed for the sick. Prince Shōtoku, a Manifest Trace of the
bodhisattva Kannon, says in the *Autograph History of the Tennōji*[88]
that the sick monk is permitted to take the five spicy roots [onions,
scallions, leeks, garlic, and ginger],[89] meat, and *sake.* But when the
sickness is relieved he must return to the approved diet.

The prohibition against lying is one of the Ten Major Commandments. How can we condone the attitude of blithely breaking it
without reason? . . . At secular parties people force liquor on you,
and then, roaring drunk, spill their drinks — it is like a flood. On the
other hand, the monk who strictly observes the discipline does not
drink at all: this is like a drought. My drinking is a little like an evening shower on parched ground. It makes me feel mellow but never
wild. This is certainly not a serious excess. I use it to treat my illness,
and it helps a bit. (*CD* 3:1)

The weakness in his legs may have inhibited Mujū's practice of
meditation, but not his ability or zest for traveling. Late in life he
frequently visited Rengeji in Kuwana, the stage just to the west of
Atsuta Shrine. It could easily be reached within a day from Chōboji,
partly by land and partly by sea, to avoid several river crossings. The
temple no longer exists and its records have long since been scattered. The biographer Tainin tried unsuccessfully to find the temple
two centuries ago:

When I inquired recently, I found that a mile or so west of
Kuwana there is a village called Rengeji-mura. The temple has
disappeared and left only its name to the place. There is also an area
called "Temple Ruins" (Teraato), but it is a complete wasteland,
having been left unattended for so many generations. No one knows
anything about it.

Fifteen minutes west of Nishi-Kuwana station on the Mie Kōtsū

Line at the Rengeji stop is the hamlet of Harina-shi Rengeji, formerly Ōaza Rengeji of Ariyoshi-mura in the Kuwana district. This is the site of the Rengeji temple visited by Mujū, but no trace of the temple remains. A walk of five or six minutes to the north of this place brings one to a temple called Sōfutsuzan Rengeji, belonging to the Ōtani Shinshū sect. This temple, of recent origin, took its name from that of the old village and has no relationship to the Rengeji of Mujū's time.[90]

Apart from occasional side trips, Mujū had been at Chōboji since 1262, or perhaps a year earlier. By the first decade of the fourteenth century, his life there had grown stale — which may partly account for his attraction to Rengeji.

> Apparently I have a karmic affinity with this temple [Chōboji], for I have frequented it for forty-three years. At this temple without a patron the smoke of prosperity never rises; apart from my robe, bowl, and religious implements, I have no material assets. The world considers me an outcast and feels that there is an unquestionable discrepancy between that dream of good fortune at my birth and the facts. But when I ponder the matter carefully, I must conclude that I have indeed had great good fortune in having abandoned the world for the priesthood, and to have heard the principles of Buddhism from the great scholars of the day . . . (CD 3:5; Traces)

> Having lived at this temple for over forty years, perhaps I have exhausted this karma. And so I compose this verse on the myriad affairs in which I have lost interest:
>
> | | |
> |---|---|
> | Hito wa fuwa | Estranged from others, |
> | Tera wa muen ni | My temple without supporters, |
> | Takigi nashi | I have no twigs to burn: |
> | Kigasaki ni koso | Here at Kigasaki |
> | Korihatenikere | I have had enough! |
>
> (CD 4:11; Traces)

What had gone wrong? When Mujū re-established Chōboji in 1262 as a Zen temple affiliated with Enni's prospering Tōjukuji in Kyoto, the prospects seemed bright indeed. He had the continuing support of the Yamada family, and even the military dictator had made a contribution. He had gone to Kigasaki at the express command of the Atsuta Deity, who continued to provide material as well as moral encouragement. The temple was ideally located near, but not too near, a major travel artery and one of the major shrines in the country. One would expect to see Mujū in the evening years of

his life surrounded by eager disciples in a temple where the smoke of
prosperity never stopped rising from kitchen and hearth. But it was
not to be. Elsewhere he says:

> All day long this temple is without support or those who care. With
> not a single item in reserve, I have no fear of burglary. Some years
> ago a robber broke into the temple warehouse and asked where
> everything was. "There's not even a dog's turd here!" I replied. Since
> then burglars have avoided this place. . . .
>
> I have been around this province for forty-three years, and
> everyone must be tired of me by now. As the years pass, my close ac-
> quaintances, both laymen and priests, have become few. This is only
> natural. But because of some old karmic connections, perhaps, there
> are still a few people who are kind to me. Have my karmic ties with
> this place not yet been exhausted? After one gets old perhaps it is bet-
> ter to think to oneself that worldly success and the way things happen
> have their own rationale, and that one should not give himself over to
> many things. Following one's destiny and abandoning religious prac-
> tices, he should leave the rest to the will of heaven. That we do not
> get what we want no matter how hard we try is a fact of life . . . (CD
> 3:5)

The decline of Chōboji even during Mujū's lifetime no doubt
resulted from a complex of causes, and we should not deduce from it
too severe an indictment of Mujū's character. The Yamada family
which had been the temple's patron since its founding was probably
in a depressed financial position after its unhappy involvement in
the Jōkyū War. And after Dōen and his wife donated "their entire
worldly possessions and household goods," they could hardly do
more. On the other hand, the association of Chōboji with the
rebellious Yamadas did not dissuade Hōjō Tokiyori, of the
Kamakura military establishment, from making a substantial contribution to the temple. Had Mujū been a stern religious master like
his teacher Enni, he might have attracted a following of dedicated
disciples. But being as he was — concerned with religious practice
but rather relaxed about it — his next line of support would have to
be the local farmers and craftsmen. The sense of humor which we
find in Sand and Pebbles and his initiation of the Owari Manzai folk
performance suggest the genial pastor loved by his flock. Yet in the
Mirror for Women (1300) we find him scolding those who, "disliking
the local priest, send to a distance to invite a celebrant for their service, snubbing the priest with whom they are out of favor for one
with whom they are on friendly terms." And we have seen that even-

tually he could not even attract burglars. A clue to his evident alienation from the community may be seen in the fact that his works, although purporting to be about the everyday affairs of life, contain few references to events in his immediate neighborhood, even to Atsuta Shrine. In the end we must conclude that the fault lay more in himself than in his stars.

What was special about Rengeji that attracted Mujū? We do not know. Probably he had a friend there, although Mujū never mentions him. There is also an old tradition that Mujū died and was buried at Rengeji,[91] but Tainin disputes this, suggesting that the notion came about from Mujū's close association with the temple. The "Temple of the Lotus Flowers" became Mujū's second home. Near the middle of *Casual Digressions* (4:11), just after his verse of weariness at having lived at Chōboji for over forty years, he composed an allusive variation on an earlier verse by Bishop Henjō (816–890) recalling a phrase from the *Lotus Sutra*:

Yo no naka no	Heart unstained
Nigori ni shimanu	By all the muddiness
Kokoro mote	Of worldly life,
Hachisu no hana no	Ah, to live here at this
Tera ni sumu kana	Temple of Lotus Flowers![92]

And what of his friends and disciples? The record is skimpy. Manuscript notations (*shikigo*) by an author or later copier which are carried forward in subsequent manuscripts and printed editions are a minor source of information, but not to be neglected in the absence of detailed sources. As we saw earlier, certain copies of *Sand and Pebbles* tell of a disciple called Mujin Dōshō, who in 1283 took that work to Saihōji in Kyoto for copying. Notations dated 1293, 1294, 1295, and 1303 tell of a Dōe copying portions of *Sand and Pebbles* at various places in Kyoto, and of giving certain chapters to Dōshō in 1303. Another disciple named Jigen is said to have taken *Casual Digressons* to Mantokuji Temple in Owari Province for copying in 1305. From these scattered notations we can at least learn the names of several of Mujū's disciples: Mujin Dōshō, Dōe, and Jigen. And we also know of Muō, to whom Mujū transferred Chōboji in 1305. Eventually, when the voluminous travel accounts, temple records, diaries, and other miscellanea of the times are fed into an enormous memory bank sometime within the next century, we will know more about these individuals. The pieces to the puzzle exist as does the technology to assemble them.

Tainin's *Traces* says that "the Venerable Jōen who restored
Mantokuji in Owari Province at that time was also from Sagami
Province and belonged to the Kajiwara family. His accomplished
disciple, the Venerable Kūen, was also his nephew; and he founded
the Jizōjiin Ichinomiya. These three men from the same family were
likewise adepts in the esoteric teaching, and from time to time
would meet for elevated conversation. The public called them the
'Three En's.' "

In 1305, Mujū was eighty and it was a busy year for him. In the
third month he handed over the administration of Chōboji to Muō
(=Jun'ichibō), who may have been the great-grandson of Yamada
Shigetada, founder of the temple, and the grandson of Sukeko, his
son Shigetsugu's wife. The *Deed of Transfer* (Figure 3), thought to
be in Mujū's hand, is extant. It says that Muō had been raised by
Mujū since he was six; and this is consistent with other known
details. If Muō came to stay at Chōboji as early as 1262 when Mujū
became its abbot, he could chronologically have been a child of
Sukeko's offspring; in 1305, he would have been about fifty. The
Deed states that although Muō was not very learned, he had practiced *zazen* for many years and was competent enough to take
charge of the affairs of the temple. Although Mujū professes to have
a close relationship with Muō, he evidently has reservations about
the transfer.

Deed of Transfer (Yuzurijō)

This temple was the legacy to the Venerable Jōgambō from his
teacher, the Venerable Keihōkyō, and it became a temple where the
regulations were strictly observed. He then transferred it to me, who
was at the time an unaffiliated monk. When fire destroyed the temple, Dōembō (i.e., Dōen) restored and gave it to me, constructing the
Buddha Hall and other buildings, including an Assembly Hall and
monks' residence. Was it perhaps fate that my unworthy self then
became the temple's founder?

Often when I could not depend on support, I have sometimes
thought of transferring the temple to someone else, and sometimes
thought simply of resigning. But it was well known to people that by
virtue of the dream which I had, I could not sever my connections.
It is my lot to have lived here for forty-four years, diligent even now
in the theory and practice of both the overt and esoteric methods in
these Latter Days when both men and the Law decline. At the feet of
the late founder of Tōfukuji I heard the basic principles of the overt,
esoteric and Zen teachings. Although I did not grasp the essence of

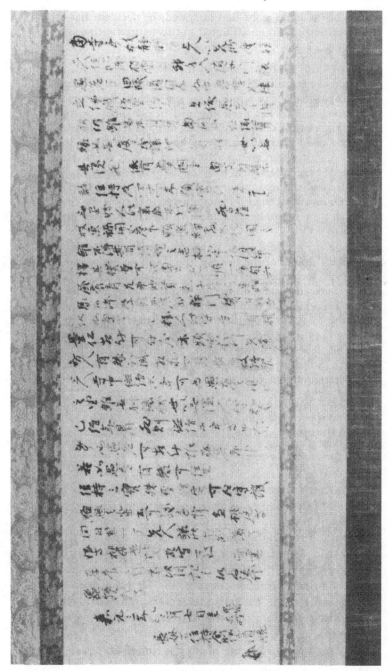

Figure 3. Deed of Transfer (*Yuzurijō*) by which Mujū ceded the Chōboji to Muō in 1305. (Chōboji, Important Cultural Property.)
Photo by Kawabe Ryōsuke.

the transmission of the lamp as he had intended, he decided that I had understood sufficiently to be affiliated to this temple within his tradition.

This Jun'ichibō (Muō) has been raised by me since he was six years old. Being as close as natural kin, our relationship has been as deep as that of brothers, as teacher to pupil, as parent to child. His learning is not extensive, but he has been engaged in Zen practice for years. He can be elder of the temple by seeking out a group to decide matters together, senior men in the overt and esoteric methods, friends in the faith with whom he has affinities. The late Venerable Jōgambō explained to me how to deal with the monks and other matters in the temple; and the reason he offered the temple to me was that even without a formal deed of transfer, everyone knew of the circumstances, which were not to be concealed. In the end I passed my years here.

So if you manage as I have the great and small matters concerning the monks and other affairs of the temple, there will be nothing to object to. If, like me, you maintain connections with people, you will be able to abide here. If, maintaining this temple, you guard the Three Treasures, especially the tradition of the sage priests, then the wicked cannot harm you. Together with the deed from my predecessor giving me the lands belonging to the Momooji as well as the abbot's parasol, I bequeath this temple to you as the legacy of your grandmother [Sukeko?]. By maintaining this temple you will carry on the discharge of your filial duties.

> Recorded at Mt. Kikyō [Momooji's "mountain"] for posterity
> on the seventh day of the third month in Kangen 3 (1305).
> Kongō Busshi (Son of the Diamond Buddha),
> Dōgyō (i.e., Mujū)
> (SEAL)[93]

Mujū then moved to the reconstructed Momooji within the Chōboji compound. Both Tokugawa biographers state that he then fashioned a likeness of himself, Tainin noting that a papier maché statue is still extant. Presumably he has confused this with the wooden statue of the founder (Frontispiece) now enshrined at Chōboji. Kenryō says that Mujū inserted a copy of an esoteric charm, the Jewel-box Spell (Hōkyōin darani; cf. S&P 2:8) into the image after having written the Sanskrit characters himself. A copy of this text was discovered in the wooden statue when it was dismantled for repairs in 1951.[94]

In the years after his retirement, Mujū continued to revise his writings and to visit Rengeji. Finally in 1312

. . . on the tenth day of the tenth month he made the following declaration to his assembled disciples and followers: "All beings will eventually achieve liberation. Be each of you mindful of this and propagate it to later generations." When his followers begged the National Teacher for his death verse, he wrote:

Ichiō umi ni ukite	A single bubble floating on the sea
Hachijū shichinen	Of life for eighty-seven years:
Kaze yami nami shizuka ni	Now the wind abates, the waves subside,
Kyū ni yorite tanzen[95]	And all is tranquil as of old.

Mujū passed away in his eighty-seventh year after placing himself in a square casket in an earthen sarcophagus nine feet long, on the shelves of whose four sides were assembled the implements of the Eight Sects.[96] Seating himself within, he took leave of the world (*Sketch*).

In 1546, ex-Emperor Gonara gave Mujū the posthumous title of Daien Kokushi, "National Teacher of Great Perfection." Along with his writings, the Chōboji which he reconstructed in 1262 survived through the next seven centuries. Today, his carved likeness[97] is enshrined in the Founder's Hall. Naturally, it is the likeness of an elderly monk, although we would not guess that its model was eighty-six years of age. His look is serene enough but lacks the air of austerity and determination often seen in the features of other eminent clerics whose likenesses have come down to us. Over the left eye is a wen, the mouth is full and relaxed with the suggestion of a smile. In his right hand he holds a *hossu*, a ritual fly whisk symbolizing spiritual authority, with whose hairs the fingers of Mujū's left hand appear to be playing, appropriately enough. The old monk often regretted his lack of religious zeal; but had he been less worldly, the loss would have been ours. Instead of *Sand and Pebbles* and *Casual Digressions*, the corpus of Japanese Buddhist literature might include two more opaquely serious discourses on the meaning of time or methods of meditation, of interest only to the student of religious history. Mujū's touch of worldliness which is part of his charm for us today would surely have disappeared in the austerity of Self-Realization. Had Mujū been a better monk he would have been less of a writer.

Mujū's World of Ideas

Mujū the storyteller is still approachable after seven centuries of social and ideological change during which his Buddhist-Confucian-Shintō worldview largely was replaced in Japan by an understanding of the human condition not dissimilar to that of the modern West. Mujū the monk and moralist requires of us somewhat more patience, and a willingness to meet him half-way between our respective word games by which we rationalize experience. His concerns are the same human problems to which we attempt to find answers today: life's frustrations, its pain, and its brevity. But the complex of ideas in which he dealt with these problems has no easy parallel in our modern Western consciousness.

For Mujū the cure for life's pain lay in modifying our subjective attitudes rather than in changing the condition of the external world. Although this approach is not uncommon today, Western thought patterns do not provide us with a fund of easily borrowed words and equivalent metaphors with which to reconstruct Mujū's worldview in English. Only gradually are we developing the vocabulary which will permit us to appreciate Buddhist thought as a perfectly straightforward and plausible rationalization of human experience. Even the central Buddhist concept of Nirvāṇa has found no generally-accepted English equivalent, and its interpretation is still debatable.[98] Meanwhile, words continue "to strain, crack and sometimes break, under the burden." The translator is only partly to blame. Sometimes he chooses a word, a phrase, a metaphor, which may not jar the ears of his audience, but which inevitably ignores the context of the original. At other times he must choose an unfamiliar but parallel construction which mirrors the original well enough, only to be charged with obscurantism. The middle way is difficult to achieve, and often little of an improvement.

The dilemma is neither new nor surprising. The acculturation of Buddhism to Chinese ways of thinking began with the simple transliteration of the Sanskrit terms, proceeded to the "method of analogy" with the use of Taoist vocabulary,[99] and finally, four hundred year after its appearance in China, arrived at a distinctive

Chinese vocabulary for Buddhist concepts. Japan benefited from the Chinese experience, but the Japanese assimilation of Buddhist thought was also very gradual. The writer of English today cannot avoid the same problem of communication and must be wary of the apparent similarity of concepts plucked from different contexts.[100]

Often the best course of action may be stay as close as possible to the intractable word or metaphor, resigning ourselves to the realization that every complex of ideas—whether it be the methodology of a discipline or a system of philosophy or religion—has its irreducible expressions which appear as jargon to the outsider; and that if we wish to penetrate that structure of ideas, we may be required simply to accept its peculiar mode of expression. No one asks the Freudian to translate the word, "id", into everyday English; so perhaps we can sometimes extend the same courtesy to Mujū.

For Mujū and his contemporaries, the stage on which sentient beings played the drama of illusion consisted of three major regions: the Realms of Desire, of Form, and of the Formless. The Realm of Desire (*yokkai*) consisted of Six Paths (*rokudō*; or-*shu*, "Destinies") through which beings impelled by desire transmigrated (*rinne*) through the round of birth-and-death (*shōji*) until the karma of their evil action was exhausted and they attained liberation (*gedatsu*), nirvāṇa (*nehan*). According to the Mahāyāna all sentient beings would eventually attain nirvana, but it would take time. The Six Paths were:

1. The heavens of desire
2. The human world
3. The world of fighting-spirits (*asuras*)
4. The animal world
5. The world of hungry-ghosts (*pretas*)
6. The hells.

The Tendai sect, and also Mujū, sometimes referred to the Ten Stations of Being (*jippōkai*), which included the stages of *srāvaka* (*shōmon*), *pratyeka-buddha* (*engaku*), bodhisattva (*bosatsu*), and Buddha beyond the Six Paths. These four stages were not subject to the round of birth-and-death.

Good conduct would lead to rebirth in human form, or in one of the heavens; bad action led to rebirth in one of the Three Evil Destinies (*san'akushu*): of the animals, hungry-ghosts, or the hells. (The world of the fighting-spirits was ambiguous and in some accounts was included among the hells.) The advantage of being born in human form — see, for example, the opening statement of the *Mirror for Women*[101] — is that only in this state can beings perform acts which might lead to an improved stage of rebirth, or even to the final release of nirvana. In the Three Evil Destinies one could only wait passively until his karmic debt was repaid, or until chance brought him into proximity with the Buddhist Teaching. (See, for example, the story of the small clam who was ultimately reborn as the Shingon scholar, Kakukai; *S&P* 2:10.)

The Three Poisons (*sandoku*) of anger, covetousness, and delusion are the sources of bad action; but they may be overcome by any of the variety of religious practice which the Buddha in his compassion has accommodated to specific human biases and needs. We may practice meditation in order to realize our inherent Buddha-nature. Such methods were promoted by the traditional schools of Buddhism, but especially by the newly-introduced Zen sects. Or, by calling on the name of the Buddha Amida (*nembutsu*), we may opt for birth in his Pure Land (*ōjō*), from which there will be no backsliding into the Three Evil Destinies. (Originally, birth in Amida's Pure Land was not considered to be identical with the attainment of Perfect Enlightenment, but came to be so with Shinran.)

Another method through which to attain liberation was esotericism (*mikkyō*), which conceived of the religious life in terms of "the attainment of Buddhahood in the very existence" (*sokushin jōbutsu*) by integrating the three aspects of human action (*sangō*) — deeds, words, and thought — with the parallel functions of the Great Sun Buddha, the Three Mysteries (*sammitsu*) of Mahāvairocana (Dainichi Nyorai).[102] This method was especially associated with Kūkai's Shingon sect, but it was also widely accommodated to other sectarian positions. Tendai had for centuries had an esoteric component; and among the leaders of Kamakura Buddhism, Myōe (Kegon), Eizon (Shingon-Ritsu), Eisai and Enni (both Rinzai Zen) cultivated these traditional practices, which also appealed to Mujū.

The spiritual life might be rationalized in a variety of ways. As Mujū would say: "There is not just one method for entering the Way, the causes and conditions for enlightenment being many" (*S&P* Preface). His syncretism, his conviction that truth not only can, but must, assume a variety of forms is reflected throughout his life and writings. The gods of the native Japanese Shintō pantheon "soften their light to identify with the dust of human affairs." The buddhas and bodhisattvas in their essential nature (*honji*) are ineffable, inaccessible to ordinary human understanding; accordingly, they assume familiar, local guises, "manifesting their traces" (*suijaku*) as a means of leading sentient beings to enlightenment.[103] They assume the forms of Shintō gods, Confucian sages, Taoist immortals, or any other shapes appropriate to the expectations of the devotee, because the underlying Reality transcends all particular manifestations. And yet it is through these particular forms that we, symbolizing animals, are led to the Ineffable. As Kūkai remarked with respect to all expedients: "The Dharma is beyond speech, but without speech it cannot be revealed. Suchness transcends forms, but without depending on forms it cannot be realized. Though one may at times err by taking the finger pointing at the moon to be the moon itself, the Buddha's teachings which guide people are limitless."[104] "Wild words and specious phrases" (*kyōgen kigo*) may also be provisional methods, as the words of poetry are no different than mystic phrases (*dhāraṇī*), all pointing to the same experiential goal beyond all words, all concepts, all symbols.

Common to every Buddhist teaching is the recognition that all conditioned beings are in flux, evanescent, impermanent (*mujō*); and because each exists only interdependently with all other beings, it is intrinsically self-less (*muga*). To strive for *one's own* enlightenment is, in effect, to deny this basic principle of self-lessness. So the Mahāyānists proposed as their spiritual model the bodhisattva, "a being compounded of the two contradictory forces of wisdom and compassion. In his wisdom he sees no persons; in his compassion he is resolved to save them."[105] This compassion arises neither from any desire for profit nor from a sense of altruism — without an *alter*, an "other", the word itself has no meaning. It springs rather from an awareness of the underlying identity between what is conventionally distinguished as "self" and "other."

The compassion of the Buddha is revealed in the manifold Accommodations (*hōben*) which he makes to human frailties, expedients and "skillful means" which include not only the varieties of Buddhist teaching but the mythology of Shintō as well. The importance of the syncretism theme in Mujū's thought is to be seen in the fact that when, fairly late in life, he began to write, this was the first subject which he chose to elaborate. Most of his arguments and illustrations of this topic are conveniently concentrated in the ten chapters of the first book of *Sand and Pebbles*. After the preface and opening chapter, in which Mujū sets forth the general argument for the identity of the gods and buddhas as applied to the Ise shrines, a series of anecdotes interspersed with doctrinal digressions

sets the tone of the work. *Sand and Pebbles* is thus classified as Bud
dhist Tale Literature (*bukkyō setsuwa*), but also occasionally as a Vernacular Tract (*kana hōgo*). The only major item on the syncretism
theme not appearing in the first book is Mujū's defense of poetry.

The Mahāyāna set Buddhists a tantalizing paradox: the sensual
world which obscures our apprehension of enlightenment is at the
same time that in and through which it is to be apprehended. In
doctrinal shorthand: nirvana, the goal of religious activity, is identical with the world of birth-and-death to be transcended. Early
Buddhism had rationalized nirvana as a state *apart from* the world
of everyday affairs. As the agitated elements constituting the
phenomenal world were gradually suppressed through right action,
the unconditioned reality of nirvana emerged. The mechanics of
this process are still debated by scholars, but we can at least say that
nirvana differed from the world of ever-recombining elements.[106]

Then Mahāyāna introduced perspective. The world *seen* from
one point of view was nirvana, from another, birth-and-death; the
difference was not between two physical places but between two
modes of understanding. And it was in and through the common
referent, the world given to immediate experience, that one was
either deluded or enlightened. The cloud of conceptualization
obscuring the Real from us may also be the means through which I
become aware of It — bearing in mind that ultimately there is no "I"
nor any nirvana to be apprehended; both are convenient fictions.
"Those who stumble and fall to the ground also arise by virtue of the
support which the ground provides." The finger pointing at the
moon may be a distraction or a guide, depending on the use to
which we put it. Moreover, the absolutes of morality are only conventional wisdom, useful but not intrinsically fixed. More often than
not they are a help to enlightenment, but as objects of attachment
they are obstacles — as in the story of Chikō and Raikō. And the
bodhisattva, who stands beyond the conventional distinctions of
morality, may bring about good through apparent evil — as did Lady
Mallikā, Vasumitrā, and Prince Shōtoku.[107] Appearances are
deceptive. Behavior with all the outward marks of conformity to the
precepts might lead straight to hell, while apparent wickedness
might in fact be the inspired action of the bodhisattva beyond all
conventional good and evil. The final criterion of right is not the in-
trinsic quality of the act, but the *attitude* of the agent. Thus the difference in behavior between the two monks who committed suicide
in order to attain speedy birth in Amida's Pure Land lay in their attitudes of attachment or freedom from attachment (*S&P* 4:7, 4:8).

The Kade-no-kōji lady who believed that the young monk's deception was a visitation from Jizō was rewarded for her attitude of trust
(S&P 2:6). And in the several anecdotes of extramarital affairs (S&P
7:1, 7:17, rufubon 7B:6), Mujū does not condemn the infidelity or
sexual excess as proscribed by conventional morality; rather, he is
concerned with the *mental state* of those involved. Conventional
morality is not to be dismissed lightly, inasmuch as bad action
creates the karma of birth-and-death; but even more important is
the presence or lack of a state of attachment (anger, jealousy) which
blocks spiritual awareness.

Conventional morality held that "wild words and specious
phrases" (*kyōgen kigo*) were to be avoided as impediments to
enlightenment: hence the condemnation of literature as so much
distraction from right views.[108] But if nirvana were to be realized
within the world of everyday affairs, then these same "wild words
and specious phrases" could be cause for praising the vehicle of the
Buddha and condition for turning the Wheel of the Law. The concept was rooted in Indian Buddhism, but the phrase itself originated
with the Chinese poet Po Chü-i (772–846), from whom it was borrowed by Japanese Buddhists as a catch phrase to express the concept of the noumenal realized through the phenomenal. It appears
throughout Mujū's works, beginning with the Preface to *Sand and
Pebbles*: "Through the wanton sport of wild words and specious
phrases I wish to bring people into the marvelous Way of the Buddha's Teaching." Still, the tension in the paradox remained: delusions of word and thought were certainly to be eschewed (— and,
strictly speaking, even the most "sacred" words and thoughts were
ultimately impediments to enlightenment); but on the other hand,
they might be utilized as expedients, accommodations. "Those who
search for gold extract it from sand; those who take pleasure in
jewels gather pebbles and polish them." Truth was a middle way
between the poles of morality as conventionally (but necessarily)
fixed, and morality as ultimately indeterminate. Literature was to
serve the needs of society—the ultimate goal of both individual and
society, in Mujū's view, being the enlightenment of all sentient beings. What could be said of the inspiring anecdote as a means to
lead people along the path of spiritual realization was even more appropriate for poetry, which was nothing less than *dhāraṇī*, mystic
phrases to establish rapport with the divine.

Mujū had a lively interest in the thirty-one syllable *waka* as well
as in the related linked-verse. His defense of the Way of Poetry as a
religious exercise is an extension of his argument for Shintō-

Buddhist syncretism. Scattered throughout *Sand and Pebbles* and *Casual Digressions* are *waka* by himself and others, and a separate section of *Sand and Pebbles* — from 5A:9 through 5B:11 — is devoted to this theme. The poems are chosen for the most part to illustrate some moral or religious point. Mujū himself was not an outstanding poet, although of sufficient merit to have prompted a modern scholar to compile eighty-three *waka* gleaned from his works.[109] Of greater interest to us is his defense of *waka*, especially as articulated in *Sand and Pebbles* 5A:12.

For him to have defended the Way of Poetry as a method of religious realization was not unusual for his time — Shunzei (1114–1204) and Teika (1162–1241), among others, having but recently seriously applied Tendai religious ideals to their poetic practice.[110] But Mujū's position is a curious by-product of the *honji-suijaku* movement, and his argument is that of a scholar rather than that of a poet.[111]

> Japanese poems do not differ from the words of the Buddha. The *dhāraṇī* of India are simply the words used by the people of that country which the Buddha took and interpreted as mystic formulas. . . . Had the Buddha appeared in Japan, he would simply have used Japanese for mystic verses. . . . (*S&P* 5A:12)

In her famous defense of the novel in *The Tale of Genji*, Murasaki also appeals to the doctrine of accommodation as the rationale for finding the sacred in the profane. Mujū starts from the same premise, but, as a well-educated cleric, could be expected to carry the argument a step further, for better or worse. Mujū's poetry was much like his meditation: better defended than practiced. His few experiments with linked verse are perhaps of some historical interest in the shift of focus to that poetic form from court-centered *waka* during succeeding centuries. These appear mainly in *Sand and Pebbles* 5B:7.

Sand and Pebbles consists of ten books (*kan*), each illustrating one or two major themes. The length and organization of chapters within these books do not follow a consistent pattern. A few are almost fragmentary while others seem excessively long. We may suppose that in some cases a chapter merely reflects the amount of work Mujū produced at one sitting; at other times it is clear that he saw the episodes of a lengthy chapter as all illustrating a central theme, even when their relationship might seem tenuous. Characteristically, his initial anecedote, or *exemplum*, is followed by a religious discourse which it illuminates. This in turn may be followed by another, or series of anecdotes, which are related to each other for the most part by the religious theme under consideration, although sometimes by apparently extraneous factors. At other times a string of short anecdotes appears, like a chain of linked verse, each related to a central theme perhaps, but to one another by additional connecting ideas. The sequence can be described as a controlled stream of consciousness, in which each item is related to what precedes and follows it, although not always to other items in the series. Long didactic interludes often push the work in the direction of the vernacular tract, but even these are often leavened by a spritely humor. Even this selection, consciously focussed on the literary, cannot exclude the message which is Mujū's conscious rationale for writing at all. At other times, Mujū seems to have been attracted mainly by the story, and the moral is incidental or difficult to find.

The major themes of the ten books of *Sand and Pebbles*, according to the organization of the unabbreviated version, are as follows:

Book One. Ten chapters, beginning with "The Great Shrine at Ise," argue that the gods are local manifestations of the buddhas and bodhisattvas. Chapter 10 tells of an Amidist devotee who is punished for his intolerance of other religious practices.

Book Two. Ten chapters relating miracles performed by various buddhas and bodhisattvas: Yakushi, Amida, Kannon, Jizō, Fudō, and Miroku; also diverse sectarian practices.

Book Three. Eight chapters on several doctrinal and moral issues, including the paradox that the apparent good is not always the real good, Confucian anecdotes, and the importance of the appropriate.

Book Four. Nine chapters on the dangers of attachment to mental biases as well as material things.

Book Five. In two parts, Book 5A (twelve chapters) is mainly about scholars. A long section on poetry begins with 5A:9 and continues through the eleven chapters of 5B.

Book Six. Eighteen chapters on preaching. Chapters 1-8, 12-13, which include the earliest tales in the collection, are lacking in the abbreviated versions. If we assume that these were later deleted as being improper, perhaps by Mujū himself, we have the problem of explaining the presence of equally indiscreet episodes in abbreviated but not unabbreviated versions.

Book Seven. Twenty-five chapters on karmic retribution and the evils of envy, carnal attachment, murder, greed and stupidity.

Book Eight. Twenty-three chapters on stupidity and resourcefulness.

Book Nine. Thirteen chapters on honesty, loyalty, and filial piety.

Book Ten. In two parts, 10A (ten chapters) and 10B (three chapters) largely consists of stories of people who have entered the religious life. The concluding anecdotes tell of the final moments of contemporary virtuous monks, especially the Zen followers of Eisai.

We cannot yet clearly assess the extent of Mujū's audience during the seven centuries that separate us from Kamakura Japan, nor can we comprehensively describe the influence of his writings on subsequent literature and thought. Some of the correspondences between his works, especially *Sand and Pebbles*, and later literary productions are close enough to imply a direct influence; others are suggestive but far from convincing. Eventually when we have pieced together the fragments of the puzzle hidden in hundreds of volumes of neglected collectanea, a pattern will emerge. But for the present we can only speculate from a few details and correspondences.

The fifty narratives of the *Shintōshū* (Collection of the Way of the Gods, ca. 1358-61) are a major bridge between the Buddhist *setsuwa* of Kamakura and the short stories (*otogizōshi*) of the Muromachi period.[112] It was used, and perhaps composed, by members of the Agui school of preachers, which included Shōgaku (1167-1235), son of the movement's founder, Chōgen. Whatever other influences *Sand and Pebbles* may or may not have had on *Shintoshū*, we do find a close parallel between passages in *S&P* 1:1 and the latter.[113] The story of the faithful mandarin duck killed by a hunter (*S&P* 7:14) reappears in *Ikkyū's Travels All Over* (Ikkyū shokoku monogatari, 1672).[114] And there is a close similarity between the most famous of Muromachi short stories, *The Three Priests* (*Sannin hōshi*) and *S&P* 10A:7. The explanation for these apparent influences await further study.

A minor detail which suggests that *Sand and Pebbles* was known to the Nō dramatist Zeami (1363-1443) appears in his play *Kasuga ryūjin* (The Dragon God of Kasuga).[115] Here the *kyōgen* actor refers to Myōe and Gedatsu (Jōkei) as his sons, his "Tarō and Jirō"—a phrase which appears in *S&P* 1:5, but not in four other literary sources likely to have provided background for the play. And in a related theatrical form, the theme for the *kyōgen*, *Busu*, is generally regarded as having originated in *S&P* 8:11.

Whisperings (1463), a landmark of linked-verse criticism by Shinkei (1406-75), includes more than thirty allusions to *Sand and*

Pebbles in a work of some eighty-three pages in a modern printed edition. It is unlikely that an artist of Shinkei's sensibility was impressed by Mujū's poetic practice, but his ideas *about* poetry are a different matter. Shinkei remarks in discussing the unity of religious and poetic practice:

> Essentially the Way of Poetry is the *dhāranī* of our country. Compared to discoursing in "specious phrases" (*kigyo*), the reading of scripture and the practice of Zen is so much delusion.[116]

In isolation the statement is rather cryptic. But against the background of Mujū's defense of the Way of Poetry in *Sand and Pebbles*, and the related concept of attaining religious realization *through* "wild words and specious phrases" (*kyōgen kigo*), it does not obtrude in any way.[117]

The Ōbaku Zen monk, Tetsugen Dōkō (1630-1682), as editor of a massive edition of Buddhist writings, was in a position to evaluate the plethora of works produced up to the early Tokugawa period. In a postscript to a doctrinal tract which attempted to accommodate Buddhist doctrine to the level of popular understanding, one of his disciples had this to say:

> Since the Zen sect was introduced into this country, there have been few other men [aside from Tetsugen] who have in this fashion presented the essence of it in the Japanese language. The *Collection of Sand and Pebbles* by the Zen master Mujū and the *Dialogue in a Dream*[118] by the master Musō are about the only good books there are; although there are many others, few of them are worth mentioning.[119]

Later in the period the haiku poet, Kobayashi Issa (1763-1827), begins his *Year of My Life* (Oraga haru, 1819) with a retelling of Mujū's account of "The Amida Welcome Service" (*S&P* 10A:9). The anecdote about the nun with the impossibly long name (*S&P* 8:13) is perhaps the ancestor of the popular *rakugo* story, *Jugemu*; and scholars of folklore find variants of popular formulas in both *S&P* and *Casual Digressions* (e.g., *CD* 5:1).

At present some fourteen manuscript copies of *Sand and Pebbles* from the Kamakura through the Edo periods are extant; and there are eleven Tokugawa printed editions—the *Konjaku* has one![120]—and thirteen modern printed editions. Although Mujū's other works have not been as popular, it is curious to note that there have been at least seven modern printings of the *Mirror for Women*. Obviously, Mujū has had some kind of following.

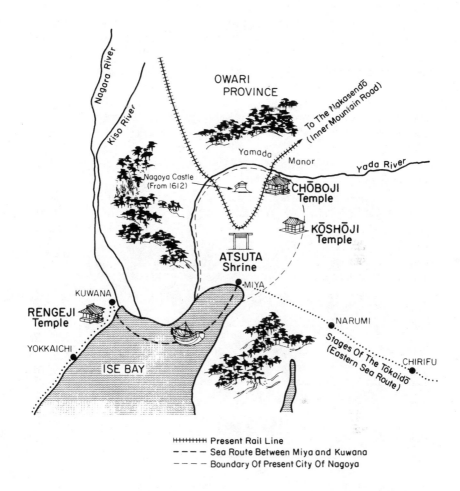

Figure 4. Map of Miya (Nagoya) showing the relationship of Atsuta Shrine, Chōboji, Rengeji, and Tainin's Kōshōji.

The principle of Accommodation so earnestly defended by Mujū gradually lost ground as Japanese Buddhism became increasingly
parochial and the sense of unity underlying difference which had
characterized Heian's Tendai and Shingon was gradually eroded.
The Shintō-Buddhist synthesis continued throughout the Tokugawa
period in spite of Shintō attacks, which eventually culminated in the
official separation of Shintō and Buddhism (*shimbutsu bunri*) in
early Meiji (1868) and in the subsequent persecution of Buddhsm

(*haibutsu kishaku*).[121] Japan was to become a modern nation, and one of the casualties to progress was an institution which had succeeded in accommodating a broad spectrum of beliefs and practices for over a millennium. Once again the zealot was to pay a high price for his single-mindedness.

But Mujū's message of Accommodation is as relevant to our own day as to his. Today we live in an expanding pluralistic society, each of us acting within our own conceptual constructs, myths, illusions — convinced that our own surely have a kind of objectivity denied to others. But Mujū would remind us that there is not just one method for entering the Way, the causes and conditions for enlightenment being many.

Just as each of us strives to attain the goal of his or her own illusion, let us hope that Mujū reached the goal as he imagined it for himself. Having turned the Wheel of the Law by means of "wild words and specious phrases," may he have left this village of Birth-and-death for the great city of Nirvana.

I have based my translations and summaries (in italics) of *Sand and Pebbles* on Watanabe Tsunaya, ed. *Shasekishū* (1966); and, for a few minor items from the abbreviated *rufubon*, on the editions by Tsukudo Reikan and Fujii Otoo. For *Casual Digressions* I have used Yamada and Miki, eds. *Zōtanshū* (1973). See Selected Bibliography, Part A, for additional details.

Part II. Sand and Pebbles
(Shasekishū)

Translations and Summaries

Collection of Sand and Pebbles

Prologue

Coarse words and refined expressions both proceed from the First Principle,[122] nor are the everyday affairs of life at variance with the True Reality. Through the wanton sport of wild words and specious phrases, I wish to bring people into the marvelous Way of the Buddha's teaching; and with unpretentious examples taken from the common ordinary affairs of life I should like to illustrate the profound significance of this splendid doctrine. So I rouse myself from the drowsiness of old age, and with an idle hand have assembled at random that which I have seen and heard. I have recorded incidents just as they have come to mind, without selecting the good from the bad.[123]

At a time when he should be aware of the things of impermanence which thought-by-thought obstruct his apprehension of Reality, and when he should be concerned over his step-by-step approach to the nether world, piling up provisions for the long journey to the subterranean regions and preparing the boat to carry him over the deep currents of the troubled seas of life, this old priest is writing down incidents that strike his fancy, and recording frivolous worldly anecdotes. He does not care how he wastes his time in the present, nor does he feel shame at what the wise and learned may say of him later on. But though it may seem useless, for the sake of those foolish people who are not aware of the great benefits of Buddhism, who do not know the profound intent of the gods who soften their light,[124] who do not discriminate between wise and foolish, and who do not believe that the operation of moral causality is determined and fixed, he has selected clear passages from the sutras and commentaries and set down the admonitions left by the wise of former times.

There is not just one method for entering the Way, the causes and conditions for enlightenment being many. Once a person understands their general significance, he will see that the purport of the various teachings does not vary. And when he puts them into

71

Figure 5. Woodblocks of the Jōkyō 3 (1686) edition of the *Shasekishū. Photo by Kawabe Ryōsuke.*

practice, he will find that the goal of the myriad religious exercises is the same. So from among casual digressions this old monk extracts the sacred teaching, and among humorous anecdotes he points out the theory and practice of Buddhism. May those who have occasion to see it not despise this poorly-written work by means of which they may come to comprehend the significance of Buddhism; nor should they blame the inclusion of extraneous material through which they may come to understand the operation of moral causality. May they use this work as a means by which to leave this village of Birth-and-death and as a signpost to reach the great city of Nirvana—such is the hope of this foolish old man.

Those who search for gold extract it from sand; those who take pleasure in jewels gather pebbles and polish them. So I call this book the *Collection of Sand and Pebbles.* It consists of ten chapters and includes over a hundred items.

Collected in midsummer in the second year of Kōan [1279] by a humble monk in the grove of letters, Mujū.

1:1 The Great Shrine at Ise

While I was on a pilgrimage to the Great Shrine during the Kōchō era [1261–64], an official explained to me why words associated with the Three Treasures of Buddhism [the Buddha, the Law, and the Order] were forbidden at the shrine, and why monks could not closely approach the sacred buildings.

In antiquity, when this country did not yet exist, the deity of the Great Shrine [the Sun Goddess, Amaterasu], guided by a seal of the Great Sun Buddha inscribed on the ocean floor, thrust down her august spear. Brine from the spear coagulated like drops of dew, and this was seen from afar by Māra, the Evil One, in the Sixth Heaven of Desire.[125] "It appears that these drops are forming into a land where Buddhism will be propagated and people will escape from the round of birth-and-death," he said, and came down to prevent it.

Then the deity of the Great Shrine met with the demon king. "I promise not to utter the names of the Three Treasures, nor will I permit them near my person. So return quickly back to the heavens." Being thus mollified, he withdrew.

Monks to this very day, not wishing to violate that august promise, do not approach the sacred shrine, and the sutras are not carried openly in its precincts. Things associated with the Three Treasures are referred to obliquely: Buddha is called "The Cramp-Legged One" [*tachisukumi*]; the sutras, "colored paper" [*somegami*]; monks, "longhairs" [*kaminaga*]; and temples, "incense burners" [*koritaki*], etc.[126] Outwardly the deity is estranged from the Law, but inwardly she profoundly supports the Three Treasures. Thus, Japanese Buddhism is under the special protection of the deity of the Great Shrine.

This shrine is father and mother to all the gods of this land. When Amaterasu closed the Rock Door of Heaven and dwelt in seclusion, disgusted by the heavenly improprieties committed by Susa-no-o, all the world was plunged in darkness. In their distress the eight hundred myriad deities built a ceremonial fire and performed the sacred dance [*kagura*], that they might coax her forth. When the Sun Goddess, curious at the sport of the divine maidens, narrowly opened the Rock Door and looked out, the world was illuminated. As everyone was thus enabled to distinguish the faces of others once more, they exclaimed: "*Ara omoshiroshi!*" ["How delightful it is again to see each other's faces!"] This was the origin of the expression.[127]

Then the god Tajikara-no-o carried her forth and drew a sacred rope across the Rock, asking her not to enter again into the cave. On being brought forth, she immediately became sun and moon, and illumined the earth. Thus, even our now being affected by the light of the sun and moon is through the benevolent virtue of this deity. Since all of this arose by virtue of the seal of the Great Sun Buddha on the ocean floor, we have come to identify the deities of the Inner and Outer Shrines[128] with the Great Sun Buddha of the

Two-Part Mandala;[129] and that which is called the Rock Door of
Heaven is the Tuṣita Heaven [of the Buddha Maitreya],[130] also
known as the High Plain of Heaven.[131]

Events which took place during the Age of the Gods all have
their Buddhist interpretation. In the Shingon view the Tuṣita
Heaven, indeed, is spoken of as the Great Sun Buddha's World-of-
Dharma Palace of Inner Realization,[132] his Land of Esoteric
Grandeur (mitsugonkoku). The Great Sun Buddha came forth from
this capital of Inner Realization to assume local manifestations in
the land of the sun [Japan]. Thus, the deity of the Inner Shrine at
Ise is the Great Sun of the Matrix World; and patterned after the
Four-Enclosure Mandala[133] are the several shrine fences: tamagaki,
mizugaki, aragaki, etc.[134] Likewise, there are nine logs (katsuogi) on
the roof of the main hall of the Inner Shrine symbolizing the nine
Holy Ones of the Matrix World.[135] We are accustomed to identify
the deity of the Outer Shrine with the Great Sun Buddha of the Diamond World; and also with Amida. It is doubtless to symbolize the
Five Wisdoms (gochi) of the Diamond World that its design consists
of five moon-circles.[136] When the Two-Part Matrix-Diamond Mandala is viewed in the light of the Yin-Yang teaching, wherein the
Yin is female and the Yang male, the eight petals of the Matrix
parallel the shrine's Eight Maidens;[137] and it is because the Five
Wisdoms of the Diamond World are represented by male divinities
that there is a group of five male shrine dancers [kagurōdo].

Moreover, out of consideration of its burden on the people and
its expense to the country, the shrine sanctuaries are thatched simply with miscanthus and it uses ceremonial offerings of thrice-
pounded unpolished rice.[138]. The crosspieces [katsuogi] are straight
and the roof beams uncurved — so that the hearts of men may be rectified. Thus, those who with upright hearts consider the effect of
their actions on the plight of the people and its expense to the country conform to the will of the gods. One who serves at this shrine
quite naturally refrains from the Ten Grave Offenses proscribed by
the Net of Brahma Sutra. If he murders, he is exiled from his clan
for a long period of time, just as a monk is no longer counted among
the sons of the Buddha if he commits one of the Ten Grave Offenses. Having struck a man and drawn blood, a Shinto priest is expelled from his office, just as if he had been charged with one of the
Lesser Offenses prescribed for the Buddhist clergy.

The tabus observed at Ise differ somewhat from those of other
shrines. Childbirth[139] is spoken of as "bearing spirit" [shōki], and
those involved are under a fifty-day pollution; likewise, death is
spoken of as "death-spirit,"[140] and also creates a fifty-day pollution.

Death proceeds from life, and life is the beginning of death. The shrine official informed me that this was handed down as the reason for birth and death to be both tabu.

Now the Great Sun Buddha is not subject to birth-and-death; and the original purpose for his coming forth from the Inner Realization of the Law Body[141] and manifesting his traces in order to save the ignorant and deluded masses produced through the four forms of birth [i.e., from womb, egg, moisture, or by metamorphosis] was to put a stop to the round of birth-and-death, and to lead people to the Buddha's Path of eternal life. Thus, to speak of placing both birth and death under a tabu is the same as saying that we do not foolishly create the karma of delusive conduct which causes the painful cycle of birth-and-death. It is to say that we wisely practice the marvelous Law of the Buddha, and that we aspire to birth in a Pure Land[142] and to enlightenment. While it is entirely in conformity with the will of the deity of the Great Shrine that we believe in and practice the Way of the Buddha, it is contrary to the divine will for us to concern ourselves with the glories of this life, to pray for prosperity and longevity, to observe the tabus with a heart still deeply attached to the things of the world, and to be devoid of any sense of religious aspiration.

The august forms of the Traces Manifest by the Original Ground may vary, but their purpose is assuredly the same. In order to propagate Buddhism in China, the three bodhisattvas Māṇava, Kāśyapa and Dīpamkara[143] — appearing as Confucius, Lao-tzu and Yen Hui[144] — first softened the people's hearts by means of non-Buddhist teachings. later, when Buddhism was propagated, everyone believed in it.

In Japan the illustrious native deities who soften their light first manifested their traces — the Buddha using this as a skillful means to soften the rough disposition of the people and to lead them to belief in the Law. If we rely on the profound efficacy of the Original Ground while believing in the skillful means, close to hand, of gods who soften their light, we will realize our hope for peace and the end of calamities in this life, and attain the eternal enlightenment, not subject to birth-and-death, in the next. Those born in our land should be thoroughly aware of this fact.

1:2 The Venerable Gedatsubō of Kasagi's Pilgrimage to the Great Shrine

A shrine official informed me that the late holy man of Kasagi

[Jōkei, 1155-1213] once confined himself in the Iwashimizu Hachiman Shrine to pray for his enlightenment, and the deity revealed itself to him. "It is not within my power to arrange this. Go to the Great Shrine at Ise to make your request," said the god in his dream. And he was given explicit travel instructions.

In the dream he imagined setting forth and before long he was traversing the mountain to the south of the Outer Shrine. On the mountain peak he saw a pond full of lotuses, large and small, some in bloom and others budding whose color and fragrance were truly wonderful.

"The lotuses in bloom are the priests of this shrine who have already been born into the Pure Land," someone remarked. "Those yet to attain this are the buds. By the skillful means of the gods who soften their light, many are born into the Pure Land. The large lotus there is a deacon known as Tsunemoto who is to attain that blessed birth." Gedatsubō then entered the shrine and even heard the sound of Buddhist scriptures being chanted.

Upon waking he strapped on his implement box and set out alone, following the instructions he had received. His course did not deviate in the slightest from what he had seen in the dream, except that there was a wide road winding around the foot of the mountain south of the Outer Shrine, and no trail leading to the summit. But this was the only point of difference, the layout of the mountain being exactly as he had envisioned it.

He spoke to a young layman, inquiring if there was a deacon at that place called Tsunemoto.

"Truly, that is my own name," came the reply. "But although I will eventually become a deacon, I am not one now." Gedatsubō then took three measures of gold from his implement box; presenting them to the man, he took lodging at his house and questioned him in detail about the shrine. Tsunemoto told him that when he had not attained release from the round of birth-and-death, he vowed that when he was again born into the human world, he would come as a priest of the shrine and rely on the skillful means of the gods who soften their light for his salvation.

Since I heard this from a shrine priest who was close to Tsunemoto, I know that it actually happened.

1:3 Praying to the Gods for Release from Birth-and-Death

Abbot Kōken [Hongakubō, 1110-93], Superintendent of

Miidera, was a master of both exoteric and esoteric doctrine. He was a man of such renown for sanctity that priest Myōhen [Rengedani Sōzu, 1142–1224] of Mount Kōya, having certain doubts about the abbot's religious practices, told the recluse Zen'amidabutsu to go and observe his behavior. Zen'amidabutsu traveled to the abbot's residence dressed strangely in a hat woven of Kōya cypress strips and a knee-length robe, entered the temple compound, and announced his arrival. When the abbot heard that he was a holy man from Mount Kōya, toward which he had cordial feelings, he called Zen'amidabutsu to his humble, low-eved sitting room. All night long they discussed the affairs of Kōya and stories of the next life.

When morning came the abbot donned a white Shintō robe and, with Shintō offerings, stood between a curtained space between two pillars and performed ritual gestures. To Zen'amidabutsu they appeared to be most irregular. After carefully noting the abbot's un-varying behavior for three days, he spoke to him. "Your morning observances appear quite unusual. What kind of ritual is it?"

"Even had you not broached the subject, I should have ex-plained," replied the abbot. "I am pleased to be asked such a ques-tion. Although I studied both the overt and secret teachings of Bud-dhism determined to enter upon the Path of release from birth-and-death, my self-power was weak and my capacity for understanding shallow. Apart from the power of my exceptional karmic affinities, my hopes for release could not be realized. So I wrote down the sacred names of the major and minor deities throughout the entire country of Japan, not only those spoken of in the capital, but also those I heard about in remote areas and distant provinces. In this two-pillared space I present my petition, reciting the *Heart of Wisdom Sutra* thirty times a session, as well as performing various incantations to the gods and making offerings of that which is con-ducive to delight in the Law. Apart from earnestly relying on the skillful means of the gods who soften their light to lead me to the path of release from birth-and-death, I perform no other practices.

The accommodations of the Blessed One vary according to country and occasion and has no fixed mode of operation. Just as [*The Way and Its Power*] says: "The Sage has no heart of his own; he uses the heart of the people as his heart," so also has the Law Body no fixed form but takes the myriad forms of the phenomenal world as its body. Its ten worlds[145] constituted by the formless Law Body are all the perfect body of the Great Sun Buddha. To express this in Tendai terms, the karmas conditioning person and environment in the ten worlds, the natures of whose inhabitants are composed of the three thousand dharmas, are all myriad capacities of the Law Body immanent in them. Thus, through action It manifests the ten worlds, in which the natural capacity for good or ill is latent, and saves those deluded natures in the nine worlds by virtue of Its assuming a variety of bodies and forms.

"Moreover, if we use the thought of the esoteric teaching, we may say that the Four-Enclosure Mandala is also the ten-fold world constituted by the Law Body. Its Inner Realization reflects the basic assemblage of Its self-nature; Its Outer Function manifests the benefits of Its great compassion. I have worked it out according to both the exoteric and esoteric doctrines: from the Law Body the Buddha manifests bodies in the ten worlds and benefits all sentient beings. The marvelous function [yū] which complements the marvelous substance [tai] is like the wave which does not exist apart from its water. Apart from the Real [shinnyo], no causes arise.

"Accordingly, long ago in the West — in India — the buddhas and bodhisattvas made their appearance and saved the people of that land. Ours is a country as remote from this center as the small, scattered millet seed, where rough, fierce creatures were unaware of moral causation. For those who did not believe in the Dharma, the impartially outflowing Law Body, acting in accordance with the same spontaneous compassion as elsewhere, employed that which was appropriate to the time and place. Manifesting the shapes of evil demons and wicked spirits and showing forth the forms of poisonous serpents and fierce beasts, it subdued this ferocious and evil lot and thereby brought people to the Way of the Buddha.[146]

"Thus, other lands attach importance to those bodies which have an affinity to the Law, and in this country we should not disparage those forms which are appropriate. In our country, as the land of the gods, the provisional manifestations of the Buddha leave their traces. Moreover, we are all their descendants; and it is no trivial fate to share with them a common spirit. If we pray to other blessed beings, their response will be ever so far distant from us. Consequently, there can be nothing so profitable as relying on the skillful means of the gods who soften their light in response to our potential for good, praying to them to lead us to the path essential for release from birth-and-death.

"When we see an image of man or beast made of gold and pay no attention to the gold, then we say that the image is superior or inferior. But when we pay attention to the gold and neglect the form, it is as though there were no difference between a superior and an inferior image. As the occasion dictates, the Law Body creates the various forms in the ten-fold world of the Four-Enclosure Mandala. If we ignore the forms and hold to the essential substance, then what is there that does not participate in the benefits of the Law Body? The gate of Wisdom takes the highest attainment to be most excellent; the gate of Compassion takes benefit to the lowest to be most wonderful—as when midgets compare heights, the smallest is the winner. The benefit of the great compassion is such that the impartially outflowing Law Body draws near especially to those of feeble capacity, and the compassion which profits those creatures of strong and violent disposition is most excellent. Thus, I trust in the gods who soften their light and identify with the dust as the ultimate in compassion from the various Buddhas; and although my religious practice is unusual in this respect, it has been my custom for many years." So spoke the abbot.

Zen'amidabutsu, rejoicing at his truly noble aspiration, returned to Kōya and reported the incident to Myōhen. "Because he is a wise man, I knew that he could not be involved in any foolish practices. But now I have the highest admiration for him," replied the priest, shedding tears of sympathetic joy.

The holy recluse related this incident to me.

The Great Teacher Chih-i explains in the *Great Cessation and Insight*, "With respect to concentration and insight, the wise man will act wisely and the foolish man, foolishly." Similarly, the wise man will act wisely toward the Manifest Traces, the gods who soften their light. The profound sense of the esoteric doctrine is that since the ten worlds are all the manifestation of the formless Law Body, the body of Emma [king of the nether world] and that of the Great Sun Buddha are both constituted through the Law Body of the Four-Enclosure Mandala and accompany the Five Limitless Wisdoms[147] of the Buddha. When absorbed in Inner Realization, Emma exhibits the mind-ground of his self-nature, the Law Body, without altering his demonic appearance. Thus, a virtuous ancient [Chan-jan in the *Diamond Stick*] remarked: "The karma of person and place which bring one to the lowest hell are entirely in the Mind of the Blessed One, and the karma of person and place of the Great Sun Buddha are no more than a single unenlightened thought."

Moreover, we speak of the three aspects of "attaining Buddhahood in this very existence."[148] [1] The "attainment of Buddhahood because its principle is inherent"[149] means that humans are essentially Buddha, but they are not aware of this because of egoistic attachments. [2] The various Buddhas, having realized "the attainment of Buddhahood by 'revealing and acquiring' [this inherent nature through successful practice]",[150] freely dispense its benefits. And [3] the "attainment of Buddhahood through the grace of the Three Mysteries of Mahāvairocana being 'retained' "[151] means that we learn to integrate with the marvelous activity of the Three Actions [Body, Speech, Mind] of the Buddhas who have already attained enlightenment, and to establish favorable affinities with them. What is realized in my own mind is that which manifests benefits as infinite and limitless as the sands of the Ganges.

Perhaps it was during the reign of Emperor Murakami [926-967] that a Five-Pedestal Ceremony[152] was held at the palace with Bishop Jie [Ryōgen, 912-85] acting as Esoteric Master at the central platform. The emperor secretly observed the performance, during which he saw Jie assume the form of Fudō, so that there was not the slightest difference between him and the object of worship. Abbot Kanchō [Hirosawa no Daisōjō, 918-98] performed as Esoteric Master before Gōzanze, at times appearing as the deity and at times as abbot. At seeing this the emperor remarked: "How unfortunate! Kanchō is troubled by delusive thoughts!" The other priests simply retained their original forms. The scripture[153] says: "All sentient beings proceed from the womb of the Tathāgata, because the very body of Samantabhadra[154] is everywhere."

Although it is said that we ourselves are entirely the Law Body, the distinction is made (or not) depending on whether the viewpoint is from delusion or enlightenment. Thus, the *Sutra of Neither Increase Nor Decrease*[155] states: "On the one hand we speak of the Law Body transmigrating through the Five Paths of existence[156] and call It 'sentient beings'. Or we assign the name 'bodhisattva' to the Law Body's practice of the Six Virtues. Or again, we speak of the Law Body turning back the current of rebirth and exhausting its source [i.e., karma], and we call It 'Buddha'." Now when we consider the Manifest Traces, this can be understood as follows: "The Law Body softens Its light and identifies with the dust, and we give It the name 'gods'."

Thus, although the body of the Original Ground and the Manifest Traces are identical, their effects, which vary with the occasion, will sometimes be superior and sometimes inferior. As for its effects in our country, how superlative is the appearance of the Manifest Traces! This is because, in antiquity, when En no Gyōja[157] was practicing austerities on Mt. Yoshino and the form of

Śākyamuni appeared before him, the ascetic said: "In this august form it will be difficult to convert the people of this country. You should conceal yourself." Then the shape of Maitreya appeared to him, but En said: "This likewise will not do." However, when the Buddha manifested a fearsome shape as Zaō Gongen, En responded, "Truly, this is one who can convert our land to Buddhism." And today the Buddha manifests this Trace.

The significance of this fearsome aspect is that as his period of influence is exhausted Śākyamuni comes as a demon to devour the unconverted and to encourage men to strive for enlightenment. When the devotee venerates this manifestation wholeheartedly with deep faith, he enjoys its benefits. It is the custom in our country that since the gods clearly reveal their decisions for better or worse, people have warm faith and reverence toward them. There are foolish people who seldom place their reliance on the buddhas and bodhisattvas, whose benefits are more moderate than those of the skillful means of the gods who soften their light. But there are also benefits from afar to be received from buddhas and bodhisattvas which flow from their fundamental essence—the benefits of the various buddhas being especially effective for those in distress. In any case, the accommodations which benefit the foolish masses truly have the color of deep compassion and the form of tender versatility. Just as the blue material is bluer than the indigo plant from which its color derives, so the spiritually-valued is more precious than the Buddha from whom this value proceeds—such is the benefit of the gods who soften their light!

When the ancient men of virtue built a temple, without fail they began by venerating a propitious manifestation of the gods. This is because without the "skillful means" of the gods who soften their light it is difficult to establish Buddhism. The vows of Abbot Kōken were undertaken in such a spirit, and men of sensitivity will learn from his experience.

1:4 The Gods Esteem Compassion

The venerable Jōgambō[158] of Miwa in Yamato province, a man of compassion, concentrated on the practices of the Shingon sect and was thoroughly initiated in the spells for establishing relationships between man and Buddha [kechien]. Once when he was traveling on a pilgrimage to Yoshino,[159] he was moved at finding several children crying by the side of the road. 'Why are you crying?'

asked Jōgambō. A girl of eleven or twelve replied, her tears flowing ceaselessly. "My mother became sick and died, and my father has gone far away and is not here to help us. The neighbors wish to have nothing to do with such nasty, unpleasant business, and so there is no one to look after the burial. I am only a girl, and my little brother is useless. I am so heartbroken that I can only cry."

Feeling pity in his heart for the children, Jōgambō decided to forgo the pilgrimage and to help them — he could make it to Yoshino some other time. Carrying the corpse to a field conveniently nearby, he set it down, recited some incantations, and quickly buried it. Then, as he was about to return to Miwa, his body became paralyzed and he was unable to move. "Just as I expected," he thought fearfully. "While realizing the importance of strict ritual purity before the Manifest Traces, by acting as I have done I have incurred divine retribution!"

But when he tried to walk in the direction of Yoshino he had not the slightest difficulty. Thinking that perhaps it was the god's wish that he continue, Jōgambō journeyed on without fear. Then suddenly apprehensive, he stopped under a tree some distance from the shrine and recited sutras and spells as homage to the gods. Presently an attendant possessed by the deity danced forth from the shrine and approached him.

"What is the meaning of this, worthy monk?" she inquired. Jōgambō trembled with fear. "Alas, how short-sighted of me! I should not have come so far, and now I shall be chastised." "Why are you late, worthy monk, when I have been expecting you for so long?" asked the deity as she approached. "I certainly do not abhor what you have done. On the contrary, I respect compassion." And taking the monk by the sleeve, the deity led him to the Worship Hall.

Jōgambō was overcome with awe and gratitude, so that his black sleeves were soaked with tears. After hearing the Buddhist teachings expounded, he returned from his pilgrimage shedding tears of gratitude.

Formerly when Priest Eshin was visiting a shrine, the deity revealed itself to him through a vestal virgin. When Eshin spoke concerning doctrinal matters, she responded graciously; and when questioned about Tendai philosophy, she replied with clarity. Then Eshin, having gradually won his way into the god's favor, put a profound doctrinal matter before her. The vestal stood by a pillar and assumed a thoughtful stance with her ankles crossed. "I have softened the light and identified with the dust for such a long time that I have quite forgotten!" said the deity, looking rather magnificent.

"I am a manifestation of Kannon." declared Ishihijiri Kyōjū of Tōdaiji. And, since no one believed him, he drew up a lengthy manifesto. "You claim to be a manifestation of Kannon," someone remarked, "but since no one believes you, you ought to demonstrate some miraculous powers. As for this manifesto, it is simply impertinent!" Replied Ishihijiri, "I have not assumed the form of Kannon for a very long time, and now I have forgotten even how to employ the miraculous powers."

I find the matter quite an interesting contrast as I turn it over in my mind. Behaving as the occasion dictates in these Latter Days, even the avatars find it difficult to distinguish between their earlier and present states. And so it was said: "You should not evaluate sentient beings with your stupid cow- and goat-like eyes."[160] This is truly difficult to comprehend.

An official of the Atsuta Shrine in Owari province tells the story of a holy man called Shōrembō who planned to stop over near the shrine precincts on his way to Mt. Kōya with his mother's ashes. But everyone knew what he carried, and no one would give him lodging. That night, while Shōrembō was keeping vigil by the gate to the south of the main shrine, a shrine official came in a dream to the head priest as a messenger of the august deity.

"Tonight I have a most important guest," said the god. "It is my wish that you treat him well." The head priest awoke and sent a messenger to the sanctuary to inquire if anyone had arrived during the night. He returned to report that no one had come but Shōrembō; so the head priest invited the monk in. "Since I am carrying my mother's ashes, I cannot enter," he replied. Then the head priest said, "Where the Great Deity resides, all things are done in accordance with the will of the gods. By virtue of a revelation which I received this night, I am not to consider your presence as tabu." He invited the monk into the shrine precincts, where he entertained him lavishly. Then ordering horse, saddle, and traveling expenses, he sent him on to Kōya. This happened really quite recently.

Moreover, during the Jōkyū War the frightened people living in the area assembled within the Atsuta Shrine's outer mud-wall enclosure. They brought their valuables and various utensils with them, and, crowded together without room to move, one youth preceded his parents to the grave and a young girl was in labor.[161] The officials were unable to restrain the people, and, in order to call down the Great Deity that they might seek his advice, had sacred dances performed and the god was petitioned by those who shared this concern. Speaking through one of the shrine priests, the deity declared: "The reason for my coming down from heaven to this land is that I might help the multitude of people. In the light of the present circumstances these actions are not tabu." When he had said this, the people raised their voices in unison and shed tears of joy and sympathetic admiration. A person who was present at the time is alive today and related the incident to me.

Thus, the will of the gods is everywhere the same. If only the heart is pure, the body likewise is not defiled.

1:5 The Gods Esteem Those with Wisdom and Compassion

"I regard Myōebō[162] and Gedatsubō as my sons," the Great Deity of Kasuga Shrine[163] declared. When the two men were once on a pilgrimage to the great shrine, the deer on Kasuga Plain all bent their knees and knelt out of respect for them. When the venerable Myōe was merely thinking of making a trip to India, the Kasuga deity communicated with him through an oracle at Yuasa to prevent his departure. Indeed, I hear that there is written record of this communication. The deity explained that he would be sad if they were to be separated by such a distance, and Myōe was impressed that the god disapproved of his leaving. "But if I should decide to go," he inquired, would I reach India safely?" "If I am protecting you, what could go wrong?" replied the deity. At that time he touched the holy man's hand, which is said to have remained fragrant throughout his lifetime.

When the venerable Gedatsubō, living at Kasagi in a secluded retreat which he called Wisdom Heights, invited the deity for a visit, it assumed the form of a child and rode on his shoulders. The god composed this verse:

Ware yukan	I will come,
Yukite maboran	And having arrived will protect
Hannyadai	Wisdom Heights
Shaka no minori no	As long as the Holy Law
Aran kagiri wa	Of Śākyamuni may survive.[164]

Once, in a vacant practice hall at Wisdom Heights, the voice of
the deity proclaimed:

Ware wo shire	Know who I am!
Shakamuni butsu no	Now that Śākyamuni Buddha
Yo ni idete	Has appeared,
Sayakeki tsuki no	Think of me as the clear moon
Yo wo terasu to wa	Shining over the land.[165]

It is said that the deity constantly discoursed on Buddhist doctrine. Indeed, how fortunate and enviable the experience of those
who actually heard what took place when Śākyamuni was in the
world.

It is said, "Those having the light of wisdom accompany those
having the light of wisdom." Internally, the bright wisdom of the
gods is unobscured; externally, their compassion is marvelous. If we
have wisdom and compassion, we should feel that the gods consider
us as their companions. In a certain book it says, "Fire breaks out
where it is dry, and water flows where it is moist."[166] If we dry up the
attachments of the heart, the fire of wisdom will break out; if we
have the moisture of sympathy, the water of compassion will issue
forth.

1:6 Profound is the Grace of the Gods Who Soften their Light

In Nara a disciple of the venerable Gedatsubō known as the
Undersecretary Monk Shōen was a great scholar, but fell into one of
the evil paths. His spirit took possession of a woman, and among
various things which he said through her was this: "By virtue of the
excellence of this illustrious deity's skillful means, he does not send
to other hells those who have shown the least devotion to him,
whatever their crimes may be. Rather, he deposits them in the hell
directly beneath Kasuga Plain, and early every morning the
bodhisattva Jizō from the Third Shrine[167] brings water in a lustra-
tion vessel and scatters it with a ritual sprinkler. If a single drop of
water reaches the mouth of a sinner, his misery is temporarily re-

lieved. And when for even a short time a man's thoughts dwell on the Truth, the god does not neglect to have him daily hear the exposition of the Mahāyāna sutras and the chanting of the sacred spells. Through this skillful means, in the end one rises out of hell. The scholars hear discourses on the *Great Wisdom Sutra*[168] held at Kōsen Hall east of Mt. Kasuga, and their debates and discussions are the same as those of living men. Scholars in the past, they are all still scholars. And they are most grateful to hear the illustrious deity expounding the Law before their very eyes."

Jizō occupies one of the four sites of the Kasuga Shrine, and his grace is said to be truly efficacious. He is the bodhisattva who leads and is entrusted [with mankind during the interval between the death of Śākyamuni and the coming of Maitreya], when there is no Buddha in the world. His Original Ground and Trace Manifestations are equally to be relied on; consequently, the benefits of the gods who soften their light are everywhere identical. A number of monks from Enryakuji who had been turned into goblins[169] somewhere behind the great shrine of the Hiyoshi deity were restored by the "skillful means" of this god who softened his light. There, too, among the various shrines, the god Jūzenji frequently manifests himself, his Original Ground being the bodhisattva Jizō.[170]

When we consider that somehow or other we have had the good fortune to have received a human form in this life, we should aspire for release by employing the skillful means of a single method if we are to succeed in meeting the Law of the Buddha. "It is important to place reliance on the skillful means of a single Buddha and a single bodhisattva," says the *Sutra on Viewing the Mind-Ground*.[171] Inwardly, we should rely on the fact that our Buddha-nature provides us with the condition for eternal life; outwardly, we should rely on the compassion and "skillful means" of the Original Grounds who Manifest their Traces, centering our thoughts deeply on the way of release from birth-and-death.

The horrors of the Three Evil Destinies lie just beneath our feet; we have not yet awakened from the long night's dream of rebirth through the Six Paths of phenomenal existence. It we return to our old haunts in the Three Evil Destinies, having once had the exceptional good fortune to have received a human body and to have heard the Buddha's teaching,[172] of what avail will be a thousand regrets and a hundred laments? During many lives it is rare to float up into the human world, and we encounter the Buddha's teaching once in a hundred million aeons. Do not waste the days vainly following your whims. Time waits for no one, and we cannot know when death will come. Let us seriously exert ourselves.

1:7 The Native Gods Esteem the Sincere Desire for Enlightenment

In Nara lived a learned priest known as Eichō [1014-95]. After years of burning the midnight oil he developed a reputation for being a great scholar. Once when he was at the great Kasuga Shrine on a pilgrimage the deity spoke to him in a dream. Eichō questioned him about the doctrines of the *Treatise on Yoga* and the *Completion of Mere Ideation*[173] and was vouchsafed a reply. However, the monk was not able to see the august countenance.

"For many years I have devoted myself to the way of learning, carrying on the Idealist (*yuishiki*) tradition which is the light of the Law, and offering up those rites in which the gods delight," he remarked. "As a result, I perceive your august form before me and hear the sound of your sublime words; and I should like to think that this is an effect of good karma from earlier lives. If I could likewise view your noble countenance, how deeply my heart would rejoice."

"Your pursuit of learning is admirable," came the reply. "and because of this I have held discourse with you. But since you have no sincere desire for enlightenment, I do not wish to meet you face to face."

Eichō woke from his dream overwhelmed with compunction. Indeed, the doctrines of Buddhism, whatever the sect, are for the purpose of liberation from the cycle of birth-and-death; one should not think of fame and profit. The conduct of the scholars in the seminaries of Nara and Kyoto has only fame and profit as its objective, and the pursuit of enlightenment is outside its purview. To fall into heresy and sink into the lower realms of existence because of this would be most regrettable. With this in mind, Eichō forthwith became a recluse, and, with singleness of purpose, devoted himself to the way of release.

Long ago [1081] Miidera was burned down by monks from Enryakuji, and nothing remained of halls and pagodas, monks' quarters, Buddhist images, or sutras. The monks were dispersed through the fields and mountains, and the Miidera became a completely uninhabited temple. One of the monks made a pilgrimage to the shrine of the illustrious god Shinra[174] and there spent the night. In a dream he saw the bright deity push open the doors of the shrine. Because the god appeared to be in a very good humor, the monk in his dream made bold to address him.

"When I consider your august vow to protect the Buddhist teachings of this temple and think how profound must be your sorrow at what has been completely lost, why is this not reflected on your countenance?"

"How could I not feel grieved?" replied the god. "But even so, it pleases me that this incident should give rise to a genuine desire for enlightenment in a single monk. One can always restore the halls, pagodas, images and sutras if one has the money. But it is the man aspiring to Buddhahood, though one in ten million, who is to be valued highly."

It is related that the monk awoke from his dream pondering how wondrous was the divine will, and developed a sincere desire for enlightenment. The divine will, which delights in men awakening the desire for enlightenment and entering upon the True Way, does not vary regardless of the deity. Nor does it seem to be in conformity with the will of the gods for us to pray for the things of this life — poverty and prosperity being determined by one's actions in former lives. It is shameful simply to petition the gods and buddhas for good fortune in this world; in fact, it is stupid. One ought to direct this same amount of merit from religious practice toward the attainment of perfect wisdom. And even if he receives no sign from the gods, he should continue to pray for a genuine desire for enlightenment.

A poor monk at Enryakuji living in the East Pagoda's Northern Valley made a hundred-day pilgrimage to the Hiyoshi shrine in order to improve his lot. He was vouchsafed a revelation in which the god informed him that he would make suitable arrangements. Then, while happily passing the time in anticipation, he was evicted for some trifling reason from the quarters where he had lived for many years. As there was nowhere else for him to go, the monk took identical lodgings in the West Pagoda's Southern Valley. After having received his revelation, he had waited expectantly. Now not only was there no such good fortune as he had anticipated, but he was even expelled from his quarters by the superintendent. With a feeling of embarrassment he again confined himself in the shrine and prayed to the god. Once again he was vouchsafed a revelation.

"Because there is not the slightest chance of good fortune for you in this life by virtue of your bad karma from former lives," explained the god, "I have simply moved you to warm quarters in the West Pagoda's Southern Valley since it is cold in the East Pagoda's Northern Valley—and I consider even this a bit of a concession! Aside from this it is not within my power to affect your fortunes."

After receiving this pronouncement, the monk resigned himself and did not press the matter further. Thus it has been said, "Even the power of the gods cannot overcome the force of karma."

At the time of the Buddha, five hundred of his kinsmen were attacked by Prince Virūdhaka, and the Buddha was unable to help them. People conjectured, "Since they are relatives of Blessed Śākyamuni, he will surely employ some miraculous power to save them." In order to resolve their doubts, Śākyamuni placed one of his kinsmen in his begging bowl and hid it in the heavens. But on the day when the other kinsmen were attacked, the man died spontaneously in the holy bowl. The Buddha then explained the causes underlying the incident. "These five hundred kinsmen long ago were five hundred fishermen who pulled out a large fish from the sea and killed it. That large fish was today's Prince Virūdhaka. At that time I was a child and stroked the fish's head with a blade of grass, and, as a result, today I have a headache." On that day even the Buddha was afflicted. How then as ordinary men can we avoid the law of moral causation?

Although the bhikkhu Rigunshi was a virtuous arhat, he was destitute. Although he went out to beg, he obtained no food. Whenever he swept the dirt from the stupa where the Buddha discoursed, on that day he would receive alms. On one occasion Rigunshi overslept and Śāriputra swept the platform. Later when Rigunshi went begging, he received nothing. And with no food but sand and water for seven days, he died of hunger. The Buddha explained the reason for this as follows. "In the past Rigunshi was unfilial toward his mother, and, when she was hungry and begged for something to eat, he told her to eat sand and drink water. For seven days he gave her no food, and this finally killed her. For such bad karma, though he is a virtuous monk, he is still punished."

Because of such karma, poverty and low social position, the difficulties we encounter and the hardships of life, are all the result of past transgressions. We should envy neither society nor individuals but simply examine our own hearts with compunction and seek the Pure Land of Enlightenment, blameless and without fault. Perhaps this is the thought expressed by Nijō no In no Sanuki in her verse:

Uki mo nao	Were I not aware
Mukashi no yue to	That my present misery
Omowazu wa	Is rooted in the past,
Ikani kono yo wo	What bitterness would I then
Uramihatemashi	Feel toward the world![175]

Generally speaking, the response of the gods and buddhas operates with little effect on practical affairs. How could it be concerned with the glories of the dream world of this present life? It is in conformity with the divine will that we pray for enlightenment in the next life, even if we receive no auspicious omen.

Priest Kanshun [978–1057] was a monk of Enryakuji. Destitute, he confined himself in the Hiyoshi shrine for prayer, but the time was spent in vain as he received no auspicious sign from the god. So with bitterness toward the Sannō deity,[176] he left Mt. Hiei and traveled to the Inari shrine,[177] where he presented his petition. Before long he was delighted in a dream to see the god press to his forehead a token for a thousand measures of rice. But later Inari addressed him as follows: "In accordance with the injunction of Hiyoshi Daimyōjin, I must take back the token that I gave you earlier." "The Hiyoshi deity has no intention of helping me himself," said Kanshun in his dream, "and he even has an injunction against my receiving favors elsewhere. I don't understand." Again the deity spoke. "I am just a minor god and it is not for me to decide. Hiyoshi is an illustrious deity and has informed me, 'this time Kanshun will escape from the cycle of birth-and-death. His material prosperity would become an obstacle to his spiritual progress, and he would find it difficult to attain release. Consequently, I do not comply with any request whatever, and I grant him nothing.' So I must take back the token."

At this the monk recognized the great compassion of the deity, and, still in a dream, was filled with gratitude. Upon waking he immediately returned to Enryakuji, where, according to one report, after devoting himself exclusively to religious rites for enlightenment in the next life, he attained birth in paradise. Thus, even if we are refused a favorable omen, it is not futile to pray to the gods and buddhas. This may be part of the divine plan! We should simply keep the faith, persevere in practice, and rely on their mysterious grace.

In a dream Seal of the Law Hōchibō no Shōshin [XII cen.] met the god Jūzenji coming up Mt. Hiei from West Sakamoto. The god rode in a small palanquin with his attendants in stately array, and Shōshin, wishing to use the occasion to make some request, recalled the poverty of his aged mother and asked the deity to provide for her support. The god's countenance had been truly gracious and he appeared to be in a pleasant mood. But on hearing this request, he looked dejected and tired, and a pensiveness came over him. Shōshin then reconsidered: it certainly was not in conformity with the divine will for him to have asked for the things of this world. "Since my aged mother is not long for this world, anything will suffice. But how is she to attain enlightenment in the next life? Please give her your earnest help." At this the monk saw the god's countenance resume its original appearance; in a happy frame of mind again he smiled and nodded his assent. Gradually the hue of the mother's desire for enlightenment deepened and her end was auspicious.

It is utterly foolish to pray to the gods and buddhas with our thoughts only on worldly affairs. The intention of the gods who soften their light is to lead people into the Way of the Buddha. Worldly prosperity is only an occasional "skillful means" to this end. This incident was related to me by students of Shōshin's disciples. It is a true story.

1:8 The Dubious Custom of Presenting the Gods with Offerings of Living Beings

It has become a tradition for people to visit the Itsukushima shrine[178] in Aki province to pray for the religious conviction to pursue enlightenment. Some have attributed this to the fact that long ago Kōbō Daishi made a pilgrimage here. Having discoursed on the profundities of Buddhism, he was apprised by the deities that he would receive in recompense whatever he might request. "For myself I want nothing," he replied, "but should any in these degenerate times pray for the resolve to pursue enlightenment, please grant them religious determination." "We have heard your request," was the reply. And from that day to this even men of considerable religious attainment have constantly paid their respects to the shrine.

While inspecting the premises, a certain venerable priest who had confined himself to the shrine on retreat saw countless numbers of fish from the sea donated as offerings to the gods. Now the Original Ground of the gods who soften their light are the buddhas and bodhisattvas, who, placing compassion before all else, admonish men not to take life. This custom of making offerings of fish was so utterly questionable that the monk prayed to the gods especially that they might resolve his doubts about the matter.

This is what the deities revealed to him: "Indeed, it is a strange business! Unaware of the nature of moral causality, wantonly taking life and unable to rid themselves of delusion, there are those who hope to serve us by offerings of living beings. Because we transfer the responsibility for this to ourselves, their guilt is light. The creatures whom they kill use this as a "skillful means" to enter into the Way of the Buddha, since their lives are wantonly cast away and offered up to us, their days numbered by past karma now being exhausted. Accordingly, we gather to us those fish whose numbered days of retribution are spent." When he had heard this, the priest's doubts were immediately resolved.

This is perhaps the reason that offerings of deer and birds are made at Suwa in Nagano province, and at Utsunomiya in Tochigi province, where there is much hunting. Ordinary people cannot understand the "skillful means" of the provisional manifestations of the buddha. So also is it with the practice of using sacred formulas to subdue one's opponent. For the sake of society and for the sake of others, the exorcist, abiding in a resolve to show compassion and benefit sentient beings, subjugates the violent individual who is their enemy. It is said that this individual will then surely abide in compassion, put an end to evil thoughts, and in a future life will attain enlightenment. Were the exorcist to act simply with the thought that the man was his enemy, this would be contrary to the spirit of his religious discipline and clearly a misdeed to hinder his spiritual progress. In any case the method would not work under these circumstances. Thus, the "skillful means" of the gods will accord with this principle. Indeed, to refrain from killing, to observe the commandments as taught by Buddhism, and to devote oneself to the nectar of the Law—this truly conforms to the will of the gods!

So, concerning the fact that Confucianism and Taoism were first disseminated in Han China, and filial rites were performed using cows and goats, an ancient sage remarked: "It is not easy to spread the Law of the Buddha. Accordingly, the Indian bodhisatt-vas were born into the land of the Han and in the beginning prom-ulgated non-Buddhist scriptures, acquainted the people with the notion that their fathers and mothers were divine spirits, and taught the disposition of filial piety—all as skillful means of the Dharma." Therefore we speak of the non-Buddhist scriptures as "provisional teachings;" they are not the strict teaching of the Buddha. After Buddhism became widespread, those who followed the teachings of Śākyamuni revised these native ceremonies, converting them into Buddhist rites of filial devotion.

If we consider the matter in this way, we find that in the days when our own country had neither seen nor heard the name of Bud-dhism and was not acquainted with the principle of moral causa-tion, as accommodations to serve the Buddha and advance the Dharma, the bodhisattvas taught people what are known as Shintō ceremonies, gradually employing them as "skillful means" for the propagation of Buddhism. Had the strict Buddhist teaching reflect-ing the mind of the true nature of these deities become widespread, people would have abandoned the ancient customs and devoted themselves to the nectar of the Law; and this would certain-ly have been in conformity with the will of the gods. However, since the mind of man finds it difficult to abandon deeply-entrenched customs and hard to forget what has been dyed into one's thinking, this would have been poor strategy. People would have continued to observe the tabus and to make much of the native ceremonies, while their reverence for Buddhism would have been minimal.

To observe the Buddhist regulations in the presence of the gods who soften their light is surely compatible with the will of the gods. And to make pilgrimages to places such as Kumano[179] does not violate the Buddhist precepts. The teaching and practice of Bud-dhism at various miraculous shrines from medieval times being in accord with their Original Ground, the prestige of the gods who soften their light is likewise to be gratefully maintained.

At the foot of a certain mountain in China was a shrine with miraculous powers which the people of the country venerated with offerings of cattle, sheep, fish and birds. The shrine deity was only an old pot. Now it happened that a Zen master came and struck the pot, saying, "Whence comes the deity? Where are the miraculous spirits?" And he completely demolished it.

Then a layman in a plain blue robe appeared, tipped his hat, and bowed respectfully to the Zen master. "I have suffered many afflictions here. Now by virtue of your discoursing on the doctrine of no-rebirth in the cycle of transmigration, I am suddenly released from my painful karma and have been born into the heavens. I cannot repay your kindness." Having said this, he departed.

It has been stated that when the gods receive offerings of slain creatures, their lot is pain; but when the pure nectar of the Law is offered up in profound discourse, then they experience happiness. Bearing this in mind, we should make guiltless offerings to the gods and revere the miraculous nectar of Buddhism.

1:9 Delusion Checked by the Accommodations of the Gods Who Soften their Light

The Land Steward of Takataki[180] in Kazusa province made his yearly[181] pilgrimage to Kumano. Cherishing his one and only daughter, and feeling, moreover, that the experience would benefit her, he took her along with him on the trip. The daughter was exceptionally beautiful, and in the quarters of the Kumano priests lived a young monk from Kyoto called Ajari Something-or-other. On seeing the girl the monk was troubled at heart and longed unbearably for her. But having undertaken the practice of Buddhism at this miraculous shrine and resolved to observe the pure discipline, he was chagrined at having met such an unhappy fate and at being unable to clear his mind of delusive thoughts. He prayed both to the principal deity and to the provisional manifestations to put an end to his troubled state of mind, but as the days passed the vision of her loveliness would not leave him and he could think of nothing else. Unable to endure the torment any longer and hoping to divert his mind, he strapped on his implement box and set out vacantly for Kazusa province. He passed Kamakura, and, at a place called Mutsura, lay down on the beach while waiting for a favorable boat that would take him across the bay to Kazusa. Tired from his travels, he dozed off.

In his dream he made his way by ship to Kazusa and inquired until he came to Takataki. The Land Steward came to greet him and asked why he had traveled so far. "I wanted to visit Kamakura and I made a trip to perform certain austerities," replied the Ajari. "Having heard that your house was nearby, I have come to visit you." The Land Steward entertained him lavishly and when the Ajari remarked that he was about to be on his way, the man detained him with an invitation to spend some time getting acquainted with life in the country.

This had been the Ajari's plan from the beginning and he stayed on, calling on the girl at various times and visiting her stealthily. As their mutual affection deepened, a baby boy was born to them, to the great annoyance of the girl's parents. She was immediately disinherited as an unfilial child, and the two lovers went into hiding, staying at the house of a relative in Kamakura. As the months and years passed, the girl's parents finally relented: "She is our only daughter; and besides, there is nothing we can do to change matters." The priest, in addition to being an average young man of pleasant appearance, was quick-witted and excelled in calligraphy and like accomplishments. Accordingly, the girl's parents decided to accept him as their son-in-law, and her father sent him to Kamakura as his representative to inform the authorities. Since the grandson likewise was quite well-behaved, the grandparents entertained and pampered him. In time, several children were born to the couple.

In their son's thirteenth year they went up to Kamakura for his Coming-of-Age Ceremony. The luggage was put in order and a number of ships were outfitted. But just as they were crossing the bay, a strong wind came up and the waves ran high. The child was at the gunwale looking out and accidentally tumbled into the sea. Crying for help, he sank into the waves and was seen no more.

The Ajari woke from his dream heartbroken and in great distress. During the space of a short nap he had reviewed in detail the events of thirteen years. Even if his plan were to succeed and he attained happiness and prosperity, they would be but the dream of a moment; and though there might be pleasure, there would also be misery. Considering the futility of his plan, the Ajari immediately set out and returned to Kumano. Truly, the dream was a skillful device of the gods who soften their light.[182]

During Chuang Chou's short nap long ago, he dreamed that he became a butterfly and frolicked in a garden of flowers for a hundred years. Upon waking he found that only a short time had elapsed. The *Chuang Tzu* comments: "Did Chuang Chou in a dream become a butterfly; or did a butterfly in a dream become Chuang Chou?"

Indeed, although we consider things to be real, they are figments of a dream; and it is because they are figments of a dream that they are difficult to distinguish as such. Transmigration in the Three Realms [of desire, form, and beyond form] and the transformations through the four kinds of living beings are all a delusive dream occurring during our nap of ignorance. So the *Sutra of Perfect Enlightenment* explains, "When we first realize that all sentient beings have been Buddha from the very beginning, then 'birth-and-death' and 'nirvana' are both as figments of a dream." When we open our minds to true understanding, we see that the beginningless cycle of birth-and-death and the nirvana of attainment [*shigaku*] are both manifest in the short nap of ignorance. Only the unborn substratum of mind which is Original Enlightenment [*hongaku*] is the True Mind that knows no napping and no dreaming.

An ancient has said, "There is no difference between yesterday's reality and today's dream. When one has not crossed over to the land of enlightenment, experience is like a dream in which even the figments of a dream, depending on circumstances, resemble enlightenment. But what man of understanding will think that 'dream' and 'enlightenment' are distinguishable?" The profound reason of things is difficult to comprehend. But the thoughtful man must not entertain any doubts about the illusory things of the world.

Po [Chü-i, 772–846] says: "Flourishing and withering, all things pass away to become as a dream. To put aside both grief and delight at this is *zen*." It is not only because things pass away that they are empty. It is because they have no self-nature, even when present in time, that things are Empty—which thus is involved in the created while being itself uncreated. When we know all phenomena to be in fact a dream, and, with neither pleasure nor grief, the mind-ground is quiet and serene, we will then quite naturally be in conformity with the Gate of Emptiness [which leads to spiritual realization].

Again Po says, "The efficacy of *zen* is known to the individual but is not apparent to others—so that even at times when he is expected to grieve, he does not grieve." The meaning of this statement is as follows: "The figments of a dream are so inconsequential that pleasure and grief should not occupy the mind. The things of the world that we are wont to think of as '*satori*' are all a dream. To take pleasure in life, to grieve at death, to delight at meeting and to feel regret at parting is to have a heart which does not realize that they are all a dream. But the man whose heart is unmoved by all these things is one who enters the Gate of Emptiness. That which is spoken by the mouth we should not call 'zen', but rather, the serenity after having set aside all thoughts from the mind." The *Chuang Tzu* says: "Dogs that bark well are said not to be good; men who speak cleverly are said not to be wise."

Accordingly, he who does not rid his heart of the desire for fame and profit and the objects of the five senses is far from the Gate of Emptiness, though he may discourse eloquently on the doctrines of Buddhism. The *Net of Brahma* says, "Though he explain Emptiness with his mouth, his actions are in the phenomenal world." Those with true wisdom and religious conviction are rare in these Latter Days, and though a man may explain the Law with his mouth, he does not follow the Way with his heart. As he believes the figments of a dream to be reality, his attachment is deep and his craving strong. In the *Completion of Mere Ideation* it is said, "When one has not yet attained true enlightenment, he constantly lives in a dream. For this reason the Buddha describes birth-and-death as a long night." The Great Teacher Tz'u En[183] comments, "When the Law is external to the mind, we transmigrate through birth-and-death; but when we realize the One Mind as enlightenment, we cast birth-and-death aside forever." This is because we are constantly reborn by virtue of the erroneous state in which we experience the unrelieved darkness of the long night of birth-and-death and view the Law as something external. It is said that by our not seeing the Law as external to the mind, the Law becomes mind and the mind becomes the Law, and we will leave the cycle of birth-and-death. The thoughtful man, realizing the One Mind as the source of all phenomena, must awaken from his nap in the Three Realms [of desire, form, and beyond form].

1:10 A Pure Land Devotee Punished for Slighting the Gods

In Chinzei [Kyūshū] lived a lay scholar of the Pure Land sect who conducted a survey of the shrine lands under his jurisdiction as Land Steward. After he had appropriated certain property as in excess of what was registered, the priests and monks attached to the shrine expressed their resentment and made an appeal to the government in Kamakura. "As for the appropriation of excess lands, what the Land Steward decides has the authority of his office," was the reply. Since Kamakura would take no action, the shrine officials argued at length with the Land Steward, but he would not give in. When they threatened to put a curse on him, he simply ridiculed them. "I'm not the least bit frightened. Curse away! What does a Pure Land devotee care about the gods? How can even the gods inflict punishment on a devotee who is to receive the bright light of Amida accepting him into the Pure Land?"

The priests of the shrine were deeply angered and placed a curse on him, so that presently he was afflicted with a grave illness and began to rave. The Land Steward's mother, a nun, was greatly alarmed and pleaded with him in tears, "Consider your filial obligations to me. Return the shrine lands and tell them you have made a mistake." But all to no avail. As the sickness became progressively worse and there appeared to be little hope for the man's recovery, his mother, unable to stand the strain any longer, called upon the god, who sent a messenger to the sick man's house. "The shrine lands must be restored at all costs! Say there has been an error and return the property to the shrine." But the sick man shook his head with an air of madness. "I pay no attention to the gods," he replied, and would not relent in the slightest.

After the messenger secretly reported to the Land Steward's mother what had happened, the god finally took possession of a vestal and held discourse with the woman, who tried to placate him. "The sick man declares that he will return the shrine lands," said the nun, "Please spare his life this time." "He is one who shakes his head and says, 'I pay no attention to the gods!' " replied the vestal, laughing outright. "O what a defiled mind! I am a Transformation Body of the Eleven-Faced Kannon.[184] If one relies on the Original Vow of Amida, my primordial form, and calls upon his name with an upright heart, how endearing do I consider this, how precious! But how can such a dirty, defiled, and unrighteous mind be worthy of the Original Vow?" The vestal snapped her fingers with irritation and her tears fell quietly, so that those who heard it all wept profusely.

In the end the Land Steward did not recover from his head shaking and he expired. In his final hour his teacher and religious mentor of many years came to encourage him to say the nembutsu. "Impertinent fellow!" was his response, striking his teacher with a pillow; and the man struck him back on the head. Indeed, he seems to have had a peculiar life.

Then his mother, the nun, also fell ill and called down

Hakusan Gongen[185] to pray for recovery. "Inasmuch as I commanded him to stop behaving as he did, I do not feel that I have done
anything blameworthy in the sight of the gods." Replied the deity:
"Even though you commanded him to stop, it displeases me that in
your heart you felt ill-will toward me out of sympathy for your
child." In the end the nun also passed away.

Soon after his son succeeded the Land Steward as head of the
house, a heron came to roost on the ridgepole of the house, and this
was interpreted as an admonition from the gods. "What punishment
can the gods inflict? I can contain it," declared a resident
soothsayer. A cup still in his hands, the man's fingers were bent
backwards as though bound by cords, and crouching over, he died
on the spot. The soothsayer's descendants are living today and tell
people of the incident, which, since it happened in our own times, is
known to many. With the man's descendants and relations alive today, I hesitate to relate the matter. However, my purpose is not to
carry gossip, but simply to let people know why they should not
belittle the majesty of the gods.

The *nembutsu* sects are an important gateway to salvation appropriate to this defiled world, and provide the common man with a
direct route to release from birth-and-death. But though they are
indeed most excellent, there are those who pass judgment on other
practices, other ways of acquiring merit. They go as far as to make
light of the other buddhas, bodhisattvas, and divinities, and to
ridicule the various teachings of the Mahāyāna. These com-
monplace people have a way of thinking which does not admit that
other disciplines also lead to paradise; understanding nothing outside
their own beliefs, they disparage the other buddhas and bodhisattvas. The schools of the *nembutsu* sects are numerous, but if we
discuss the issue in the light of their common basic principles, we
find that in general their sutras and commentaries do not contest
the attainment of paradise through other disciplines. The *Sutra of
Meditation on Amida Buddha*[186] states: "Reciting the scriptures of
the Mahāyāna, expounding their fundamental principle, showing
filial devotion to one's parents, observing five, or eight, of the Buddhist commandments, or even the five social virtues of Confucianism—one will still transfer the merit of his actions to others and
attain birth in paradise."

In the *Larger Pure Land Sutra*[187] it is said: "Among my forty-
eight vows, the eighteenth is for those who make a special practice of
the *nembutsu*; by the nineteenth, I vow to meet on their deathbeds
those who devote themselves to meritorious virtues; and in accord-

ance with the twentieth vow, those who accrue merit and collect their thoughts will be born in paradise."

Thus, the *nembutsu*, being especially selected from among the various practices and established on a single vow, is primary, fundamental; but the other practices, based on the entire set of productive vows, are secondary, complementary. If one admits as much, then how can he say that the other practices do not lead to birth in paradise?

In the commentary of Shan-tao[188] it is stated, "Because they devote themselves to the myriad practices, they all can go to paradise." It thus appears that if one devotes himself to any of the myriad disciplines and virtuous activities, he will attain birth in paradise. In a commentary [*Sanzengi*] on miscellaneous practices he says, "Although we grant that birth in paradise can be attained by applying these methods, they are all called indiscriminate practices." But though it applies the terms "distant" and "familiar," it does not appear to say that birth in paradise cannot be attained through them.

Even more to the point are the many examples from India, China, and Japan based on the writings and biographies of those who achieved their objective of birth in paradise through recitation of the *Lotus Sutra* and the chanting of sacred formulas. We should not lose the efficacy of the Mahāyāna by curbing it, nor disparage and neglect the benefits of the other teachings. Thus, while respecting and relying solely on Amida's Vow and diligently seeking benefit from the *nembutsu*, we should not disparage other disciplines nor make light of other buddhas, bodhisattvas, and deities. The consequences of this offense can be seen in the final moments of the Land Steward, related above. The capsizing of the vehicle in front is a warning to those that follow—those who truly desire birth in the Pure Land should bear in mind the significance of this incident.

To speak in such a way is itself certainly a severe criticism, but I have tried to illustrate a certain way of thinking. The attitude which denies the attainments of paradise to other disciplines seems to do homage to Amida; actually, it disparages him. This is because Amida, with widespread compassion, also welcomes into his Pure Land those who cultivate the myriad disciplines and virtuous actions. The boundaries of his paradise are limitless and will encompass those groups which follow other teachings and other sects. Amida excels the other buddhas, his Pure Land surpasses theirs, his forty-eight world-transcending vows are reliable, and his great, limitless paradise is most splendid. So if one rejects the non-

nembutsu disciplines and doctrines and denies their efficacy for attaining birth in the Pure Land, he minimizes the Buddha's compassion and treats his paradise as if it had narrow boundaries.

This reminds me of a certain wet-nurse who wished to praise the little princess in her charge. "The princess I take care of has a most beautiful appearance. Her eyes are narrow and pretty." Then someone mentioned to her that narrow eyes were a defect. "Indeed? Well, one of her eyes is quite big!" Similarly, some people try unsuccessfully to praise Amida. Moreover, even among those who would deny the attainment of paradise to the other disciplines there are various viewpoints. "Those who say that other practices do not lead to the Pure Land are not in possession of the Three Qualities of Mind[189] for reaching it," explains a certain master. "When one has the Three Qualities he sees that the other disciplines all become as the *nembutsu*, and he will attain birth in Amida's Pure Land (*ōjō*). But if he lacks these three qualities, he will not attain this birth, even though he recites the Buddha's name."

If this is true, then we should not doubt that the other disciplines also lead to birth in paradise. If one utterly lacks these three qualities, then he will not attain *ōjō*, though he may say the *nembutsu*. Between the *nembutsu* and other practices there is absolutely no difference. The earlier Pure Land scholars spoke in a similar vein while propagating their sect as circumstances permitted. There is nothing to blame in this attitude. Later scholars and householders, hearing only the words [but not understanding the meaning of the doctrine], disparage other practices.

Not long ago when the *nembutsu* doctrine was becoming widespread, certain people threw copies of the *Lotus Sutra* into the river and others rubbed Jizō's head with smartweed,[190] saying that the non-Amidist buddhas and scriptures were useless. In one village the serving girls were discussing the affairs of a neighboring household: "They've already crushed smartweed on the neighbor's Jizō down as far as his eyes!" What shameful behavior! During a ceremony honoring the bodhisattva Jizō a certain priest of the Pure Land sect, because he felt the service was improper, took down a statue of Amida which was standing beside the Jizō. Another individual remarked, "Those who believe in Jizō will fall into hell, because Jizō resides in hell." If this is the case, then by virtue of the "skillful means" to benefit sentient beings and having vowed out of their great compassion vicariously to bear the sufferings of others, both Amida and Kannon are, of their own accord, also in hell! Why limit it to Jizō? Because the mind of discrimination is deeply attached to the things of this world, none of these people understands the basis of the appearances of the Buddha.

In a northern province lived a sutra-chanter who performed the Thousand-part Sutra Recitation,[191] but joined an Amidist sect at the urging of a *nembutsu* devotee: "Those who recite the *Lotus Sutra* will certainly fall into hell; it is a grave error. Those who hope for birth in the Pure Land other than through the *nembutsu* are foolish indeed!" The man trusted the words of the devotee. In all that he did, his heart and mouth had no peace, as he kept repeating, "How wretched and miserable I am for having chanted the sutras these many years, and not once having recited the *nembutsu*." The man became seriously ill — a result, no doubt, of such a perverted notion — and fell into a frenzy. "Oh, how I regret having chanted the sutras," he droned monotonously. Finally, the man gnawed off his tongue and lips, and, smeared with blood, died raving. The monk who had encouraged him then remarked, "Having repented of the sin of reciting the *Lotus Sutra* and biting off his tongue and lips in retribution, he has atoned for his crime and has certainly been born in the Pure Land."

When the *nembutsu* doctrine became popular in the capital some time ago, a mandala was painted to express the assertion that the wicked will attain *ōjō*, but not those who observe the commandments and recite the sutras. It depicted the celestial light of salvation falling on a murderer, but not on a distinguished-looking monk chanting the sutras. The work became a sensation, and a letter of protest was sent to the court from Nara, which said in part: "Those who see the traditional pictures of hell will repent of having done evil, and those who venerate this mandala will deplore having performed good works."[192]

When we interpret things according to the four terms of differentiation,[193] we find that the good man has evil propensities. Although on the surface he resembles a good man, he is not so in reality because of his desire for fame and profit. Moreover, the evil man has good roots of merit from prior existences, and though on the surface he appears to be wicked, yet in the depths of his being exists an upright heart and a desire to follow the Buddha's teachings. From such premises ignorant priests and laymen, their hearts biased and proud, criticize and slander the man who observes the commandments and cultivates the good. "He is an evil man, his religious practice is unorthodox, and he will not be born in the Pure Land." And of the man who does evil rather than good they say, "He is a good man, the light of salvation will shine upon him, and his birth in the Pure Land is assured."

These fixed delusions are a serious error. They are rare among those who have studied the Holy Teachings and become acquainted with their senior brethren in the faith, but one now and then hears of such peculiarities among laymen in remote areas. In the outlying reaches of remote provinces there are many distorted schools of thought, not only in the *nembutsu* tradition, but in Tendai, Shingon, Zen, and the rest. Accordingly, we should exert every effort to become intimate with a man of wisdom, make the Holy Teachings our own, and thus avoid entering the forest of erroneous views.

For this reason the *Sutra* [*on Viewing the Mind-Ground*] tells us: "It is not difficult to realize Enlightenment, the marvelous fruit of religious practice; but the opportunity of meeting a genuine spiritual adviser is very uncertain." And an ancient sage has remarked that "when we have not met an outstanding teacher who has made his appearance in the world, then we imbibe a distorted version of the sacred medicine of the Mahāyāna."

According to the Tendai patriarch [Chih-i], "A wise man of non-Buddhist persuasion converts falsity into truth, heterodoxy into True Law. A dull Buddhist takes the truth and turns it into falsity, making heresy of the True Law" (*Cessation and Insight*). The Sixth Zen Patriarch [Hui-neng, 638–713] states: "When the man of false views explains the True Law, the True Law becomes heterodoxy; when the man of true understanding interprets heterodoxy, then heterodoxy becomes True Law."

Nowadays those able to view things correctly are rare, and there are those who adapt the Buddha's truth to their own erroneous views, leading themselves and others into the path of error. When a cow drinks water, it becomes milk; with a serpent, it becomes poison. Though the Dharma has a single taste, the truth or falsity of its application depends on men. Understand this well, and, avoiding the error of false views, enter into the True Path.

2:1 The Man Who Was Vouchsafed a Relic of the Buddha

In Kawachi province lay priest Shōrembō, wishing to acquire a genuine relic of the Buddha, performed the relic-prayers and prostrations of Amoghavajara (Fukū, 705–774) five hundred times every day for 14–15 years. Then he visited the tomb of Prince Shōtoku (573–621), where he prayed earnestly. At midnight an old priest came forth from the tomb and told Shōrembō to take his request to a shrine vestal reclining nearby, who led him to the rear door of the Jōdo Hall. Here he was shown a crystal reliquary and given one of the ten grains which it contained. The vestal told Shōrembō that her name was Jakujō. When he inquired for her on the following morning, he was informed that the vestal had been seen around the premises for about a week, but no one knew where she came from or who she was. Truly, it was a divine manifestation. A monk who actually saw the relic related to me what he heard. This happened very recently. Although the lay priest was unschooled in the Buddhist mysteries, his deep faith caused this miraculous result. *The* Garland Sutra, Commentary on the Great Wisdom Sutra, *and the* Lotus Sutra *all teach the importance of faith.*

A householder had great faith in a certain monk, relying on his advice in worldly matters even to the point of requesting medicine of him. The monk knew nothing about medicine and would prescribe roasted wisteria nodes for every ailment. But taken with faith, it could cure many ills. Once when the man lost a horse, he went to the monk for advice and was told to roast some wisteria nodes. The man trustingly did as he was told; and while he was at the foot of a mountain collecting nodes, he spied his horse in a nearby valley.

The Net of Brahma Sutra *tells of a demon who appeared to a man in the guise of the Buddha in an attempt to deceive him; but his plan was frustrated by the man's deep faith.*

An old monk who took orders late in life went to a temple and with deep faith said that he wished to acquire the initial fruits of enlightenment. "Just follow the eating regulations!" teased the younger monks. On his head they placed a kind of handball (comparable to a zenkiku, "meditation ball," which is used to keep people alert during meditation), and told the old man that this was the initial fruit of enlightenment. The old monk maintained his deep faith and actually attained it, from there progressing through the four stages, at which time the young monks apologized for their flippant behavior.

Retired Emperor Toba (r. 1107-1123) inspected the mementos collected at the Zentōin ("Temple of Former Trips to China") on Mount Hiei. Among the effects left by Ennin (794-864) was a round object which made a sound when dropped, but no one at the monastery knew its purpose. Lay priest Shinzei[194] *identified it as a "meditation ball". His learning was so impressive that he also recognized a "Law stick" (hōjō), a pole placed in such a way as to prod a person if his posture became faulty during meditation; and an "old mans helper" (jorō), an armrest used by old monks as a support during meditation.*

Among the Buddha's disciples Cūdapanthaka (Shurihantoku) was so dull that he forgot his own name. In order to express the notion of meditation (shikan) to him, the Buddha likened kan *to a broom and* shi *to sweeping. But when Cūdapanthaka could remember "broom," he would forget "sweeping"; and when he remembered "sweeping", he would forget "broom." Finally the Five Hundred Arhats taught him a verse which said that he who guards mouth, thought and body will cross over the world of birth-and-death. Acting on this with faith, he attained spiritual realization. Faith and practice are better than much learning. The* Dharmapada (Hokkukyō, T. 210) *says that it is better conscientiously to put into practice a single stanza of the Teaching than to recite a thousand verses.*

2:2 The Efficacy of the Buddha of Healing

At Chūgun in Hitachi province a boy living near a thatched chapel dedicated to the Buddha of Healing, Yakushi Nyorai, became ill and died. He was abandoned in the fields, but for several days the animals did not molest him. It is believed that Yakushi carried the boy back to his house, where he revived. The Yakushi image was moved to the Land Steward's residence where a hull was built to house it; and the boy, having meanwhile become a monk, was given custody of it. This happened at the end of the Bun'ei period (1264-74).

A young serf of the Atsuta Shrine suddenly went blind one year on the fifteenth day of the eleventh month. On a pilgrimage to a shrine-temple (jingūji) he prayed to the Buddha Yakushi; and on the night of the fifteenth day of the third month in the following year, a priest came to him in a dream and told him to get up and open his eyes. His sight restored, the boy returned to serve at the shrine. This happened during the Bun'ei period (1264-74).

2:3 The Efficacy of Amida

In Kamakura lived a grand dame called Machi no Tsubone, who had in her intimate service a young girl who seems to have been blessed by her good actions in former lives. The girl had faith in calling on the Buddha's name and performed this practice secretly, hidden from the eyes of the world.

Her mistress was very stern and meticulous in observing the tabus and festive proprieties. One New Year's Day as the young girl was serving at table, she was praying as usual and blurted out without thinking: "Praise to the Buddha Amida!" The mistress became violently angry.

"It's as though someone had just died. How very rude it is of you to say the *nembutsu* today of all days." Taking hold of the girl, the lady heated a coin until it was red hot and touched it to her cheek. But the girl, wondering how it could possibly be a crime to recite the *nembutsu*, continued to direct her thoughts to the Buddha. And, strange to say, the coin left no scar.

Later the mistress repaired to her private oratory to perform the first rites of the year. As she prayed before the enshrined image, a standing gold statue of the Buddha Amida, she noticed a black, coin-shaped mark on its cheek. When curiosity led her to examine it carefully, she discovered that a coin mark made by burning metal was at the very place she had touched the coin to the cheek of the young girl. So the woman summoned the girl, only to find that she had not the slightest blemish on her cheek.

With shame and repentance, the mistress called in an artisan to cover the scar with quantities of gold leaf, but it would not be hidden. The statue, which exists today, is called the "Coin-Burned Buddha."[195] I have myself prayed before it, and at the time the scar appeared to be triangular. This actually happened.

Those with faith are not without hope either for the present or for the future. It is ridiculous that while many are willing to sacrifice their lives for the sake of loyalty or worldly success, none will do so for the Buddha's Teaching, whose rewards are far greater.

2:4 The Efficacy of Yakushi and Kannon

In the Yamada District of Owari Province lived Lieutenant of the Right Horse Guards Akinaga, who sided with the Imperial forces during the Jōkyū War and was severely wounded during the fighting at Kuize River.[196] Leaving him for dead, the troops rode back to the capital, but two of his friends broke away from the main force and scouted the neighborhood steathily on foot. When they came to the battlefield that night to recover Akinaga's body for burial, they found him gravely injured but still alive. So they hoisted him on their shoulders and carried him to a mountain north of Ōhaka. Among his many wounds, the most serious was one he sustained by being pinned to the ground by an arrow which penetrated his windpipe.

"Nothing can be done to save me," he told his friends. "So take my head with you and leave." But the friends sympathized with his misfortune and looked about for some way to help him. A party of warriors came to scour the area for stragglers, and, as night was breaking, the friends concealed the wounded man in the hollow of a large tree and stole away, as nothing else could be done. Looking for traces of blood, the warriors searched the area thoroughly, but they left without discovering Akinaga.

Subsequently a black-robed monk appeared to Akinaga, saying that he had come from Yokokura, and gave him some plant leaves which he had rubbed together. When Akinaga swallowed them, the blood drained from his lungs, his bodily symptoms were relieved, and he felt that he had recovered. Then the monk disappeared. The two friends again returned, inquired about his health, and carried him from the tree. It was as Akinaga had said, for he had recovered physically.

They were going down on foot to their native [Owari] province when they came to the swollen waters of the Orizu River. As they waited for the water to recede—there was nothing else to be done—they were encountered by warriors from the East and immediately apprehended. Akinaga felt that it would be mortifying to prolong his life and expose himself to shame, having already been marked for death. But when he walked to the edge of the river with the intention of hurling himself into its waters, he was addressed by a young monk.

"I have come from Ryūsenji.[197] Having thus been saved, you are not to perish. Do yourself no harm." Akinaga wondered if he were in a dream; but this was reality. Still, his wounds were painful, the day was hot, and he felt that he could not endure the agony. But when he again drew near the river to throw himself in, the monk restrained him with a rope: "You are not to die! This is not meant to be!" Thus restrained, Akinaga gave up the idea of suicide.

Akinaga was known to the congregation and officials at Atsuta Shrine, who spoke to his captors. "Let us be responsible for him. He lectures on the sutras, performs other Buddhist rites on the shrine premises, and is conscientious about public affairs—a prominent person in these parts."

But his captors would not permit this, since Akinaga was a man of wide reputation. He was taken to Kamakura and brought before Yoshitoki, who ordered that he be beheaded immediately, and he was dispatched to Yuigahama beach. Again the same monk came as before and spoke to him in a vision: "Do not grieve. You are not to die!" Nevertheless it seemed to Akinaga that he had now come to his final hour, so he called the name of Buddha with single-minded devotion.

In the vicinity of Midarebashi Bridge he met a friend of many years standing who inquired what was going on. His captors bridled their horses while Akinaga poured out his story, with flowing tears. "I, who was to have perished at Kuize River, had hoped to avoid any further shame if I could help it. But now I have come to this pass. At this very moment I am on my way to the beach to have my head severed. But it delights me that we are able to meet for the last time."

"I have been your close friend for years," replied the man. "I will go and ask Lord Sagami to place you in my custody. Just wait a bit." The man spurred on his horse and spoke to Yoshitoki, who gave him a letter of custody; then the man galloped back and secured Akinaga's release. He accompanied his friend, plied him with many kindnesses, and restored him to health. Akinaga lived in the province until he reached a ripe old age. Due to the injury to his windpipe, his voice was hoarse.

His grandchild and others of his family are alive today. A lay priest who was his adopted son told me this story. It really happened. People commonly experienced such blessings in antiquity, but in these Latter Days we consider ourselves to be most favored. To be favored even by a dream is a blessing, but to have the benefit of being helped by the divine manifesting itself in the real world is most gratifying.

The Yakushi ["Physician Buddha"] of Yokokura in Mino province is said to have been fashioned from the same block of wood as the Yakushi in the Komponchūdō [on Mt. Hiei]. It is known for its miraculous properties and over the years Akinaga had frequently visited it. They say that Ryūsenji ["Dragon Mountain Temple"] was built and dedicated in the space of one night by a dragon king who appeared to Akinaga in a dream. When dawn broke, he awoke to find that a moat had been excavated [for the dragon to live in]; its remains can be seen even today. A Horse-headed Kannon[198] resides there which attracts crowds of people who believe it to be a miraculous image. Akinaga used to make monthly pilgrimages, coming every eighteenth day to recite the *Kannon Sutra*[199] thirty-three times. It was through the causality of such meritorious actions that he received divine assistance.

Manjuśrī (Monju) extols Kannon in the Śūraṅgama *Sutra (Shuryōgongyō); and Prince Shōtoku is a manifestation of Kannon, as Kannon is a manifestation of Amida, according to the esoteric tradition. Japan has a special affinity with Amida and Kannon.*

A young lady in abject poverty made frequent visits to Kiyomizu Temple,[200] amassing much merit for her devotion. During one of her trips, a divine apparition in the form of an old monk came to her with instructions to steal the robe of a person nearby. The woman woke from her dream in great consternation, wondering how she could possibly comply. Still, the oracle was from the gods and so she decided that she would do as she was told, however shameful the act might appear to others. Taking down a white garment which hung on a nearby screen, she donned it, holding its top edge over her head to conceal her face, as decorum required, while the rest trailed down her back. The woman started home at once.

She was proceeding on her way when, at the Fifth Street Bridge, a samurai with much pomp and splendor came to walk

along with her. He appeared to be an official of the Great Watch.
When the man inquired how it was that she happened to be out
alone, being a lady of such distinction, she replied that she was
returning from a visit to the temple. Then the samurai casually
asked if she would care to go along with him out to the back country.

"I have no one to look after me," replied the woman. "If you
will offer to help me, I will go wherever you go."

"Do you really mean it?"

The woman replied that she was quite serious. When the
samurai looked at her by the light of the moon, he found the charming features of a young woman.

"Done!" he exclaimed, giving the woman a horse to mount.
And he took her with him.

There must have been a karmic bond between them for this to
have happened. Passing the years in deep mutual affection, they
bore sons and prospered, somewhere in Mutsu Province.

After ten years passed, the lady accompanied her husband to
the capital on his next tour of duty in the Great Watch. She did not
wish to admit it, but by now the lady had no relations left there
although she continued to talk as though she had. As the couple
entered the capital, they were passing a prosperous-looking house
when the wife remarked that that was where her aunt lived. Taking
the palanquin on to the premises, she entered the house and asked
for the mistress.

"Originally I am from the capital, but my relations have all
passed away and I have no one close. I told my husband that this was
my aunt's place. Please understand! We are meeting for the first
time, but I need your help." And taking out fifty pieces of gold, she
offered them to the mistress of the house, who did not demur.

"My niece will be staying with us," announced the mistress,
entertaining the woman as though she were a relative. The house
lacked nothing and the couple was lavishly entertained. Finally,
after the *sake* had been passed around, things settled down.

"How extraordinary it is," the hostess remarked to her guest,
"that among the many inhabitants of the capital we two should have
come on such intimate terms. There must be a wondrous karmic
bond between us."

"This could not have its origins only in the present life," replied
the lady. "Since the karmic bonds which lie between us from the
past are profound, I will tell you all that has happened to me just as
it occurred." And she described her life in detail from the beginning.

Suddenly the mistress clapped her hands. "How unexpected!" she exclaimed. "That was my robe. After it was stolen, I blamed the Buddha for it; and, in my foolishness, I have not since then been up to the temple. Oh, how shallow is the common mind which cannot anticipate the happy consequences of the divine plans! We are truly indebted to the skillful methods of Kannon's compassion."

The two women wrung their tear-soaked sleeves and presently went up together to Kiyomizu Temple. As the attachments between them were deep, the lady would send to her friend presents of local products, while the mistress would respond with various items from the capital. Even blood relatives would not have done as much for one another.

Wonderful are the skillful designs of the Holy One!

Faith is important. All Buddhas have a True Body (shinjin) and a Transformation Body (ōjin); likewise, sentient beings have a wisdom-mind and a delusion-mind. The True Body of Buddha is the eternal, formless Law Body (hosshin), it cannot be recognized by the delusion-mind but only with the wisdom-mind. It is the Transformation Body which employs marvelous expedients to lead us from delusion.

2:5 Jizō Nurses the Sick

In Kamakura a Shingon master known as the "Governor-monk" (Sochi Sōzu), having reached his eightieth year, wished to transmit the esoteric methods and seal of transmission to a talented young disciple. But the boy was only eighteen so the ordination ceremony (kanjō) was not permitted. As his sickness progressed, the old monk, regretting that the tradition would be lost, asked his disciples to pray to Emma, king of the world of the dead, to prolong his life until he could ordain the young monk. They replied that this was an improper request for one of his years.

"It is not my own life that I prize, but that of the Teaching," said the monk. "I don't care what people say. If I ask Emma for a respite of a hundred days for the sake of the Dharma, how can he refuse?" And the old monk had his disciples begin the cermony for prolonging life.

As it was then the beginning of the tenth month and he had decided to perform the transmission rite in the first month of the new year (when the young disciple would be a year older, by Japanese count), he likewise began the hundred-day prefatory exercises. Meanwhile he was restored to his usual heartiness and gradually instructed his successor in the precepts. "I transmit the essence of the esoteric teaching, recognizing the identity of Amida and Jizō," he said. "I follow Jizō; and reciting the "Mantra of Light" (kōmyō shingon, whose recitation is said to effect birth in Amida's Western Paradise), I embrace the souls in hell. You are to perform my memorial services on the twenty-fourth of every month (a day sacred to Jizō)."

On the fourteenth day of the new year the ordination ceremony was performed. The following day the monk's condition worsened, and he prepared for the end. While those who nursed him took their rest, he was attended by a beautiful young monk whom no one had seen before. When his disciples were informed of this, they thought that perhaps it was the ministration of the Bodhisattva Jizō. And some recalled that when the young attendant left, he carried a metal-ringed staff (shakujō), *one of Jizō's conventional accessories. On the twenty-fourth of the month the old monk sat upright, made symbolic gestures with his hands, and causing his disciples to invoke the name of Jizō, died as though entering into deep meditation. The monk's disciples recounted this story.*

The benefits of venerating Jizō are set forth in the Sutra of Ten Cakras (Jūringyō, *T. 410, 411).*[201] *Śākyamuni entrusted sentient beings to Jizō's care between the period of his death and the arrival of the next Buddha, Maitreya. Among all the buddhas and bodhisattvas Jizō is in a special way the bodhisattva of our world.*

Among the secret writings by Eisai (1141–1215) is a one-volume work known as "The Mystery of Jizō and Fudō"[202], *which states that Jizō is the ultimate expression of the lenient aspect of Mahāvairocana, Fudō being his harsh manifestation, the extreme which breaks and subdues evil. They may be likened to the administrative and military aspects of government, which applies lenient or harsh methods depending on the circumstances.*

When the nun An'yō (ca. 947–1010), Eshin's younger sister, was on the point of death, priest Shōzan (939–1011) of the Shugakuin recited the Fire-World Spell (kakai no ju) *while Eshin intoned the name of Jizō. Then they saw Fudō push the nun out of the flames and Jizō take her by the hand to lead her back to life.*

When one of Eshin's disciples died suddenly, Fudō's Spell of Compassionate Help (jiku no shu) *was intoned. The disciple returned to life and related that as he was being taken away by four or five men, a young monk begged them to forbear, but to no avail. "Though you begrudge him even to me," said the monk, "I will have him back." As he spoke, two youths, their hair done up in the old style and carrying white staves, chased away the tormentors and brought the disciple to the monk, who returned him to the land of the living. The secret writing by Eisai bears out the teaching of Jizō's lenient activity, and Fudō's saving by harsh methods.*

2:6 Various Favors of the Bodhisattva Jizō

On a beach in Kamakura was an old Jizō Hall enshrining a sixteen-foot image[203] of the bodhisattva which was frequented by the people in the neighborhood living on the beach. One day those who had been in the habit of visiting the image all had separate dreams in which a handsome young monk spoke to them.

"You often visit me. But now I have been sold and will be taken elsewhere; so I have come to bid you a fond farewell." The people were all mystified.

It happened that the owner of the hall was poor and was selling the chapel built by his forbears. In the transaction the statue was acquired by the venerable Gangyō,[204] the great restorer of Tōji. While transporting the image to the Nikaidō area for restoration, he was downcast at not having enough workers to manage the job when a powerful monk of low station came from nowhere, saying that he would do the work of ten men. Now ten ordinary workers would not have been enough, but this priest picked up the statue and carried it with ease. Then when Gangyō was about to offer him some food, he vanished into thin air. People wondered if he was a divine manifestation. One of my fellow monks actually saw this and told me about it.

Now the back of the statue's neck had deteriorated, so the priest called an artisan to repair it, but the man refused. "It is a miraculous image and I cannot bring myself to do it any harm." But just as Gangyō was about to call another artisan, the first man returned saying that a young monk had appeared to him saying: "Repair my body. It will cause me no distress."

The artisan repaired the statue and the devotees returned, donating materials to conduct religious rites. The expression of the Buddha is no different from that of a man. It is one of the marvels of our time.

The incident was relayed by one of Gangyō's disciples and became widely known. The people near the beach who had witnessed the dream made pilgrimages by foot to express their devotion; and others who heard of the affair also came to pay their respects.[205]

The Commentary on the Great Wisdom Sutra *states that it is no crime to break a Buddhist image while one is repairing it, because the intention is good. Devadatta (Chōdatsu) spilled blood and fell into the lowest hell because of his attempt to kill Śākyamuni, whereas the physician Jīva (Giba) spilled blood and was reborn in the heavens. The act was the same but the rewards were different. Good and evil depend on the direction of the heart; that which is done is in itself neither right nor wrong. So it is in our relationships with living beings and venerable works of art. It is said that the Maitreya image at Kasagi lost its miraculous powers after being painted. One can either venerate an old statue just as it is; or, if it becomes unsightly, the regulations provide that it may be hidden behind a curtain. Just as a homely woman may appear fascinating when she is concealed and cannot be seen, so also may an old image attract the faith of believers.*

Recently on Kade-no-kōji[206] Street there has been a Jizō with remarkable powers for helping people. The men and women of the capital flock to it, among whose number was a young lady, beautiful of face and figure, who often came to spend the night.

Now a young monk who frequently came to pray before the image became enamored of this lady. At his wit's end over how he could get acquainted, he came up with the idea of approaching her by pretending to be a manifestation of the enshrined bodhisattva. One night when the lady, exhausted from her devotions, was resting, the monk whispered in her ear: "When you leave the temple, put your trust in the first person you meet."

The monk withdrew and from a distance saw the lady get up as the dawn was faintly breaking, rouse her maid-servant, and quickly leave the temple. "I've done it!" he thought, preparing to intercept her.

But his clogs had been mislaid and he had difficulty finding them. He might be too late. Looking in the direction the woman had taken, the monk decided that she was proceeding east on Kade-no-kōji and ran down the street after her. But she was nowhere in sight.

It had been ordained that the lady would turn down Karasumaru Street. There in the light of the waning moon she came upon a lay priest on horseback accompanied by four or five men. At seeing her stop, looking as though she wished to speak with him, the lay priest got down from his horse and asked what she wanted.

The woman did not reply immediately, but after a time she spoke to him through her maid-servant as go-between.

"I hesitate to address you, but recently I have been visiting the Kade-no-kōji Jizō, who instructed me in a visitation to put my trust in the first person I met this morning after leaving the temple. I hesitate to speak out like this; but how could I avoid saying something?" The woman was overcome with embarrassment.

It had been three years since the lay priest had lost his wife with whom he had lived for a long time, and he had decided not to remarry until visiting the Jizō for guidance. Now that this had occurred just as he was on his way to visit the Jizō Hall, the lay priest, without further ado, provided the lady with a horse and returned home with her. He was a samurai of some means and had land in the country.

Meanwhile the monk ran first one way and then another with his clogs clattering. Sweating and panting for breath he tried to intercept the lady, inquiring of everyone he saw. It was already light when he was informed where the lady he described had gone. Unable to restrain himself, he went up to the gate of the lay priest's house.

"That was no manifestation of Jizō. I was playing a joke on you!" he yelled. But no one believed him. People merely said: "What are you doing? Are you crazy?" He had gained nothing by his dishonesty.

Because the woman, out of deep faith, took his words as those of the Buddha, she achieved her heart's desire. The ways of the Buddha are wonderful!

Similarly, an old monk of Kurama, because he feigned a miraculous manifestation, had his living quarters trampled to pieces by an ox. I will not relate the incident in detail as it is well known.

A hunter in Suruga kept a small Jizō image in his house which he venerated with flowers and incense. One day he dreamed that he was being taken away by demons and that Jizō intervened in his behalf.

"This man is to go to hell for taking life," said the demons. But Jizō secured his release by promising to admonish him. The man refrained from killing for a month or two, but then went back to his old habits.

Then the man died; and as the ox-and-horse-headed jailers of hell came for him, Jizō again begged for his life but was told that since the man had broken his promise, he could not be released. After much insistence, Jizō saved the man a second time.

The hunter kept his word for a year. When he relapsed again, he was stricken with a grave illness and died. Many demons came to carry him away, but this time Jizō did not appear. "Even Jizō has abandoned me," cried the hunter but continued to pray fervently. Finally the bodhisattva came like a shadow by his side and the man grasped the hem of his robe to detain him.

"How is it that you help such an evil man?" asked the jailers. "He always lies."

"I didn't help him," replied the Jizō. "He took hold of me."

At that, one of the jailers shot the man through the back with an arrow, while another pierced his breast with a spear. The jailers withdrew, and the man was restored to life to find wounds in his chest. Eventually he became a monk and now devotes himself to the service of Jizō. This happened during the Kōan period.[207]

At Ikoma in Yamato province a Hossō scholar called Ronshikibō observed the post-noon fast and lived in retirement reciting the Lotus Sutra. But he would not take alms for expounding the scriptures and performing other religious services, and had a small plot of land tilled to satisfy his needs. After his death his hermitage was left to a disciple, Sanikubō. The disciple also died but returned to life after a day and a night to relate the following story.

"I went to the palace of Emma, king of the dead, and as I was leaving I

met Ronshikibō, who took me to his quarters. He explained to me that as a disciple of the Buddha, he should have profited from the good karma of having expounded the Law. It was not fitting for him to have land tilled on his behalf, and for this he had been summoned to the underworld.

"When I asked what was to become of me, I was told to wait and ask Jizō, who took me to Emma. He then led me to a distant plain on which were countless hungry ghosts, looking just the way they are shown in pictures. One of them said that I was its child, and that the hunger and thirst which it suffered were the retribution for crimes committed on my behalf. It asked that I be given to it to eat, but was told that though I appeared to be its child, I was in fact a different person. When we left I was told that, in truth, this was my mother. But even if she were to have eaten me, her relief would have been short-lived. Jizō said that he rescued me through this deception because it would have been profitless to have lost my life to no purpose. I was to exert myself to relieve my mother's torment. Then Jizō sent me away, and I revived." This story was told to me by a monk who had met both Ronshikibō and his disciple. It happened very recently.

A nembutsu recluse had land tilled to support himself, and was shown the sinfulness of this in a dream. On a mountain he saw a fiery chariot drawn by a lion and driven by an infernal jailer, who remarked: "This is how I shall punish the enemy."

The monk, filled with awe, made no reply. Three young monks standing on top of a mountain asked if he heard what the jailer said, and he replied that he had. "As one who tills the soil and kills many insects you must be warned," they continued, and three times repeated a verse of admonition. I heard from the monk myself that he gave up tilling the soil.

In Kamakura lived two samurai friends who both venerated Jizō. One was poor and offered incense and flowers before an old, unrepaired statue. The other was prosperous and performed his devotions before an image which had been skillfully carved and placed in a beautiful household shrine. When the wealthy samurai died, his statue was bequeathed to his poor friend, who now transferred his attention to the new Jizō and completely neglected his old statue. When the old Jizō appeared to the man in a dream and spoke a verse of reproach, he awoke in consternation, placed the old Jizō in the shrine with the other, and venerated them together.

At the foot of Mount Tsukuba in Hitachi province lived an old lay priest who, with his own hands, fashioned an odd-looking Jizō; and the people of his household often petitioned it with considerable success. A young child living in the house accidentally fell into a well and perished. "It's too bad that while this Jizō is busy answering everybody's prayers, he takes my child's life," said the mother, weeping bitterly. That night Jizō appeared to her in a dream standing beside the well. He told her not to bear any resentment toward him since the child's death resulted from karma against which he was powerless; but he would help the child in the next life. The woman saw Jizō take the young child out of the well and carry it away, and her grief was somewhat relieved.

In the words handed down to us from an old worthy, the true body *(shinjin)* of the Buddha is formless and ineffable *(musō munen)*. Great compassion is his original vow, and he appears in various guises by virtue of the good seeds of merit which we have sown in previous lives. Whatever form he takes is a physical manifestation of Buddha *(ōjin)*. In conforming to the level of belief and understanding of the devotee, the Buddha simply assumes the form of wood and stone for those who think in terms of wood and stone. Even at the level of wood and stone, he who thinks on the Buddha will be benefited by the Buddha. When reverence and faith are genuinely deep and one feels sincerely close to the Buddha, then he is not at all far from the benefits of his living manifestations. But when one is shallow and behaves impudently, then it is difficult for the operation of grace to become manifest. Worldly behavior is such that although we show respect to men, before the Buddha we have neither fear nor shame. How than can we obtain his grace and receive his benefits? This is the way the shallow are always wont to behave.

2:7 The Blessings of Fudō

After many years of discipline at a mountain temple in Shinano province, an old monk began having hallucinations and was no longer his usual self. So his many disciples recited the Spell of Compassionate Help in order that he might meet death in the proper frame of mind. Among those present was a man from whose head issued black smoke. When the others later questioned him, the man related that he had seen many obstacles on the old monk's path; but, as he persisted in the spell, he was aware of Fudō's sword sweeping them away. The old monk calmly prepared for death, and, in appreciation of the man's help, bequeathed to him, rather than to his close disciples, a relic of the Buddha which was the principal object of worship at the temple. He then passed on peacefully.

The following day a lay priest who had been the monk's benefactor rode up to the temple and related a dream of the previous night. He had seen the hindrances to the holy man's enlightenment swept away by Fudō Myōō, and observed that he came to a happy end.

A sutra says that we should pray to Fudō because of the severity of the Three Hindrances to enlightenment. Jizō is the ultimate of Mahāvairocana's compassion; Fudō, of his wisdom. The help of the Buddhas and Bodhisattvas appears in response to the sincerity of the devotee, just as a bell sounds according to the force with which it is struck.

I-hsing (Ichigyō, 683-727) says that even though one performs religious exercises for the sake of worldly happiness, he will ultimately attain the fruits of Buddhahood. The world's waters all flow into the ocean; so also does all good return to the Buddha-nature. But a person who applies himself will achieve the goal sooner.

2:8 Maitreya's Ascetic

Recently the Shingon monk, Yuishimbō, lived at Iwashimizu in Yawata. He transmitted the Hirosawa school of Shingon, and, as a follower of Maitreya, desired birth in the Inner Court of his Tuṣita Heaven.[208] *He had many followers and encouraged a certain monk to come to him for instruction. "The efficacy of Shingon is not to be despised even in these Latter Days," he said. Yuishimbō had the monk put out his tongue and then performed some mystic gestures, whereupon the monk tasted something sweet as nectar. With another sign he caused the taste to disappear. Then he made a "bell" gesture, which brought forth a wondrous sound. Yuishimbō told the monk that he performed these marvels in order to stimulate his faith in Shingon, and that he was to tell no one about them. This happened toward the end of the Bun'ei era (1264–74). Yuishimbō's disciples had no doubt that he was born into Maitreya's Pure Land.*

Maitreya is the Teacher of the future who will succeed Śākyamuni. The Sutra of the Bodhisattva Maitreya's Birth in the Tuṣita Heaven (Jōshōkyō, T. 452) *describes the ease of birth in that land. Many long for rebirth in India,*[209] *but since this is not a land of reward, ordinary desire is sufficient to accomplish this. Aspiration for Enlightenment*[210] *is not necessary for birth either in the Tuṣita Heaven nor in Amida's Pure Land; but from the latter there is no backsliding (futai) into the world of transmigration. In the Tuṣita Heaven the Inner and Outer Courts differ. In the Outer Court there is regression, but progress is possible. But among the forty-nine palaces of the Inner Court is the Pavilion of Everlasting Life (muryōjuin)*[211] *which is the same as Amida's Pure land of Supreme Bliss (gokuraku). When one has been born in the Pure Land of one Buddha, he is not far from those of the others. If one does have the Aspiration for Enlightenment he is assured of birth in Amida's Pure Land. The* Treatise on the Pure Land[212] *says that the Aspiration for Enlightenment is to be cultivated. And the commentary (Ōjōronchū, T. 1819) on this work by T'an-luan (Donran, 476–542) says the same thing. But the Aspiration for Enlightenment is not absolutely required, only serious intention and a few good deeds. And there is no writing which says that Aspiration for Enlightenment is necessary for birth in Maitreya's Pure Land. The esoteric tradition considers that Amida's Pure Land (an'yō) and the Tuṣita Heaven are overt names for the land of Esoteric Grandeur of the Lotus Womb (mitsugon kezō).*[213] *It is customary to identify Maitreya with Mahāvairocana of the Matrix World and Amida with the Mahāvairocana of the Diamond World Mandala. But the Mahāvairocana of this dual aspect is a single reality, as are Maitreya and Amida.*

The great pagoda and other buildings on Mount Kōya reflect the patterns of the Shingon mandalas. The efficacy of Shingon in these Latter Days is upheld by scripture, verified by current happenings, and is not to be doubted. The Sutra of the Six Virtues (Rokuharamitsukyō, *T. 261) classifies the Buddha's teachings in five groups: sutras, regulations, commentaries* (abhidharma), *wisdom treatises, and mystic symbols. The Hīnayāna had only the first three, the fourth is common to the Mahāyāna, and the fifth to the esoteric traditions. During the Period of the True Law the first three divisions flourished, and many followed the Way. They were like weak medicine for curing a light illness. During the Period of the Imitation Law, a stronger medicine was required, and so the various exoteric Mahāyāna methods were promulgated. But in these Latter Days a high grade of medicine is necessary to cure our grave spiritual illness. And so we have the esoteric teachings.*

It is the custom in Japan that the emperor and his ministers perform the Water-sprinkling (kanjō) *Ceremony and practice Shingon. Although it is believed that the ordinary man should not study these methods, the sutras do not distinguish between nobel and base. Since Shingon is an unusual, secret method, it is only natural that such an attitude should exist. According to* Kūkai's Collected Works of Prose and Poetry (Shōryōshū), *Hui-kuo (Keika, 746-805) said that among the Buddhist teachings the esoteric method is most exalted, as is a king among the people.*

Some Pure Land devotees say that during these Latter Days the methods of the Holy Path are not effective, but this is completely at variance with the scriptures. Even Hōnen, founder of the Pure Land movement in Japan, states in his Collection of Passages (Senjakushū, *1198-1212) that the* nembutsu *will be efficacious during the Latter Days, just as is the Shingon teaching.*

When Jōgambō (1168-1251) of Takedani in Daigo, a noted scholar of the Jōdo sect, was asked by the emperor for the best method to console the spirits of the dead, he recommended the Jewel-box Spell (Hōkyōin darani) *and the* Mantra of Light (Kōmyō shingon). *He defended this view against the criticism of a disciple who said that as a teacher of Pure Land doctrine he should not praise the methods of another sect. The* Full Rope of Salvation Sutra (Fukūkensakukyō, *T. 1092), where the Mantra of Light is revealed, states that if it is chanted while sand is sprinkled on the body of a dead person, the spirit of that person will be born in Amida's Land of Supreme Bliss* (gokuraku). *Such written proof is not available concerning the efficacy of the* nembutsu *in these circumstances; and one should not reply to the emperor without written proof. The* Hanjusan *hymn (T. 1981) of Shan-tao (Zendō, 613-81) states that those who cannot be saved by any other teaching can profit from* dhāraṇī. *The Shingon and* nembutsu *teachings are compatible. It is said that at the present time, members of the Seizan branch of the Jōdo sect study Shingon.*

2:9 The Vicarious Suffering of the Bodhisattva

Although many in misery petition the buddhas and bodhisattvas, they rarely elicit a response. The reason is that although we speak of the vows and activities of the bodhisattvas against the inexorable effects of our own karma, how can they help us? The power of the gods likewise does not obtain against the force of karma. If the bodhisattvas were not constrained by this, no one would ever fall into suffering. The concept of vicarious suffering (daijuku) has seven modes.

During the time of the Buddha there was a woman who faithfully supported the Order. A monk became ill and required meat to be used as medicine, but none was to be found anywhere. So the woman cut flesh from her own thigh and gave it to him. The monk recovered. But the woman's pain was unendurable, and she called on the Buddha with deep faith. Śākyamuni came and gave her medicine to stop the pain. After hearing the Law expounded, the woman came to understand the Way; so she traveled to where the Buddha was staying to speak with him about his visitation.

"I did not come to you nor was there any medicine or indoctrination," said the Buddha. "It was merely that my compassion was moved by your faith and you saw this thing." The Buddha's action was an incidental cause (zō-jōen).

The help of the buddhas and bodhisattvas is only action as incidental cause. Without it and without good roots of merit on the part of sentient beings, it is impossible to rescue them from their suffering. Even if the bodhisattva has deep compassion, there may be nothing to build on. The moon may be bright, but if the water is muddy it will not float there; and the sun may be warm, but if it is cut off by clouds, the frost will not evaporate.

Once Śākyamuni was reborn as a large snake. One noon as he was resting while observing the abstinential rules, a hunter came to flay him for the sake of his gold-colored skin. At first the snake spit forth poison to harm the man; but then he reconsidered that he was observing the abstinential rules and should not harm others. So the hunter removed his skin, and while being devoured by many insects, the Buddha prayed that in the future he might be able to save all those who were eating him. The snake died, and it is related that by his good action he effected the salvation of all those insects. This too is vicarious suffering.

The natural capacity for understanding among sentient beings is like wood; the Bodhisattva's compassion, like fire. The fire brought from without to light the firewood is an example of incidental causation: it has the power to release the fire already in the wood. Given the same cause, the extent to which there is no capacity for burning in various pieces of wood (depending on dryness and greenness) determines their flammability. Similarly the effectiveness of the compassionate help of the buddhas and bodhisattvas depends on the faith of those who petition.

2:10 Karmic Affinities with the Buddha's Law not without Effect

Kakukai[214], steward of Nanshōbō on Mount Kōya, had a

reputation as a prominent contemporary scholar of the Esoteric Sect. Wishing to know about his earlier existence, he prayed to the Great Teacher [Kūkai] and was shown the circumstances of seven of his former lives.

"First of all you were a small clam in the sea west of Tennōji Temple tossed in by the waves. While you were lying on the beach, a small child picked you up and brought you to the front of the Golden Hall where you heard the chanting of the *Hymn in Praise of Relics* (*Sharisanden*). By virtue of this you were reborn as a dog living at Tennōji who constantly heard the sutras and mystic formulas being chanted. Then you were reborn as an ox; and because of having carried paper used for the copying of the *Great Wisdom Sutra*, you were reborn as a horse. The horse carried pilgrims to Kumano and was reborn as a votive-fire attendant, who lit the way for people by always keeping the fires bright. Having gradually become suffused by the karmic activity of wisdom, you were reborn as caretaker of the Inner Chapel (Oku no In), where constantly your ears were moved and your eyes exposed to the practice of the Three Mysteries. And now you are living as the steward Kakukai."

Having heard of this incident, we can clearly see the value of establishing affinities with the Buddha's Law.

In the *Vinaya*[215] *it is recorded that a snake hid in the grass to hear the Buddha's discourse and was accidentally killed by a herdsman's staff. Through the merit of having heard the Law, the snake was reborn into the Tōriten Heaven and there accompanied the gods to visit the Buddha. The snake heard the Law expounded and attained the first fruit of arhatship.*

In India lived a Brahmin who bought skulls. He would place a copper chopstick into the ear sockets and pay most for those in which it penetrated deeply, less for those which it penetrated slightly, and nothing for those in which it would not go in at all. His reasoning was that the ear-holes of those who heard the Law in ancient times were deep, the ear-holes of those who heard little were shallow, and the ear-holes of those who heard nothing were impenetrable. The man bought the skulls of those who heard the Law, erected stupa, and performed services for them. For this he was born into the heavens. How much better it is for a person to hear the Law himself and to cultivate the discipline, as the (Shō)zenjūtenshishomongyō (T. 341) *advises.*

Although there are various schools of Buddhism, they do not go beyond the "Three Baskets" (Tripiṭaka): the sutras *emphasize meditation, the* vinaya *explains the precepts, and the* abhidharma *discusses wisdom. There are strict and modified interpretations of doctrine, and karmic affinities are not without importance. We find these ideas expressed in the* Nirvana Sutra, *the* Sutra of Ten Cakras, *the* Sutra on Viewing the Mind-Ground, *the* Compassion Flower Sutra (Hikekyō, T. 157), *and the* Great Collection of Sutras (Daijikkyō, T. 397).

Although something may be forbidden by the regulations, do not neglect to form a favorable karmic affinity with it if you believe that such an affinity will bear fruit; and even though something may be advocated in the sutras, if you suspect that it may contain an impediment to salvation, eschew it.

3:1 The Epileptic's Clever Remark

In a certain village lived a man who was subject to fits of madness. The peculiarity of his illness is that it causes agitation and discomfort when one is in the presence of fire or water, or in a large crowd of people. The condition is commonly called epilepsy (*kutsu-chi*).

On one occasion the chronic illness flared up when the man was on the bank of a great river. He appeared to have had a seizure and fell into the stream; but because his breathing had stopped, he floated on the water. Carried far out on the current, he washed up on the edge of a river shoal. After a long while the man revived. When he looked around, he found to his surprise that he was in the middle of the river.

"How did I get here?" he wondered, collecting his wits. "I remember being on the river bank . . . and then what happened?" As the man pondered the question, his sickness returned and again he fell into the stream.

"What a precarious life this is!" he thought in amazement. "Having lost my life, I found it. Had I gone on living, I surely would have died. How fortunate it was for me to have lost my life! How unexpected the results!"

Indeed, the current of the great river being swift and the bottom deep, the man had stopped breathing and submerged to die; then, having died (i.e., the vital signs having stopped), he came to float on the water and was carried away. Hence, his speaking in this way—a most clever remark, truly wonderful! These words were limited to a particular event. But in a broad sense, I feel that they penetrate even to the profound meaning of the Holy Law in both sacred and secular affairs.

When I related this incident to a monk at a mountain temple, this is what he said to me. "I had an experience just like that. An old monk who was my teacher had a servant taken from him by the

Land Steward, and he took the matter straight to the authorities. But there was nothing to be done. Though the monk brought his suit to court, he could not get a ruling in his favor. His disciples told him to drop the matter; but the man, who had always been obstinate, was now old and perverse and would not follow their advice. He was angry and upset; so, to appease him, I paid a visit to the Land Steward.

" 'Our teacher, the old monk, told us all about the trouble you have been having over the servant,' I said. 'We urged him to give in since you had every right to take the man into your service. But he is old and perverse and will not listen. Since he is so overwrought, I have come to your place in order to humor him. But the old monk is entirely at fault. You had a perfect right to take the servant, and I have simply come here to tell you so. I think I can pacify the old monk when I give him your reply. And I sincerely apologize for having brought the matter up.' "

Since the disciple deliberately backed down, the Land Steward called to him in reply: "You are a sensible monk and a discriminating individual. I don't have to, but I will give you the servant since I like what you have said." The disciple declined his offer three times but was forced to accept, and he returned with the servant. He remarked that what had happened might be described this way: "Because I lost, I won. Had I won, I would have lost. How fortunate it was for me to have lost! How unexpected the results!" It was a most interesting parallel.

When we observe the condition of the monk who conscientiously follows the rules and regulations of his calling, we see him giving up family and cherished home, leaving behind his manor, his fields, and his domestic animals. The only things he keeps are the three garments and the single bowl[216] of the monk. But, by so doing, he makes the land within the four seas his home; and when he stands to beg at the gates of many households, his provisions are inexhaustible. His house is enormous—the temples and monastic establishments are all his house. And the produce of field and garden are all his food. If one owns one specific house, this is not a house bounded by the four seas. And when one actually owns fields, they are limited to what he gets as his lot from all the land throughout the provinces. So also, concerning this we can say: "Having no home, he has a home. And were he to own a home, then perhaps he would have none."

It is the foolish attitude of the worldly man to be forever entangled with parents, relatives, family, and household, that their happiness might be maximized. But the killer-demon of impermanence is ruthless, and we cannot avoid the pain of separation. Old age and youth are without guarantees, and whether we die early or late is a variable condition of life. To assume the role of the truly-concerned by severing the fetters of affection, leaving home and casting aside social obligation to enter into Non-Action is to leave the village of Transmigration through the Three Worlds. Worldly sentiment has come to hold that to turn our backs on the world and to enter the True Path is mad and nonsensical. This is really foolish!

· During the T'ang the Meditation Master Chih-yen,[217] a prominent general during the Wu-te period (617–626) who frequently distinguished himself in the art of war, was to have been invested with many rewards. But in his fortieth year he took orders and retired into the mountains. Two of his old friends sought him out.

"Your Excellency is mad!" they said to him. "Why in the world do you live in this way?"

"You say that I should awaken from my madness," he replied. "But *your* madness is the greatest. Coveting the sensual, desiring fame, being proud of one's prosperity, and seeking patronage is action which leads to the transmigration of birth and death. How will you extricate yourselves?"

The two men left full of admiration.

Moreover, in India the Philosopher Jayasena was the disciple of Sthiramati and Śīlabhadra, and a teacher of Tripiṭaka Hsüan-tsang.[218] He had mastered Astronomy and Geography, and the scriptures of Buddhists and non-Buddhists alike, including both the Hīnayāna and Mahāyāna teachings. Though a layman, he had abandoned the world and secluded himself at a place called Walking Stick Forest Vihara, not neglecting his progress toward detachment for a single moment. King Śīlāditya[219] summoned him to be State Philosopher, offering him eighty large estates. But Jayasena would not go. Though he was firmly requested, he steadfastly declined. "When one has accepted payment from others," he said, "he worries himself over their affairs. But I am busily concerned with putting away that which binds and envelops me in birth-and-death. What time do I have to serve you?" And he was not forced to go.

Indeed, when we depend on the favors of others, we become as those people and are not ourselves. Taking the grief and troubles of others onto ourselves, even in the present life we bring pain to our bodies and discomfort to our minds. And then, in spite of all our concern, either no favor is bestowed; or, if it is, the favor is good for nothing. The bigger the favor, the bigger the discontent: there are penalties and assessments are heavy. Not only is there no pleasure in this world, but there is also no leisure. And when there is no leisure, we are unable to strive for our future enlightenment nor establish the determination to perform Buddhist practices. Neither aware of the misery in which we live nor comprehending our painful plight, we simply accept these as inevitable. Throwing away the chance of a lifetime, the chance for enlightenment which comes to us from being born as a human being, we return in the end to the Three Evil Paths of rebirth. How utterly foolish. Consider seriously the words of the Philosopher Jayasena. The person of sensibility will learn about the aftereffects of his behavior. The monk at heart, one who has renounced the world though his external appearance be that of a layman, is truly enviable. Lamentable is the moral decline in these Latter Days. There are those who give the physical appearance of leaving hearth and home, take the tonsure, dress in the dyed robes of a monk, and study the pure and unsullied Law; but only as a means to acquire fame and prosperity. Making success the road they would follow, wealth and status as their goal, they proceed to become National Teachers and covet high office. But the sensible man will realize that being born in human form is as rare as the dirt under one's nails when compared with the entire earth, and to meet a Buddha is as rare as the flowering of the udumbara flower.[220] Praying to the gods and buddhas, cultivating good companions in the faith, he will awaken the Aspiration for Enlightenment and pursue the practice of detachment.

Shan-tao's Hanjusan hymn also warns of the dangers of familial and social attachments.

After Śākyamuni had abandoned his kingly status and had gone to Mount Dandaloka, he sent his servant Chandaka back to the palace. Chandaka said: "You grew up in a spacious palace, admired by many. How can you live alone on such a secluded mountain? I will stay and serve you."

"We are born alone and we die alone," replied Śākyamuni. "In the interim what need is there for a companion? When I attain the unexcelled Way, all living beings will accompany me." We repay our family and friends best by encouraging their religious aspirations.

The Hossō sect distinguishes three modes of consciousness: (1) False existence, whereby things exist in imagination but not in reality (henge); (2)

Existence having the character of dependence on others (eta); *and (3) Existence as the ultimate reality of things.* (enjō). *For example, (1) one may imagine a hemp rope to be a snake, or (2) see the "rope" as a temporary aggregate of hemp, or (3) view the hemp as its basic substance. Vasubandhu (Tenjin, ca. 320-400) urges the elimination of discursive thought [in his* Thirty Stanzas on Mere Ideation (Yuishiki sanjūju, *T. 1586)].*

From the Mere Ideation viewpoint we can say: "Because things do not exist, they exist. If they existed, then perhaps they would not exist. How fortunate that they do not exist." (That is, the gross forms of dependent existence, being temporary, "do not exist"—at least in any ultimate sense. But at the same time we take the temporary, provisional existence at face value as "existing.")

According to the Diamond Sutra (Kongōkyō, *T. 235), when Śākyamuni was attending the Buddha Dīpamkara as a bodhisattva, he had not the least attainment of Supreme Enlightenment. If he had, then Dīpamkara would not have told him that in the future he would become a buddha called Śākyamuni. It was when he had no attainment that he received notice. Thus, "because there was no attainment, he attained. Had there been attainment, then perhaps he would not have attained."*

Tendai doctrine shows the paradox: "Because there is no causality (en), *there is causality. . . ." Shingon: "Because there is no enlightenment* (kaku), *there is enlightenment. . . ."*

Likewise the Zen sect speaks of "direct pointing to one's Mind, seeing into one's nature and attaining Buddhahood" (jikishi ninshin kenshō jōbutsu). According to the statement, we see into our own nature to attain Buddhahood. But that nature which is seen is Buddha from the very beginning (so what is to be "attained"?) The Sutra of Heroic Deed (Shuryōgonkyō, *T. 945; Śūrangama) states the paradox that knowing is the root of ignorance. And the Zen patriarch, Bodhidharma (Bodaidaruma, d. 528?) says that not to comprehend a single doctrine is to see the Way of the Buddha, and not to perform a single religious exercise is to practice the Way. So with respect to seeing into one's true nature: "Because we did not see it, therefore we saw it. Had we seen it, then perhaps we would not have seen it." The paradox has many applications.*

3:2 The Man Who Lost a Lawsuit on Purpose

In Shimōsa province a vassal of the shōgun had a dispute with the representative of the manor, and confronted him at court in Kamakura. This was during the administration of Hōjō Yasutoki (regent 1224-42). When a strong argument was advanced by the representative of the manor, the Land Steward (i.e., the vassal) clapped his hands, and, turning to Yasutoki, admitted his defeat. While everyone in the assembly laughed, Yasutoki remarked that in the many years he had been hearing cases, there had never been a person who admitted being in the wrong.

"It is customary that even those who have lost a case will say a word in their own behalf. You are an honest man." Seeing that Yasutoki spoke with tears of admiration in his eyes, those who were laughing put on a pained expression. The representative of the manor stated that the facts in the case had not hitherto been clearly explained, and that the Land Steward had not acted out of bad faith; and he exempted him from three of the six years' allotment from the manor which was overdue. Here again: "Because he lost, he won. . . ."

We should admit our errors. The Sutra on Viewing the Mind-Ground states that if evil is hidden, it proliferates; but if it is disclosed and repented of, it disappears. It is said that hiding one's fault is like burying the root of a tree in the ground, where it flourishes; repentance is like exposing the root so that the tree withers.

The Hundred Parable Sutra (Hyakuyukyō, T. 209) tells of a foolish man long ago who married into a family. Although various entertainments were provided for him, he put on affected airs and took very little to eat, although he was famished. His wife left the room for a moment, and the man took a large mouthful of rice which he was about to eat, when she returned. The man's face turned red with embarrassment. Seeing that his cheeks were swollen, the wife asked what the trouble was. But the man's face only grew redder and redder and he could not reply. The wife then called her parents, the neighbors, and finally a doctor, who lanced the man's cheek with a red-hot needle. Out spilled the rice, and the man's shame knew no bounds.

A Land Steward in Kyūshū fell on hard times and found it necessary to sell his property. His legitimate heir, a man of means, bought the property and returned it to his father. But when the father died, the land was bequeathed not to the legitimate heir, but to the second son. The elder brother took the matter to court at Kamakura, where the authorities reluctantly awarded the decision to the younger brother. Yasutoki, however, felt sympathy for the elder brother and decided to provide for him in his own house.

The elder brother lived with a woman who was cultivated but poor. She did not have a single hair on her head, and when Yasutoki asked the reason for this, he was told that it resulted from her carrying water on her head since she had no servants. After two or three years a fief became vacant in the man's province, even larger than the one held by his father, and Yasutoki gave it to him. When the man was asked why he was taking his woman companion along with him, he replied that for years he had shown her an unhappy time and he wished to make up for this. Yasutoki, impressed by the man's loyalty, made ample provision for his maintenance. Yasutoki was truly a wise and sympathetic man who made the troubles of the people his own troubles.

The History of the Later Han Dynasty (Hou Han Shu) tells us not to forget the friends we knew in poverty nor to cast off the wife married in adversity. The attitude of the elder brother was in conformity with the teaching of the ancients. The Confucian Analects speaks of "the poor man who yet does not flatter, and the rich man who is not proud." The History of the Later Han Dynasty states that if a thousand people point accusing fingers at a man, he will die even if he does not happen to be sick.

Yasutoki always used to say that a poor man might not flatter, but that a prosperous man was sure to be proud. While he was looked up to by many, he respected others and acted prudently, so that for a period of twenty years (1224-42) he kept the nation at peace.[221] *Because he considered the hardship it would cause people, he did not engage in building projects. Once it was rumored that Yasutoki was admonished by the shōgun (Yoritsune, 1218-56) to build a fence around his house. People came and offered to build a wall and a moat, saying that if everyone contributed a little, they could be completed in ten days. Yasutoki thanked them for their good will but replied that even though they thought that the work could be done easily, it would entail bringing laborers from various provinces and the hardships would be incalculable.*

"They are said to be for my protection," he remarked. "But when my fortune is exhausted, even mounds of iron will not avail. And while my fortune holds and I serve my lord, what is there to fear? I shall repair the fence; but I have no intention of constructing a moat or a wall."

Yoritomo (1147-99) planned to go to Kyoto. Although many opposed the move, none dared to voice their objections. Hatta Tomoie was asked his opinion and replied: "In India the lion is king of beasts. Even when he does not intend to harm the other animals, those who hear him roar lose their courage, and some even die of fright. Even though you do not mean to trouble people, how could they not be upset?"

(The Way and its Power, Tao Te Ching 49 says): "The sage has no mind of his own but makes the mind of the people his mind." The sage ruler conforms to men's thinking and will consider their inconvenience.

King Wen of Wei (186-226) considered himself to be a wise king. When he asked his ministers if this were so, Jen Tso replied that it was not: "A wise king is one who receives his position from heaven, but you acquired yours by force. This is not the behavior of a wise king." Jen Tso spoke bearing in mind that King Wen had seized the throne from his uncle and taken the empress as his wife.

The king became angry and sent Jen Tso away. Then he asked Ti Huang if he were a wise king. "A wise king is one who lives among wise ministers," was the reply. "Since you employ such a person as Jen Tso, you are indeed a wise king." Shamed by this remark, King Wen recalled Jen Tso, reformed his government, and acquired the reputation for being a wise king. (Cf., Sasamegoto, NKBT 66, pp. 185, 264).

3:3 The Conversation between Gon'yūbō and his Younger Sister, the Lady-in-Waiting

Some time ago in Kai province lived a scholar called Gon'yūbō who was very irascible. But since he was a good scholar, his disciples put up with him. His younger sister lost her only child whom she loved dearly. Her grief was so excessive that even outsiders came to console her, but not Gon'yūbō. When his disciples criticized him for lack of sympathy, he lost his temper as usual.

"Inconsiderate woman! The sister of a monk is not like an ordinary householder. Does she think that while we live in this world of birth, old age, sickness and death, we will not have grief at the separation from those we love? I will speak to her."

"I hear that you reproach me for not having sympathized with you in your grief," Gon'yūbō said to his sister.

"In my misery I may have said as much," she replied.

"Inconsiderate woman!" scolded the monk. *"What is born must perish; those who meet must part. Are mother and child never separated in this world? This should not surprise and distress you. It is really useless to discuss it."*

The woman apologized for her weakness but was again berated by the monk. *"If you understand the reason for things happening as they do and you still grieve, what is the use of understanding?"*

"Well then," replied his sister, drying her tears. *"Is it wrong for a person to lose his temper, or is it permissible?"*

"It is one of the basic illusions, being one of the Three Poisons of covetousness, anger, and delusion. How can there be any doubt about this? It is a fearful sin."

"If you have such understanding," retorted his sister. *"Then how is it that you have such a bad temper?"* Gon'yūbō was completely bested. *"Well then, wail to your heart's content!"* he growled as he beat his retreat.

To understand the reason of things and then to act as if one did not understand is at variance with the Way. A person may be very learned; but if he does not correct the faults of his body and rectify the biases of his mind, it is as though he vainly counted other people's jewels. Wisdom (chie) and learning (tamon) are to be distinguished. The Classic of Documents (Shu Ching) states that everyone knows that men should be courageous in battle, but few are. Our holy man, not comprehending the reason of things, was completely beaten by a housewife. His sister was a person of inferior learning but superior wisdom and turned the tables on him.

After Śākyamuni's death Aniruddha (Zenshi Bosatsu) saw Ānanda (Anan) grieving in the Jetavana park which the Buddha had often frequented, and he rebuked him for behaving just like an ordinary unenlightened man. Ānanda replied that although he understood the problem, he nevertheless was attached to the Form which he had served faithfully for twenty-five years. Then Aniruddha also wept.

How is the ordinary man then to make his heart act in accordance with the reason of things? Not to be moved by the eight winds that fan the passions is to have the virtue of a sage, but even the virtuous occasionally act in an unenlightened manner. Did not Gon'yūbō understand this?

During the time of the Buddha a similar incident took place. A wise layman called Citta (Shitta Koji) supported the Buddhist community, and a monk known as Kusaladhamma (Zembō Bikku) frequently came to his house to receive alms. Once when Citta was visited by a monk from a distant region, he treated his guest especially well and Kusaladhamma became jealous.

"Today's fare looks delightful," he remarked sarcastically. "You have exhausted the delicacies of mountain and sea. The only thing lacking is oil-cake." By this he let it be known that the householder made a living by selling oil.

"What you have just said reminds me of something," Citta replied. "In a certain country where I travel on business lives a fowl which has the shape of an ordinary chicken and the voice of a crow. When I asked about this, I was told that the fowl took the shape of its father, a chicken, and the voice of its mother, a crow. They call it a 'crow-chicken.' Now when I look at you, the form is that of a monk, but the speech, that of a layman. You remind me of a crow-chicken." Kusaladhamma said nothing but got up in a rage and left without eating. Gon'yūbō's attitude was similar to this—perhaps he was Kusaladhamma's reincarnation.

The Final Admonition Sutra (Yuikyōgyō, *T. 389*) says that without wisdom a monk is not a follower of the Way of the Buddha, nor is he a layman. There is no name for him. He is a hunter wearing a monk's scarf.

3:4 Good and Bad Distinguished in the Dialogues of the Zen Masters

The late Shinkan of Kusakawa spent thirteen years in China studying various doctrines. Among those who visited him on his return to Japan was a certain hermit who remarked that he did not understand the Tendai doctrine of the "grasses and trees attaining Buddhahood" (sōmoku jōbutsu). For some time Shinkan did not reply, and then he said: "Let us put aside for the time being the question of the grasses and trees attaining Buddhahood. What about your attainment of Buddhahood?"

"I have not yet achieved this," replied the hermit.

"Take care of that first," said Shinkan, and retired. The hermit frowned and left without saying a word. The Zen method is to ask directly and to answer directly, keeping in mind the basic purpose of the religious life.

Long ago monk Ta-chu (Daiju, VIII cen.) went to see Ma-tsu (Baso, 707–86), who asked why he had come.

"To seek the Dharma," Ta-chu replied.

"How is it that you cast away your own treasure and look for it elsewhere?"

"What is this treasure of mine?" asked Ta-chu.

"The very thing which you ask of me—that is your treasure," Ma-tsu replied. At these words, Ta-chu understood the Way. And from that time on when students would ask him about the Dharma, he would tell them to open up their own treasure and make use of their own riches.

In Japan learning has been pursued for the sake of prestige, and the practice which leads to an understanding of the True Way has been on the decline for some time. Learning at most of the temples is solely for prestige and not from any desire for liberation.

Still, there are those who awaken to the religious life through the study of doctrine. I have heard that after Eshin (Genshin, 942–1017) aroused the Aspiration for Enlightenment, he venerated the two characters myō-ri ("fame"). He considered that it was from a desire for prestige that he had studied; and it was by virtue of his learning that his Aspiration for Enlightenment arose. Without his desire for fame, there would have been no learning; and without learning, no wisdom. Without wisdom it would have been difficult for the Desire for Enlightenment to have arisen. The Vimalakīrti Sutra (Yuimakitsu-shosetsu-gyō, T. 475) speaks of entering the Way after being caught on the fish-hook of desire. It says that when there is attachment to the sensuous, the bodhisattva becomes a beautiful woman as a device for leading people into the Way of the Buddha.

The Mikawa lay priest (Ōe Sadamoto, 962–1034), Moroie no Ben, and Bridge-of-the-Law Tōbō and others all experienced religious awakening as a result of their distress at separation from women they loved. Their women were no doubt manifestations of bodhisattvas.

3:5 The Discrepancy between Doctrine and Practice among the Vinaya Scholars

Chien Chen (Ganjin, 687–763) came to Japan during the reign of Emperor Shōmu and established three ordination platforms, one at the Tōdaiji in Nara, one at the Kannonji in Kyūshū, and one at the Yakushiji in Shimotsuke. He instituted the orthodox regulations for the priesthood, but in time they fell into disuse. Since the early Heian period people have taken the precepts in name only, and have come up from the provinces and run around the ordination platform without being aware of the major and minor precepts, and without even knowing when they are violating the injunctions.

So the late Gedatsu Shōnin (Jōkei, 1155–1213) selected six men of quality to maintain the fast and study the regulations. Perhaps because the times were not right, none of them followed the strict procedures. However, there was one who studied the precepts and observed the fast during the summer retreat (ango, held from the 15th day of the fourth month to the 15th day of the seventh month). And while he gave up the observances after the retreat was over, recently there have been many among the scholars who have raised the Aspiration for Enlightenment and who observe the precepts.[222]

Among these six men was one who broke the fast and maintained many young temple-pages (chigo) in the monks' quarters. For food he would send them out to the Saogawa River to catch fish. While one was cooking a live fish, it jumped out of the pot. Whereupon the monk's favorite page washed it off and returned it. The monk applauded him, saying that it was well for young boys not to be too fastidious about such small matters. Another monk asked how the monastic rules classified such an act and was told that it was a lesser offense (ha'itsudai) in the Hīnayānist regulations and a major offense (harai) according to the Bodhisattva precepts. The divorce between theory and practice has long been common throughout the country. The decline of

Buddhism will come from within, from those who use it for fame and profit but do not practice it.

3:6 Good Advice from a Child

In Nara a Ritsu monk returned to the life of a layman and had many sons. His favorite, a child of four, climbed up on his father's knee once when two or three acquaintances were visiting.

"Here is a dull fellow," remarked his father. "As big as he is, he sleeps only with his mother, not with his father."

"My father says that I sleep with my mother, but so does he!" answered the child. It was as though he were teaching his father a lesson by shaming him.

In China lived a man named Yüan Ch'i (Genkei). When he was ten his father, at the wife's urging, made preparations to abandon his aged father in the mountains. Yüan Ch'i protested, but to no avail. So the two of them took the old man in a palanquin deep into the mountains and left him there. When Yüan Ch'i suggested that they return with the palanquin, his father asked what he would do with it and suggested that he leave it.

"When you are old," replied Yüan Ch'i, "I will use it again to take you away." The man reconsidered and took his father back home. The incident became known and the boy was called "The Filial Grandson" for having in-structed his father, and for having saved his grandfather. (From the Biographies of Filial Sons.)

Among Confucius' four leading disciples was Min Tsu-ch'ien (Bin Shiken), who was disliked by his stepmother. While she clothed her own two children in the usual cotton cloth, she made Ch'ien wear clothes whose thread was made from the tassels of wild reeds. Ch'ien bore this without bit-terness, but his father eventually found out about it and angrily dismissed his wife. Ch'ien then admonished his father: "With a mother in the house, one child wears simple clothes; without a mother, three children wear them." And if the man remarried, all three would be stepchildren. The father listened to reason and prevented his wife's leaving. Later, the woman had a change of heart and came to favor Ch'ien even more than her own children. Ch'ien acquired the reputation for being a wise man and ultimately became one of Confucius' leading disciples. (From the Historical Records.)

In the state of Lu a woman and her two sons lived together in poverty. During the sons' absence a neighbor subjected the woman to humiliation, and when the sons returned home, they killed the man to vindicate their mother's honor and then reported the matter to the authorities.

"My mother and younger brother have committed no crime," said the eldest. "I am the one to be punished."

"My mother and elder brother are not to blame," said the younger son. "I am the one to be punished.

And when the mother was summoned and questioned she said: "My two sons are not to blame. It is my fault for not having raised them properly. They should both be spared."

The official then announced that although they had all made the same claim to exonerate the others, one of the sons would have to bear the punishment; and the mother was to make the choice. She chose the younger. Since parents usually cherish their youngest, the king asked why she gave up this one.

"The younger brother is my natural son; the elder is my stepson. When his father was dying, he asked me to raise him as my own child. I cannot forget his words, so I hope to save the elder by sacrificing the younger."

The king was impressed: "Within one gate, three sages; within one house, three just men." He took the two sons into his service and the mother likewise prospered.

By setting aside self-interest, we completely attain it. That which harms others, harms us; that which benefits others, benefits us. Those who do not understand this principle are animals in human skin. (From the Biographies of Filial Sons.*)*

3:7 A Story about Confucius

Confucius (551-479 B.C.) was a manifestation during the Chou period of the Bodhisattva Māṇava and taught the Way of the Former Kings as a device (hōben) to accommodate the Dharma to mankind. He taught benevolence and righteousness and rectified their hearts. Duke Ai of Lu once remarked that the most forgetful man he ever heard of was the man who forgot his own wife when he moved. Confucius replied that he knew of two who were even more forgetful—Chieh and Chou forgot their own persons. King Chieh (1818-1766 B.C.) of the Hsia and King Chou (1154-1123) of the Yin were rulers lacking benevolence and wisdom who brought their countries to ruin and oppressed the people. They incurred the punishment of heaven and suddenly were exterminated. These were men who forgot their own persons. A wife, being outside one's own person, might conceivably be mislaid. But it is ridiculous to forget one's own self. Duke Ai felt shame at these words, reformed his government, and became known as a wise king. (From the Sayings of the Confucian School.*)*

Those who do not forget their own persons, that is, their own best interests, are rare. Those who maintain their families or manage the country bringing to perfection the Five Constant Virtues of benevolence, righteousness, propriety of demeanor, wisdom, and good faith, are those who do not forget their own persons. These five Confucian virtues correspond to the Buddhist virtues. The Classic of Filial Piety (Hsiao Ching) *says that when we are in a superior position, we should not be arrogant, and when we are in an inferior position we should not be quarrelsome; but that everywhere we should make way for others. Extravagance is to be avoided.*

The likelihood of having the good fortune to be born in human form may be likened to the amount of dirt on a toe-nail compared to that of the entire world (Nirvana Sutra). *The opportunity to encounter the teaching of the Buddha is rarer than the appearance of the flower of the Udumbara tree which blooms only once in three thousand years* (Lotus Sutra). *He who does not perfect the body given him by his parents is a man who forgets the body of this one life. But a person who neglects the practices of Buddhism forgets the bodies of many lives.*

3:8 The Discourse of the Sage of Toga-no-o

A number of recluses from Mount Kōya made a pilgrimage to Toga-no-o[223] to establish karmic affinities with the venerable Myōe [Kōben, 1173–1232], sending in word of their arrival. At first they were told that he had a cold and would not hold an audience. But presently Myōe appeared on the heels of his messenger. The group was hustled in and the sage addressed them.

"The way this monk Myōe pampers himself is so gross that he goes about with an attendant. All of you have come a long distance from Kōya to visit this old priest. When you wanted to come in to see me, I acted like an ordinary layman by saying that I had a cold. Even if I had been laid up with a grave illness, I should have agreed to meet with you to discuss the Law of the Buddha. If my condition were any less serious, there could be no conceivable justification for my behavior. I have simply lost sight of *that which is appropriate*[224] for a person in my circumstances.

"If I were to write in simple characters what to teach people, after having examined the sacred writings over the many years of my life, it would be the six syllables, "Do what is suitable." I teach that which is appropriate according to the ways and methods of what is suitable for the layman, or for the priest, or for the recluse. But in these Latter Days people are confused about what is appropriate. The king and ministers, those acquainted with the uses of external support, should protect the Law and respect it, not losing sight of the fact that Lord Śākyamuni has entrusted it to their care. That is what is appropriate for the emperor. And other laymen should not act contrary to his purposes.

"The sects and the teachings of monks who have left their homes for various temples on many mountains may differ, but they are all children of Śākyamuni. So once they take their vows, shave their heads and dye their garments, they should abandon desire and cut off attachment, being mindful of the Five Aggregates of the elements of which we are constituted and pursuing the practice of the Three Teachings [morality, wisdom, meditation]. But although they shave their heads, they do not shave their desires; and they dye their clothes but not their hearts. Some assume the responsibilities for wife and child, while others buckle on armor. The country is gradually being overrun with monks who act just as the Three Poisons [of covetousness, anger, and delusion] and the Five Desires [for property, sex, food, fame, and sleep] lead them; so that in the end they do not maintain the Five Commandments nor engage in the Ten Good Deeds. They are not mindful of what is appropriate to those who have abandoned the life of the householder (*shukke*).

"The recluse in particular should cast away pride and attachment and obliterate worldly thoughts, training mind and body according to what is appropriate to the teaching of the Law instead of acting like men of the world. To behave as everyone else does truly violates the teaching of the Buddha."

Thus Myōe spoke tearfully on the profound meaning of the Law as what was appropriate for those who had entered upon the Way of release and liberation, and on what was essential in the teaching for this generation, so that the venerable recluses wrung out their black, tear-drenched sleeves. Myōe spoke from the evening of that day throughout the night until morning, then during the following day until they heard the sound of a bell. On inquiring which it was, he was told that it was the vesper bell. "What a long time I've been talking," he remarked, and then retired.

It had seemed that the discourse had lasted only a moment. The monks recalled that the Buddha's sermon of sixty short kalpas[225] had seemed to his audience as only half a day long; and they all felt that had they lived at that time and heard him preach, it would have been just like this. Deeply impressed, they returned to Mount Kōya.

A venerable recluse who was observing the post-noon fast was invited to perform a religious service in Kawachi province. It was a wintry day over a seven-league stretch of road, and he was asked to come before noon. The recluse was mounted on a horse which could not move very fast; and, although the day was cloudy and he could not see the sun, it seemed to have been high in the sky for a considerable time.

The monk remarked that the sun seemed to have passed the meridian; but his host replied that it was still before noon, and, with various delicacies, encouraged him to eat. By nature a gourmand, he ate with gusto until he was sated, finishing up with dessert. As he was picking his teeth, he heard the sound of a bell; and when he made inquiry was informed that it was the vesper bell. This can be compared to Myōe's being startled by the vesper bell, but the recluse's diversion by food was downright reprehensible compared with Myōe's forgetting the time while discussing the Law.

When we view the present world using the past as our mirror, we find genuine differences among what prospers and what is rejected. The recluse of old imbued his heart with the Buddha's Law and set aside the myriad matters of the world, while in the present age men abandon the Buddha's Law but do not neglect worldly fame and profit. Under such circumstances they only bear the name of "recluse" (*tonsei*), but do not know its reality. Year after year we can see an increasing number of people who "escape the world" (*tonsei*) simply to get ahead in life and in spite of the fact that they have no religious aspiration at all. While in the world they are nobodies without either fame or profit, but on entering the gate of the recluse they now have both! So nowadays perhaps we ought to change the character *ton* in *tonsei* ("to escape the world") and write it with a homonym so as to read *tonsei* ("to covet the world").

Tonsei no	Let us change
Ton wa tokiyo ni	The character *ton* in *tonsei*
Kakikaen	To accord with the times:
Mukashi wa nogare	Of old it meant "to escape,"
Ima wa musaboru	And now it means "to covet."

Forgetting one's Buddha-nature is the ordinary way of birth-and-death; not to forget the Great Self of the Law Body of the Buddha is what is appropriate to the true follower of the Way. The Zen master Kuei-feng Tsung-mi (Keihō Shūmitsu, 780-841) said that the discriminations of the deluded intellect are mad ramblings by which we forget our True Mind; when a single thought does not arise, this is understanding which manifests our Original Mind. Te-shan Hsüan-chien (Tokusan Senkan, 772-865) said that only when you have nothing in your mind, and no mind in things, are you vacant and spiritual, empty and marvelous. The sayings of Confucius are a means to lead people to Buddhism. Once a person distinguishes what is appropriate to one who follows the Way, then he will appreciate what it means to be born in human form.

I was indeed fortunate to have heard the essentials of the various doctrines from the late founder of the Tōfukuji, the priest Shōichi (Enni Ben'en, 1202-80). I only regret having met him in his late years and that I could not

*sit at his feet for long. Once when he was going down to the Kantō (in 1264?)
I prepared a meal which an ordinary person would have said was excellent.
But Ben'en only remarked: "Why did you do such a thing? This is not* what is
appropriate *for me. It is said that when the incipent Bodhisattva is diverted
by mundane matters, he destroys the bud of the Way." I was deeply impressed by his words.* He was alluding to the Profound Meaning of the Lotus
Sutra (Hokke gengi, *T. 1716) which says that we should concentrate on inner
reflection to the exclusion of all else, even the practice of the Buddhist virtues; otherwise the bud of Mind Concentration (kanjin) is destroyed. Those
who are suddenly enlightened and immediately manifest this in practice are
rare, like the Dragon Girl who aspired for enlightenment and presently attained Buddhahood.*[226] *But those of sudden awakening and gradual realization are many, as we can also see from a statement in the* Sutra of Heroic
Deed. *Although we speak of being enlightened suddenly, one's natural
disposition toward illusion is difficult to exhaust. Although the wind ceases,
the waves still rise; and although the sun comes out, the frost only gradually
disappears.*

4:1 The Silent Clerics

At a mountain temple were four monks who wished to experience the Reality which is beyond words and practice the silence
of Vimalakīrti.[227] Vowing their intention, the four adorned the
practice hall, and, cutting off the myriad worldly attachments and
quieting the activities of body, word, and thought, they entered the
hall to begin seven days of silence. A single attendant had access to
the room.

It had grown late and the night was dark. Seeing that the lamp
was about to go out, the monk in the lowest seat called out: "Attendant. Raise the taper!"

"In the hall of silence there is to be no talking," said the monk
seated next to him.

The monk in the third seat was extremely annoyed at hearing
the two speaking. "You have lost your senses!" he cried.

The old monk in the senior seat thought it shameful and ir-
ritating that the others had spoken out, though each had done so for
different reasons.

"I alone have said nothing!" he remarked, nodding his head.
With his superior air he looked especially foolish.

When we consider this incident, we are reminded that for
everyone it is difficult to avoid such attitudes. When we hear people
talking about the affairs of others, we find that a person will criticize

another mercilessly for something which he himself enjoys doing. Lenient toward his own failings, he excuses himself by saying: "How self-indulgent of me!"—or some such remark, unaware of the fact that he is criticizing others while overlooking his own cherished flaws. Thus it is written: "Censure others bearing in mind your own faults; endanger others considering your own downfall. . . ."

Rakuten (Po Chü-i, 772-846) said: "Everyone has one bad habit; my bad habit is literature." Good habits are important.

We all cherish and overlook the shortcomings of that to which we are partial while searching out and condemning the defects of that of which we disapprove. But there are defects in that which pleases me, and I should not become strongly attached to it, taking heed of the fact that others may criticize its shortcomings. Neither should I violently condemn that with which I have no rapport, but recognize that it has its virtues. This will be the attitude of the superior man. Although there are differences in degree, in all things nothing is without its merits and its shortcomings. At no time are the Goddess of Virtue and the Goddess of Darkness apart. This is the heavenly order of things. And so it is said that it is water which bears the boat up, and water which capsizes it; the ruler it is who benefits the people, but he also causes them distress;[228] water, fire, and the like benefit man, but they also harm him—these all illustrate the same point and should be borne in mind. The power of the Buddha's Law is such, that when it is embraced, the benefit is great; when it is rejected, the punishment is likewise great. Compared to this, the profit and loss of things of the world are as nothing; the loss, moreover, is relatively greater than the profit. With Buddhism, on the other hand, the loss is small and the profit great. We ought to abandon our worldly condition of great loss—also inasmuch as it becomes the occasion of our disparaging the Buddha's Law—and enter upon that Path of great profit. But there are many who are attached to the things of the world, having become habituated to them from beginningless time. Those people are rare, who, meeting the Law of the Buddha for the first time, are attracted to it and practice it. What a pity!

A certain lay priest was fond of playing *go*, and would play on to the end of a winter's night. Because his hands were cold, on top of a rheumatic condition, he played the "stones" (*ishi*) after heating them first in an earthenware cup. When the oil from the lamp was consumed, he burned reeds and continued to play. When the ashes blew over him, he donned a bamboo hat and kept on going. I heard that this occurred only recently. A man who applied himself to meditation and other religious practices with such zeal would not find the path to enlightenment difficult.

There was a lowly monk who, having a taste for *sake* but not the price of it, tore off one of his sleeves for its purchase. Were he as ungrudging in his support of the Three Treasures, in filial behavior toward his parents, and in almsgiving to the unfortunate, there would be no lack of divine response. If one neglects to perform a good deed with the excuse that there is nothing to be done, it is not that there is really nothing to be done, but only that he lacks the will to do it.

A lay priest, who was also a doctor, loved rice-cakes (*mochi*). Called for his services to a man's home where it happened that they were being prepared, the lay priest, at the sound of the pounding, began moaning in a low voice and ended up gripping the edge of a straw mat.

"You ought to make the rice-cakes somewhere where I can't hear the noise," he remarked. "The sound of the pounding drives me wild with anticipation."

I heard about this incident from the man who owned the house. There can be no doubt that one who would so love the Law and utterly delight in the words of the Buddha would attain the goal of his religious endeavors. Although such cases as this are rare, everyone has that of which he is enamored. Those relatively free of attachments may like to sleep in late, or may be given to fooling around.

There was a monk at a temple in Nara, who, instead of eating his morning gruel, was accustomed to sleep until the sun was high in the sky. When someone asked why he did not eat the gruel, he replied that sleep was far tastier. Had one such a taste for the delights of the Law and of meditation, the path of the Buddha would not be distant.

Similarly, there are those who like poetry and music, those who enjoy gambling and hunting, those given to sensual pleasures, or to food and drink, who are unmindful of the fact that by these things their wealth will be exhausted, their health ruined, and that sickness will arise and misfortune follow. Just as there are differences in the things of the world which men value, so also it is with respect to that which will bring them to the path of the Buddha: the various gates of the Law differ according to people's tastes and the level of their faith and interpretation of the doctrines. For this reason the Buddha, without exhausting the myriad expedients (*ki*), bestows the Accommodated Truths (*hōben*) and sets up the unnumerable (literally, 84,000) gates of the Law. If people would delight in and practice the Buddha's Teaching just as they enjoy *sake* and *go*, they would easily come to an understanding of the Way.

> *The Buddha has provided many methods to accommodate the doctrine to many tastes, so it is foolish to be exclusively attached to one's own method while despising others.*

Recently a monk with a reputation as a scholar of the Three-Treatise (Sanron) doctrines remarked to a colleague: "While each of the other sects holds to the one-sided view that its teacher is superior, only my Three-Treatise position does not have this bias."

The statement itself is biased! He is saying in effect that the other sects, because each maintains a particular viewpoint, are inferior. *His* sect does not support any particular philosophical position and is therefore superior. This is bias indeed! It is like saying in the Hall of Silence: "There is to be no talking." For the most part, each sect says the same about its own position. Here is a rough example. The Three-Treatise scholar says: "The Hossō sect holds to Three Vehicles and the Tendai to One; for my sect there is neither three nor one." This has all the look of one-sidedness. Even the wise are not aware that they adopt this attitude, nor do they escape the fault of holding various views concerning "right" and "wrong". All the more so do those who have learned a little of the methods of one particular sect criticize and slander the deliberations of other sects which they do not understand. The crime of slandering the Law is thus difficult to avoid.

> *It is difficult for the wise to avoid prejudice; how much more so the uninformed. If one practices the Tendai method of Mind Concentration (kanjin), it is essential that he put aside doctrinal distinctions and conform to the level impartiality of Pure Consciousness. But like the four "silent" monks who had discourse by the very act of saying there should be none, so also, if one arouses the mind to the notion of non-arising, then by that very act thought arises. The statement in the* Sutra on Perfect Enlightenment *(Engakukyō, T. 842) that we should never permit distracting thoughts to arise is like saying in the Hall of Silence: "There is to be no talking." And if one becomes attached to the notion of nondiscrimination, this person too has delusive attachment. He is like the monk in the senior seat who said: "I alone have said nothing."*
>
> *The Tendai patriarch (Chih-i, 538-97) comments on the essential unity*

of the earlier Indian schools of Buddhism. The commentaries of the various sects each see something of the other's weakness and censure it in the light of what they take to be their own superior principles. It is like a wrestler who takes his own strong points and compares them with his opponent's weaknesses. According to the Great Cessation and Insight, *Gunavarman (Gunabatsuma Sanzō, 367-431) said that although the various Buddhas differ, the object of their practice is identical; and that while the biased man distinguishes between this and that doctrine, the adept is not contentious.* The Garland Sutra *illustrates the position of the Hossō and Sanron schools on the nature of Mere Ideation.*

Two nuns passing by Ōtsu saw a vehicle on the side of the road with only one wheel. "This carriage slanders the Great Vehicle of the Mahāyāna, for (it proclaims that with one wheel) it is defective," said one. "Perhaps not so," responded the other." For (it says that with only one wheel) there is nothing wanting."[229]

In Kyoto lived a physiognomist called Ben'a, one of whose legs was shorter than the other so that he limped. "Is it true that people laugh at me because my one leg is too short?" he asked his apprentice. "I can't imagine why they do this," was the reply. "But they say that one of your legs is longer than the other.

Although the words may differ in worldly reasoning, the reality does not. A carriage with one wheel does not move whether we say that it has one wheel or that it lacks one wheel. Whether he is criticized for having a short leg or a long leg, Ben'a's body was as it was. And whatever the sectarian differences, the substance of the Dharma is the same. Bhāvaviveka (Shōben, ca. 490-570) said: "As opposed to your speaking of consciousness only (yuishiki), I contend that only the objective world (yuikyō) exists. In fact, there is neither consciousness-only nor objective-world only. When Maitreya becomes the Buddha of our world, I will prove it to you. Since we shall be Bodhisattvas at that time, we will not employ these distinctions." It is said that he then entered a rock cave, sealed the entrance, and expired.

The Zen master Wei K'uan (Ikan, 755-817?), a disciple of Ma-tsu (Baso), was questioned by Po Chü-i (Haku Kyoi): "As Zen master, how do you explain the doctrine of the Buddha?" The point of the question was that Zen is a sect which does not rely on words. But the Doctrine is thought of as something discussed by a teacher.

The Zen master replied: "When enlightenment is realized through the body, this is morality (kai); when it is realized through words, this is doctrine (hō); and when it is realized through mind, this is meditation (zen). although enlightenment has three applications, its substance is not divisible. Although the Yangtze, Yellow, Huai, and Han Rivers have different names, the substance of their water is the same. Morality, doctrine, and meditation are inseparable. How could they exist as separate entities?"

Kuei-feng Tsung-mi said that meditation (zen) was the Buddha's thought, and doctrine (kyō) the Buddha's words; and that among the various

*buddhas, heart and mind were compatible. This statement appears both in
the* Mirror of Sectarian Differences (Sugyōroku, *T. 2016) and in the* Collected Sayings on Zen Principles (Zengenshosenshū, *T. 2015). The three
kinds of learning—morality* (kai), *meditation* (jō) *and wisdom* (e)—*are essentially one, although methods may vary. Their interdependence can be seen
from the words of Kuei-feng, Nanzan Risshi (Tao hsüan, 596–667), the*
Dharmapada, *the* Perfection of Wisdom in 25,000 Lines (Daibongyō, *T.
223), the* Net of Brahma Sutra, Chih-i, *the* Lotus Meditation Sutra (Hokke
sammaikyō, *T. 269), the* Sutra to Resolve Doubts about the Imitative Law
(Zōbōketsugikyō, *T. 2870), and the* Hundred Parable Sutra.

*The Buddhist regulations are the rules of deportment for the sons of the
Buddha; the* vinaya *is the life of the Dharma. Ching-ch'i Chan-jan (Keikei
Tannen, 711–82) said that there was no difference between the regulations of
the Hīnayāna and those of the Mahāyāna, but that their benefit depended
on the recipient's state of mind.*

*When Kāśyapa smiled faintly in response to the Buddha's holding out
the flower* (nenge mishō) *on Eagle Peak, the Buddha transmitted to him the
Eye of the True Law* (shōbō genzō). *If the discourses and the regulations were
of no value, they would not have been assembled. The compilation of the
Three Baskets (Tripiṭaka, Sanzō) was the work of the first patriarch (of the
Zen sect) Kāśyapa. The regulations* (ritsu) *were recited by Upāli (Ubari), the
discourses* (kyō) *by Ānanda (Anan). And these were then collected by
Kāśyapa. This is recorded in the first book of the* Commentary on the Great
Wisdom Sutra (Daichidoron, *T. 1509).*

*Among those who follow the Zen methods nowadays are some who
disparage the doctrinal approach. This is at variance with the intentions of
the patriarchs. Zen scholars, denigrating the precepts as proper to the
Hīnayāna, liken Ritsu scholars to beasts. Then the Ritsu scholars say that
Mahāyānists do not understand the operation of moral causation and violate
the regulations, so that they are like non-Buddhists. Thus, by mutual vilification both bring about the extinction of the Dharma.*

*Some perform Buddhist services for profit, saying: "I am a disciple of
the Buddha. This is what must be done." But when it comes to observing the
precepts and correcting their faults, then they say: "I follow the Mahāyāna,
not the Hīnayāna." The* Buddha Treasury Sutra (Butsuzōkyō, *T. 653) calls
such people "bat-monks"* (chōso biku). *If one says that they are to be
numbered among the birds, they reply that they live in the ground, and go
into their holes. But to escape the duties of living on the ground, they say
they live in the sky. Indeed, they are neither bird nor beast. So also the Law-
breaking monk says that he is a follower of the Buddha in order to escape his
secular duties. But then he does not observe the precepts, claiming to be an
adherent of the Mahāyāna.*

The followers of the various sects should not criticize one another. The
Commentary on the Great Wisdom Sutra *says that even if a man observes the
regulations in their purity, if he delights in his own methods and vilifies those*

of others, he cannot avoid falling into the Three Evil Destinies.
The general principle of the Law of the Buddha is this:

Shoaku makusa	Avoid all evil,
Shuzen bugyō	Cultivate every good,
Jijō koi	And purify your thoughts—
Ze shobutsu kyō	This all Buddhas teach.[230]

Mahāyāna scholars should not disparage this statement, which has been handed down by the seven Buddhas. "Avoid all evil" may be translated as kai (morality); "cultivate every good," as jō (meditation); and "purify the mind", as e (wisdom). Kai is like apprehending a thief, jō is like binding him, and e is like executing him.

Criticism abounds both among the followers of the Pure Land and those of the Holy Path (shōdō, that is, the non-nembutsu sects which emphasize "self-power," jiriki). Those who practice the nembutsu despise the Shingon and Tendai methods as trivialities; and those who follow the Shingon and Tendai despise the nembutsu. But this ignores the "skillful means" (hōben) of the Buddha and violates the injunctions of the patriarchs. Pure Land devotees are told in various writings not to disparage other practices. Shan-tao says in his Hanjusan hymn: "Śākyamuni is our father and mother. For our sake he has explained the Law with skillful means. If a person acts according to the Teaching, he will see Buddha in all sects, and will be born into Amida's Pure Land."

It is indeed difficult to understand those who disparage other practices and other sects in spite of the admonitions of the founders of their own sects. Among the followers of the Lotus are also those who vilify the nembutsu. This is contrary to the views of the Tendai patriarch (Chih-i). In the Perpetually-moving samādhi (jōgyō sammai) of the Tendai practice, for ninety days one intones the name of Amida with the mouth and sees the form of Amida in the mind. Some chant first and then meditate; others meditate first and then chant; and still others do both simultaneously. But whether walking, chanting, or meditating, they abide in Amida. Ching-ch'i Chan-jan says that praise of Amida is frequently to be found among the various teachings of Buddhism.

This practice is exemplified in the Tendai doctrine of the Three Truths. Because Amida is enlightened as to the Three Truths and manifests the three corresponding virtues, he is called Amida in the language of India, and Muryōju in Chinese. A is equivalent to Mu and signifies Emptiness (kū); its related virtue is wisdom (hannya). Mi is equivalent to ryō and signifies the Conditioned (ke); its related virtue is liberation from the bonds of Illusion and suffering (gedatsu). Da is equivalent to ju and signifies the Middle Way (chūdō); its virtue is the eternal life of the Law Body.

The T'ien T'ai monk Yang Chieh (Yōketsu, 11th cen.) believed in Amida's Pure Land, as we see in his death-verse. Chih-i likewise had Pure

Land texts recited at his deathbed, and in dying declared that Kannon had arrived to escort him to the Pure Land.

Recently Kenshin (1132–92) of Ōhara would sometimes say that he was going to recite the nembutsu *in assembly, and then would go into the hall and read the* Lotus Sutra. *Or he would say that he was going to recite the* Lotus Sutra *and then do the* nembutsu. *Earlier scholars did not make sharp distinctions among the various practices, Amida being identified with certain aspects of Shingon and Tendai doctrine. Among Zen Masters, Chikuku Zenji (Yung-ming Yen-shou, 904–975) practiced the* nembutsu *and encouraged others to.*

A statement in the Oral Instructions of the Ancient Sages (Kotoku no kuden; *not identified) speaking of Kannon as a manifestation of Amida corresponds to Kōya Daishi's (Kūkai's) remark in his* Explanatory Notes to the Lotus Sutra (Hokke no gokaidai). *Citing the* Diamond Head Sutra (Kongōchōgyō, T. *865) he states that the* Lotus Sutra *has the esoteric name, Kanjizai-ō ("The All-seeing Lord"), and that this Buddha is known as Muryōju, that is, Amida. The identity of the* Lotus Sutra, *Amida and Kannon is argued in this work.*

Jizō is also identical to Amida and Kannon. Keiso (955–1019) of the Miidera wrote on a pillar of the Jizō Hall: "The appearance of priest Hōzō (i.e., Amida) long ago is just like that of Jizō today, who is represented as a monk. And consider the character 'zō' in both of their names." Kan'in Kubu of the Enryakuji saw the writing and ordered it removed. He should have been acquainted with the identity of Amida and Jizō.

Among those who study the doctrines broadly there is no prejudice. We ought to put a stop to such biased thoughts as "right" and "wrong," and instead be diligent in practice. In writing of these matters, my criticism of others may also appear as a bias. On the other hand, perhaps the person who thinks that he alone is without prejudice is like the priest who declared that he was the only one who had not broken the rule of silence.

4:2 The Monk Who Had Children

A monk of Shinano province had three children, each by a different woman. When the mother of the first child brought it to him, the monk had doubts since he had been very circumspect in his affair with her. So he named the child "Unexpected" (Omoiyorazu). Since the mother of the second child used to visit him secretly from time to time in his quarters, there was little doubt that the child was his. So he called it "Probably" (Samoaruran). He had maintained the third woman in a house, so there was no doubt that he had fathered her child. He called it "Unquestionably" (Shisainashi). This happened only recently.

A monk's having children is not without precedent. The monk Kumārāyana (Kumaraen) of India was transporting to China the sandalwood image of the Buddha made by King Udyāna (Uden-ō), the original of the

Śākyamuni at the Seiryōji in Saga. Then the King of Kucha joined Kumārāyana to his daughter in marriage, and from that union Kumārājīva (344-413) was born. Kumārājīva went to China and had four children: Shō, Chō, Yū and Ei [that is, Chu Tao-sheng (ca. 360-434), Seng-chao (374-414), Tao-jung (IV-V cen.) and Seng-jui (378-444?)]. They collaborated with him in translating the Lotus Sutra. *Although there are instances of such behavior among the sages in antiquity, they were men of such parts that their children were also wise and distinguished. But today, when the father is foolish, how can a son amount to anything?*

The times decline and men degenerate. As the years go by, men of wisdom and virtuous practice become rare. In antiquity there were many distinguished monks and sages. And although the ways of monk and layman differ, warriors of an earlier age acted with such high-handed pride as even to try to usurp the position of emperor. Masakado (d. 940) was styled "Prince of the Tairas." And it is related that such was the self-discipline of Hatakeyama Shigetada (1164-1205) that he did not permit smoke to rise in his mansion because he aspired to become governor of the northern military prefecture. His son (Shigeyoshi?), who became a monk, was also a man of parts.

Nowadays people are an inferior breed. In the (Nirvana) Sutra *the Buddha says: "After my extinction many will become monks merely to relieve their hunger. I call these 'those who harm the joy of the mind' (igyō songai)." Worthless monks are also called "bald householders" (kafuro koji), and "thieves wearing surplices" (kesa wo kitaru zoku).*

4:3 The Monk Who was Nursed by His Daughter

The abbot of a mountain temple in the Eastern Provinces was distinguished as a scholar and had many disciples and followers. But in his old age he became paralyzed and lay on his bed passing the years and months barely alive while his body no longer responded to his wishes. His disciples grew tired of nursing, and finally abandoned him. Then from nowhere appeared a woman who asked if she could take care of the old monk. "As you wish," replied the disciples, and gave their permission. The old monk was unable to speak, but the woman nursed him with a great deal of loving care.

When asked her identity, the woman vaguely replied that she was just a shiftless person not worth knowing about. But as she continued to nurse him with rare solicitude over the days and months, the invalid had to speak to her.

"When I have been abandoned even by my disciples of many years who have both religious and worldly obligations to me, I am extremely grateful for the tender care you have given me. I believe that we surely must have bonds from some previous life to have brought this to pass, and it troubles me that you are so secretive. Who are you, anyhow?"

"Now I will tell you frankly," the woman replied in tears. "I have an unsuspected relationship with you, since I am the daughter of Such-and-such, a person with whom you had a chance affair. Although she said nothing to you, my mother informed me that I was the child of this union. Considering that I am your daughter in body and soul, I have thought over the years that I would like to see you and be recognized by others as your daughter. I considered this for many years, but inasmuch as I was illegitimate, I was hesitant. When I heard that those who nursed you in your illness had tired of it and that you were destitute, I made up my mind that out of filial obligation I would tenderly care for you until your death."

The invalid, impressed by such devotion, was unable to wipe away his tears. "How wondrous are the bonds between parent and child to have brought this to pass."

They were very close to each other. The monk was nursed until the end of his life and died in the woman's tender care. Her extreme sense of filial piety is to be highly esteemed. The saying is indeed true that daughters have a greater sense of filial piety than sons and are more obliging in providing support.

4:4 The Monk Who Encouraged Marriage

At a mountain temple called Matsu-no-o in Yamato province lived the monk Chūrembō, who after having become paralyzed, put up a small hut near the highway in Takita. Whenever monks from the mountain temple passed along the road, he would inquire if they were single; and if they replied that they were, this is how he would encourage them.

"Get yourself a wife right away! It was my lot to be a scholar, and I have been single since my youth. I had a great many disciples and followers, but after I became paralyzed and crippled, these people no longer care about me. I have ended up as a destitute old beggar who has a hard time making ends meet, carrying on barely alive by the side of the road. I feel that if I had a wife and children I might not have come to such a bitter pass. Now, when you are just the right youthful age, get together with someone. As the years go by, the affection between husband and wife deepens. Don't think that such illness as mine just happens to other people."

An unexpected piece of advice to be sure; but since the monk spoke from personal experience, perhaps there was some truth to it.

4:5 The Wife Who was an Impediment in the Final Hour

A priest at a mountain temple fell into the ways of the world and exchanged vows with a certain woman. While they were living together with deep mutual affection, the priest fell gravely ill and was sick for many days. Because his wife had nursed him ever so tenderly, he was very close to her and had few contacts with his disciples or any others. He felt that he had been most wise to have established this mutual relationship and looked forward to a peaceful demise. Finally, in the fullness of time, his original desire to follow the Way returned and he continually repeated the name of the Buddha. Thinking that his end was at hand, he sat up in the posture of meditation and joined his hands. Facing the west, he recited the *nembutsu.*

"Oh no! You are leaving me. Where are you going?" cried his wife, throwing her arms around the monk's neck and pulling him down.

"For heaven's sake, let me die in peace!" pleaded the monk, lifting himself up to recite the *nembutsu.* But again she toppled him over. Although the monk lifted his voice to recite the name of the Buddha, he died on his back, wrestling with his wife. The manner of his passing was most unbecoming. I wonder if it was an obstacle to his obtaining salvation?

Such incidents are rare. But when wife and child are lined up before us and we see their grief and yearning, how could they not be an impediment for those of inferior capacities? Those who truly wish to be freed from illusion should cast off the impediments to the Way which leads to the mountain of Enlightenment, and loosen the mooring lines of the boat which crosses the sea of the passions [to the Other Shore].

4:6 The Monk Whose Wife Tried To Kill Him

At a mountain village in the Eastern Provinces was a monk who lived the life of a recluse. Originally he had been a priest of the Kōfukuji in Nara and used to tell how in his youth he had witnessed

Shunjōbō's reconstruction of the Great Buddha Hall at the Tōdaiji. He remained single until late in life, but when he reached seventy he exchanged vows with a young nun and put her up in his quarters, probably with the thought that she would take care of him.

This nun was about thirty years of age; and, being from the capital, had a witty comment about everything. She held nothing back and discussed the old monk's behavior with others.

"The Lord Abbot of the house calls out to me, 'Well, the passion's up. Heat the water and prepare a bath.' So I hurry and tell him the bath is ready and he says to me: 'All of a sudden my passion has cooled.' It's always the same; and then he gets mad, loses interest, and is in a bad mood." It is amusing that while his temper rises with the temperature of the water, his sexual interest cools along with his passion.

Instead of the nun taking care of the old monk, she secretly carried on an affair with a young ascetic. The old monk's quarters were pleasantly appointed and there were also money and provisions for the needs of every season. So the nun decided to get rid of the old monk and live in his quarters after exchanging vows with the young ascetic. At an opportune moment she brought the old monk to the ground; then with all the strength of her vigorous young body in its prime, she twisted the old monk's genitals until he thought he was dead for sure.

"Have pity! Help!" he cried at the top of his voice. "She's killing me!"

The sound of his screaming was heard faintly at a hermitage on the other side of the ridge. The recluse who lived there was startled and ran to the old monk's place to find him already changing color and apparently not breathing. The recluse gave the nun a powerful kick and pulled her away.

The old monk recovered. Since the scandal could not be hushed up, he appealed to the local Land Steward who held a trial by confrontation (monchū). The nun was clearly in the wrong and had nothing to say. Her crime was serious and the court could have exacted whatever penalty it wished — the severing of a hand, a foot, or even her neck. But since the monk was already a recluse [and thus somewhat outside the pale of the law] and the Land Steward was a man of compassion, he merely banished her from his territory.

I often saw both the old monk and the nun. I wasn't there when this incident took place, but I heard about it in detail. When we consider such an incident as this, it is hard to follow the advice of the monk with paralysis.[231] We should weigh the options carefully.

4:7 One Should Be Wary of Attachment at the Time of Death

In Ōhara lived a monk who had religious aspirations, but who was without understanding. Deciding that there was no point in continuing to live in this miserable, floating world, he prepared himself to observe thirty-seven days of silence, and then, on the final day of services, to meet his end by hanging. He discussed his plan with two or three fellow-monks and retired into the practice hall.

News of the affair having spread abroad, the Ōhara Superintendant of Priests,[232] moved by admiration and respect, conducted an Expounding-on-Birth-in-the-Pure-Land (ōjōkō) and other services in order to establish karmic affinities with the holy man. As the event was newsworthy, Kenshin wrote to high-ranking prelates in the capital, inviting them to attend, in the hope that the holy man might hear their recitation of Amida's name and his desire for birth in the Pure Land would be reinforced. Then he inaugurated a seven-day service for the continuous repetition of the nembutsu.[233]

When word reached the capital, laymen and clerics of both sexes assembled that they might establish a karmic bond with the holy man. They asked to meet with him, and the monk went out to receive them, although this confidants did not approve, considering his behavior unseemly and ostentatious.

The allotted number of days having been fulfilled, the monk's final bath was prepared.

"Now that you have come this far, nothing should be bothering you," said one of his companions. "But the mind of man is fickle; so if there are any attachments standing in your way, speak up. You must face death with no mental blocks. Now is not the time for silence."

"When I first made my decision, I was stout-hearted," replied the monk. "And when I heard about the fellow who died the other day in the bath-house fire, I thought that I should like to go as soon as possible, that I would no longer know such tragedy. But now my resolution fails me and I am no longer in any hurry."

Among the monk's long-standing disciples was a sharp-witted lay priest who lived in the capital and who had come to Ōhara for the occasion. Perhaps because he was piqued at not being permitted into the practice hall, he edged up close to the sliding panel and, when he heard the holy man speak, called out in a loud voice.

"Deliberations are in order before the affair has been decided. But having made a noisy announcement of your intentions, and having set the day and the hour, you cannot now come out with sage reasons for changing your mind. This is the work of the devil, so take your bath and get on with it. You're just trying to stall!"

Thus reproached, the monk was silent. Then, making a wry face, he performed his ablutions, hung a rope from a nettle-tree in front of the hall, and hanged himself by the neck. The people venerated and revered him, each taking something which he left behind as a memento.

Some six months after this affair, the Abbot Superintendent fell ill. Signs indicated that a supernatural force was at work, so they protected his body by covering it with mystic formulas. The Abbot babbled, saying many strange things. The ghost of the monk who had hanged himself had taken possession of his faculties.

"Alas! You should have stopped me," said the voice. "It irks me that when I wanted to abandon my plan, you did nothing to help!"

Unable to forget and to cast off his delusive thoughts and attachments, the monk had entered into the path of the demons. What a futile undertaking! We should be well aware and fearful of delusive and binding thoughts.

This is a true story, having been related to me by an Ōhara monk of my acquaintance who witnessed it with his own eyes.

4:8 The Monk Who Drowned Himself

On a mountain lived a monk with a deep understanding of the Way whose heart was not fixed on this floating world. Wishing to enter quickly into Paradise, he decided to meet his end by drowning. With the support of a fellow-monk, he prepared a boat and rowed out on a lake.

"The moment of death is the most important in one's entire life," said the holy man. "Now even when one is accustomed to a situation, mistakes occur, and he may blunder through carelessness. Since I have never before attained birth in the Pure Land nor experienced death, I am uncertain how I shall behave. If, after I go into the water, delusive and binding thoughts arise so that I begrudge my life, and should extraneous notions distract me from my purpose, my birth in the Pure Land is not assured. Should I want to return after I enter the water, I will jerk the line. Then pull me out."

The monk tied a rope to his side and dived into the water, reciting the name of Amida, but soon felt uncomfortable. So he jerked the line and his campanion hauled him out, soaking wet.

Although his friend did not know what was going through his mind, he brought him back as promised.

"It was painful in the water and when delusive thoughts arose, I knew that in this state of mind I should never attain birth in the Pure Land. So I came back," explained the monk.

After several days passed, the monk decided that this time he would surely not fail, and again rode out in the boat. But after diving in, he pulled on the line as before, and his companion hauled him back. Two or three unsuccessful attempts later the monk went out again without any high hopes.

But this time after diving in, he did not jerk the rope. In the sky, celestial music was heard and a purple cloud trailed over the waves. When his friend beheld these auspicious signs, tears of gratitude fell with the water dripping from the oars.

Truly, the mind which clings to the thought of self and desires fame cannot be born into the Pure Land. But with genuine faith one can realize his cherished desire. Unlike the monk who hanged himself, wise indeed was this one who kept trying and attained birth in the Pure Land!

4:9 One Who Would Aspire to Enlightenment Should Cast Off Attachment

Kenshin of Ōhara held a discussion for forty-eight days on the Essentials of Salvation *(Ōjōyōshū, T. 2682) with Hōnen and Shunjō (1121–1206). After the ceremony was over, Hōnen asked Shunjō what he thought was the gist of the discussion. Shunjō replied: "I understand it to be that attachment which can be stopped should be stopped—be it only for a miserable pot of rice-bran paste." Kenshin was impressed and said that he had not heard such a splendid comment during the entire discussion.*

Truly the round of transmigration arises from a single thought of attachment. However broad their program of accommodation, the various teachings have no other object than to eliminate the attachment of sentient beings. In the Lotus Sutra *the Buddha says that he makes it possible for sentient beings to withdraw from that to which they are attached. By burning the firewood of the passions in the fire of wisdom, we leave the bitterness of desire and know enlightenment. All imperfection is merely attachment.*

The Commentary on the Great Wisdom Sutra, *commenting on the eighteen kinds of Emptiness[234] says that although Emptiness is one, it is called by eighteen names because of the eighteen attachments of sentient beings. Although fire is one, there is a pine fire or a bamboo fire, depending on the nature of the firewood.*

The Sage of Toga-no-o (Myōe) comments on the difficulty of ridding the self of stubborn passions. Nan-shan (Tao-hsüan, 596-667) says that the Holy Teachings exist to be practiced, not merely to be read about. Myōzen (1184-1225), while discoursing on Tendai's practice of Cessation and Insight (shikan), *cited a line of Rakuten's (Po Chü-i's) poetry on nonattachment. Upon hearing it, a lay priest remarked: "Now I understand Cessation and Insight." "Hearing one part, he understands all," said Myōzen.*

Po Chü-i also said that even when one is prosperous, he suffers; because suffering is the mind's anxiety. Moreover, a person can be happy in poverty, because happiness is in one's freedom from anxiety. Hsien-shou (Genju; Fa-tsang, 643-712) has a similar comment.

In the Imperial Palace is a screen on which is written, in the calligraphy of Empress Kōmyō (702-760): "The poor are always happy, the rich always wretched." The Final Admonition Sutra (Yuikyōgyō, *T. 389) says that a man of wisdom is rich even though he is poor, and a fool is poor even if he is wealthy.*

While some Ritsu monks from Nara were eating at the temple of Shō-getsubō (d. 1268) of Matsu-no-o, he chanted a passage from the Lotus Sutra *which counseled abstention. The monks lost interest in their food and withdrew.*

Attachment is to be avoided. Daie Zenji (I-hsing, 683-727) said that if you have time to be critical of others, be critical of yourself and there will be nothing in your study of Buddhism which cannot be achieved. The Sayings of the Confucian School, *compares being with a good man to entering a room full of fragrant herbs, and being with a bad man to entering a fish-market.*

Po Chü-i spoke of water and bamboo as his friends, because they cleansed his heart—water, because of its fleeting nature; and bamboo, because it understood the inner Emptiness.

The Lao Tzu *says that there is no worse sin than desire, and no worse misfortune than dissatisfaction. (In the* Rules to Purify Mind and Maintain Insight) *Nan-shan observes; "The four hundred and four grave illnesses have their origin in last night's undigested food; the suffering in the eight places where one is unable to see the Buddha or listen to the Dharma has as its source—woman.'"*[235]

5A:1 The Tendai Scholar Who Escaped the Demon-Sickness

A monk in retreat at the Great Hiei Shrine was visited during the night by an array of pestilential spirits. "All under heaven is calamity," they said. "and this mountain monk will also have a share."

Then in his dream the monk beheld a shrine priest come forth and tell the spirits to leave him alone. "However, among those who live on this mountain is a certain monk who intends soon to go down to his home country. Harrass him to prevent his leaving, but you are not to take his life." The priest then told the spirits the monk's name, and they departed.

The monk in question was just about to depart. But feeling regret at leaving Mount Hiei, he had that night composed his mind and recited the "Perfect and Sudden" (Endon) *chapter of the* Great Cessation and Insight *until late. Because of this, the evil spirits were unable to approach him; and they returned to the shrine saying that they had no power over him.*

Hearing all this in his dream, the first monk later went to the other's quarters and told what he had witnessed. "I am honored that the god should feel this way about my leaving," was the reply. The second monk decided to stay, and lived for many years on the mountain.

This chapter describes the "Perfect and Sudden" meditation practice, one of the three kinds which Nan-yüeh (Nangaku Eshi, 515-77) transmitted to Chih-i. Tendai scholars all recite it verbally; and although this does not suffice to enlighten their hearts, there is merit in it. The Nirvana Sutra *states that the light from that scripture enters the pores of living beings to help bring about their enlightenment. The* Net of Brahma Sutra *says that when we see the lower animals, we should speak to them about raising the Aspiration for Enlightenment. Even if they do not comprehend the words, the sound of the Law enters through their pores and at length contributes to their enlightenment.*

5A:2 The Benefit of Expounding the Perfect and Sudden Teaching

Long ago lived a Hiei monk who was distinguished for his accomplishment. After his death his disciples had no doubt that he would be born in some auspicious place. But the monk appeared to one of them in a dream as a demon.

"Because you delighted in the Perfect and Sudden doctrine," said a disciple in surprise, "we expected that you would be born either into a Pure Land, or into a human or heavenly world. What has become of you?"

"This is the Perfect and Sudden Teaching which I believed and expounded," replied the monk. And as he opened his clenched fist, it shed light all around with the brilliance of a precious gem. "Because I rubbed this jewel up against myself, my suffering is alleviated." Then the demonic form flew away.

Although one may fall into the Evil Destinies because his observance of the discipline is lax, if he strives zealously for understanding, he will attain wisdom and enlightenment. The dragon spirits and demons who benefited by attending the assemblies held by the Buddha when he was in the world belong to this class. But even if one is zealous in the observance of the discipline, if he has no background in meditation and wisdom, it will be difficult for him to be reborn into the human or heavenly worlds, or to enter on to the Way of the Buddha. The Final Admonition Sutra *says that if one does not observe the discipline, his potential for good cannot be realized. By observing the regulations (kai), we acquire the capacity for meditation (jō); and through meditation, wisdom (chie). Our scholar cultivated the Perfect and Sudden practices; but it seems that he was delayed in the Evil Directions by his attachments. Nevertheless, his release seems to be at hand.*

5A:3 The Scholar Who Was Reborn as a Beast

On Mount Hiei lived two scholars who were alike in all respects. Because of this they made a vow to each other saying: "We belong to the same religious tradition, and since our behavior does not differ in a great many ways, we ought to receive the same treatment in the afterlife. If one of us dies before the other, he must return and reveal the place of his rebirth." One of the monks died and revealed to the other in a dream that he had been reborn as a field-hammer (nozuchi). *The field-hammer is an unusual animal; it is said to exist as a rarity deep in the mountains. Its body is large, and it has neither eyes, nose, hands, nor feet. They say that it only has a mouth, and that it feeds on human beings.*

The monk who died had diligently studied Buddhism for the sake of honor and profit. But in disputation there was anger, no weakening of delusive attachments, and no equanimity. His mouth was clever, but he did not have the eyes of wisdom, the hands of faith, nor the legs of righteous behavior. And so he was reborn as this fearsome thing.

Even minor causes are not without their effects. The Lotus Sutra says that even those who gather sand for a Buddha's stupa will all attain Buddhahood. If a person studies Buddhism for the sake of enlightenment, the profit is great; if for the sake of reputation, the loss is great. Whether one remains in the world or abandons it, his attitude determines the good or evil of his actions. A world-transcender (shussesha) is one who truly intends to attain the Way of the Buddha and liberation; a person who uses Buddhism for worldly gain is a worldling (sekensha). Just as in music when a certain tone is taken as the melody and the remaining four are subsidiary, so the man of the world, although he studies the Buddha's Law, subordinates it to worldly concerns.

A person who enters on the Way of the Buddha should have neither the entanglements of tools, clothing and food, nor dwelling-place and material goods. But with the human body it is difficult to maintain oneself without them. Since it is difficult to be blessed with the opportunity of being born as a human being, we should use this opportunity to practice the Buddhist Way. The sages of old sowed seeds and plowed fields so that the world became a thing of the Dharma. Worldly activity does not run contrary to reality if performed with the proper attitude. Strictly speaking, only the Buddha maintained the discipline. But in the broad sense, all activities can be directed to this end.

5A:4 The Compassionate Man Who Avoided the Demon-Sickness

Some time ago at Miidera lived two young monks called Shikibu and Jijū. Shikibu excelled in scholastic ability; Jijū was noted for his genial disposition. When young pages came to the temple for the first time, Jijū would put them at ease by showing them pictures and playing games with them.

A certain prelate made a pilgrimage to Shinra Myōjin, the guardian dei-

ty of the Miidera. In a dream he saw an array of spirits come before the shrine, from which a priest came forth to address them: "You are to spare Ji-jū and visit the affliction on Shikibu." The prelate was unable to com-prehend the reason for this order inasmuch as Shikibu, unlike Jijū, was a talented scholar. So he challenged the priest, who replied: "Although Shikibu is indeed a scholar, he acts for his own advantage rather than for the benefit of others. Jijū is a man of compassion, and there are more than a hundred monks who might not be living in this temple but for him." The prelate awoke from his dream and sent a messenger to Jijū to inquire of him what had occurred.

"For two or three days I was laid low with a grave illness," replied Jijū. "But from daybreak this morning I broke into a sweat and was relieved." Then he sent a messenger to Shikibu's quarters and heard that he had been seized by a serious illness at daybreak and had perished. Shikibu ought to have excelled in wisdom (chie); but since his mind was set on personal gain, there was no advantage to all his learning. There is little profit in learning (tamon: "the hearing of many things") because it is worldly wisdom. Com-passion (jihi) is the body of the Bodhisattva, the heart of the Buddha.

In a narrow sense we speak of benevolence (jin), in larger sense, we speak of compassion. Just as with burning: although the fire is the same, when the fuel is meager, the flame is small; and when the fuel is abundant, the flame is intense. The Sutra of Meditation on Amida Buddha (Kam-muryōjukyō, *T. 365*) *says that the heart of the Buddha is great compassion. The* Treatise on Yoga (Yugaron, *T. 1579*), *in answer to the question, "What is the essence of the Bodhisattva?" replies: "Compassion."*

In the Deer Park in ancient times lived a deer-king who ruled over a herd of five hundred animals. This was Śākyamuni during his career as a bodhisattva. Devadatta (Daibadatta) also ruled over a herd of five hundred. After the emperor of the country had gone hunting and killed many deer in the space of a day, the bodhisattva deer-king spoke to him of his sorrow over such useless slaughter. He then offered to present the emperor a deer a day for his table; and the emperor agreed. Every day a single deer was delivered up until eventually the choice fell on one in Devadatta's herd who was with child. "There is no way for me to avoid my responsibility," said the grieving mother. "But it is not the child whose time has come. Let one of the others exchange places with me, and after I have delivered the child, I will go."

"Who is not reluctant to give up his life?" replied Devadatta. "If it is your turn, you ought to go."

Then the woman spoke to the bodhisattva deer-king, who took her place and went up to the emperor's palace. People recognized him from the golden pattern on his fur and informed the emperor that the deer-king had come. "Is the herd exhausted?" asked the emperor. The deer-king related the cir-cumstances of his coming, adding: "It is immeasurably rewarding to succour others through compassion. If a person does not have compassion, he is no different from the foxes and wolves."

"It is I who am the beast—a human-headed deer," said the emperor.

"And you are the man—a deer-headed man. It is compassion, not physical appearance, which makes the man." The emperor sent the deer back to his herd, and forever after refrained from killing.

At the time of Śākyamuni's death in the Sal-tree grove, Cunda (Junda) wished to offer a bowl of food to the Buddha. And as a result of his doing this out of compassion for all living beings, a single bowl of food fed the great assembly. When the Buddha told the assembly of Cunda's intention, they praised him with one voice, though in diverse tongues: "Praise be to Cunda. Although his body is that of a man, his heart is that of a Buddha." If one's heart is pure, he will escape manifold temptations, just as the wisteria and willow bend but are not broken before the wind.

Long ago in India the king's consort was a person of deep compassion and respected the Three Treasures of Buddhism, while the king was a wicked man and envied her. When he took his bow in hand to shoot her, the empress felt only compassion in her heart for the king's erroneous views. When the arrow was shot, it turned backwards and lodged in the king's breast, killing him. At the maxim says; "The clenched fist does not touch the smiling face."

5A:5 The Scholar Dispels Ill-will

At the Miidera lived two young Kusha scholars who were great friends. One of them having been offended by the other over some trifling matter, he ran at him with his sword drawn. "What's this?" asked his friend, smiling and unperturbed. "The other day you spoke ill of me," said the first monk. "And now I shall get even."

"It is because I thought of you as a learned scholar that what you did seemed stupid. But that's over and done with. For what am I now to blame?" The first monk put up his sword and the two were reconciled.

Although they had merely studied the Dharma, yet it was because they understood and believed in the principle that the phenomenal disappears from thought to thought[236] and does not long persist that the offended monk's anger was quickly soothed.

Long ago in China a king wished to test the wise men of the land. So he invited a hundred high-ranking priests to the palace, where he had concealed a large number of warriors. When they suddenly surrounded the monks, making as if to slay them, the monks scattered in all directions. Only one remained seated and composed.

"The others are all terrified. Why are you alone not afraid?" asked the king. "In the process of living," replied the monk, "we die from thought to thought.[237] Why should I now begin to fear?" The king recognized him as a wise man and honored him with the title of National Teacher.

Although we imagine that things of the past do not change, they begin and cease from moment to moment. The former is extinguished and born anew. Its appearance continues because of karma; and when this is exhausted, it disappears. There is light as long as there is oil, but the fire is ex-

tinguished from moment to moment. Springing to life again and again by virtue of the oil, it constantly burns out. It is like a stream of water which appears to be the same but never stops flowing. (According to the Mirror of Sectarian Differences) *Confucius remarked that at the end of the day he saw Yen Hui (Gankai, 513–482) as a new person, meaning that the former body vanishes thought by thought. An ancient remarked that the body which had red cheeks in childhood now had gray hair in old age.*

Once there was an ascetic who went to another country in his youth and returned to his home town after he had become old. People said: "The man of old has returned." But the ascetic replied: "I resemble the one of old, but I am not he." People are aware that the years and months pass, but they are not conscious that as the years go by, the body of old passes away.

Long ago Zen master Tao-lin (Dōrin, 741–824) lived in a tall pine tree on Ch'in Wang Mountain. People called him the "Bird-nest monk." When Po Chü-i came to that part of the country, he spoke to Tao-lin and told him that the place where he lived was quite dangerous.

"In what way is it dangerous for me?" replied the monk. "Your position is considerably more dangerous than this."

"I administer the Chiang Mountain," said Po. "How is this dangerous?"

"Firewood and fire intermingle; perception and object do not remain distinct. How could this not be a dangerous situation?"

Po continued: "What is the meaning of Buddhism?"

"To avoid evil and do good."

"A child of three knows enough to say that."

"A child of three may be able to say it," replied the master. "But even an old man of eighty years is unable to practice it."

It has been handed down from earlier men of virtue that whatever differs from the admonition to avoid all evil is not the true Dharma. I-hsing (Daie Zenji, 683–727), the esoteric master, said that the familiar paradox that the passions are identical with enlightenment is like the lotus which does not grow on high ground but in a muddy pool; however, it is an error to extend this in order to condone that which violates the precepts. Yung-chia (Yōka, 665–713), (in his Song of Enlightenment, T. 2014), *said that it is wrong to extol Emptiness at the expense of moral causality.*

"To avoid all evil" (shoaku makusa; cf., 4:1) does not merely mean not to perform evil; nor does it mean to do what is formally good. "To cultivate every good" means that even if one performs good works all day long, he does them "without doing" them; nor does he even abide in the place of "no-doing." Tendai (Chih-i) says that the true immortal is not even blessed, much less sinful.

Long ago a wise man admonished his son: "Be careful not to do good."

"Shall I do evil then?" asked the son. The father replied: "You shouldn't even do good, let alone evil."

This is the import of all the scriptures. In the words of the "Bird-nest monk": "Firewood and fire intermingle; perception and object do not remain distinct." Although the mind, facing the objective world, has the semblance of being a continuing existence inasmuch as the appearances of things persist from thought to thought, yet the mind is discrete from moment to moment. Like the fire and firewood which vanish together, mind and its perceptions last but a short time.

The doctrines of the aforementioned scholars of the Mïidera are comparable to the attitude of Confucius. We should set our minds intently on the fact of impermanence. There are many ways to enter upon the Buddha's Law, but the understanding of impermanence is basic. Chih-i says that a truly virtuous man does not even create blessings, much less evils. By constantly fixing our minds on impermanence, we discard attachments. By forgetting delusive sentiment, we enter the Way of "no-mind" (mushin), and will come to know egolessness (muga).

5A:6 The Scholar Who Had Distorted Views

On Mount Izu a scholar was approached by a salt-vendor. The monk knew that salt was an important commodity and agreed to buy some. When he asked the price of a bagful, the vendor replied that he would leave it to the monk's judgment.

"Will you trade it for a bolt of fine silk?" asked the scholar. The vendor was happy to do so, and left.

When the scholar's disciples heard what had happened, they upbraided him. "With a bolt of fine silk one can buy fourteen or fifteen bags of salt."

"How mortifying," mused the scholar, scratching his head.

On the following day a lumber-dealer came by on his horse and asked the monk if he wished to buy some wood.

"Unload it!" cried the monk, laying hands on him.

"What's the matter?" asked the lumber-dealer in surprise.

"Yesterday you tricked me."

"That's not so."

Then his disciples spoke to the scholar. "What a mistake to make! The man yesterday was a salt-vendor; this man is a lumber dealer."

"You are all unscholarly, impertinent fellows who understand nothing," scolded the monk. "To say that a salt-vendor is a salt-vendor and that a lumber-dealer is a lumber-dealer is the attitude of the Special Teaching (bekkyō). But in the mind of one who understands the Perfect Teaching (enkyō), a lumber-dealer is a salt-vendor and a salt-vendor is a lumber-dealer."

The monk's disciples quietly paid the dealer what was owed him and sent the man away.

The scholar's views were truly distorted and came about because of his misunderstanding of the doctrine of the Two Truths, absolute and phenomenal (shinzoku no nitai). A similar position is maintained by the Tendai doctrine of the Three Truths and in the Vimalakīrti Sutra (Yuimakyō, T. 475).

Our scholar misunderstood the notion of the Undifferentiated (byōdō).
If he is speaking of phenomenal identity in the light of the absolute, then how
can he show the identity only between salt-vendor and lumber-dealer? The
monk, those who lived with him, and his retainers are all identical in this
sense. Since everything in the Ten Worlds is one-aspect-without-
differentiation, who is it that deceives and who is deceived? But if, in the
light of the phenomenal truth, we consider the phenomenal aspect of things,
then the salt-vendor and the lumber-dealer are separate beings. Why should
he suppress this side of it? Needless to say, his views were biased. And his
disciples likewise were not scholarly: why didn't they carry through the
reasoning?

5A:7 The Scholar Who Neglected Worldly Affairs

At Tōjōji in Hitachi Province lived Bridge-of-the-Law Enkō
Kyōōbō, scholar of Miidera. To the exclusion of all else, he pored
over the Holy Teachings, diligently pursuing both esoteric and overt
practices. But in practical matters he was hopeless.

A young monk was loading up a horse with manure to take to
the fields, as is the custom in the country. Seeing this, the scholar
stopped him.

"What are you doing with manure?" he inquired. "In my
prayers I recite the *Benevolent Kings Sutra*[238] for the prosperity of
the land. Is the *Benevolent Kings Sutra* inferior to horse-manure
that the fields need fertilizing?"

On another occasion he said to his disciples: "People in the
world are foolish and not careful about managing things. Now I
have invented something interesting: a way to pound two mortars
with one pestle. Place one mortar in the usual way, and suspend the
other from above, facing downwards. As you move the pestle up and
down, it will pound both mortars."

"If the materials to be ground would only stay in place in the
upper mortar," replied his disciples, "then indeed you might do it."

"That's a problem!" admitted the scholar, at a loss for words.

5A:8 The Discussion of the Ant and Tick Scholars

On Kasuga Plain in Nara near the scholars' quarters lived an
ant and a tick. Naturally, both were scholars, living as they did in
this learned neighborhood. Having heard of each other, they

wanted to get together for a discussion of views, and one day when they happened to meet on the road, both were overjoyed. The tick then formally[239] addressed the ant.

"What is the rationale of denominating ants, 'ants' (*ari*)?"

"It is because the ant has (*ari*) fore and aft parts on either side of a constricted waist that they are called 'ants' (*ari*)," was the reply.

"If that which has fore and aft parts is to be called 'ant'," pursued the tick, "then drum-shaped instruments[240] and the like ought to be so called."

"It is because we already had the name 'drum-shaped instrument' that they are not called 'ants'. By the same token, tom-toms[241] and the like are called as they are.

Then the ant questioned the tick.

"What is the rationale of denominating ticks, 'ticks' (*tani*)?"

"It is because they have depressions in their back like valleys (*tani*) that they are called 'ticks' (*tani*)."

"If things are called 'ticks' because their backs are troughed, then dumplings, whose backs are troughed, ought to be called *tani*."

"Not so! Because formerly we already had the name 'dumpling', they are not called *tani*. Similarly, cymbals are called as they are."

Someone from Nara related this anecdote and I have recorded it as an example of the workings of intellect. Probably the ant and tick were scholars in a former life. Certainly they are more admirable than the fieldhammer.[242].

Discussions among animals often appear in the sacred writings. The *Commentary on the Great Wisdom Sutra* tells of a snake, a turtle, and a frog who lived together as friends in a pond. Then came a drought, the water in the pond dried up, and there was no food. Hungry and brooding, the snake sent the turtle as his messenger to where the frog was staying.

"Come over and pay me a little visit," he said. "Let's get together!"

The frog replied with a maxim: "When we are tortured by hunger and thirst, we forget about morality and think only of food. Sympathy and friendship are for normal times, and this is not such a time. I cannot come to see you."

Indeed, it would have been a dangerous visit! Down in one

gulp, and with the best will in the world there would be no bringing him back.

In the ocean lives a creature called a *kiku*.[243] They say it is like a large snake and has no horns. Now the wife of one of these creatures was pregnant and had a craving for fresh monkey liver; so the serpent went to a mountainous region where a monkey was living.

"Are there many nuts on this mountain?" he inquired.

"They are rather difficult to come by."

"In the middle of the ocean is a mountain with lots of nuts," said the *kiku*. "You really ought to go there."

"How am I supposed to get to the middle of the ocean?" asked the monkey.

"Ride on my back." So the monkey rode on the serpent's back and they went far out into the ocean, but he saw no mountain.

"Where in the world is the mountain?" asked the monkey.

"Really!" the serpent replied. "How could there be a mountain in the middle of the ocean? I have brought you here because my wife has a craving for fresh monkey liver."

The monkey paled and spoke in desperation: "If you had only mentioned this when we were on the mountain, I could easily have obliged you. I keep my fresh liver high in a tree on the mountain where I live, and I was in such a hurry that I forgot it."

"Well, go back and get it!" said the serpent, reflecting that it was only for the sake of the liver that he had gone to all this trouble.

"No problem," was the reply. And so they returned to the mountain.

There the monkey climbed up a tree and disappeared into the mountain with these words: "In the middle of the ocean there is no mountain and apart from the body there is no liver."

Nonplussed, the serpent returned to the sea. As set forth in the scriptures, here is an example of wiliness even among animals.

> A crow, a dove, and a deer were discussing life's troubles. "There is nothing so irritating as being hungry," said the crow. "When I am hungry I lose my wits and am in danger of being snared in a net."
>
> "For me there is nothing so troublesome as sensual desire," said the dove. "The pain in my breast is difficult to bear."
>
> "For me there is nothing worse than the pain of fear," said the deer. "At the sound of men and the sight of a bow, I race over the mountain peaks and valleys, heedless of the fact that my body may be dashed to pieces."

A centipede, a one-legged mountain-spirit, and a snake lived together on a mountain. "Although I have a hundred legs, I do not consider this to be excessive," said the centipede to the mountain-spirit. "How do you get about with only one leg? You ought to have ninety-nine more."

"I have only one leg," replied the mountain-spirit, "but this does not prevent me from dancing and walking. Cut off your ninety-nine legs and throw them away."

Then the snake said: "I have neither one nor a hundred legs but I move about on my stomach and am not at a disadvantage. Get rid of both the hundred legs and the one leg!" (Cf., Chuang Tzu 17)

For those with many possessions in this world, they do not appear excessive; these people are like the centipede. Others know a single place; and because they are satisfied with this, they are not lacking. They are like the mountain-spirit. Then there are those completely without worldly fortune; but they do not starve to death. They are like the snake. (Chuang Tzu 8:2) says that we cannot shorten a crane's legs nor lengthen a duck's.

When we hear such anecdotes of long ago, why should not the ant and tick scholars have their discussions?

5A:9 The Scholars Who Composed Verse

Two Lecturer (ikō) monks returning from a court ceremony put on each other's straw sandals by mistake. On returning them they exchanged poor waka full of "ifs", "ands" and "buts"—typical of pedantic priests.

5A:10 The Scholar Who Took Everything as a Philosophical Argument

Some time ago at the Miidera lived a scholar called Kyōgetsubō. He was very learned; but about the Way of Poetry he had not the slightest understanding. His disciples complained to him that he knew nothing about the Way of Poetry as it was then practiced. When he asked for an example, his disciples quoted a verse (Kokinshū I:1, by Ariwara Motokata, 883-953) which asks two questions. The monk responded with appreciation for its rhetorical qualities but complete incomprehension of its poetic ones.

The man who has entered the Way sees all things as means toward liberation. The preacher sees all things as texts for expounding the scriptures. And those who study the traditional doctrines see all things as argument (rongi). This is far from the path of release. Although practices which foster the growth of Wisdom are to be taken seriously, disputatiousness is a cause of rebirth.

5A:11 The Scholar Who Loved Poetry

Because Assistant High Priest Eshin was a deeply religious man who was lacking neither in the theory nor the practice of Buddhism, he abhorred the frivolity of "mad words and specious phrases." His disciples included a young page who day and night devoted himself to the composition of poetry.

"Young boys ought to pursue their studies, but this page only likes poetry and nothing can be done with him," Eshin was informed by his colleagues. "With a person like this around, the others will imitate his behavior and that would be troublesome. Tomorrow morning he will be sent back to his village."

The page, unaware of what had been decided, went out on the veranda that night where the moon was serene and everything peaceful. Cupping his hands as though to scoop up water, the page recited this verse:

Te ni musubu	Like the moon
Mizu ni yadoreru	Reflected on the water
Tsuki kage wa	Cupped in my hands,
Aru ka naki ka no	Is it real or not—
Yo ni mo sumu kana	This world in which we live?[244]

The Assistant High Priest was deeply impressed and moved by the appropriate spirit and style of the verse. Subsequently he retained the page and he himself came to love poetry. His verse can be found in the collections of many reigns.[245]

According to another tradition, Eshin heard the page recite this poem on seeing a boat moving on Lake [Biwa in] Ōmi:

Yo no naka wo	To what shall I
Nani ni tatoemu	Compare this human life?
Asaborake	To the white wake
Kogiyuku fune no	Of a boat rowing away
Ato no shiranami	At the break of dawn.[246]

It is said that Eshin thus came to love poetry. The earlier verse was written when Tsurayuki was depressed by a serious illness; the latter is a poem by Mansei. In a most appropriate spirit the poets composed these old verses, which are both in the *Collection of Gleanings*.

The Assistant High Priest also composed this verse:

Urayamashi	As the moon
Ikanaru sora no	For every season,
Tsuki nareba	How enviable
Kokoro no mama ni	That it moves as it pleases
Nishi ni yukuran	Toward the Western Paradise.[247]

Now we refer to the poetry of "wild words and specious phrases" as "defiled poetry," because it lures us to attachment, imbues us with vain sensuality, and decks us out with empty words. But poetry may express the principles of the Holy Teaching, accompany a sense of impermanence, weaken our worldly ties and profane thoughts, and cause us to forget fame and profit. If, on seeing the leaves scattered by the wind, we come to know the vanity of the world; and if, on composing a verse on the moon hidden in the clouds, we become aware of the unsullied Principle within our hearts, then poetry mediates our entry upon the path of Buddha and becomes a reliable tool for understanding the Law. Accordingly, men of old practiced the Law of Buddha without rejecting the Way of Poetry.

We hear many poems on Personal Grievance *(jukkai)*. At a gathering attended by the venerable priest of Ōhara [Jakunen, fl.ca. 1170], Priest Saigyō (1118–90) and others, someone [Ennin Shōnin] wrote this verse on the grievances of old age.

Yama no ha ni	As the light sinks
Kage katabukite	Through the leaves at the rim
Kuyashiki wa	Of the mountain,
Munashiku sugishi	I am vexed by the months
Tsukihi narikeri	Which have vainly slipped away.[248]

As we enter into the writer's feelings, hearing his words at this distance in time, even one whose heart has renounced the world experiences a sense of wonder.[249]

The Final Admonition Sutra *expresses a similar sentiment. Be diligent while you are young. It may have been during the reign of Murakami that a poet (the monk Dōin, ca. 1093–ca. 1182) who closely served the emperor composed a poem of regret at old age (Senzaishū XVII: 1077). It is said to have raised the emperor's Aspiration for Enlightenment. Kanemori (d. 990) also composed a verse (Shūishū IV: 261) which had a similar effect. Although anything can be a cause for religious awakening,* waka *is ideal.*

5A:12 The Profound Reason for the Way of Poetry

When we consider *waka* as a means to religious realization, we see that it has the virtue of serenity and peace, of putting a stop to the distractions and undisciplined movements of the mind. With a few words, it encompasses its sentiment. This is the very nature of mystic verses,[250] or *dhāraṇī*.

The gods of Japan are Manifest Traces, the unexcelled Transformation Bodies (*ōjin*) of buddhas and bodhisattvas. The god Susa-no-o initiated composition in thirty-one syllables with the "many-layered fence at Izumo."[251] Japanese poems do not differ from the words of the Buddha. The *dhāraṇī* of India are simply the words used by the people of that country which the Buddha took and interpreted as mystic formulas. For this reason the Meditation Master I-hsing in his *Commentary on the Great Sun Sutra* says: "The languages of every region are all *dhāraṇī*." Had the Buddha appeared in Japan, he would simply have used Japanese for mystic verses.

Essentially, mystic spells have no characters; the characters *express* the spells. Do not the characters of every country have the ability to express mystic spells? The Great Teacher of Mount Kōya [Kūkai] said:

> The five great elements have vibrations;
> [Each of the ten worlds has its language;]
> The six kinds of objects are expressive symbols;
> [The Dharmakaya Buddha is the Reality.][252]

Apart from the Five Tones[253] there is no pitch, and apart from the letter "A"[254] there are no words. The letter "A" is the basis of the *mantras* of esoteric Buddhism. And so the scripture [the *Commentary on the Great Wisdom Sutra*] says: "Everything spoken by the tongue is a mystic formula." The thirty-one chapters of the *Great Sun Sutra*[255] likewise parallel the thirty-one syllable of *waka*. The principles of secular and religious life are contained in thirty-one syllables: they are that which moves ($ō$)[256] the Buddhas and Bodhisattvas and elicits a response (*kan*) from the gods to men. Although *dhāraṇī* employ the ordinary language of India, when the words are maintained *as dhāraṇī*, they have the capacity to destroy wickedness and remove suffering. Japanese poetry also uses the ordinary words of the world; and when we use *waka* to convey religious intent, there will necessarily be a favorable response. When they embody the spirit of the Buddha's Law, there can be no doubt that they are *dhāraṇī*.

The words of India, China, and Japan differ, but their meanings are mutual and their results the same. Through them Buddhism spread, its doctrines were accepted, and the benefits have not been without avail. Among words there are no fixed standards. If only the meaning is grasped and the thought conveyed, there will necessarily be a favorable response (*kannō*).

Great sages have appeared in our country and composed *waka*. There is even the poem of the Kiyomizu Kannon:

Tada tanome	Although your pain
Shimeji ga hara no	Be as the burning moxa grass
Sasemogusa	On Shimeji's fields,
Waga yo no naka ni	Still trust in me while yet
Aran kagiri wa	I remain in this world.[257]

This is certainly a *dhāraṇī*; there can be no doubt about it.

Likewise the gods, greatly admiring a man's poetry, will grant him his wish. The efficacy of Japanese poetry and the nature of mystic verses are in every respect to be understood as identical with *dhāraṇī*. If one levels the charge that poetry is "specious talk" (*kigo*), he should be aware that the fault lies in the defiled mind of the subject. Even the sacred teachings, when exploited for prestige and profit, generate evil karma. This is *man's* defect. Consequently, the efficacy of mystic verses is not to be lost. In the *Completion of Truth* it says that even the sutras, when they are read at inappropriate occasions, become empty words.

Having come to understand these principles, I have written them down here for a very good reason. Moreover, the same principles appear in sutras and commentaries, so please do not think they are just my personal opinions.

> *The phenomenal is the absolute* (shohō jissō). *The* (Great Cessation and Insight *says that) a single taste or odor is the Middle Way of Buddhism; and (the* Nirvana Sutra *says that) coarse words and refined expressions both proceed from the First Principle; nor are the everyday affairs of life at variance with the True Reality.*[258] *I composed a poem to this effect on hearing the belling of deer. A line (from the* Sutra of Heroic Deed) *also expresses this idea.*

> *Shingon teaches that all things are a mystic configuration* (mandara) *leading to delusion or enlightenment depending on one's karma. There is a* waka *to the effect that some people call burning fields of pampas grass, "mandara"; in the Kantō it is called "matara."*

> Waka *can express the Mahāyāna teaching. (The* Way and Its Power *49) says that "the sage has no invariable mind of his own; he makes the mind of the people his mind" (Legge, tr.). The sage has no language of his own but makes the language of the people his language. Are these words of the sage not then truly the words with which to expound the Law? The gods and buddhas certainly do use* waka *as mantras!*

5B:1 The Gods Help People in Response to their Poetry

In the days of Cloistered Sovereign Toba (r. 1107–1123; d. 1156), a person called Kodaijin served as lady-in-waiting to the empress Taikenmon'in.

One of the royal garments having disappeared, Kodaijin was unjustly suspected of theft, and made a seven-day pilgrimage to Kitano. As she was writing her petition to the deity, she accidentally spilled some perfumed water and was reprimanded but pardoned. In her depressed state, she protested her innocence of the theft to the deity in a poem [which is included in Kiyosuke's Shokushikashū *(ca. 1165), VIII]. That night the sovereign was visited in a dream by a distinguished old man who announced that he was from Kitano and requested that a royal messenger be sent as there was something of interest to be seen. The messenger went to Kitano where he found Kodaijin's poem; and, as he was returning to report to Toba, a serving girl called Shikishima and a priest came into the women's apartments with the missing garment to perform the Lion Dance. Kodaijin was recalled after the incident, but she retired to the Ninnaji and did not return to court.*

An impoverished lady-in-waiting accompanied her mother on a pilgrimage to the Iwashimizu Hachiman shrine to pray for prosperity. After their arrival the exhausted woman lay down and slept through the night. When her mother chided her next morning, the daughter replied with a verse which employed a pun on the name Iwashimizu. She said that although her suffering was beyond words, the god could read her heart. On their return mother and daughter were met on the road by a prosperous courtier who took them under his protection.

Once when she was gravely ill, Koshikibu Naishi (d. 1025) composed a verse regretting that she would be so unfilial as to precede her mother in death. The gods heard her and she recovered.

Ōe no Takachika (d. 1046) was seriously ill and had no hope for recovery. But since his illness was retribution by the deity of Sumiyoshi, his mother, Akazome Emon, proposed that the god take her life and spare his. She presented votive strips at the shrine with the verse (Shikashū X:361):

Kawaran to	The life I pray
Inoru inochi wa	Be taken in place of his
Oshikarazu	I do not begrudge;
Satemo wakaren	But oh the parting
Koto zo kanashiki	Is so bitter!

That night in a dream she saw a white-haired old man take the votive strip. Takachika recovered.

5B:2 The Admiration Which People Have Felt for Poetry

Monk Ryūson, son of Lord Ietaka (1157-1231) traveled throughout the Kantō region following the religious life. On one occasion he broke off a sprig of cherry blossoms from a tree in front of the house of the Land Steward, who ordered that he be seized as a thief. When Ryūson submitted a poem alluding to a verse by Saigyō, the official set him free. The monk remained at the house, where he instructed the Land Steward in poetry and other literary pursuits and was lavishly entertained.

Whey Ryūson set out on the religious life, he left the capital with a companion and traveled to a hamlet in Ōmi prefecture. Darkness came, and as there were no better lodgings available, the two squeezed into a hovel and spent the night there. As they were leaving in the morning, their host offered them some coarse food with an apologetic verse, to which they suitably responded.

While Ryūson was traveling in the Musashino Plain, he became thirsty and dropped in at what appeared to be a shack, asking for a glass of water. From a window a boy of eleven or twelve offered him some water in a chipped bowl. Ryūson remarked:

Mochinagara	Although it is full,
Kataware tsuki ni	It seems but a half-moon
Miyuru kana	In the bowl I hold.

The boy immediately capped the verse:

Mada yama no ha wo	Since it has not yet emerged
Ide mo yaraneba	Above the mountain ridge.

Daishimbō, a native of Tsukushi, was imprisoned in Kamakura eight years for larceny. But after having composed a skillful poem at a Tanabata festival, he was rewarded by being made a magistrate in Ōshū.

The son of an archivist was sent to Mount Hiei and lived in the quarters of a monk who was practicing austerities. He was a handsome child, and once when his mentor had sent him to the capital on an errand, he was inveigled by a monk from Miidera to stay at his temple. When the monks on Hiei heard what had happened, an angry crowd assembled. The situation was saved by the boy's mentor, who sent a poem to the Miidera which the monks there greatly admired. Without further ado they returned the boy to Hiei.

In Kamakura a novice became dissatisfied with his mentor and went over to another monk. Seeing that the boy had left behind a copy of the Shikashū (Collection of Verbal Flowers), *the teacher returned it to him with this verse:*

Ika ni shite	How is it
Kotoba no hana no	That the Verbal Flowers
Nokoriken	Be left behind
Utsuroihateshi	When the hue of affection
Hito no kokoro ni	Has faded in your heart?

On reading the poem the boy returned.
A Provincial Governor of Iwami province, having been informed that

the women divers at Iwamigata were adept at singing, summoned several before him. An attractive girl of about seventeen composed a verse and was awarded a purple garment. When she responded with a verse asking what a diving-girl could do with a purple coat worn by nobility, the official was so impressed that he took the girl and her parents back with him to the capital. She became his wife and bore him many sons.

At the house of an aristocrat a grasshopper began chirping in the area where the ladies- in- waiting were amusing themselves. They playfully suggested that a young servant compose a poem on this unlikely subject. The ladies tittered when she began but were soon put to shame by the servant's skillful creation. As the ancients have said, we should be careful about ridiculing others.

On a clear moonlit night in autumn when Fujiwara Toshitsuna (1028-1094) was composing poetry on the topic, "Moon on the Pond," he asked a country servant if he knew anything about waka. Amused at the servant's ignorance, Toshitsuna offered him a leave of absence if he composed a verse. "Do it any way you like. The topic is 'Moon on the Pond,' and the idea is for you to compose a poem describing the way the moon rests on the pond." Toshitsuna even agreed to give him a prize. After a while the servant produced the following:

Sora ya mizu	"Is it sky,
Mizu ya sora to mo	Or is it water?"—
Obooezu	I cannot say:
Kayoite sumeru	Shining intermingled,
Aki no yo no tsuki	Moon of an autumn night.

Toshitsuna was impressed and richly rewarded the servant.

At the death of his wife, Ōe Sadamoto (Jakushō, 962-1034), governor of Mikawa, was brooding on the vanity of life when he was visited by a woman selling mirrors. A poem wrapped around one of the mirrors turned his heart to the religious life (Shūishu VIII:469). And a request from monk Ryōzen to Toshitsuna (see above) was sent as a poem (Shikashū X: 366).

A menial living in Mikawa was also a poet and was given a lined garment after writing a waka about Mt. Iimori. And the prelates Kenshō and Shinkō both received advancement by writing poems. Ureshisa, servant of the Lay Priest of Uji (Fujiwara Morozane, 1042-1101), sent a clever poem to Akisuke (1090-1155). Subsequently, the Lay Priest presented Akisuke with the servant.

On a pilgrimage to the Inari Shrine, Izumi Shikibu (b. ca. 976) borrowed a garment from a peasant boy to protect her from the rain. Some days later he appeared at her house with a poem declaring his love for her.

When the Cloistered Sovereign Gosaga (r. 1242-1246) was on a pilgrimage to Kumano, a peasant of Ise province composed a poem on seeing the plum trees blossoming at Otonashigawa in Hongū. The emperor sent his retainers to find the author, who was brought before him and told to make a request. When the man asked to have enough to support his mother, Gosaga presented him with a document exempting him forever from property taxes. It is said that although the man was the son of a farmer, he had been educated as a page and understood the Way of Poetry.

5B:3 Poems Composed in the Spirit of the Man'yōshū

Some time ago in Hitachi province lived a mountain ascetic called Kōkambō who secretly would visit a certain Tōtsui, wife of a farmer in the area. The affair came to the attention of the husband, who decided that it would be the best policy not to shame the hermit, a well-known leader of pilgrims to Kumano. But while Kōkambō was on a pilgrimage, the farmer quietly went to visit relatives at Sembuku in the province of Mutsu. The hermit returned to find the woman gone, and no one in the area knew her whereabouts. While Kōkambō was standing in the bedroom of her house, he saw the wife's handwriting on a pillar:

Koishikuwa	Though it is far,
Toutemo wase yo	Come if you love me,
Kōkambō	Kōkambō.
Sembuku ni aru zo	I am in Sembuku
Tōshiro no moto ni	At Tōshiro's place!

Kōkambō was moved and felt that he should make a reply, even though the woman would not see it. On the pillar he wrote a reply in an unusual format upbraiding the woman for not having notified him earlier. The conception of the poem was unusual although the style was indeed displeasing. However, poems in the Man'yōshū are not always in thirty-one syllables; but if the sentiment is expressed, perhaps they may be considered as poems. On a sign-board at the Tōdaiji there are also a number of old-style verses.

5B:4 About Saigyō

A shrine maiden known as Lady Heigo composed poetry spontaneously, expressing the idea of whatever she saw or heard, although her poems did not always follow the usual thirty-one syllable pattern. On viewing a scroll illustrating the life of priest Saigyō (1118–1190), she composed verses expressing the meaning of the pictures. On the illustration of Saigyō's farewell to Cloistered Sovereign Toba (r. 1107–1123) she wrote:

    Samo koso wa   To be sure,
    Aware otoko ya   What a splendid man
      To mieshi ni   He seemed to be!
    Yo no ma ni kawaru   But how pitiful overnight
    Kokoro no itoushi ya   To have changed his mind.

On an illustration of cherry-blossom viewing on an old tree, she wrote a poem about a woodpecker. Perhaps there was one drawn on the scroll. She also wrote a verse on the provisions Saigyō had prepared for a trip to the capital having been eaten by deer during the night. These poems were in the spirit of the Man'yōshū.

At Iso no Kamifuru in Yamato province a man called Genjirō lost his first wife and had an affair with another just as he remarried. The woman of the affair became despondent and hanged herself. Genjirō then taught himself to write so that he could inscribe on her grave marker the following verse:

    Kono yo ni wa   It is not to be —
    Ika ni omoedo   Whatever we might hope for
     Kanaumaji   In this world;
    Raise ni wa kanarazu But in the next, without fail,
    Mairiawau yo   We will get together.

At least the conception of the poem was unusual. It is like Lady Heigo's verses, which reminded me of it. Then there is the poem by the peasant girl who used a bottle of cloudy sake for a comparison, the lady who exchanged poems with an admirer which cleverly incorporated the names of various animals, and the lay priest who exchanged whimsical poems about chestnuts with an attractive young nun.

A man crossed the Western Valley River at the Fuwa Barrier and inquired at a hut as to the name of the river. An old woman replied that it was the river referred to in a poem which she cited as being included in the Man'yōshū [but it is not and the source is unknown]. The man was moved, as though he had met the great poetess Ono no Komachi (fl. ca. 850). A person's sensitivity does not depend on social status. In the words of an ancient: "The distinction between noble and base is in the good or evil of people's actions."

In Saga lived an indigent courtier whose land faced that of a lady of the aristocracy who acted high-handedly toward her social inferiors. Year by year the lady pushed her boundary line into the courtier's property; and though the man wanted to take the matter to court, he felt that this would not be easy to do. He finally sent the lady a protest in the form of a poem which could also be read as an indecent proposition. The lady was so embarrassed *that she left house and property and moved to the capital. As no provision was made for the house, it became the courtier's. In antiquity men were sensitive and conscious of shame. Nowadays such people are rare.*

5B:5 Poems in Dreams

A samurai, unacquainted with the history of Anrahuji's Flying Plum Tree, which flew there on the occasion of a poem by Sugawara Michizane (843-903) during his banishment from the capital to Tsukushi,[259] *broke a twig from it. That night he was visited in a dream by a distinguished lady who upbraided him for his behavior* (Shinkokinshū XIX: 1853).

Nasakenaku	It is a cruel man
Oru hito tsurashi	Who breaks without pity
Waga yado no	The high-grown twig
Aruji wasurenu	From the plum which forgets not
Ume no tachie wo	The master of our house.

After a son of my acquaintance, a page at Kokawa Temple, died, someone who worked in the house of the boy's mother had a dream in which she heard his voice reciting a poem.

After the death of Fujiwara Takatō (949-1013), a poem was revealed to someone in a dream (Fukuro sōshi IV). Such instances of poems being revealed in dreams are known from antiquity.

5B:6 Losing One's Life Over Poetry

Fujiwara Nagatō (fl. ca. 980) died of chagrin after his poem was criticized by Kintō (966-1041). Moreover, at the Tentoku poetry competition (960) Taira no Kanemori (d. 990) and Mibu no Tadami (Tadamine's son, fl. ca. 960) each composed a verse on the topic, "First Love." Both poems were of superior quality and the judging was difficult, but Kanemori's was given the decision. Chagrined, Tadami became hopelessly ill and passed away, after explaining the cause of his illness to Kanemori. Although it is not good that the mind be attached to things, we consider Tadami's fondness for the Way of Poetry to be touching. Both poems were included in the Collection of Gleanings *(Shūishū XI: 621, 622).*

5B:7 Linked Verse

When the late lay priest of the Tō family[260] was ill unto death, he called together those with whom he had composed poetry over the years. Prostrate on his sickbed in the bright moonlight, and considering that this would be their last meeting, the master of the house composed the opening stanza of a linked verse.

Aware ge ni	Alas! how often
Ima ikutabi ka	After today will I be
Tsuki wo mimu	Seeing the moon?

The party was at a loss as to how to cap the verse, when someone from within the women's quarters replied:

Tatoeba nagaki	So is it even when
Inochi naritomo	One's life is long.

Everyone admired the response as novel and apposite[261] to the occasion inasmuch as the lay priest had indeed lived a long life; they had been saved from embarrassment. It is said that the priest's younger sister, Lady Wakasa, may have supplied the lines.

At Gokurakuji in Kamakura the bodhisattva Mañjuśrī appeared to a monk in a dream and said:

Iza kaerinamu	Let us then return
Moto no miyako e	To the Original Capital.

One of the monks at the temple composed the following stanza:

Omoitatsu	Apart from
Kokoro no hoka ni	The conceptualizing mind
Michi mo nashi	There is no Way.

This is most apposite to the notion that our very mind is itself the Way; there is no Way apart from the operation of the senses. The idea is that apart from this there is no place at which to enter upon the path of the Buddha.

A certain Ben no Ajari from a mountain temple in Momo-no-o in Yamato province made a trip to Hasedera. Finding the crimson leaves of autumn most compelling at a mountain temple called

"Kettle Mouth" (*Kama no kuchi*), the young monk attending him took his master's horse by the mouth with these words:

Kama no kuchi	At Kettle Mouth
Kogarete miyuru	Looking as though scorched,
Momiji kana	Those crimson leaves!

Ben was at a loss for words, but he felt that a reply was in order.

Nabete no yo ni wa	I think there's none like it
Araji to zo omou	In all your world.[262]

To a stanza written many years ago at Hearth Mountain [Kamadoyama in Kyūshū]

Haru wa moe	Hearth Mountain:
Aki wa kogaruru	Aflame in spring, scorched
Kamado yama	In autumn.

someone added the line:

Kasumi mo kiri mo	We see both mist
Kemuri to zo miru	And fog as smoke!

This capping is said to have been extraordinarily poor.

One winter some years ago, I was traveling along the Eastern Sea Route. On seeing a ring of clouds at the foot of Mount Fuji, a young priest who accompanied me made this stanza:

Fuji no yama	Mount Fuji
Kumo no hakama wo	Is wearing trousers
Kitaru kana	Of clouds.

I thought this was quite apposite, and I could not let it pass without a reply.

Yuki no katabira	While donning
Uchikazuki tsutsu	An upper robe of snow.

It is not a good poem; but since it goes well with the other items here, I have written it down.

Sakuradō ("Cherry Hall") at Toki in Mino Province is famous for its blossoms. When they were at their prime, someone wrote this stanza and attached it to the branch of a cherry tree.

Toki ni kitaredo	I came to Toki to unwind (*toku*), but here
Musubime mo nashi	Are neither stress nor artificial flowers.[263]

As there was no one else to supply the opening stanza, Kamata Jirozaemon Jō Yoshiyuki composed this:

Fukimusubu	Drooping cherry blossoms
Kaze ni midaruru	Are scattered by the wind which
Itozakura	Blows them into clusters.

This happened while Gotō Ikinokami Motomasa (1214–1267) of Kamakura was living in the capital. Once when returning from the mountains west of the city where he had been flower viewing, he placed a sprig of blossoms in his quiver. As he was proceeding on his way, a lady-in-waiting, seated on a high viewing platform, called out:

Yasashiku miyuru	Ah! The quiver of blossoms
Hanautsubo kana	So pleasant to look at!

Motomasa got down from his horse and replied:

Mononofu no	The warriors,
Sakuragarite shite	Gone hunting for cherry blossoms:
Kaeru niwa	Their return baggage.

At Bishamon Hall on the road to Izumo a group of people were composing linked verse. One stanza proved difficult to cap:

Usukurenai ni	Into a pale crimson
Nareru sora kana	Is the sky transformed!

After more than thirty attempts without an interesting response, the lay priest Tō was heard in a low voice.

> *Amatobu ya*   Sky-flying!
> *Inaoosetori no*   Silhouettes of wagtails
> *Kage miete*   Suddenly appear.

Tradition says that he answered what was apposite to the occasion. In the audience of commoners was Jūnembō. As soon as Tō said "Sky-flying," he exclaimed with excitement, "Great! He's capped it!" He was really sharp.

Somewhere or other there was a linked verse meeting which centered on reciting the name of Amida Buddha. A difficult stanza was put forward:

> *Nanorite izuru*   Ah! the cuckoo
> *Hototogisu kana*   Announces himself!

to which was attached [antithetically]:

> *Mononofu no*   On Bird-Snare Mount[264]
> *Tate wo naraburu*   Where side-by-side stand shields
> *Tonamiyama*   Of warriors

On the hill east of Kyoto some people came together to compose linked verse all night long. Among some "harsh stanzas"[265] proposed was this:

> *Zeso no zōshi mo*   The maid in the kitchen
> *Akamo wo zo kiru*   Also wears a red skirt.

to which was appended to everyone's delight:

> *Ōebi no*   Peeling shells
> *Kara mukiokeru*   And seated in the midst
> *Naka ni ite*   Of lobsters.

At a linked verse gathering of commoner poets[266] this stanza was spoken:

> *Futatabi chigo ni* Once again
> *Nari ni keru kana* Becoming a child.

Among various replies to this difficult phrase was one by a certain ascetic:

> *Nogoite wa* The doll seller:
> *Mata kakinaosu* Wiping off the wooden face,
> *Kaouri no* He paints it afresh.[267]

Splendid! . . . and among the difficult stanzas:

> *Fune no naka nite* Growing old
> *Oi ni keru kana* In a tub (= boat/vat)

This was attached:

> *Ukikusa no* Floating weeds
> *Kakehi no mizu ni* Carried in with the water
> *Nagarekite* From the conduit.[268]

On seeing eight bees, someone wrote:

> *Yatsu areba koso* Because they are eight
>   (*yatsu = hachi*)
> *Hachi to iurame* We doubtless call them bees
>   (*hachi*).[269]

This was added:

> *Hatachi iba* If twenty (*hatachi*)
> *Hataori nite zo* Then they would have to be
> *Aru beki ni* Crickets (*hataori*).

In Nara lived four temple priests who always got together to pass the time by making linked verse. People called them the "Four Heavenly Kings"; so one of them wrote:

> *Warera wo ba* We are the ones:
> *Shitennō to zo* "The Four Heavenly Kings,"
> *Hito wa iu* People call us.

Another of them capped it:

> *Shikashi Bishamon*   Perhaps, but surely I see
> *Nashi to koso mire*   No God of Wealth before me![270]

All were indigent monks.

Lord Takasuke[271] handed down a fine literary tradition within his family and was known as a splendid poet. On one occasion, when both serious (*ushin*) and "comic" (*mushin*) linked verse[272] were being composed, the following difficult stanza was set forth:

> *Ko-o ko-o ko-o to*   "Ko-o ko-o ko-o,"
> *Hara zo narikeru*   Rumbles the belly.

To which he replied:

> *Kawafune no*   Thus rumbles
> *Asase mo chikaku*   The belly of the river boat
> *Naru mama ni*   Approaching shallows.

It was most apposite!
Once, in a group of commoner poets, there were many who responded to this stanza:

> *Tsukuri-kaetaru*   On the eaves
> *Yado no nokiba ni*   Of my rebuilt house.

Takasuke completed it with this line:

> *Mayourashi*   They seem perplexed:
> *Kozo no sudachi no*   Returning to last year's nest,
> *Tsubakurame*   Swallows.

For the occasion it was splendid.
While this man was on a trip east, someone at Samegae in Ōmi province with whom he used to compose poetry, died. On his return, Takasuke thought of this person and wrote this on a rock in (the Amano?) river.

> Hito naraba
> Katarite sode wa
> Nurenamashi
> Iwa moru mizu no
> Aware yo no naka

> Were you human,
> Your sleeves would be drenched
> When I spoke of him:
> Water dripping from the rock
> In this world of sadness.[273]

I have recorded these matters just as they have occurred to me.

5B:8 Poems With a Deeper Significance

A verse by the Great Minister of Kamakura[274] reads:

> Naruko woba
> Onoga hakaze ni
> Makasetsutsu
> Kokoro to sewagu
> Murasuzume kana

> Bird-clappers
> Moved to sound by the wind
> Of their own wings,
> The flock of sparrows
> Simply frightens itself.

This poem has deep significance. In the Lotus Sutra *it is said that "all things in their essential nature are ever unconditioned and quiet" (Ch. 2). An ancient has said that things are by nature at rest, and that man puts them into turmoil. This is like the sparrows who activate the clappers and throw themselves into confusion. A similar moral is illustrated by a poem by Superintendent of Priests Dōkei (13th c.): things are as we see them.*

5B:9 Poems of Sorrow

Although poetry can be specious words (kigyō), *it may also be a means* (hōben) *to enter upon the Way of the Buddha. When we read old poems and see their relevance to our own lives, we are moved. Here are some of them: the verse on a mother's death* (Shinshūishu X:860 *in a variant form), Bishop Henjō's poem on retiring from the world at the death of Nimmyō (810-850) (Kokinshū XVI: 847), the poem composed by Izumi Shikibu (b. ca. 976) after the death of her daughter Koshikibu no Naishi (Kinyōshū X: 660), the poem on leaving a child behind in the old Nara capital (Gosenshū XV: 1103), the Ozasawara poem (Shinkokinshū XVIII: 1822) by Fujiwara Shunzei (1114-1204), two poems by Tameie (1198-1275) on the death of his daughter, and two by priest Saion to the exiled Gotoba (1180-1239) (one is Shokusenzaishū XVIII: 1963).*

On visiting the tomb of Sutoku (1119-1164), priest Saigyō (1118-1190) composed a poem expressing his feelings on the transience of worldly pomp (Sankashū 1355). He was answered with a poem by a faint voice from the grave.[275]

Although such poems are often quoted in common parlance, when recited quietly they gradually pacify the mind. The Way and Its Power *says: "The things which from old have got the One (the Tao) are—Heaven by which it is bright and pure; Earth rendered thereby firm and sure . . ." (Ch. 39; Legge's translation.) Although the methods for entering the Way are various, they attain the same end. Grasping the phenomenal with one mind, we understand the single nature underlying it. This notion is found in various doctrines and scriptural writings.*

There is nothing like poetry as a preliminary method for attaining singleness of mind. When we ponder it, we relax our attachment to worldly affairs; composing it, we forget profit and prestige. Seeing the floating blossoms, we recognize that it is difficult to evade the winds of impermanence. Seeing the bright moon, we come to understand how easy it is to obscure Reality with the clouds of the passions. The extent to which we do not attain true awareness is the extent to which feelings and thoughts are not checked. Starting from expedients having form, we ultimately enter into the formless Reality. This is the basic principle of the various teachings, the central rule of all sects. It is the state of mind attained in the Zen sect through the kōan, and in the esoteric sects through contemplation on the letter "A."

After Priest Saigyō became a recluse (*tonsei*), the innermost meaning of the Tendai *mantras (shingon)* was transmitted to him. When Abbot Jichin (Jien, 1155-1225) asked Saigyō to pass them on to him, he was told: "To begin with, become adept at poetry. If you don't grasp the meaning of poetry, you will not understand the meaning of the mantras." It is said that after Jichin became adept at poetry, Saigyō revealed this to him.

The truth of Buddhism transcends verbal explanation, nor is it to be grasped conceptually. When the mind is pacified and the emotions emptied, then the spiritual light which we possess from the very beginning will shine forth, and the sea of enlightenment which is our self-nature will be manifest. Thus the Great Teacher of Kōya[276] said: "The essence of the esoteric teaching is transmitted directly from mind to mind. Words are rubble, dregs." The words "transmit mind" do not mean that someone's thoughts are transmitted to me; they mean that that which makes my mind equal to the teacher's is transmitted. Thus, we do not understand it as "to transmit mind", but to transmit to the mind. The Zen doctrine is paralled in the esoteric A-ji practice.

The Way of Poetry is superior as an expedient method by which to leave this wretched sphere of worldly trouble and to enter into the marvelous realm of liberation. This is why it has been practiced from antiquity by the avatars who have left their traces in our country.

5B:10 The Avatars Delight in Poetry

The history of the Tōdaiji states that Bishop Rōben (689-773) as a child lived at the top of a tree where he was cared for by an eagle. He vowed to build a large temple on the site but realized that he could not accomplish his purpose without imperial assistance. He prayed aloud for the peace and longevity of the sovereign, so that the sound of his voice reached the ears of Shōmu (701-756), who sent a messenger to inquire whence it came. In reply to the messenger's inquiry, the boy told of his vow; and when the sovereign was so informed he sent Gyōgi Bosatsu (668-749) to take up a subscription for building the temple. Gyōgi was appointed to lead the dedication services but declined. As the day for the dedication approached, he went down to the beach at Naniwa with a hundred monks. Just then, Bodhisena (704-760) arrived in a boat from India. He made his way to Gyōgi and took him by the hand. The two exchanged verses referring to their meeting in an earlier existence (Shūishū XX: 1348, 1349). The Tōdaiji is called the "Temple of the Unanimous Intention of the Four Sages" (shishō dōshin no tera): Boshisena (Fugen), Gyōgi (Monju), Shōmu (Kannon), and Rōben (Miroku). Both the bodhisattvas of India and the sages of Japan delight in poetry.

Once when Prince Shōtoku (574-621) was sitting inconspicuously in a group of children, the Korean monk Nichira saluted him as an incarnation of Kannon. On another occasion, when Shōtoku was crossing Kataoka Mountain, he came upon a starving monk. Alighting from his horse, he covered him with his purple robe and they exchanged verses (Shūishū XX: 1350, 1351). The starving man was Bodhidharma (Daruma Daishi, d. 528?), according to the Heishi Biography of the Crown Prince *(i.e., the* Shōtoku Taishi denryaku). *In a former life Shōtoku lived in China, at which time he was told by Bodhidharma: "The people of the eastern sea are ignorant of the operations of the law of karma and have not yet heard the Buddha's teaching. You have an affinity with that country. Be born there, propagate the Law, and help all sentient beings." Thus, Prince Shōtoku's promulgation of Buddhism in Japan was from the encouragement of Bodhidharma. In the Zen sect Bodhidharma is said to be Kannon; Shōtoku is seen as Monju (Mañjuśrī). Monju and Kannon are both "skillful means" (hōben) of Mahāvairocana's wisdom and compassion.*

The distinction between meditation (zen) and philosophical explanation (kyō) is based on the principle of "skillful means." An ancient remarked that Buddhist philosophy is the speech of the Buddha; meditation, his mind. Both are compatible with each other. From its inception when Kāśyapa (Kashō) transmitted the Eye of the True Dharma (shōbōgenzō), the Zen sect has been a special transmission of the teaching which does not rely on the written word. Other sects speak of the ultimate as beyond conceptualization, but they nonetheless set up successive levels and classifications of understanding. This is like a turtle which drags its tail in the sand, leaving a trace after hiding its eggs. It was for this reason that Bodhidharma came to the West and propagated the teaching of "direct pointing" (jikiji) [to the heart of man]. This is "transmission from mind to mind." An ancient has said: "The gate of liberation is no-gate; the thought of the sage is no-thought."

Today's scholars are not like those of old. Those who follow Zen despise the doctrinal approach, and the followers of the doctrinal sects disparage the Zen schools. The methods may differ, but the understanding of the Way should be the same.

5B:11 The Hymn about Gyōgi Bosatsu

Gyōgi Bosatsu was conceived in Izumi province by a servant girl named Yakushi. When her time came, what she brought forth had an uncanny, gelatinous appearance.[277] In astonishment she deposited the object in a bowl which she placed in a fork in the branches of a nettle tree by the gate of a house, where a mendicant monk heard a voice within the bowl reciting the Buddha-Head Spell.[278] Realizing that there must be some profound significance in this, he notified the girl and had her take care of the substance. After some days a handsome child came forth who grew up to be the Subscription Saint who took up collections for the construction of the Great Buddha Hall at Tōdaiji.[279]

From ancient times services have been held at Gyōgi's birthplace; and a hymn[280] was composed which begins as follows, I am told:

Yakushi Gozen ni/gotanjō	When Yakushi Gozen gave birth to him,
Kokorobuto ni zo/nitarikeru	He looked like raw gelatin;
Surikobachi ni/sashiirete	So she placed him in an earthen bowl
Enoki no mata ni/okitekeri	In the crotch of a nettle tree.

Although the circumstances of Gyōgi's birth are indeed strange, the wording of the hymn is most unsuitable. Even the heart of the devotee freezes up. Just as a miraculous image of the Buddha which is unsightly is concealed behind a curtain, so should this hymn be stored away in a box!

Some years ago I had occasion to see Gyōgi's deathbed admonitions written in his own hand. They counsel us to be diligent in controlling speech, mind and body.

Karisome no	Think as naught
Yado karu ware wo	The self which borrows
Imasara ni	This temporary lodging,
Mono na omoi so	And now presently
Hotoke to onaji	You are Buddha.[281]

That which borrows (karu) *the temporary lodging* (karisome no yado) *is the delusive mind; and the dwelling borrowed is the illusory body. In the body the four great elements of earth, water, fire and wind temporarily* (kari ni) *come together. The hard bone and flesh is earth; that which is moist, water; that which is warm, fire; and that which moves, wind. Apart from these there is nothing to be called "body"* (shin). *Accordingly, when the breath stops and the spirit departs, the body returns to the original four elements. Delusive thoughts and the discriminations of desire, anger, and stupidity are like floating clouds and the flash of lightning: they appear to exist but they have no reality. They move in accordance with the environment, change according to situation. There is no thing to be called a "self"* (ga). *Apart from the Great Self of Selflessness* (muga no taiga) *there is no reality. The True Self lives eternally and is not subject to the flux of birth-and-death.*

Thus, if there is no delusive conceptualization, one's self-nature which is the Buddha will appear spontaneously. Kōbō Daishi and others remind us that by avoiding delusive affinities, we become the Buddha.

Izumi Shikibu, alienated from her husband's affections, retired to the Kibune Shrine. On seeing a flight of fireflies she composed a verse which was answered from within the shrine (Goshūishū XX: 1164, 1165).

An oracle delivered to me in Kii province during the Kenji period (1275-1277) by Hachiman Daibosatsu lamented people's involvement in worldly concerns, and extolled the practice of meditation (zazen). *While noting that his own Original Ground* (honji) *was Amida, he said that all methods, if performed single-mindedly, would lead one from birth-and-death.*

Someone remarked that it was common to observe the behavior of the three monkeys; but one who entered the Way of the Buddha ought to follow four monkeys. Of special importance was the injunction against conceptualization:

Iwazaru to	There are those
Mizaru to kikazaru	Who speak, see, and hear
Yo ni wa aru	No evil—
Omowazaru wo ba	But those without delusive thought
Imada minu kana	Have yet to be seen![282]

The Commentary on the Great Wisdom Sutra *says that thought is birth-and-death; no-thought, nirvana.*

6:1 The Preacher Who Was Taken the Wrong Way by his Patron

In the Eastern Provinces[283] a lay nun,[284] the widow of a certain great landholder, held a religious service, inviting as celebrant an old monk who had been a liturgist for many years. The ceremony was performed before the Great Sun Buddha, and while discoursing in detail on the sectarian views of his patron, the monk had this to say:

"According to Shingon doctrine, the Power of Spiritual Integration (*kajiriki*)[285] refers to the responsive communion between the body of the Buddha and those of sentient beings, not unlike the moon lodging in the water by reflection. Moreover, when the burning embers and the charcoal are intermingled and we poke the embers along with the charcoal, then the charcoal presently becomes embers. Similarly when those who practice the religious life with faith come into contact with the august body of the Buddha, the devotee presently becomes the Buddha. This is what is called 'The Power of Spiritual Integration.' " It is an excellent method.

"Now the Great Sun Buddha illumines the great devotion of this lay nun, is moved by it, and feels intimately towards her. If the forehead of the Great Sun Buddha and the forehead of this lay nun were to come together, then hers would assume a golden hue. If the bosom of the Great Sun Buddha and the bosom of this lay nun were to come together, then hers would assume a golden hue. If the abdomen of the Great Sun Buddha and the abdomen of this lay nun were to come together, then hers would assume a golden hue. If the navel of the Great Sun Buddha . . ."

As he was about to continue, the lay priest supervising the service and monitoring from the corridor could not bear to listen. "What in the world are you talking about?" he called out in severe reprimand. "This is in bad taste and impossible to listen to. Get down from the lectern!"

"How can he stop the sermon now without finishing it?" asked the nun. "Hurry and get on with it."

The celebrant looked up at the ceiling in perplexity. "What shall I do? The lay priest tells me to step down while the nun tells me to press on. I've never been in such a difficult situation." It was indeed an amusing state of affairs.

I hesitate to mention the names of those involved since some of their grandchildren are alive today. But this actually happened. Perhaps we can generalize that if one goes into detail about the donor's circumstances, such difficulties are likely to occur. And when a priest tries too hard to please a donor, they are inevitable. It's a pity!

In Shinano a similar incident occurred. At a memorial service held after the death of a land steward in Sarashina by his three daughters, an old monk who knew them well gave the sermon. He complimented each of the donors in turn for a special act of filial piety which they had performed. But his words could also be construed as indecent remarks, and were a general embarrassment.

In Kai province a certain Uma no Shiro succeeded as head of the household on his father's death. At the memorial service the preacher discussed the donor's merits and his close affection with his father. The remarks became so embarrassing that the audience fled. Even Shiro tried to escape but was prevented by someone sitting nearby. "If you don't listen to it, who will?" he was told.

A nun in Mutsu province lost her son called Saemon no Jō and held a memorial service, at which the celebrant spoke of the causes of resemblance between parent and child. "The causal relationship between mother and child is splendid. When the father and mother have relations, a boy is produced through love on the part of the mother; a girl, when that of the father predominates. If at the time of conception the father's mood is ecstatic, the child will resemble him; if this is the mother's mood, then the child will resemble her. Since Saemon looked exactly like his mother, she must of had a good time conceiving him!"

It is embarrassing to go into so much detail about a person who sponsors a religious service.

6:2 The Nun who Praised a Preacher

A nun from Shinano province held a Buddhist service in Kamakura and asked a monk from Jufukuji, whom she had known since childhood, to deliver the sermon. The donor found it to her liking. On returning from the service she extolled the monk to a group of ladies.

"Since I raised him from the time he was a little boy and used to run around with his member hanging out, I was wondering how far he would go. And then he stood erect at the lectern. I had not expected anything extraordinary, but he did very well. As I was thinking to myself how wonderfully he was doing, he pushed forward ardently to the end. I felt as though I had lost my senses."

A truly unhappy choice of words! It became the topic of conversation in Kamakura. I forget the names of the nun and the priest involved.

6:3 The Preacher's Poor Choice of Words

In Mutsu a priest held a dedication service for a grave tablet (sotoba). He was thoroughly incompetent, but the ceremony had to be performed. And so he improvised.

"With respect to the sotoba, *I should speak concerning the reason for its name, and its religious function. It is called* soto- *because it stands outside* (soto); *and* -ba *refers to the sound it makes when it falls down The top of the* sotoba *cannot be sharpened enough, so that it may pentrate through the bottom of the pot of hell!"*

There was a preacher like this in Shinano province. An association of farmers whose object was to promote good works had constructed a bridge. One of their number having passed away, they decided to erect a grave tablet in his memory, and the priest spoke at the dedication ceremony. "The merit of having constructed this bridge and this grave tablet join together. If the spirit of this man is not born into the Pure Land, may my head be cut off with seven slices!"
For a vow this is really too much.

6:4 A Humble Donation for a Preacher

A preacher in Yamato province went to many poor homes; and, as he was easily approached, he was invited everywhere to give sermons. Once he was invited by a woodcutter in Ohara in Yamashiro province. While the monk waited after the sermon for his donation, he heard a rustling sound. He realized that it was out of the question that he would be presented with a robe. Still, it would be an elegant gesture in such rustic surroundings. When he finally looked to see what was placed before him, he was astonished to find a bundle of dried taro stalks. But though he received taro stalks (imo no kuki; in the on *reading,* zuiki), *he felt no gratitude (*zuiki).

Once he spoke at an old temple in Yamato province which had no ceremonial platform, so he seated himself on an old drum. In the middle of the sermon the drum head split and the monk fell in. His son, who was also a priest, witnessed this. It is a true story.

6:5 The Long Sermon

In Hitachi Province lived a Shingon Master called the Ajari Kanchi, who chanted the sutras and performed other rites with great refinement and charm; only he did not realize that his parishioners were severely critical of his long sermons.

Now this priest was invited to be the celebrant at a service dedicating a temple building. Ceremonial dance music (*bugaku*) had been prearranged and there were to be child dancers, so an unusually large number of spectators of both sexes assembled for this rare event. They were waiting for the sermon to end, but it dragged on until the sun was going down and the audience was bored stiff.

"My, oh my! Will this sermon never end?" some asked. To which others replied: "Not as long as that calamity is in the pulpit!" Finally after the sun had set, the spectators simply called for the dance, and the music started up.

[*The Way and Its Power*] says: "The Sage has no heart of his own; he uses the heart of the people as his heart."[286] In all matters we should pay attention to the feelings of others and follow what is opportune to the occasion. It is a principle of Buddhism that it be expounded respectfully in a tranquil place of assembly in accordance with the disposition of the audience. At a service with dancing and music, one should use common sense. The *Lotus Sutra* says: "Even to those who love the Dharma, he [the bodhisattva] is not to preach overmuch."[287] There can be too much of even a good thing; we should simply act in accordance with the feelings of others. This attitude applies not only to explaining the scriptures but also to being a guest. An ancient said that if you go to someone's house, you should not stay long even if your host asks you to. Whatever the circumstances, you are to return home quickly.

In Nara someone had been marooned by a heavy rain and had become a house guest for two or three days. He was in the toilet when he heard several of his host's servants washing burdock at a nearby pond. Servants from a neighboring house called to them over a fence.

"What are you doing there?"

"We're washing this long burdock to serve to the calamity who's staying so long!" came the reply.

When he heard this, the man quickly returned home in the rain. Even though the master of the house did not mind his staying, the servants considered him a nuisance.

We should be considerate and pay attention to the feelings of others. General insensitivity to others is the rule which governs animal behavior. The basic purpose of preaching is to elucidate our other lives of past and future in terms of the present; we should bring people to the Buddha's Law by knowing their dispositions, acting so as to arouse them to a desire for enlightenment. We should never act without entering into the feelings of others and without doing what is appropriate to the occasion. Make careful note of this.

6:6 Speaking to Donors According to Circumstances

Fishermen in Ōtsu invited many preachers to officiate at their Buddhist services, but few were satisfactory. But one of the preachers knew what they wanted. "The fact that you catch fish in Lake Biwa is meritorious,"[288] he said. "This lake is the eye of the Great Tendai Teacher (Chih-i, 538-597), and to remove dust from the eye of a Buddha is a virtuous act." This pleased the fishermen, who made generous donations.

At the dedication of a temple built by fishermen in a northern province, the celebrant did not satisfy them. But there was one who knew what they wanted. "You who have contributed to this temple will without doubt attain birth in the Pure Land because to recite the name of the Buddha is the way to get there. Morning and night you chant 'ami, ami' with your fishing nets (ami), and the waves answer, 'tabu, tabu.' So you are always chanting the nembutsu: (Namu) amidabu (tsu)." This pleased the fishermen, who made generous offerings.

If a preacher uses these tricks in the hope of getting a good livelihood, he preaches from a distorted viewpoint (cf., 6:17). But if, like the bodhisattva, he employs them altruistically as devices to lead men to the good, then they are acceptable.

6:7 The Lecturer's Happy Remark

At an Eight Expoundings of the Lotus (hakkō) ceremony held at the Kiyomizu temple, the lecturer was an old monk eighty years of age. During the sermon on the first day he stepped down from the platform and then reascended to continue the proceedings. Then, during the sermon on the following day, he looked up perplexed.

"Ah. What shall I do?" he remarked.

The audience asked what the trouble was.

"Yesterday I passed gas induced by stool; today I passed stool induced by gas."

The audience left in disgust, the platform was cleaned and the sermon was terminated. It was a clever remark but a disgraceful thing to do. When an old man goes out to work, care must be taken.

6:8 The Preacher Who Praised a Breaking of Wind

When the Hexagonal Hall[289] was destroyed by fire, a series of daily sermons was given to raise funds for its reconstruction. In a large audience which had assembled on the day that Shōgaku[290] spoke, a young lady-in-waiting by the worship platform dozed off and broke wind so loudly that it was heard throughout the hall. Moreover, the odor was so overpowering that people lost interest in the proceedings.

The celebrant was undaunted by the noise. " 'The sounding flutes, of many reeds or of one only, and lyres, mounted on stands or not, and lutes and cymbals'[291] all produce a wondrous sound, but they have no scent. The incense of precious woods and resins, on the other hand, have a fragrant aroma but they make no sound. But to-day's worthy exhalation has both sound and fragrance; hear it and note its aroma!"

On being so excessively praised, the woman removed one of her garments. "Along with this," she said, "make it an offering to the Buddha from Lady Orange Blossom."[292]

Even the unpraiseworthy has praised! This is true eloquence. The lady was pleased with what had happened and began to call herself "Lady Orange Blossom", as was only fitting.

But what a god-forsaken offering!

During an Amida Welcome Service (mukaekō; cf., S&P 10A:9) held at a village in Yamato province the performer dressed as Kannon was approaching the Human World (shabadō). *The Lotus Platform had already sunk out of sight, and the performer was touching the ground with the tips of his fingers when he broke wind loudly, although the sound was muffled by the chanting of the* nembutsu. *But the actor playing the bodhisattva Seishi giggled and before long the* nembutsu *stopped and everyone burst out laughing.*

During the Kanki period (1229-1231) a woodcutter in Kazusa province, seeing a farmer in a neighboring village planting rice, asked how he had the energy to work in view of the current famine. The farmer replied that he subsisted on the wild (and usually constipating) Nawashiro berry. The woodcutter consumed a large quantity of the berries on an empty stomach and became fatally constipated.

"I don't mind dying,"he remarked. "But my swollen stomach presses unbearably against my chest and I cannot say the nembutsu. *All I want to do is to break wind once before I die." And with these last words he expired. If, because of the famine, he had died thinking of food, then perhaps he would have fallen into the path of the hungry ghosts. But under the circumstances he probably fell into the animal realm, to become a fart-bug (hehirimushi). Or, if he merely changed his human form, perhaps he was reborn like the lady of the Hexagonal Hall or the Kannon of the Amida's Welcome Service.*

6:9 Benefit from Abuse at an Expounding of the Precepts[293]

Once when the Preceptor Eichō, founder of Serada Chōrakuji on Nitta Manor in Kōzuke province was speaking to a large group of people at a meeting to expound the precepts, he lamented the current decline in the observance of the regulations.

"Although monks today talk of receiving the precepts, they do not know what it means to observe them. While half-heartedly calling themselves priests, taking alms, and performing services, it is a strange breed of priest which abounds throughout the country, bringing disgrace to the disciples of the Buddha. Some have families and others bear arms, or go hunting and fishing. In these wretched latter days there are those who do not even know the meaning of the word 'repentance.'

"I see one from where I am sitting. I look and ask myself if he is a layman—but he wears a priest's scarf. He is neither adult, child, priest, nor menial. He isn't even shit, but something like diarrhea!"

Because his remarks were directed at a fierce mountain ascetic who was present, some of the monks feared that he might be made to pay for them. But since he did not speak out of spite but out of compassion, they brought forth a sympathetic response. The mountain ascetic repented and abandoned his worldly ways.

6:10 The Preacher Who Fell Among Thieves

In the capital (Rakuyō) lived a celebrated monk known as "The Kiyomizu Priest"; some say it was Shōgaku (cf., S&P 6:8). Returning to his quarters one dark night with many donations, he was waylaid by robbers. The monk harangued the robbers all night and they were so moved by his eloquence and sincerity that they became lay priests.

His arguments were those of Hsüan-tsang (Genjō, 602-664), known as Tripiṭaka, who crossed over to India in order to bring Buddhism back to the Chinese.[294] Hsüan-tsang was seized by the inhabitants of a country who worshipped evil spirits and was about to be offered as a sacrifice. Entering deep meditation he rose in spirit to the Tuṣita heaven to ask Maitreya for help. There was a great storm and the people trembled with fear. Hsüan-tsang then exhorted them: "Why, for the sake of a body that lives but a short time like lightning or the morning dew, do you create endless suffering for yourselves?" With such words as these even the foolish robbers attained religious awakening.

Long ago in China the pirate Tai Yüan (Taien) stopped a boat in which the Prime Minister was riding. Seeing him to be man of ability, the minister remarked that it was sad that a man of such competence should be involved in piracy. Tai Yüan had a change of heart, went with the minister to see the emperor, and was made a general.[295]

Nembutsu *devotees are too scornful of all religious devotions but the* nembutsu, *and too tolerant of the flesh. There is a need for serious religious concern. In the* Great Cessation and Insight *Chih-i says that even scholarly pursuits must be abandoned; how much more so does this apply to worldly affairs! Chi-ts'ang (Kichizō, 643-712) speaks of learning being for the sake of practice. Practice, however, is the essence of liberation from this world of illusion. Hui-ssu (Eshi, 514-577) says that the essence of Buddhism is simply practice, not literary activity. None of the sects contradict this notion. In the* Shōryōshū *[or Seireishū; see S&P 5B:9, and note 276], Kūkai states that the esoteric teaching is transmitted from mind to mind, and that words are rubble, dregs. Even more so is Zen the sect which does not rely on words. And the Amidist sects teach single-minded devotion to the* nembutsu, *as is expressed in the* Hanjusan.

Today's Pure Land devotees for the most part vilify other practices and meritorious deeds as so much busywork; but they have no fear of worldliness. This is very foolish and goes against the spirit of Buddhism which is "to avoid evil and do good."[296] *In the preface to the* Hanjusan, *Shan-tao (Zendō, 613-681) says not to slander other sects. In his* Praise of Birth in the Pure Land[297] *he does counsel against becoming involved with practices other than the* nembutsu. *But this is so that the devotee can attain single-minded devotion, and he does not condemn other practices. Life is a dream and deep understanding is difficult to attain. So we should be alert.*

An ancient has remarked that there is no difference between the reality of yesterday and the dream of today. [In the Commentary on the Great Wisdom Sutra*] Nāgārjuna (Ryūju) says that one who has no intention to practice the Buddha's Law is simply an animal wearing the skin of a man. We should heed the admonitions of the founders of the various sects. Even foolish robbers, hearing their teachings, are awakened and repent of their sins.*

6:11 The Robber Who Inquired About the Sacred Teaching

Recently in Kamakura lived a Shingon master known, I believe, as the Ajari Mimbu, who served at the Wakamiya Shrine. One night when he was returning with a large donation he was surprised by five or six robbers. One of them was a priest and questioned Mimbu about Shingon doctrine. When it came to the secret mysteries of the sect, however, Mimbu would reveal nothing, even though the robber held a large sword to his chest.

"You are a true believer," remarked the robber, handing him ten bundles of cash. "Here is a donation." This happened only recently.

6:12 The Lowly Monk's Temple Dedication

In Shimōsa province a man called Nakanuma no Awaji no Kami built an oratory in memory of his father but made no arrangements to engage a celebrant for the dedication service. When the time arrived he instructed a menial monk who had prepared hot water during the thousand days of purification to strike the gong and conduct the service: "Say 'Hear this, Buddha! This is the oratory built for the late Nakanuma,' and strike the gong." The trembling monk did as he was told and was presented with a handsome donation.

"The Buddha, who understands my way of thinking, will hear what this monk has to say better than the flattery of some famous priest," remarked the man. "He has served me for a thousand days, and so I have invited him to be the celebrant."

The oratory still stands today.

The leader of the service dedicating the Amida Hall of Lord Uji's (Fujiwara Yorimichi, 992-1074) Byōdōin was a monk from Mount Hiei. Commenting on the donor's merit during the sermon he said: "For having built this temple he will fall into hell!" Later when he was asked what was to be done, the monk replied that Lord Uji should compensate those who had been inconvenienced by the construction. This he did.

6:13 Taking the Donation Without Giving the Sermon

A nun in Kamakura held a pre-death rite (gyakushu) and invited a monk who was not accustomed to preaching to perform the service. He accepted, perhaps because he wanted the donation. The monk ascended the ceremonial platform, performed the service, and then it was time for him to discourse on its significance. Frantically but in vain he searched his pockets for his notes, as smoke began to rise from his head, like the top of a boiled potato. Finally he was told to step down from the platform, and as he did, the notes fell from the folds of his skirt and were blown away by the wind. He simply picked them up and sat down. And when he was offered a donation, he accepted it without demur. It was impossible for him to say a word from memory. But, as people observed at the time, embarrassment rarely proves fatal.

A certain evangelist had his notes suddenly blown up into the branches of a citron tree and was unable to retrieve them. "The details of the matter under consideration are to be found in the branches of the citron tree," he remarked, descending from the platform. He took the donation.

The head monk at a mountain temple was incompetent, but the other monks sympathized with the old man's bungling. Invited to perform a service, he replied that he was not capable.

"We know all about it," said the patron. "We will write the sermon down on paper, and you just read it off."

"I can't even do that," was his reply.

"In that case, sit below the lectern and read it while the Amida Sutra *is being recited."* This he did, but the congregation never heard a word of what he said. He took the donation.

The mistress of a household in Shinano province asked a monk attached to the private chapel to perform a service before the guardian Buddha. The monk pleaded that he was utterly incapable of delivering a sermon, but the woman told him to consecrate a new image, performing the service in any way he wanted. The monk agreed to do so as long as there was to be no audience for the sermon. But when he ascended the ceremonial platform, a group of ladies entered the room to amuse themselves at his expense.

"I won't do it if there is an audience," said the monk, descending from the platform. The ladies retired, but every time he returned to the platform they came back in. In the end the monk did not perform the service.

I heard the incident from someone who witnessed it. The monk is to be commended for not taking the donation.

6:14 The Sermon at Saga

When the Shakadō (at the Seiryōji) in Saga burned down (1217), a series of fifty daily sermons was given to raise funds for its restoration. After they had gone on for more than forty days, Jōhen (1166-1224) spoke.

"Śākyamuni stated that all sentient beings are his children. Our worldly parents benefit us only in this life, but Śākyamuni's compassion extends much further. Now when the house of one's worldly parents burns down, the child rebuilds it—though he be only a single man. How much more so when the house of our True Parent burns down should we rebuild it." Jōhen went on to urge that those who wished to make a contribution bring it forward immediately, before their ardor cooled. The offerings were many, and in a short time the building was reconstructed.

6:15 Shōgaku's Remarks Toward a Donor

A request written in Sanskrit was sent from the Oki Palace[298] to Kōya no Omuro (Dōjo, Gotoba's second son, 1196-1249) requesting that a pre-death rite (gyakushu; cf., 6:13) be performed on the exiled sovereign's behalf for forty-eight days by Kōya no Omuro and the (second) son (Gotakakura, 1179-1223) of the late Jimyōin Cloistered Soveriegn (Takakura, 1161-1181). During the service Seal-of-the-Law Shōgaku (1167-1235; or, Seikaku) made some startling remarks.

"Gotoba is a sovereign who will receive favorable recompense for his actions; Jimyōin (Takakura) will not. Gotoba was exiled to a distant province (Oki), but used the occasion to expiate his former karma. His now having

*rites performed for the afterlife makes his future prospects bright. But
Takakura passed his years unprofitably and his rewards will be unfortunate. "*

*Adversity has its uses; misfortune in this life may be a blessing with
respect to the religious life. Cloistered Sovereign Goshirakawa (1127–1192),
expecting to be killed, retired into the Toba Palace and prepared to meet his
end. This was a blessing in that it led him to the Way of the Buddha.*

6:16 Nōsetsubō's Sermon

In Saga lived a preacher named Nōsetsubō who was a monk of
considerable eloquence. His neighbor was a prosperous nun who ran
a wine shop. Nōsetsubō, being very fond of spirits, spent all his
donations on it.

On one occasion, having run up a bill, Nōsetsubō presented her
with a donation which he had received. Then, since the nun had a
Buddhist service to be performed, she invited Nōsetsubō to be the
celebrant. The people in the neighborhood got wind of the matter
and spoke to the preacher.

"This good nun sells fine wine," they told him, "but there is
only one problem. She has no qualms about cutting it with water. In
today's sermon please dwell on the wickedness of selling watered-
down wine. It's for our benefit as well as yours."

"Even before you called this to my attention, I have been aware
of the problem and it has troubled me of late," replied Nōsetsubō.
"I will speak my mind on the matter." So for his explanation of the
scriptural reading, Nōsetsubō gave merely a cursory outline. Then
he called to mind all he could about the evils of adulterating wine,
relating them in detail and even making up a few things which were
not true.

After the sermon the nun filled up a large tub with wine, inviting everyone to help himself. Nōsetsubō, at the urging of the congregation, took the first cupful and drank it down.

"How shameful of me!" the nun was saying. "I didn't realize it
was sinful to add water to wine." And everyone was thinking to
himself how fine it would be that day, since it was good wine even
when she added some water.

"Ahhh!" exclaimed Nōsetsubō. People wondered in anticipation how delicious it must be. "See how he is enjoying himself!"

"Lately you have been serving wine flavored with a little
water," observed Nōsetsubō. "But this is water flavored with a little
wine!"

"So it is," replied the nun. "Since I heard you say that it was wrong to add water to wine, I have added wine to the water."

Indeed, filling a large pail of water, she had merely added a small potful of spirits. Did she do it out of fun? Or was her thinking warped?

So too in Buddhism, when words are wrongly understood heresy arises, as in the case of the Tachikawa sect, which advocates sexual relations as a means to enlightenment. Condoning ordinary behavior and performing acts of delusion are contrary to the Law of the Buddha. The Buddha Head Sutra (Butchōkyō) states that disasters will visit the country where such things occur.

6:17 Preaching for a Livelihood

The expression "improper livelihood through preaching" (jamyō seppō) comes from the Buddha Treasury Sutra (cf., S&P 4:1). It is also called "acting merely for profit" (ushotoku). Laymen think of this as giving sermons with the hope of getting alms. But the sutra says that to preach about the phenomenal without speaking about the Formless Reality (musō no kotowari) is to make an "improper livelihood through preaching," "acting merely for profit." Such preaching is a great crime. The Sutra of Mediation on the True Law (Shōbōnenshokyō, T. 721) says that to expound the Law for the sake of others in order to cause their roots of merit to grow without seeking fame and profit for oneself is best; to preach from a desire to surpass others is second best; and to do so for fame and profit is third best. This assumes, of course, that the Law is being correctly expounded, although from ulterior motives. In the Buddha Treasury Sutra the Buddha states that after serving another Buddha of great virtue for many eons he attained the rank of Wheel-Rolling King (Cakravartin, Tenrinnō), but not enlightenment. Only after having come to realize the true significance of expounding the Law did he become a Buddha. The Sutra of Ten Cakras (Jūringyō, T. 410, 411) says that in the Latter Days of the Law a monk of genuine understanding who expounds the Law correctly can accomplish good, although he himself may be degenerate. The Sutra on Viewing the Mind-Ground calls such a monk a "priestly jewel" (sōhō). And Kumārajīva (344-413), after being involved with women (cf., S&P 4:2), remarked that his body was like mud, but the words he spoke were like lotus flowers.

6:18 The Power of the Surplice

On the seventeenth day of the seventh month in Bun'ei 7 (1270) lightning struck an inn at Oritsu in Owari province, injuring three horses which *were walking in the street. Stampeding into a small house, they clambered over the back of a monk who was playing backgammon* (sugoroku) *dressed in a thin kimono and wearing a surplice* (kesa). *The kimono was torn to shreds, but the surplice was not damaged at all. The monk too escaped injury. I heard of the incident on the following day, when he happened to be in the neighborhood on business.*

The power of the surplice is discussed in detail in the Sutra of Ten Cakras, *the* Compassion Flower Sutra *(Hikekyō, T. 157), the* Sutra of Great Compassion (Daihikyō, *T. 380), and the* Sutra on Viewing the Mind-Ground. *The power is properly to be found in the regulation surplice; the short one which we see today is not regulation. However, the surplice also has power today. The* Great Collection of Sutras *(Daijikkyō, T. 397) says that it is to be found at the hem. The* Mind-Ground *states that if one ties himself with a single thread from a surplice, he will not be threatened by poisonous dragons when crossing the broad seas.*

In the Sutra of Ten Cakras *it is related that a monk who had violated the regulations was sent off to an island inhabited by hungry ghosts. But he escaped being devoured because of the power of his surplice.*

Long ago lived a lion called Kensei who had golden markings on his fur. A hunter, wishing to skin the lion and present his pelt to the king, assumed the appearance of a monk but concealed a bow and arrow in his surplice. Seeing a monk, the lion came forth tamely. But when the hunter drew his bow to shoot, the lion realized his mistake and rushed forward to devour him. Then he reflected that even if a person's intention is not good, he who wears the surplice will eventually become a Buddha. The lion, who was Śākyamuni in an earlier existence, met his end steadfastly.[299]

The nun Keshiki attained the fruit of arhatship after donning a surplice in sport.[300]

The deity Itenshōgun told Nan-shan (Tao-hsüan, 596–667) that the spirit of penitence was greater among monks in China than in India and that accordingly the gods and buddhas tended to be lenient with them. Although the observance of the precepts is slack in Japan, the surplice still has its virtues. The sutra says that "a country without gold treasures silver; and land without silver cherishes copper—and so on to the point where even wax may become valuable. So also in a country without good monks: without considering whether or not they observe the regulations, we should respect even the appearance of goodness." The lion Kensei respected the outer form without looking into the state of the hunter's mind.

At Nakashima in Owari province when a large old tree was being cut down to build a temple, the spirits of the tree took possession of a nearby householder and asked him to have the monks stop. The man protested that since he had nothing to do with the matter, they should bother the monks.

"Having been touched by the wind stirred up by their surplices and robes, and having heard the sound of their incantations, we are relieved of torment. So how can we disturb them? Please just relay our message."
The monks spared the tree. This was over ten years ago.

The same thing happened at Ajima in Owari province. A monk was cutting a tree to repair one of the halls when the spirit of the tree took possession of a man.
"I fear the monk and cannot speak to him," said the spirit. "Please tell him to stop cutting the tree." This happened recently during the Bun'ei period (1264-1275).

We should establish karmic affinities with the Buddha's Law and respect the surplice as the representative of the teaching. The Great Teacher of Kōya said that although preachers of the Law commit the most serious crimes from morning to night, we should not slander them or, through them, the Law which they propound.[301].

A preacher once remarked: "Nowadays the burden of sin is light. Because people everywhere chant the nembutsu, *hell has disappeared."*
"In that case," replied a donor, "there is no need to accululate merit. Let's not give this monk all of the donation—just a third or a fourth."
"Even so, gentlemen," continued the preacher, "this does not mean that there is no hell at all. The pot of hell is wide and deep. It used to be that when one was boiling in it, there might be an occasional cooling breeze and one could take a breather after he had been thoroughly boiled. But nowadays the pot you enter is cracked and will not hold water, and there is no respite from torment. So it behooves you to pray for your enlightenment in the afterlife."

7:1 Two Whose Hearts Were Free of Envy

A nobleman went down to his estate in the country, and, on returning to the capital accompanied by a courtesan, sent a messenger ahead to notify his wife. "I am returning with someone. Since she will be made uncomfortable by your presence, please leave."

Even after having been addressed so cruelly, the woman did not show the least sign of bitterness. "The master is returning with another woman. Prepare for her arrival," she announced, giving detailed instructions. She removed everything that might prove embarrassing; then, after seeing that every last detail was suitably taken care of, the wife withdrew.

On being apprised of what had happened, the courtesan was dumbfounded and spoke to the nobleman. "Your wife's behavior reveals a most gracious disposition, as I have been informed. Having seen what she has done, how could I live here in her place? I would surely forfeit the divine protection. So call your wife back as before, and provide me with other accommodations where you can visit me from time to time. That will be all right. Otherwise, how could I stay here even for one day?"

After the courtesan repeatedly sent the nobleman written pledges[302] in support of the wife, the nobleman bowed to reason. Recalling his wife's unusual generosity, he sent a messenger to bring her back. At first he received no reply, but after repeated appeals, she returned to live with him. The courtesan being also a person of sensitivity, the two women shared each other's company and were inseparable. Their attitude is unprecedented.

In Tōtomi province a divorced wife was already mounted on her horse and starting to leave when her husband said: "It is customary that when a woman is divorced, she is to take with her something of her choosing from the house. So take whatever you like."

"What could I want, having lost such a fine man as yourself?" she replied. The appearance of the woman smiling without rancour was so endearing that the husband relented, and they were separated only by death.

While we may say that our being disliked by others is caused by events in former lives, it also depends on one's present disposition. "Hsi Shih loved a river and Momu hated a mirror."[303] Hsi Shih, who had good features, saw her reflection in the river and loved it; Momu, whose features were unsightly, saw that her reflection in the mirror was ugly, and so disliked the mirror. The excellence, however, lay in Hsi Shih's features, not in the river; likewise, the fault lay not in the mirror but in Momu's unsightly appearance.

So also, without reproaching others, consider that your present state is influenced both by the karma which you have created in past and present lives, and by your own state of mind; and be neither angry nor bitter. It is the way of the world that many are deeply jealous, quick to anger, and suspicious; they nag and alienate others, put on a sour face, turn red with anger, make their eyes glint, and use violent language. As a result, their attitude becomes increasingly disagreeable and their disposition that of a demon. Some are reborn as malignant spirits and others as serpents. And their state becomes progressively worse. But if we learn from what has been handed down from the ancient men of sensibility, in the present life they will bestow upon us the power of commanding respect and love, and in the future we shall certainly escape the calamity of rebirth as a serpent.

With his first wife still on the premises, a man took another woman to be his wife and brought her home to stay with him. He lived with his new wife separated from the former only by a single partition.[304] On hearing the sound of deer crying one autumn night, he asked his first wife if she too heard it. She replied with a poem:

Ware mo shika	Once I was thus
Nakite zo hito ni	Called to and cherished
Koirareba	By another;
Ima koso yoso ni	But now I only hear
Koe bakari kake	His voice from afar.[305]

The man was touched and returned to live with her, dismissing his second wife. If we are neither bitter, jaundiced, nor resentful, then with deep affection we will quite naturally realize our wishes.

A man in Shinano province, hearing that an admirer was frequenting his wife's quarters, concealed himself in the ceiling. The admirer came as usual; and as the man was observing the two talking and carrying on, he missed his footing and fell to the floor, injuring his hip and losing consciousness. The admirer picked the man up in arms and nursed him back to health, helping him in every possible way. As they were both mild-tempered individuals, the affair was overlooked, and, according to report, they became close friends.

In Kyoto a monk known as the Ajari of Asahi paid frequent visits to the quarters of the wife of a certain Doctor of Astrology.[306] On one occasion when he had slipped into the room, knowing that the woman's husband was absent, the husband suddenly returned.

There was no way to escape unnoticed and the husband, coming upon the Ajari opening a sliding door in the west wall of the apartment, accosted him.

Ayashiku mo	It is incredible
Nishi ni asahi no	To see the Morning Sun (*asahi*)
Izuru kana	Rising in the West!

To which the Ajari responded:

| *Temmon hakase* | But how could this be observed |
| *Ika ni miruran* | By a Doctor of Astrology? |

The husband called to him to stop, and together they made merry composing linked-verse. The incident was overlooked, and the Ajari frequently visited the man's house.

There was a preacher of the Pure Land school who traveled on foot throughout the provinces. The wife of a certain Land Steward fell ill from the deep love she felt for this priest, and, after some days, believed that she was about to die.

"If to no purpose I were to lose my life by keeping this matter bottled up inside," she reasoned, "then even in the next life the penalties would be severe." And so she confessed everything to her husband of many years.

"For you thus to confide in me is the result of our long-standing relationship," he replied. "Anyone can have a problem like this, and I am most grateful that you have completely opened your heart to me. It would be regrettable were you to lose your life unnecessarily over this. Without telling anyone, I will call the priest, inform him privately, and make the arrangements."

The man called the priest for an audience and told him the facts in detail. "We have many children, and because of our affection over the years, I would feel sad to lose her. Please save her life." The priest replied that he understood.

In anticipation the wife tidied up and waited. Then the priest came and looked her squarely in the face. "So this is the shameless woman! You have many children; and do you think that you are still good-looking at your age to be hankering after this beggar monk? What an unpleasant countenance. How disgusting!" And he brushed her aside and left the room.

All the earlier fondness and lust vanished and she recovered from her illness, to the delight of her husband.[307]

7:2 The Girl Who Became a Serpent Through Delusive Attachment

In Kamakura a young girl became sick with love over a page who lived at the monks' quarters on Wakamiya Street. But the boy showed no interest and she finally died of love. Her parents placed her cremated remains in a box to be sent to the Zenkōji in Nagano.

Then the page went mad and was put away in a small room. He seemed to be conversing, and his parents peeked through a small crack to see him facing a large snake. Finally the boy died; and when they placed his remains in the coffin to be buried in the mountains west of Wakamiya, there in the box was a large snake entwined around his body. They were interred together.

When the parents of the girl went to divide up her remains so that they might retain a portion at a temple in Kamakura, they discovered that the bones had all changed into small snakes. The parents disclosed this to the monk whom they asked to perform the memorial service. This actually happened within the last ten years. I know the names of the people concerned, but I hesitate to make them known for fear of causing embarrassment.

Nothing is to be so feared as attachment and desire. A nun married off her own husband to a young woman. Living in the same house and depending on the woman for support, the nun concealed the fact that her fingers had turned into snakes. The Collected Tales of Pious Resolution *(Hosshin-shū, ca. 1216) records such happenings in antiquity.*

7:3 The Woman Who Tried to Marry Her Stepdaughter to a Serpent

In Shimōsa province a woman took her eleven or twelve year old step-daughter to a large lake and offered her in marriage to the resident deity. The lake was rough from the blowing wind as the woman repeated her request, and the frightened girl took to her heels and quickly ran back to her house. As she was telling her father what had happened, the stepmother rushed in, followed by a large serpent, its head high and its tongue darting in and out. But the father was a man of spirit and he addressed the creature.

"This girl is my daughter and the woman is only her stepmother. How can you take my daughter without my permission? Take the stepmother instead."

As the serpent crawled toward the woman the father and daughter escaped. It is said to have wrapped itself around the stepmother, who also changed into a serpent. This happened one summer during the Bun'ei period

(1264-1274). There was a rumor that the serpents were to appear on the third day of the eighth month of that year. The wind and rain were unusually rough on the day in question but I didn't hear if they actually came forth. Spite toward others soon rebounds to one's self—no doubt about it!

7:4 The Snake Who Violated a Man's Wife

Some years ago in a mountain village in Tōtōmi province the wife of an official was violated by a snake during his absence. The man returned to find the snake lying with her, and chased it away with a stick.

"I ought to kill you, but this time I will let you off. If you ever do this again," he warned the snake, "your life is forfeit."

A few days later the couple was visited by a large company of snakes, and the husband went into the parlor to confront them.

"Why have you come here?" he asked. "One day while my wife was sleeping late, she was violated by a snake. Seeing this before my very eyes I should have killed him, but out of compassion I let him go with a warning. Do you think that I am guilty of some fault? Men and beasts may differ, but the ethical realities do not."

At this, each of the serpents, beginning with the largest, took a bite at the culprit until he was chewed to pieces. The snakes returned to the mountain and the couple had no further trouble. By arguing the reasonableness of his position, the man avoided the disaster which would have befallen him had he defended himself by force. We should take care not to harm living creatures.

7:5 The Man Who Died Suddenly After Killing a Snake

In Shimotsuke province a man saw a large snake put its head out of a hole in a tree and he shot it with an arrow. Later as he was walking beside a large pond, the man saw a big ten-foot snake with an arrow in its neck swimming across the water. With another arrow he killed it. But the man never reached home, for presently he became deranged and died babbling. I heard the name of the man and the place where this happened only recently. It was rumored that the snake was a deity of a certain shrine.

In the same province lived a man who caught fish at a certain pond. From a hole beneath its banks they came forth in large numbers, and the man peered in to discover that they emerged from a small pot. While he was pondering the strangeness of the matter, a small foot-long snake emerged, which the man impaled on a skewer, sticking it in the ground by the side of the road. He returned home and was cooking his fish when the skewered snake appeared. The man killed it, but as he did, another and then another appeared. The man died raving.

7:6 A Jealous Woman's Possession by an Avenging Spirit

The wife of a Kyoto nobleman, jealous of her husband's paramour, sent a carriage for the lady saying that the husband had summoned her. The lady was with child, and when she arrived the jealous wife confined her in a small area and had a hot iron applied to her stomach. Then she was returned to her mother's house barely alive, where she expired as she was being carried from the carriage. Her mother made pilgrimages to various shrines, lamenting and vowing revenge, and presently passed away.

The jealous wife was possessed by the mother's spirit, her body became bloated, and she died in agony. It is said that the spirit of the mother continues to torment her from life to life. I hesitate to record this, but I suppose there is no harm to be done since I do not know the precise circumstances nor the names of the people involved. I mention it merely to show the operation of karma, and not to describe the error of a particular person. It is indeed foolish not to realize that to harm others is to harm oneself.

7:7 Retribution for Killing a Man

The retainer of a Kyoto samurai discovered a servant stealing a halberd, tied him to a post, and taunted him as he cut the man's body with the tip of the weapon. Although the servant pleaded to be dispatched at once, the retainer tortured him for three days until he died. This occurred within the forty-nine day memorial period (chūin) after the death of one of the samurai's parents, and the retainer had been instructed to pardon the man. When the samurai heard that he had been disobeyed, he expelled the retainer, who then went to live with relatives in Owari province. But presently he is said to have felt a stabbing over his entire body and he died miserably.

Karma is a fearsome matter and the taking of life will be requited. The Sūtra [of Meditation on the True Law?] describes the tortures of hell for those who have taken life. The inexorability of moral causality is like a shadow following an object, or the echo of a sound.

7:8 Wickedness Requited

A menial, coveting the horse of a fellow-servant, dragged his rival from his mount with the help of an accomplice one dark night and bound him.

"Our master has ordered me to slit your throat," he said. The man pleaded that he had done no wrong but the wicked servant told him to repeat the nembutsu for the last time and then struck him down, making off with the horse.

Although the man was thought to be dead, he revived and went to his master's house, where he related in detail what had transpired. The two *villains were seized and ordered to be put to death by the injured servant. Thus, the evil of the former night was requited in the morning.*

A samurai who was decapitated at Kamakura sometime during the Bun'ei period (1264–1274) had the previous year taken the head of an innocent man during the Hour of the Monkey (3–5 p.m.) on the seventeenth day of the second month. At exactly the same time the following year he lost his own, no doubt as a result of the resentment and indignation of the man he had murdered.

Two prelates traveling together on the road stopped for lodging. During the night one of them went secretly to the landlord, claimed that his companion was indentured to serve him, and offered to sell him. The landlord agreed.

But the other monk overheard the conversation, and at dawn when his partner had returned to sleep, he went to the landlord.

"Please give me the price which we agreed on earlier this evening. I am in a hurry and my companion is still sleeping." The second monk took the money and left. When the first monk awoke, his partner was gone. Contrary to his plan, he had sold himself into slavery.

7:9 The Rewards of Past Karma

At a mountain temple in Shinano province a dog gave birth to five puppies. Among them was one whom the mother disliked and to whom she refused her milk, growling and snapping at it until it became wretchedly skinny. The residents at the temple were annoyed with her behavior until one night many of them — chief priest, monks, and pages — all had a dream in which the mother dog appeared.

"In my former life I was a courtesan. I had five patrons, four of whom always behaved well toward me so that we had a deep relationship. The fifth one, an insensitive fellow, only caused me trouble, and I passed my life detesting him.

"Now my five puppies are these five patrons. Because four of them formerly were very kind to me, I am delighted that they take my milk and it is no trouble. But as the other was disagreeable, I begrudge him my milk. You may blame me, but that's how I feel. Tomorrow the nephew of that late detested patron will come to take this puppy away. I should not have mentioned this, but I feel that you will not consider my behavior strange if you are aware that it is the natural result of former karma."

Next morning all agreed with what they had seen in their dreams. There was not the slightest disparity among them. Then came a layman who asked for one of the dog's puppies. Recalling that it was just as had been fortold in their dreams the night before, the monks inquired if he knew of a courtesan with a certain name.

"There was such a person. In fact, she was my uncle's mistress."

"Did this lady have many patrons?"

"There were four aside from my uncle with whom she met frequently in spite of his vehement jealousy."

As this completely corraborated their dreams, the monks told the man about them.

"How sad!" he replied. "I will requite my debt of gratitude to my uncle for having raised me. And in any case, he is a nice-looking dog, so I'll take him!" Hugging the puppy in his arms, the man departed.

This is a strange occurrence of recent times. A certain person related the incident to me, stating that those who had had the dream at the mountain temple were still alive.

Although the retributions of past karma should not surprise us, when we hear of such things actually taking place, the operation of moral causality is all the more believable. Whether one is hated or dearly loved may not be simply the result of conditions of the present life. If you are disliked, you should not consider it the fault of others but simply as past karma, moral causality. We should resolve all doubts, abandon delusive thoughts, do away with the obstacles to the attainment of good, erase old evils, and refrain from creating new ones.

7:10 Killing One's Parent of a Former Life

At Tōyama in Mino province the wife of a farmer had a dream in which her deceased father-in-law appeared to her. "Tomorrow morning during the Land Steward's hunt my life will be in jeopardy. If I come to your house, please conceal me. You will recognize me from the fact that I am blind in one eye, as I was in my former life."

On the following day during the hunt a pheasant flew into the house. Her husband was out; but the woman, recognizing the bird as the reincarnation of her father-in-law who had appeared in her dream, hid it in a pot and put the lid on. The hunters came to look around, but it did not occur to them to look there. That night when her husband returned, the woman told him what had happened. They took the pheasant out of the pot to find that it was blind in one eye, as the dream had foretold. When the man stroked it, the bird did not appear to be frightened.

"It is indeed my father," he remarked. "When formerly he was alive as a human being, he was partially blind. Now, from the compassion of our filial relationship, he wishes to be eaten by his child." Then the man killed the bird.

His wife reported the matter to the Land Steward, who expelled the husband for his inhumanity and gave the estate to the woman. I heard that this happened within the last four or five years.

7:11 A Heartless Layman

In Mutsu province lived a greedy farmer who had no consideration even for his wife and child. As a result his wife had run away from him several times, but was always apprehended and returned. Finally she took her child of four or five years and went to see the Land Steward.

"My husband is so greedy that I don't wish to put up with him anymore. I want a decree permitting me to leave him."

"It is the husband who divorces the wife," said the Land Steward. "As a wife, what grounds do you have for divorcing your husband?"

"It would be impossible to list the many times he has been inconsiderate," replied the woman. "But from one example you can infer the rest. The other day my husband went up to a mountain stream and brought back thirty large trout. He cooked some to eat and put the rest aside for pickling. While his only child here clung to his father begging for a bite, all he said was: 'It isn't cooked yet.' He just kept nibbling at it and gave none to the child. Of course it never occurred to him to give me any. I thought he might at least let us have some pickled fish. But he would say, 'It's not ready yet . . . not ready yet.' We didn't get a single piece. From this you can imagine the rest of his behavior."

When the man was summoned to appear he admitted that he had acted just as his wife had said. The Land Steward denounced him as an outrageous fellow and banished him from the region, commending the wife for having lived with the man so long. In sympathy with her plight the Land Steward required her to pay only her own head tax, exempting her from her husband's.

When we consider that the only reason men value wealth is for the sake of wife and child, how heartless indeed is such behavior as that described above. Covetousness is bad economy.

A virtuous monk with many disciples died suddenly without having pro-
vided for the division of his property. His disciples wrangled over its disposi-
tion without even burying the man. After this had gone on for two or three
days and the stench became unbearable, he was interred. The person who
buried him told me about the incident. It happened very recently.

7:12 The Falconer Who Was Devoured by Pheasants

In Shimotsuke province a man who had spent his life hunting became
gravely ill. He cried out that pheasants were devouring his thighs; and,
although nothing was to be seen from without, his flesh was cut through as
though with a knife. I heard that this actually happened. There are many
such incidents, but this one will suffice here. Such a thing happened recently
in Tōtōmi; and in Shimotsuke a man was eaten by quail. Moreover, the birds
and animals killed by a certain falconer to feed the young falcons appeared
before his very eyes when he lay ill, besetting him on all sides. This happened
to someone connected with a personage of some importance, so I refrain
from mentioning names. Again, there are innumerable instances of retribu-
tion for killing dogs, tortoises, and the like.

7:13 The Recompense for Killing Young Chickens

A young woman in Owari province killed many chicks to feed her
children. In a dream a lady appeared to her, lamenting the loss of her off-
spring. Later, two of the young woman's children died. The person who told
me this said that it happened recently, but concealed the woman's name.

7:14 Killing a Mandarin Duck[308]

A man of Asonuma in Shimotsuke province liked to hunt with hawks.
One day he bagged a mandarin duck, and that night was visited in a dream
by a woman who accused him of killing her husband. The woman expressed
her grief in a waka *and then flew away, revealing herself to be a mandarin*
duck. On the following morning the man discovered a female duck and the
male duck which he had killed the day before lying side by side in death. It is
said that the sight caused a religious awakening in the man, who gave up kill-
ing and became a lay-priest.

7:15 Animals Also Have Understanding

During the Kangen period (1243-1246) there was a disturbance in the
capital and warriors came up from the east. One of them spoke to a horse

which he had recently selected.

"Animals also have understanding, so listen to me. If anything happens, I depend on you to serve me faithfully. That is why you are treated better than the other horses. Don't forget that I rely on you!" And the warrior entrusted a groom with special provisions for the horse.

But when they arrived at the capital, the groom was suddenly seized with a fit and spoke wildly, possessed by the spirit of the horse. ". . . Since you appropriated the provisions intended for me, then you meet the crisis if you can. You are a despicable fellow!"

I was told this story by the groom's son. Although animals do not speak, they are not to be deceived as if they had no understanding.

7:16 The Man Who Burned the Sutras

A monk stopping for the night at a house in Kyoto was awakened during the night by the sound of someone lamenting. The monk went to investigate and found a man among scattered sheets of a sutra with characters in gold written on blue paper. To the monk's inquiry, the man replied that while he was attempting to remove the gold dust from a copy of the Great Wisdom Sutra, *both of his eyes fell into the brazier. How unfortunate is this man's lot both in this life and in the next.*

Recently a lady went to a bath-house, and when she returned after splashing about, it was discovered that she had abandoned a statue of the Buddha there after having washed the gold from it. What a serious crime!

7:17 The Nun Who Blackened the Buddha's Nose

A certain aristocratic nun had a standing, golden image of the Buddha beautifully fashioned, and, taking it as the special object of her devotions, venerated it with religious services performed in its honor. Originally she had lived in the capital, but was compelled by circumstances to move to a remote region. Taking the sacred image with her, she installed it in a local private oratory, and attended it with flowers and incense.

This nun was extremely niggardly, distinguishing between what was hers and what belonged to others in everything she touched. As there were a number of other statues in addition to her own in the oratory, she came to the conclusion that her buddha was not getting the full benefit of the incense smoke, which dispersed in every direction. So she twisted one end of a bamboo tube into the lid of the incense burner and the other into the buddha's nostrils. Not a wisp of incense smoke was lost! As though it had been painted with lacquer, the nose of the gilded buddha became tarnished until its golden shine could not be seen.

The nun died and was reborn — her features truly fair, but her nostrils as black as India ink. It was revealed to someone in a dream that the woman was the nun reborn. Such were the operations of moral causality.

In a mountain village in Yamato province lived a farmer who built a rustic oratory and invited the monk Shiembō (Eizon) of Saidaiji to officiate at the dedication ceremony. In the dedicatory statement the farmer's declaration of intention with respect to the merit-transference read as follows: "This hall was built for the sake of my grandmother. If the merit of this act is applied to all beings, she will receive no particular benefit from it. Let the merit be transferred to her alone."

"When merit is offered up for the sake of all sentient beings," replied the monk, "its efficacy is all the greater. On no account would her benefit be lessened."

"It is indeed gratifying that this is so! Just the same, I want you to leave out Father Saburō, who lives in this neighborhood," the farmer insisted.

It seems quite unbecoming for him to have singled out one man from among all living beings because he thought of him as his sworn enemy. The incident was told to me by a holy man who witnessed it at the service.

A husband unexpectedly returned home while his wife was sleeping with her lover, and there was no way for him to make his escape. So the woman wrapped her admirer in a straw mat and carried it out, remarking that she wished to rid it of some fleas. As she was vaulting over the sunken hearth, the man, stark naked, slipped out of the mat and fell plumb into the grate.

Seeing this, the husband opened his eyes wide in surprise; but, covering his mouth in a gesture of amazement, remarked casually: "My! What a big flea!"

As the husband made no move to punish the man, he simply crawled away.

An official at the Ikeda manor in Tōtōmi province had a wife who was extremely possessive, and who virtually tied the man up so that he could not go out at all.[309] Now a deputy Land Steward for the region had come up from Kamakura and was dallying at the Ikeda stage. The husband wanted to visit him there but, as usual, could not get permission from this wife. He was a close friend of the deputy.

"Why can't I see him?" asked the man, begging his wife's permission.

"All right, you can go. But I'll put my mark on you." And she coated his private parts with flour.

The man went to the stage, where the deputy had made all kinds of preparations.

"It's great that your wife would let you come. So now call a girl and enjoy yourself."

"No man has it as hard as I do. She has even put her mark on me." The Land Steward told his friend all the details.

"Just go to my attendants and they will powder you up as good as new." So after the man had taken his pleasure, they coated him again with flour just as he had been originally, and he returned home.

"Come here and let me see you!" said his wife, rubbing off some of the flour to taste. "So you've gone and done it! I added salt to my flour, but this has none." The woman threw her husband down and bound him.

Finally deciding that his wife's affection for him was just too much of a nuisance, the man left her and went down to Kamakura. This happened only recently.

There is an old story about a man who went on a trip and drew a cow on his wife's private parts as a seal during his absence; she had been having an affair.

While the husband was away the woman told her lover what he had done.

"I'll draw another picture just like it," was his reply. But although he had a good look at the original, the lover did not draw it as it had been. The husband had drawn the cow lying down, but his was a standing cow. When the husband returned and saw it, he scolded his wife.

"This is surely the work of your lover. The cow I drew was lying down; this one is standing up."

"For heaven's sake don't get upset" the wife replied. "Do you expect a reclining cow to spend its entire life lying down?"

"Perhaps you are right," said the husband, and forgave her.
The man had a lighthearted and generous disposition. In spite of his
wife's impertinence, he was indulgent enough to make light of her
offense. He was not at all like the lady from Ikeda.

In Nara lived an aristocratic nun who for many years placed
her trust in the Jizō of Yada,[310] tending and venerating it with un-
divided attention. Whenever she invoked the name of the Buddha,
her opening statement was: "I do not rely on the Fukuchiin Jizō, the
Jūrin'in Jizō, the Chizokuin Jizō, and certainly not on the Jizōs which
stand in the city streets. Praise be to my Bodhisattva Jizō of Yada!"

Here, too, is the attitude of the nun who smoked up the Buddha's nose.

7:18 The Stupid Monk Who Became an Ox

*A monk from Ōmi province traveled back and forth to a temple in
Mikawa. He neither studied nor practiced the Way of the Buddha, but just
accepted the donations of the faithful. On one occasion he had made a trip
to his teacher's place in Mikawa and was about to enter the monks' quarters
when a servant girl struck him with a whip. When he was about to be struck a
second time, he tried to ask what was going on. But no sound came forth.*

*"For some reason this ox keeps coming back," said the servant girl,
leading him to the stable. When the monk looked at himself, he saw that he
had become an ox. Reasoning that this had happened because of his having
unworthily received alms from the faithful, he recalled that the Holy and
Virtuous Spell (Sonshō darani)[311] was effective in such cases. Although he
had heard it, he could not remember how it went and so was unable to recite
it. All he could say was: "Son—, son—."*

*People thought that the ox was sick, for it neither ate nor drank. The
monk was so upset that he completely forgot about food. After three days he
was able to say "sonshō darani" and was restored to his original form as a
monk. He untied the rope and presented himself before his teacher, to whom
he related all that had happened.*

*The Holy and Virtuous Spell is especially effective in counteracting the
retribution earned by the improper use of alms received from the faithful.
The Five Hundred Questions Sutra (Gohyaku monron)[312] tells of a follower of
the Buddha who unworthily accepted alms from the faithful and was
transformed into a mountain of flesh. During a famine the people of the
nearby village came to cut the flesh for food. People in a neighboring country*

came to steal a portion but the mountain spoke to them: "Long ago I was a follower of the Buddha who accepted alms from the people of this country without practicing the virtuous life. Now I have become a mountain of flesh to repay them. But since I took nothing from you, it would be intolerable of you to cut me." The intruders left. A similar incident occurred in China where a monk was reborn as a mushroom.

Near the Jimokuji in Owari province a young girl was picking vegetables when suddenly she fell to the ground. A man ploughing in a rice field nearby ran over to find a snake four or five feet long about to wrap itself around her. While the man was returning to get a hoe with which to chase the snake, it suddenly disappeared on approaching the girl's head.

"Just now a handsome young man came and told me to lie down," said the girl. "But when he got close to me, he became frightened for some reason or other and fled."

"Do you carry a talisman?" asked the man. The girl replied that she did not; but on closer examination a paper attached to her hair was found to have the Holy and Virtuous Spell written on it.

One should carry a talisman. It is useful even when the person is not aware that he has it. This happened during the Bun'ei period (1264-1274).

7:19 The Shingon Retribution

A monk studying Shingon lied to his teacher that he had received the initiation rite (kanjō) and subsequently he was shown certain secret materials. When the teacher discovered the truth he had them returned. After this the monk became violently ill, blind, and died in agony. This was told to me by someone who actually witnessed it.

A certain monk, concealing his misconduct, was to be initiated into an esoteric rite for which the ceremonial utensils were to be dyed red [presumably in honor of Aizen Myō-ō]. But the color did not take. This was related to me by someone who witnessed the dyeing.

7:20 The Goblin Who Taught a Man Shingon

A monk on his way to Mutsu province stopped at a mountain village for a night's lodging, but no place was available. "There's an old oratory on this mountain where you might stop, but it's said that goblins live there," warned the villagers. The monk went and seated himself on the platform behind the image of the Buddha.

That night a crowd of people came down from the mountain to the oratory. The frightened monk performed the hand gesture (mudrā) to make himself invisible (ongyō no in) and watched quietly. He saw a fat priest with a *clean white appearance draw up in a hand-cart and enter the temple with twenty or thirty attendants. The priest sent the attendants out to amuse themselves in the garden, and then called out to the monk.*

"Your hand gesture is all wrong. Come here and I will teach you." So the priest instructed him, warning him that he must not reveal the sign to any who were not worthy. The monk again sat behind the Buddha and made the sign.

"Good! Good! Now you are invisible," said the priest. Afterwards he called his companions back into the oratory where they made merry and then returned to the mountain.

The goblin (tengu) is a Japanese tradition. It is not mentioned in the scriptures or in the writings of the sages. Perhaps it is what was referred to as an "evil spirit" (maki) in the old writings. It is evidently some kind of demon. There are two kinds of goblin: good ones and bad ones. Good goblins follow the Way of the Buddha; the bad ones do not.

7:21 Attachment Dissolved by the Dharma

A lay priest in Shinano province, for many years a devotee of the nembutsu, *died in the epidemic during the summer of the first year of the Kōan period (1278). He died in a disturbed state of mind, and when they tried to cremate him, his body was like a stone and would not burn. His monk son surmised that this might have been caused by some strong attachment. He recalled that in India in ancient times there was a follower of a non-Buddhist school whose views on permanence hardened into a stone which dissolved after the Buddha and his disciples wrote some characters on it.*

The son recalled the incident, and although he could not remember the characters used at that time, wrote on a slip torn from a paper funeral flag the four lines of the verse beginning, "All conditioned things are impermanent."[313] *He attached this to the hard lump and the cremation proceeded successfully. While they were reading the first book of the* Amida Sutra, *the lump burned up without leaving a trace. This was told to me by an eyewitness.*

7:22 Poverty Expelled

In Owari province an indigent monk called Enjōbō had reached the age of fifty when he decided to improve his lot in life with some kind of esoteric (shingon) or Yin-yang (onyō) practice. With a disciple and another young monk he swept the house with peach branches on the last day of the year, saying: "Mr. Poverty, get out!" Then he closed the gate tightly.

That night a skinny monk appeared to him in a dream. "I have lived here many years," he said, "but now I have been chased out." Enveloped in the falling rain, he seemed to be crying.

It is said that after this incident Enjōbō's fortunes improved. This was told to me by someone who heard it first hand.

An impoverished monk was considering moving to a new location in the hope that his circumstances would improve. A skinny boy wearing sandals appeared to him in a dream: "I am your servant, Poverty. When you set out on your trip, I will accompany you."

A priest of Mount Hiei was extremely poor and decided to move to the countryside to improve his lot.

"A half-gallon jug takes just half a gallon, no matter where it is," argued the head priest at the quarters where he lived.

"This may be true of the Buddha's Law," replied the disciple. "But according to the law of the world it varies from place to place."

7:23 The Man Who Sold His Ears

In Nara a poor monk with thick ear lobes was told by another that he wished to buy them. They agreed on five hundred coppers. Later the monk and the buyer went to Kyoto to consult a physiognomist. The ear-buyer first had his features read, and the report was unfavorable.

I bought this monk's ears for a price. Read them in place of mine," he requested.

"From about next spring you will have good fortune," said the physiognomist.

Then the ear-selling monk had his features read. "Good fortune appears in the ears which you sold, but apart from them I see none."

The monk is poor to this day and wanders about Nara and the eastern regions preaching and doing odd jobs.

An old monk told another priest that he had received an offer to perform a Buddhist service. "But the way is far and I am too old. You may take my place if you wish. It takes three days on the road, and the offering will not exceed a mere twenty kan. There is also a priest at a shrine a day's journey away who wishes to have a death rite (gyakushu) performed for seven days. He is prosperous and has many sons. At worst they will pay five kan a day, and possibly as high as ten. To which place do you choose to go?"

"No need to ask!" was the reply. "Why should I make a three-day trip for twenty kan? I'll take the seventy kan for a day's travel."

So in a day the second monk crossed the waters in a boat to the residence of the shrine priest. The old man was eighty and had been lying down unable to eat for a long time. The sons requested that the monk perform an abbreviated recitation of the Great Wisdom Sutra. *Although the monk enjoyed sake, he declined when they offered him a drink, believing that the donation would be increased if he maintained a virtuous air. So they gave him a warm cake. And when presently he began reading the* Great Wisdom Sutra, *he took a small bite with the remark:*

"This is the flavor of wisdom, the medicine of immortality." He offered a piece to the sick man, who accepted it gratefully and swallowed it in one gulp. But the old man had not eaten for a long time, and he choked to death on it. His sons then sent the monk away, asking him to return to perform the memorial service.

The wind was rough as the monk started back, and presently he fell into the water, so that his belongings were soaked. Meanwhile, the sons decided to have the monk stay with them until the time for the service and to present him with a donation. They set out to overtake him, but the monk, believing that he was being pursued by pirates, rowed out into the rough sea. He barely escaped with his life. The monk later heard that the donation for the single memorial service was fifty kan.

One's heart should be clean. Such things happen when it is crooked and besmirched.

7:24 The Efficacy of Shingon

The disciples of Daiembō (Ryōin, 1212–1291) of the Kanshōji frequently employed the Jewel-box Spell[314] with success. While reciting it for a woman who had become possessed, the spirit spoke through the sick woman.

"Buddhism helps others, but me it afflicts. I am a shrine priestess of Kyoto, and I make a living by placing spells on people. This lady through whom I am speaking took away her elder sister's husband, and, at the elder sister's request, I prepared an amulet and placed a spell on her. This darani recitation attacks both the amulet and myself. How am I going to make a living?"

This was told to me by a monk who actually witnessed the incident.

The things that I record I have heard to be true, and I tell them in order to illustrate the teachings of Buddhism. Since many of these happenings have occurred in my own time, I have concealed the names of those involved, unless the incident was not painful.

During the epidemic in the Bandō area in the summer of the first year of the Kōan period (1278) many people died. A young child was cured while some monks chanted the Spell of the Thousand-Armed [Kannon].[315] And according to the monks at the Ordination Hall in Nara, a sick woman vomited up something resembling a sword while the Thousand-Armed Spell was being recited.

Some monks who recited a spell for a woman say that a snake came forth from her and entered a lady-in-waiting, who went mad.

The late Jissōbō (1001–1084) had some interesting experiences with Shingon. A woman of Shirakawa had a hard lump in her stomach as big as a handball which was cured by an elaborate Fire Ceremony (goma). I heard this from a reliable monk.

7:25 Priest Former-Life

In Shimōsa province lived a monk of low status but good disposition called Zenzebō, "Priest Former-Life." He did not court the world's favor and was neither depressed nor elated over events, seeing everything simply as the result of actions in a former life. When his house caught fire, he said that this too was something from the past. Thus he was called "Priest Former-Life."

Present good and evil are determined by our actions in former lives. The [Garland Sutra] states that the Three Worlds are simply One Mind, and apart from Mind there is no thing.

A certain worthy remarked that the perception of the senses was affected by the good or bad state of one's mind. Once he had the impression that everything smelled of excrement, even the Buddha image in the oratory where he had gone to pray. Believing that this must have been the result of his having fallen into evil ways, he performed the Spell of Saving Compassion[316] *and prayed to Fudō, but without results. On leaving the oratory he brushed his face and discovered a piece of excrement on the tip of his nose. After he washed it off, things no longer smelled bad. He noted that ignorance and enlightenment is much the same: good and bad are not in what is seen but in the mind of the observer. We should become neither depressed nor elated by the things of this world.*

In China Pei Sou (Hokusō)[317] *never showed any emotion. When his only horse disappeared and people came to console him, he said: "Perhaps this will prove to be a blessing. Shall I then grieve over it?" And when he acquired an exceptional horse a few days later and people congratulated him, he maintained his composure, saying that it might prove to be a misfortune.*

When his beloved child fell from the horse and broke its elbow, Pei Sou remarked that this too might prove to be blessing, and refused to grieve. A great disturbance came to the country and many were called into military service to die in battle. But because the child was crippled, he survived. This is the way things happen.

Lao Tzu says: "Misery!—happiness is to be found by its side! Happiness!— misery lurks beneath it!" (Tao Te Ching 58; Legge's translation).

The Nirvana Sutra *sets forth this parable. A beautiful woman came to a man's house and announced that she was the Goddess of Virtue (Kudokuten), because wherever she went there was happiness and good fortune.*

The man was pleased and invited her in. But a second woman, who was ugly, entered with her. She said that she was the Goddess of Darkness (Kokuanten), because wherever she went there was misfortune and calamity. When the man ordered her to leave, she replied: "My elder sister and I are inseparable. If you love her, love me. If you chase me away, chase her away as well." The man expelled them both.

Living and meeting are like the elder sister; death and parting like the younger. There is no life without death, and no meeting without parting. It is a virtue to love one's family, but one may also become a slave to love and duty.

In India lived a devout layman so devoted to his wife that after he died he was reborn as a worm in her nose. When the woman blew her nose and was about to step on the worm, a holy man explained to her that it was her husband.

"My husband was a devout man and should have been born in the heavens. How could he have become a worm?" she inquired.

"Because of his strong attachment at the moment of death, he must first be so reborn."

It is said that by virtue of having heard the Law expounded, the worm died and was reborn into the heavens.[318]

Wife and child may be a misfortune, like being shot with an arrow shaped like a flower. Although pleasant to look at, it may take your life.

Han Shan (Kanzan, T'ang period) says that one who fills his warehouse with a thousand pieces of gold has less than the poor man who practices meditation. Po Chü-i tells us neither to lament our poverty, nor to be proud of our wealth. When the rich and the poor return to dust, what difference is there between them? [*In the* Commentary on the Great Wisdom Sutra] Nāgārjuna says that a man who does not practice the Dharma is no different from the animals (cf., S&P 6:10). We should follow the example of Pei Sou and Zenzebō.

Shan-tao (Zendō) states that those who do not cultivate the three sources of felicity by observing the commandments are beasts wearing men's skins. The Net of Brahma Sutra says that those who do not keep the precepts are no different than wooden statues; they are like animals. Although statues have the form of man, they have no mind. Animals have minds, but they have neither wisdom nor good karma. On refusing the post of Prime Minister, Jayasena told the king: "Because I accepted emoluments, I have become involved in people's problems. Now I am feverishly trying to cut the entanglements of birth-and-death. What leisure do I have to devote to you?" (cf., 3:1).

Po Chü-i says that even when one is prosperous, he suffers; because suffering is the mind's anxiety. Likewise, a person can be happy in poverty, because happiness is in being free (cf., 4:9). among the poems expressing personal grievance (jukkai) in Po's Collected Writings (Hakushi monjū), he writes of his early interest in literature and his later devotion to meditation. Han Shan says that just as ice and water are inseparable, so life and death alike are beautiful. And Po Chü-i admonishes us neither to cherish nor to dislike ourselves. As the source of all worldly troubles, how can the self be loved? But as all is empty dust, how can it be despised?

Through neither attachment nor aversion to things, we come to realize that all things have the same Self-nature. This is the basis of the Buddhist teaching, the reason for religious practice.

8:1 Chūkan

A monk called Chūkan Shōshimbō lived in the quarters of the Hongan Bishop (?Shin'en, 1153-1224) of [the Shōryakuji][319] *on Mount Bodai in Yamato province. Because he was always nodding, he was called "Sleepy Shōshin." Once during a performance of a Relic Venerating Ceremony (sharikō), the flowers were about to be scattered when Shōshin, having dozed off as usual, suddenly awoke and began to intone the concluding anthem: "With my hand I grasp the staff . . ." He thought the assembly was singing the hymn.*

One night he awoke to some birds chirping and thought the superior was calling him. When Shin'en said that he had not summoned him, Shōshin replied that the birds had told him.

On another occasion when the Bishop was taking a bath, Shōshin spread his damp garments over a drying cage (fusego), wet side up, and heating them over a blazing fire. Then he nodded off as usual. When the Bishop called for his clothes, Shōshin awoke to find that the pattern of the drying frame had been scorched onto the white garment. Rolling it up wet side out, he took it to the Bishop.

"Inside it's well toasted," was his explanation.

Recently a boy living in the East Gate Quarters at the Kōfukuji was in the privy when a large kite flew in from the direction of Kasuga Mountain, set itself down in front of him, and dozed off. The frightened boy killed the bird and then fainted dead away. The spirit of the dead kite had taken possession of him.

"I, Chūkan, was just taking an innocent nap when this boy killed me," said the voice. "I am angry." But suitable prayers and spells were said which averted evil from the boy.

If a person was torpid in a former life, the fault persists through successive rebirths.

This is what is called the continuity of cause and effect (shūin shūka). Among the Buddha's disciples, Śāriputra (Sharihotsu) gave the appearance of anger because during five-hundred lifetimes he had been a serpent. Nanda (Nanda)[320] *had been deeply immersed in sensuality, and even after he attained the fruit of arhatship, he still had an eye for women. When wise men are so, who among ordinary men will not have this flaw?*

Once when the Buddha and Ānanda (Anan) were walking along the road, they came upon two men ploughing a field. One went to greet the Buddha while the other kept on ploughing.

"Both men had the opportunity to meet the seven Buddhas when they came into this world," explained Gautama. "One of them, just as today, never came out to pay his respects and so today does not have the root of merit (zengon) *which would induce him to come." (Source undetermined.)*

This is the result (shūka) *of being remiss; the mind of long ago we call the cause* (shūin). *When I think of Shōshin's sleeping, I am reminded of my own faults. My intention in collecting foolish anecdotes in this book is to lead people to the path of wisdom. Po Yang* (Hakuyō, Sung period) *said that if one's desire for enlightenment were as strong as his sensual thoughts, there would be many opportunities to attain Buddhahood.*

8:2 Chiumbō of the Kōfukuji

In Nara a monk called Chiumbō was such a wild man that people called him "Noisy Chiumbō"—a good match for "Sleepy Shōshin" (see 8:1). Once when the temple was aroused by rumors of a robber, Chiumbō beat a stick against a pillar, shouting: "This will get him out!" When asked what he was doing, he replied: "Well, I think it's a robber!"[321]

Once during a fire Chiumbō poured a bucket of water down another monk's neck on seeing the light reflected of the monk's face.

During a banquet Chiumbō went to have a bucket filled with sake. When he returned and the contents were emptied into the dispenser, grass was seen floating on top. It was found to be water.

"This cannot be. I scooped it up immediately. I slipped by Sarusawa Pond and the sake fell into the water. Without losing a moment, I scooped it out from the bottom of the pond." This fellow not only had a loud mouth. He also didn't think clearly.

8:3 Iyobō

At Kofu in Hitachi province lived a Scripture Reader (jigyōja) called Iyobō who decided to smooth his roof thatched with miscanthus by burning off a portion. Suddenly a wind blew up and burned both his and another person's house down. When people collected to watch, he remarked: "In these parts such a splendid fire seldom occurs. Come close and have a good look."

Iyobō used to put horses to pasture in the morning and return for them in the evening. Any horse that happened to be in the pasture at the time would be led away with the others. Once on meeting another priest riding a horse he inquired if the chestnut-colored horse belonging to the priest was his own brown horse. How comical!

8:4 The Man Who Did Not Know His Own Horse

At an archery meet in Kai province a man was boasting about his chestnut-colored horse, and a companion asked if it was a stallion. It was, but the man thought it was a mare although he had had it for three years. He was subsequently expelled from his master's house. Nothing can be said for a man who doesn't know his own horse after three years.

8:5 Exchanging Horses

A monk in Owari province had a mare that he wished to exchange for a stallion, because he thought that mares were difficult to maintain. On his way to the market in Orizu he exchanged his horse for another inferior to his own, but one which he thought was a stallion. A lay disciple overtook the monk on the road and was told of the trade.

"This horse is also a mare. Take a look," said the disciple. The monk dismounted to discover that it was indeed.

"Go find a new owner!" said the monk, reprimanding the horse. But it was hardly the horse's fault. If the horse could have spoken, it might have replied: "Call me anything you like, blind man!"

8:6 A Bad Buy in a Horse

A monk of Shimōsa province called Yuishimbō went to Kamakura to buy a horse and returned with an animal blind in one eye. The horse dealer, seeing a stupid-looking monk, had walked the animal around in a circle so that the eye would not be noticed.

8:7 The Man Who Did Not Understand About Riding a Horse

In Hitachi province a monk riding alone came to a bridge which his horse would not cross. The horse retreated backwards, as horses are wont to do. But the monk, thinking that it wished to cross the bridge tail end first, faced it about without dismounting and tried unsuccessfully to coax it over. After an hour or so of this a man came by who led the horse over the bridge on foot. "What a clever idea," remarked the monk.

A nun in the same province was riding a horse—as is the custom even for nuns in the Bandō region. When the owner of the horse told her to stop, she whipped the animal, which then only ran faster. Later the nun explained that when she whipped the horse, she told it to stop. She thought it was the horse's fault that it didn't understand what she meant. It is common for people not to be aware of their own faults.

8:8 A Discrepancy Between Intentions and Words

At a mountain temple in Hitachi province lived a venerable recluse. Among a great number of ascetics who had assembled at the temple was a priest who claimed that from the moment of his birth he had never been angry. The recluse was a scholar and did not believe that this was possible according to the principles of the Buddhist teaching.

"The ordinary man is affected by the Three Poisons of covetousness, anger and delusion. If one is a sage then it goes without saying that this does not apply; but as for the ordinary man, no one has ever been untouched by anger. How could you have avoided the Three Poisons?"

"Nevertheless, I have never been the least bit angry," replied the priest.

But the recluse did not believe him. "This can't be true. I think you're lying."

"Look! If I say I don't get angry, then I don't get angry! What do you say to that?" scolded the monk, his face reddening.

On another occasion a certain ascetic monk remarked that from the moment of his birth he had never taken the life of any creature. As he was being congratulated on having such good karma from a previous life, a horse-fly stung him on the head. Taking aim, he struck it dead with a great splattering.

"How could you take this creature's life even while saying that you don't kill?" he was asked.

"Well, I thought it was a bee!"

8:9 Discrepancy Between Beginning and End

Someone commented on a Curtain Opening [to display a sacred image for a fixed period of time] which had occurred at the Hasedera the previous year from the first day of the eleventh month to the middle of the third month in the following year. A monk from a mountain temple in Owari province then remarked: "That makes thirty-three days."

This monk once mentioned that he had lived at a temple in the Bandō, and someone asked him how long he had been there. "A year and a half—that is to say, ninety days," was his reply.

When he was asked why he recited the Great Amida Spell[322] forty-nine times a day, he replied that it was because of Amida's forty-eight vows. The discrepancy is less than the others, but it is amusing all the same.

Once when he attended an Urabon service on the fourteenth day of the seventh month, he decided on entering the hall to hide his clogs under the veranda, lest they be stolen by some unseemly characters who were present. As he was putting them back on after the service he remarked: "I was sure they would be lost, so I put them under the veranda. And just as I expected, here they are!"

The monk had a friend at the Atsuta Shrine who spoke to him of someone who had a disorder of the testicles. "Is it serious?" asked the monk. "Is this person a woman?"

At a temple in Kamakura he said that he had met a certain monk on the road looking like a beggar. The second monk heard the report and before a large assembly angrily demanded when it was that the first had seen him.

"It was on Wakamiya Street that I saw you."

"When did you see me?"

"On the twenty-third of next month." The reply was so silly that the offended monk laughed the matter away.

8:10 The Apprentice-Monk's Wit

At a mountain temple in Hitachi province all the monks at mealtime had leftovers for their apprentices—except Genjōbō, who never left anything. "I am more embarrassed about this than he is," remarked the apprentice.

Likewise in Owari province there was a monk who never left anything. Once it seemed that he might, but while everyone waited expectantly, his apprentice remarked: "Just wait and see. He'll finish it off with some hot water." He did.

A famous nembutsu monk in Shimōsa called Shōkambō also left nothing behind. But his apprentice remarked to his colleagues without bitterness: "I am really not hungry. It's strange, but I think of the days when my mother cuddled me in her arms, and I am all right."

An impertinent apprentice-monk at a mountain temple in Yamato was reprimanded for urinating in the drinking-water tank. "How could I piss into the water-tank?" he replied. "I pissed over it!"

In the same province an apprentice was walking downstream along a river. When his superior, who was walking ahead of him, stopped for a drink he was asked to wait a while. The apprentice had relieved himself upstream and was waiting until the water cleared.

A stingy monk at a mountain temple constantly suspected and reprimanded his apprentice. Once when he accused him of stealing some parched rice (yakigome), the apprentice denied the charge.

"What evidence do you have?" asked the boy.

"When you broke wind, it smelled of parched rice," replied the monk.

"Does a fart, then, have the odor of what was eaten?"

"Unquestionably!"

"Well, the other day when you broke wind, it smelled like crap, so does that mean . . ."

The monk was at a loss for words.

8:11 The Page Who Ate the Rice-Jelly[323]

At a certain mountain temple the head monk, a stingy man, made some rice-jelly[324] for his own personal use. He often nibbled at it, but, placing it high up on a shelf, would not share it even with his single solitary page. "When a person eats this, death is sure to follow," he admonished.

"My, how I would like to try some!" thought the page to himself. Then one day when the head monk happened to be absent from the temple, while taking the jar down from the shelf, he spilled the jelly all over his hair and clothing.

"I've waited a long time for this," he reflected, ravenously gulping down several cupfuls of the jelly, and knocking down one of the monk's treasured water-bottles, which struck a drain-stone and shattered.

When the monk returned, the page was sobbing and blubbering. "Why are you crying?" he asked.

"By accident I broke your treasured water-bottle. And then I thought how you would reprimand me, and felt so miserable that I saw no reason even to go on living. You told me that if a person ate this he would perish. So I took a cupful—but nothing happened. Even after eating two or three cupfuls, I didn't die in the least. Finally, I smeared it over my hair and clothes, but I still haven't died!"

The rice-jelly was eaten, the water-bottle broken, and the stingy monk gained nothing. The wit of the page was exceptional—no doubt he turned out to be no contemptible scholar as well.

A townsman from Kyoto brought his son to serve as a page to a rather undistinguished monk at a temple in Musashi province. The monk proposed giving the boy an unusual name, and, after many days, he told the boy's father that he had decided on something suitable: Burachi. The father had never heard the name and asked which characters were used.

"Bura- is from kabura *('turnip') and -chi is from* kukutachi *('stalk').''*
Truly a rare combination.

8:12 The Princess

*A princess about to move into her husband's residence was counseled by
her wet nurse to be gentle and restrained in speech.*
"Speak sweetly like a spring nightingale on a bamboo fence."
*After the princess moved to her husband's house, she said nothing for
two or three days. Then, while eating with her husband one day and wishing
to have some pickled radishes, she raised her knees, shrugged her shoulders
as if arranging her wings, and stretched out her neck.*
*"I should like to have some pickled radishes," she said twice, imitating
the voice of a nightingale.*
*In both the secular and religious life one may thus follow the letter of an
injunction without understanding its spirit. When one follows the words of
Buddhism literally without understanding their purpose, he is sure to go
astray.*

8:13 The Nun's Name[325]

A woman went to a certain mountain temple to become a nun.
"Let me confer a religious name upon you," suggested her ad-
viser.
"For some time already I have decided on a name," she replied.
"What is it?"
"I place my trust in the many gods and buddhas. And, as they
are all precious to me, I have composed my name by taking a
character from each of theirs—Ashamyōkanjihakuyūhihatake—
delighting in the holy names of Amida, Shaka, Myōhō, Kannon, Jizō,
Hakuzan, Kumano, Hiyoshi, Haguro, and Ontake."
This is just too long!

8:14 The Servant Who Acted Foolishly

*In Kamakura a man from Mikawa province whose name I do not recall
sent out a servant for delicacies to entertain his guests. Taking off a pair of
ceremonial pants, he told the servant to take them to the city and exchange
them for some fowl. But the pants were so expensive that he was unable to
sell them.*
The servant happened to see a monk carrying a small Jizō in a portable

shrine; and he overheard someone say that the monk would take a bird in exchange for the Jizō. So he offered to trade the pants and the monk agreed. Then he tried to exchange the Jizō for some fowl, but the merchant merely laughed at his foolishness without replying. The servant returned to his master's house with the Jizō in his tunic.

In the end he explained what had happened, but the matter was so preposterous that his master could not even come to disown him. The man bit off the head of the Jizō, saying: "Interesting! This is some hors d'oeuvre." and he laughed until his sides split. This is a true story, told to me by someone who saw this man.

8:15 A Ridiculous Commoner

When the late Imadegawa (Saionji Kinsuke, 1223-1267) was visiting the Tennōji, a commoner came to his residence near Kawajiri, asked to be employed, and was taken on.

"My name is Onikurō, and I am also called Tsukamu," said the man, who had a large scar on his face. At a banquet after the return from Tennōji someone inquired how he came to be called as he was, and how he received his scar.

"Some years ago on my way to Watanabe I was frightened out of my wits during a frightful thunderstorm," he replied. "As I was clutching the statue of a devil (oni) under the foot of the guardian deity Niō, a child remarked: 'He grabs the devil' (onikurō tsukamu). The scar comes from being stepped on by a horse." Imadegawa was informed of this ill-bred fellow and released him from his service. What a silly story it is!

8:16 A Clever Fellow[326]

An elderly man seeking employment called at the mansion of a certain nobleman. "What are you qualified to do?" he was asked.

"Though I have no special accomplishments, when it comes to anything at all out of the ordinary, there is nothing with which I am not acquainted. Knowing this to be the case, people refer to me as 'Mr. Philosopher'." The official was impressed and took him into his employ.

When the nobleman went down from the capital to serve as Provincial Governor of Harima the man accompanied him. At Akashi Bay a large net was drawn in to reveal a slimy creature rolling about, shaped like a soccer ball and having neither eyes nor mouth. Everyone, including the fishermen, agreed that they had never seen its likes before; and though inquiries were made far and wide, people all replied that they did not know what it was.

"Indeed?" said the Governor. "Well, then, call Mr. Philosopher." And the question was put to him.

Now Mr. Philosopher likewise did not know what the animal was, but not wishing to lose the reputation he had built up for himself, replied: "Such things do exist."

"Yes, but what is its name?"

"It's called a *'kugurugutsu.'* "

"Evidently that's what it's called," said the Governor. "You are preeminently well-informed. Enter this in the official diary." The year, month, and day were recorded, and it was written that in the opinion of Mr. Philosopher such was the name of the creature.

Having finished his four-year tour of duty, the nobleman returned to the capital with tales of life in the back country. "At Akashi Bay we pulled in a most remarkable organism which I told my men to dry and bring back. Do we have it?" he asked, ordering the creature to be brought forth.

"What was its name, anyhow?" he inquired. But everyone had forgotten, and no one could say. Moreover, the official diary could not be located. So he summoned the Philosopher, who was brought before him and questioned.

Mr. Philosopher also had forgotten the name he had given the creature on that earlier occasion, but as it looked dry and brittle, he took a guess. "It's called a *'hihirihitsu'*." The consensus among everyone, of high and low station, was that this was not the name, but Mr. Philosopher stoutly insisted that the creature was a *hihirihitsu.*

Then it was reported that the official diary had been found, and it read: "On this day and month in this year, a creature was pulled up at Akashi Bay in Harima. Its name is *'kugurugutsu.'* This is the opinion of Mr. Philosopher."

"What do you say to this?" asked the Governor.

"When the creature is alive," the Philosopher replied, "it is called *'kugurugutsu.'* When it is dried out, it is called *'hihirihitsu.'* "

"So be it!" rejoined the governor, putting an end to the discussion.

This was a more resourceful fellow than Onikurō (*S&P* 8:15).

8:17 Spirited Behavior

A slightly-built man from the Hatsuse River region in Yamato province

Owari Manzai

was employed by the steward of the Kumano temples. During a drinking party at which about a hundred people were present, the man without hesitation took the seat below the steward's eldest son, but above the others. And when the steward offered the new employee some sake, *he gulped it down without ceremony.*

"What a disagreeable rascal!" said the steward's son, striking the man with his fist. Immediately the man struck the person sitting next to him.

"I thought it was my turn," was his explanation. Impressed by his artless remark, everyone laughed heartily.

Foolish men make big incidents out of trifles; the wise take serious matters in stride.

8:18 The Foolish Boy

The teenage son of a Nara craftsman was of unsound mind and said foolish things. Once at a neighbor's house he remarked casually that he did not feel very well.

"My mother just now died suddenly so I am rather depressed. Imagine how my father will feel when he returns from Kyoto."

What a dumb thing to say!

8:19 The Monk Who Took a Boat

A young monk came to a ferry in Shimōsa and was asked where he was from.

"From Yuirembō's place in Kazahaya."

The boatman, who was careful to avoid inauspicious language, replied: "To mention Kazahaya ('strong winds') is bad enough, but Yuirembō (suggesting 'to take water') is even more disturbing." The monk made several other slips but was finally permitted to board.

8:20 The Boatman Who Rode a Horse

The residents of Nakajima in Ise province use only boats and never ride horses. A boatman called Yatarō rode a horse for the first time in his life while visiting a temple in Owari province. The man fell from the horse and returned to the temple to tell of his mishaps in nautical terms. This was told to me by an eyewitness.

8:21 The Monk Who Concealed His Age

When the Ajari Saigyoku of Mushashi province was asked his age, he replied that he was "over sixty."

"How much over sixty?"

"Fourteen years." Quite a bit over! By saying sixty instead of seventy he felt somewhat younger, which is the way with us all. If someone says in flattery: "You look younger than your age," we are pleased. But if he says: "You look very old," we are disheartened. It is because of our attachments to this world that the sickness of old age and the pain of death are considered frightening and disagreeable. But this body which we receive as a legacy from our parents is a temporary aggregate of earth, water, fire, and wind. Its solidity is earth; its moistness, water; its warmth, fire; and its movement, wind. Among these there is nothing to be looked on as the "I". When the breath stops, the mind passes away and the body returns to its origins: warmth to fire, moisture to water, movement to wind, and solidity to earth. And the mind, whether it be gentle and affectionate, or bold and clever—where does it go? It is like a tree which burns to ashes and is buried to become earth. Exalted or humble, who can escape the nature of things?

Hakurakuten (Po Chü-i, 772-846) says:

The old grave—from what era the man who lies there?
We know neither his family nor his personal name.
He has dissolved into the wayside dust from which
Every spring the grasses come forth.[327]

There are also lines (of an imayō) and another verse by Po which express this sentiment.

Long ago a follower of the Buddha came upon two mountaineers, father and son, one lying on the ground and the other tending a garden. He discovered that the son had suddenly been bitten by a poisonous snake and had died. Showing no signs of grief, the father spoke to the pilgrim.

"On the side of the road where you are walking is a house. It is mine, and someone will be coming from there with food. Please tell the woman that our son has just now died and to bring only one serving."

"The parting of parent is supposed to be distressing," said the pilgrim. "How is it that you show no emotion?"

"The bond between parent and child is fragile. They are like birds who stop together in the forest at night and at dawn fly away with a flapping of wings.[328] What is there to lament?"

When the pilgrim relayed the message to the mountaineer's house, where the dead man's wife and mother were living, he received a similar response. And so he was reminded that causality among the myriad elements creates temporary configurations, and that the attachment-mind is not to be aroused by them. He felt compunction that among laymen there should be such deep understanding.[329]

8:22 The Monk Who Did Not Know the Way of Death

In Kyūshū a monk called the Temple-Master of Tosa (Tosa no Jishu) remarked to an acquaintance: "For many years I have not thought of reciting the nembutsu or of performing meritorious acts. The reason is that I did not expect to die, and I believed that one should prepare for the afterlife when he felt that this was going to happen. Now I am having premonitions so I will begin to recite the nembutsu and perform good deeds. First my father died, then my mother, my aunts and uncles, and my brother. The fact that my entire family is now dead raises doubts about my own longevity."

This monk was a clever fellow and was expressing the worldly frame of mind. Death is one thing that people do not really understand.

Long ago King Aśoka (Aiku Daiō, r. ca. 269–232 B.C.) was an ardent champion of Buddhism. Since he lived only a century after the death of the Buddha, during the period of the True Law (shōbō),[330] there were many holy arhats in his day. Twenty thousand from the monastery of Kukkutārāma were constantly maintained at the palace. The king's younger brother Vītāśoka (Ashuka-ō) did not believe in Buddhism and resented this. Aśoka assured him that although the monks received support, they were not attached to the world of the Five Desires.

But Vītāśoka was still dissatisfied and attempted to usurp the throne. For this he was condemned to die. "But since you wish to rule," said Aśoka, "you may do so for seven days. Sate yourself with the enjoyment of the Five Desires, and after a week you will be executed." The king confined his brother to the palace, and at the gate placed a guard who was ordered to ring a bell every day and announce the passing of time left for him to live. By the time the last day arrived, he had been frightened out of his wits and lost all interest in worldly affairs. He began to cultivate the Way and after seven days attained the first fruit of arhatship. After this Aśoka pardoned him.[331]

It is said that monk Nyomu (10th c.), while accompanying an imperial progress at the Oi River, took the precaution of placing a courtier's hat at the bottom of his vestment hamper. When General Izumi's (Fujiwara Sadakuni, 867-906) hat was blown into the water, Nyomu attained renown by presenting it to the general. How foolish it is, then, that even seemingly wise people neglect preparing for the road which we all must travel. We should be diligent.

After the Emperor Daigo (885-930) died, Nichizō Shōnin (d. 985) went into seclusion at Shō no Iwaya in Shōhei 14 (944). At noon on the first day of the eighth month he suddenly dropped dead, but later revived to tell of his experiences in the land of darkness. He said that he saw Daigo living in a thatched hut surrounded by four iron mountains, each fifty to sixty feet high. The emperor told Nichizō that during his lifetime he had committed the Five Serious Offenses, and now was suffering retribution—especially for having unjustly exiled Sugawara Michizane (845-903). The emperor and the three ministers who had slandered Michizane were crouched over a bed of red coals, and Daigo alone was clothed. "In the land of darkness, we do not speak of rank," said the emperor. "So do not tender your respects to me."

Prince Takaoka (799-845) wrote a verse expresing this idea:

Iunaraku	It is said
Naraku no soko ni	That when a person enters
Irinureba	The depths of hell,
Setsuri mo shuda mo	He becomes neither
Kawarazarikeri	Brahmin nor outcast.[332]

8:23 The Man Who Had His Teeth Pulled

In Nara lived a Chinese who pulled teeth. Now a certain greedy layman, putting profit before all else, was quite successful by applying a business mentality to every possible situation. So that he might have a rotten tooth removed, he went to the dentist's house, where the price of an extraction was two coppers.

"Take it out for one," he bargained. It was a trifling matter and the dentist could easily have complied; but he had a mean disposition and replied that he was not about to pull the tooth for a single copper.

"All right, then. Take out two teeth for three coppers." And two teeth were removed, including a perfectly good one without any decay. The man thought he had a bargain, but it was a great waste to have lost a tooth which had nothing wrong with it. This was a most ridiculous and silly thing to do.

However, the deep attachment which people of the world have for material gain is such that in all they do they think only of profit, without concern for the principle of moral cause and effect and without discerning the painful results which their present acts will engender in the future. Many are the instances of people being intent on the profit which is before their eyes while losing the jewel of enlightenment and not acquiring the benefits of the Buddha's Law. In ancient times the minds of men were frank and guileless, their actions produced good karma, and all lived with upright hearts.

At the dedication of the Amida Hall after the Lord of Uji had constructed the Byōdōin,[333] it seems that there was some Holy Teacher or other from Mount Hiei with quite a reputation, whom Yorimichi invited to conduct the service.

"It is most unfortunate," remarked the celebrant during the donor eulogy (seshubun), "that he should fall into hell for having constructed this hall." The entire congregation wondered in amazement at this statement, and after the service was over, Yorimichi inquired what he might do to make up for any wrongs he had committed.

"During the construction of this hall you have caused an unreasonable inconvenience for people. It would be well for you to recompense them on the day following this event from your own resources."

Yorimichi made a thorough search for those who had claims and gave them recompense, even to the day laborers. From having been constructed out of a pure spirit of faith, the temple has been subject neither to fire nor damage from that day until this.[334]

The pagoda at Kenninji also escaped destruction by fire on four occasions.[335] According to an old monk living at the temple, it was after the death of the late Kajiwara Kagetoki that his wife, the nun Kano, grieved excessively and was depressed and bitter toward both individuals and society in general. She frequently came to the Kenninji Bishop [Eisai] for counsel; and this is what he told her repeatedly:

"In all things one receives retribution for his actions. We harvest the karma that we ourselves create: the effect which is pleasure or pain corresponds to a good or evil cause. You should feel bitter neither toward individuals nor toward society.

"Because he was involved in many plots of battle in the days of the Great Lord General [Yoritomo], people were destroyed and perished; and while we may say that their deaths were inevitable, they were the result of his decisions. In the end he could not evade responsibility for this and was destroyed, so you should not impute the blame to others. Simply put a stop to your bitterness and grief and with all your heart pray for his enlightenment in the next life."

"However reasonable the course of events, I cannot resign myself to it but feel terribly disconsolate." The nun continued to grieve, but through constant admonition and instruction gradually came to appreciate the reason for what had happened.

"Indeed it was inevitable," she concluded. "This is what is meant by the saying that one receives retribution for his actions. Moreover, while we are in the world we accumulate much karma for rebirth in everything we touch. Having become like a recluse by virtue of my grief, I am all the better able to understand myself as a being of impermanence. If I practice the Buddha's Law for Kagetoki's salvation, then although my life may seem to be one of grief, the future will be most promising. Were I to continue to mingle in worldly affairs, my wrongdoing would gradually accumulate. I now realize that the grief of this life will become the happiness of the next, and so I feel no bitterness towards either society or individuals. I rejoice in the great kindness shown me by my good friend in the faith, [Eisai]."

The faith which developed as she practiced abstinence and performed esoteric rites manifested itself outwardly. When she was awarded a large manor of three parcels of land, the bishop accompanied her down to Kamakura.

"That's why I spoke as I did," he commented. "When the heart is unsullied, one has free access to divine blessings."

"Since the late Kajiwara was an important man, his offenses were likewise great. I would alleviate his wretched condition by whatever meritorious acts I can perform."

"Among all beneficial undertakings, the most profitable is to build a pagoda. Build one at this temple," advised the bishop. With her profit from the three parcels of land, the nun constructed the pagoda within three years, and without the least inconvenience to anyone. As for the fires that continued to plague the rest of the temple, were they not because it was brought to completion with such fraudulent "donations" as taxes levied on people's houses? And was this not contrary to the wishes of the Buddha?

Once when Śāriputra and Maudgalyāyana were passing through the Broad Plains country (Kōyajō), people fled and hid themselves as if they feared demons or ghosts. It seems that there were monks in that country, and people disliked their begging for materials to build their monasteries. They said that the Buddha's disciples were beggars. When the two returned and told the Buddha what had happened, he assembled his followers and established as the second of the Complete Commandments (gussokukai): "One is not to construct large living quarters. Large temples are not provided for in the regulations."[336]

Even animals dislike having people beg things from them. A man engaged in religious practices in a grove of trees was bothered by birds while attempting to pacify his mind. He brought the problem to the Buddha, who suggested: "Beg a feather a day from the birds." The monk returned to the grove and received a feather for his begging. But when he asked again the following day, the birds replied: "We have feathers that we may fly in the sky to seek food and maintain our lives. If they are begged off every day, they will all disappear." And away they flew.

An ascetic on the banks of the Ganges was bothered by a large serpent which would come out of the river and affectionately twine itself about his body. The man related his problem to the Buddha, who asked if the serpent possessed a jewel.

"On its neck," replied the ascetic.

"Well, then, beg to have it."

When the ascetic asked for the jewel, the serpent replied: "It is because you are satisfied with little that I was attracted to you. The jewel is the only treasure I have and I cannot give it away." After this the serpent did not return.

The ability of people in ancient times to endure adversity was such that they lived under trees, on top of rocks, in thatched huts, and in rock caves. Ever since middle antiquity (chūko) there has been an elaborate construction of temples and monasteries. This is because people's capacity to receive the Law has deteriorated. If the men of old had quarters which protected them from the wind and rain so that they could avoid sickness, this would be enough. But in recent times we exhaust every artifice and lavish every expense on temples. Even if they are built by wealthy lay donors, the conscientious follower of the Way should be concerned by the onus of the donations; and it is certainly not worthy of a follower of the Way to consider construction if his purpose be not to engage in religious practice as a child of the Bud-

dha. *The Zen Master Tz'u Ming*[337] *remarked that although he had been senior monk of a large temple five times, he never moved a single rafter: "A temple is not the Buddha's Law; it is merely protection for the living body. The Way is the Buddha's Law, with which the heart is to be deeply imbued."* In the Sutra to Resolve Doubts about the Imitative Law[338] *the Buddha says:* "*After my extinction, at the end of the period of the Apparent Law, there will be many halls, pagodas, and Buddha images crowding the thoroughfares, but among men there will be no spirit of reverence. These constructions are the semblance of my Law, which is to vanish."* *Contemporary behavior bears out the Buddha's prediction. People build temples and pagodas from the wrong motives and at other's inconvenience. Although at the time they think it profitable, they will suffer great loss. Their behavior is even more foolish than having a perfectly good tooth removed.*

In India the philosopher Śīlabhadra (Kaiken Ronji, 6-7 cen.) was stricken with a serious illness and the pain was so severe that he considered committing suicide. A sage appeared to him in a dream saying that the sickness was retribution for his behavior in a former life when, as king of a country, he had oppressed his subjects. The sage said that after three years the atonement would be completed, and three years later Śīlabhadra recovered from his illness. Retribution will follow those who accept alms without performing the duties which they entail.

The Kannon Chapter (Ch. 25) *of the* Lotus Sutra *tells of a band of merchants who were rescued from highwaymen by singlemindedly calling on the name of Kannon. The story may be applied to the operation of the mental functions.*

Lao Tzu says: "The tree which fills the arms grew from the tiniest sprout; the tower of nine storeys rose from a (small) heap of earth." (Tao Te Ching 64; Legge translation). *We should treasure the jewel which is our Self-nature and not permit it to be lost through attachment to the phenomenal world.*

9:1 An Honest Woman

The steward of a mountain temple in Mutsu province set out for the capital to purchase a statue of the Buddha. Along the way he stopped at the post town of Haranaka in Suruga province and mislaid a purse containing fifty gold ryō while taking a bath. He assumed that the purse had been stolen, and since there was nothing to be done about it, he simply continued on his trip to the capital. On his return he passed the same inn in Haranaka and happened to mention his loss to a young woman who worked there. She had found the purse and returned the entire fifty ryō, refusing even a reward of ten ryō which the steward offered to her. The monk was so impressed by her honesty that he invited the woman to accompany him. She agreed and I hear that they are still living happily together. There were also such incidents in olden times. But for a person in today's world, the woman is most forthright and honest. This happened quite recently during the Bun'ei period (1264-1274).

It behooves us to be honest. Had the woman stolen the money, it probably would have been lost or taken by a thief. And even if she had held on to it, what use would it have served? A problem in the present life and retribution for a crime against the Buddha in the next. Honesty is the best policy. The Lotus Sutra (Ch. *16) says that the meek and honest will see the body of the Buddha.*

9:2 Upright Laymen

On Yü Wang mountain in China Dharmamitra (Ren Oshō, 356-442) lectured two monks who were quarreling over alms before expelling them from the temple.

"A certain layman had custody of a hundred pieces of silver belonging to another. After the owner died the layman offered them to the man's child, but he would not take them.

" 'My father gave them to you and they are yours,' said the child.

" 'He only entrusted them to my care; he didn't give them to me. A parent's possessions belong to the child.'

"They disputed together until the matter was brought before a magistrate for a decision. The official commended them both and suggested that they donate the money to a temple to have masses said on the dead man's behalf. This was something I myself saw and heard. Although these people were laymen defiled by the dust of the world, they were not greedy for profit. How can those who have renounced the world be quarreling over worldly goods?"

In these Latter Days there are prosperous laymen who have little attachment to things but have faith and a sense of propriety, whereas there are petty monks who are covetous and possess neither wisdom nor virtue.

9:3 A Couple Which Was Rewarded for Being Upright

This was told to me by a person who heard it from a monk recently returned from China. A poor couple made a living selling rice cakes. Once when the husband was out on business, he found a purse containing six pieces of silver. The couple agreed that they should not keep the money and eventually found the owner, who offered them three pieces as a reward. But when the time came to divide the money, the man had second thoughts and decided to make trouble.

"There used to be seven pieces. Strange that now there are only six! You must have hidden one."

The couple insisted that there had been only six pieces, and the matter finally went to the district magistrate for a decision. The magistrate had a sharp eye for things and saw that the owner of the purse was dishonest. But since it was such a curious affair, he summoned the rice cake dealer's wife and questioned her about the circumstances of the case. Her report did not differ in the least from her husband's.

"It is difficult to render a decision," said the magistrate. "Both of you appear to be honest. The accounts given by husband and wife do not conflict, and the statement of the owner of the purse also seems to be true. So he should be looking for a bundle with seven pieces in it. Since this one has only six, it must belong to someone else."

He gave the six pieces of silver to the couple, and the people of the Sung loudly praised his excellent judgment.

9:4 A Man of Good Will

In Musashi province lived an affluent land steward who was known to be a man of deep compassion and good will. Year after year this man bought up the property of an unsuccessful neighbor who had to sell. When the neighbor died, his only son was left without any inheritance. The son sought help from a wide circle of relations, but without success, since they were also people of small means. But they suggested that he ask for help from the wealthy land steward, and this man gave the son the deeds to his father's land. We do not often hear of such men of feeling in these Latter Days.

Kasai Kiyoshige (13th cen.) was an accomplished master of the bow and arrow. When Wada Yoshimori (1147-1213) threw the world into disorder (1213), Kasai dispersed his forces. He was a brave and considerate man. In the days of Yoritomo (1147-1199), there was some trouble with the Edo family of Musashi and its lands were awarded to Kasai. Kasai replied that he was friends with the Edo and that if a crime had been committed, the land should be awarded to someone else. Kasai held firm against Yoritomo's scolding and in the end the Edo were not dispossessed.

In olden times there was benevolence and righteousness between lord and retainer. But in these Latter Days fathers and sons, brothers and relatives, turn against each other. The Benevolent Kings Sutra says that when there is disharmony in the family, the gods do not extend their protection.

Yamada Jirō, Minamoto no Shigetada (1165-1221)[339] of Owari province, was slain at the time of the Jōkyū Disturbance (1219-1221) while supporting the emperor [Gotoba]. He was skillful in the way of bow and arrow. Being highminded and a man of dignity, he also had a gentle disposition and was aware of the people's sufferings. In all respects he was a gentleman.

On his lands lived a priest who had some double-petaled azaleas which Shigetada coveted, but he would not ask for them. Then the monk commit-

*ted a crime for which he was to be punished, and a certain Tōhyōe was sent
as executor. Shigetada gave the monk a choice between a fine of seven bolts
of silk or the azaleas; but Tōhyōe, knowing his master's mind, advised the
monk: "If you send the silk, some doubt may remain in Shigetada's mind
about your loyalty. Send the azaleas."*

*"As executor you are entitled to half the fine," said the monk. "Take
three bolts of silk and a branch of azaleas for yourself." Tōhyōe reluctantly
agreed to take the silk, but the monk insisted on his also taking the flowers.*

The azaleas are still to be seen today.

*The double-petalled cherry blossoms of the Nara capital are to be seen
even today in front of the Tōendō. Ex-empress Jōtōmon'in (Michinaga's
daughter Shōshi, 988–1074) sent an order to the steward of the Kōfukuji req-
uisitioning a cherry tree which grew there. As it was being hauled away people grumbled that the steward was wrong to give it up. Presently a large
crowd gathered to stop the carriage and throw the steward out, regardless of
the penalties.*

*When the retired empress heard of the incident, she was touched by the
popular response and designated it as her personal property. Entrusting it to
the Yono Manor in Iga province which she named "Flower-fence"
(hanagaki), she built a fence around the cherry-tree and had it guarded during seven days at the peak of its season. Today the manor is administered as a
temple.*

9:5 The Deceased Father Who Directed His Son
to Return a Borrowed Item

*Some time ago in Musashi province lived two laymen who were intimate
neighbors. One being poor and the other rich, things were constantly being
borrowed. After they both died their children continued the friendship.*

*Now the child of the poor man had a dream in which his deceased father
appeared and ordered him to return some money to the son of the other
man. Upon waking, the son quickly collected the amount of the loan and
presented it to the son of the rich man, informing him of the circumstances.
This one, however, replied: "How can I take it? Since my father is calling
yours to account in the other world, I should not complicate the matter by
accepting the money in this one."*

*And so the matter was argued back and forth until it was taken to
Kamakura for a decision.*

*"I have never heard such a strange sad tale. Your filial concern is deep,
and you are both upright men," said the magistrate. It was decided that they
should take the money and offer it for the repose of the souls of both their
fathers.*

9:6 The Young Sons Who Slew Their Father's Enemy

A layman of Musashi province went down to Kyūshū to attend to his property. When he did not return for two or three years, his wife had an affair with another man. Then news came that the husband was returning from Kyūshū. When the wife and her lover plotted to have a servant attack the man on the road, they were overheard by his six-year-old son, who then made plans with his younger brother to dispose of their mother's lover. While he was napping, one of the boys held a sword to his chest near the heart while the other struck it with a hammer three times until the tip penetrated the floor. The man died without saying a word.

The children then went to their uncle's house and told what they had done. He praised them, but since the matter could not be concealed, referred it to Kamakura.

"Although I have heard of a six-year-old avenging his father, I have never actually witnessed it," said the magistrate. Inasmuch as no real crime had been committed, the children went to live with their father on his return home.

9:7 A Man Loyal and Filial Toward His Mother

A lady in the service of the late Zen Monk of Sagami Province (Hōjō Tokiyori, 1227–1263) had a bad temper. Once when she had become angry over some trifle, she stumbled and fell while attempting to strike her grown son. In a rage she went to Tokiyori complaining that her son had hit her. The lad was summoned and confirmed her story.

"This is outrageous," scolded Tokiyori, and determined to confiscate the son's possessions and send him away. At length the mother calmed down and, full of remorse, admitted to Tokiyori that she had lied. Again the son was interrogated.

"How could I strike my mother?" was his reply.

"Then why did you not tell me the truth from the beginning?" asked Tokiyori.

"It would have been wrong. How could I have made my mother out to be a liar?"

The man was admired for his sense of filial piety and awarded a special grant of land.

9:8 The Child Who Supported His Blind Mother

The venerable Shunjōbō[340] of Nara was having timber cut on the mountains of Aki and Suō provinces[341] for the construction of the Great Buddha Hall at Tōdaiji, and had stored up many bales of rice with which to feed the workers. One day he caught someone making off with one of the bales—a skinny, wizened boy.

"What kind of person are you to commit such a sacrilegious act against the Buddha's property?" asked the monk.

"I realize that this is no excuse," replied the boy. "But in addition to being too poor to eke out my own livelihood, I have a mother who is blind. I support her by collecting firewood and selling it in a distant village. But with my body worn out and my strength exhausted, I do not have the peace of mind of being able to care for her adequately. There is plenty of food for the lumbermen. And I figured that since this was a religious undertaking, it would not lack support and the supplies would never be used up. So I decided to pilfer just a little to help my mother. By committing such a sacrilege I have truly brought shame upon myself. My behavior, though probably occasioned by the karma of some previous life, was disgraceful and I regret it!" The child wept without restraint.

The holy man was moved by what he heard. But in order to ascertain whether or not the child was telling the truth, he took him into his employ while sending another servant to look for the mother's house on the basis of the child's description. The servant went to investigate and found a small hut at the foot of a mountain. Hearing a voice within, he approached and inquired who was living there.

"One who is blind and fallen on hard times drags out her life at the foot of this mountain," came the reply from within. "By relying on my young son who supports me by taking firewood to the village, this life which is as ephemeral as dew has not quite faded away. The child went out yesterday and I am impatient and uneasy that he has not returned. Hearing that someone had come. I thought it might be my child. But it isn't!"

Returning quickly, the servant told the holy man that he had found the situation just as the child had described it. Shunjō was deeply moved and gave the boy enough food to sustain his mother. But bearing in mind that it was a serious matter to whimsically dispose of the Buddha's property, he hired the boy for the duration of the timber-cutting.

What the boy did had the appearance of being a sacrilege. But inasmuch as he acted out of a genuine spirit of filial piety, was it perhaps only consistent with the beneficence of the Three Treasures that he should receive enough food to sustain his mother? How very extraordinary! It all happened because when the sense of filial piety is genuine, even the unseen spirits may be moved to pity!

In the days of Cloistered Sovereign Shirakawa (1053–1129) the prohibition against killing living things applied to everyone in the land, and whoever violated it was subject to severe penalties. The mother of a monk at a certain mountain temple was poor and advanced in years. She was ill from malnutrition and could eat only fish, but fish were neither bought nor sold. So the monk tied back his surplice and robe and had caught a few in the Katsura River when he was apprehended by an official and taken to Shirakawa's palace. For a monk the crime was all the worse and the punishment should be extreme.

"I sought to preserve my mother's life, whatever blame I might incur," said the monk. *"Since these fish are now beyond saving, take them to my mother. After I have heard that she has eaten, do with me as you will."*

The emperor was moved, forgave the monk, and gave him enough to support his mother. Here was a case of genuine filial concern. In antiquity there were many such.

9:9 The Boy Who Sold Himself to Support His Mother

During the long droughts of the Bun'ei period (1264–1274) Mino and Owari provinces were especially hard hit by the widespread famine, so that many people fled to other areas. In Mino lived a poor mother and son who had no one on whom to rely, and who in such troubled times could only starve to death. So the boy decided to sell himself into bondage in order to provide for his mother. But the mother could not agree. "If we are to die, let us die together."

Nevertheless, the son sold himself without his mother's consent and gave her the proceeds. After a tearful farewell, he went down to the eastern provinces with his new master. According to the report of someone who had taken lodging at an inn at Yahagi in Mikawa province, the young boy wept uncontrollably among a large company of merchants with whom he was traveling. When he explained what he had done and told of his sadness at leaving this mother, everyone at the inn was moved.

The boy's filial piety was not inferior to that in antiquity.

9:10 A Daughter's Prayer Reveals the Place of Her Mother's Rebirth

In Kyoto lived a poor woman and her daughter. Life having become difficult for them in the capital, they moved to Echigo province where they had relations. Subsequently the daughter married a man from Kyoto, a devotee of the nembutsu, *who urged her to live with him in the capital. But the daughter was reluctant to leave her mother, who had become a nun.*

Finally the daughter was persuaded by her mother to move with her husband to the capital. Then after hearing no news from the country, she made a pilgrimage to the Kiyomizu temple and prayed to know if her mother was still alive. Days passed without a response, and then in a dream she was told:

"After you left your mother died of a broken heart. She was reborn as a chestnut-colored packhorse at the residence of a certain man in Kyūshū. At present she is in Kyoto, at such-and-such an inn."

Upon waking, the daughter went straightway to the inn to discover that there was indeed a man from Kyūshū lodging there who had a chestnut-colored pack horse. The owner became suspicious when she asked if he would show it to her, so she told him of her separation from her mother, her prayer at the Kiyomizu, and her revelation. The man sent for the horse, only to be told by a servant that it had been taken off to Kamakura the day before. A messenger was dispatched and overtook the horse at an inn in Ōmi province, but on the way back to Kyoto the horse suddenly became sick and died. Rather than return empty-handed, the messenger cut off the horse's head and brought it with him.

The daughter, having carefully prepared food for the horse while counting the days until its return, received only the head. In great sorrow she took it home, buried it, and performed the rites prescribed by filial piety.

Unless it be by a revelation from the gods, children do not realize the torment which their parents receive by falling into the Evil Paths through foolish attachment to them. This girl, out of deep filial piety, prayed to the Buddha and came to know her mother's fate. The Net of Brahma Sutra says that because of our myriad previous existences there is no living creature in the world who has not been our father or mother in a past life. So when we take life and eat flesh, we are devouring our parents.

At the Kuo-ch'ing Temple in China lived a disciple of the Zen Master Feng-kan (Bukan, 8th cen.) called Shih-te (Jittoku). A householder, wishing to entertain some guests, asked the master to send Shih-te to help him with the preparations. Shih-te and Han-shan (Kanzan) went together. During the banquet Han-shan and Shih-te carried on so rudely that the host and guests were offended. Later the master reprimanded them.

"How could we be jovial?" replied Shih-te. "This man's parents in a former life were reborn with bodies of animals. Today, without knowing it, he feasted on the flesh of his parents; and the distress which Han-shan and I expressed was interpreted as laughter."

Whether or not we are aware of it, and whether they are near or far, we all, so to speak, kill and devour our parents. Animals should not be tormented and slain.

9:11 The Man Who Prospered Through Loyalty to His Superior

Some years ago it became the fashion to chose partners by lot, exchange gifts, and thus accrue spiritual merit by reason of one's liberality. The custom became widespread, reaching even to the upper classes. At the residence of a certain nobleman a poor samurai was chosen to be the partner of his lord. Not having the resources to sustain his side of the transaction, the man even *considered becoming a monk to avoid the obligation. But since he had no genuine religious aspiration, his wife discouraged him.*

"Man's fortune and happiness depend on one's state of mind," she argued. "Although you wish to escape these worldly obligations, you have already been chosen as your lord's partner. We are man and wife, and we either prosper together or suffer together. So mortgage the house and land and settle the matter."

After further discussion the man sold the property for some fifty or sixty kan *by means of which he had fashioned a silver tray and a golden orange. When the moment came to exchange gifts, the superior was impressed by the man's loyalty, although hitherto he had not been especially favored. He then gave the man a thousand* koku *manor near the capital.*

Although one is poor, he should know his shortcomings and have loyalty to his superiors.

9:12 The Man Who Prospered Through Treating a Friend Justly

In the household of the late Imadegawa Prime Minister (Saionji Kinsuke; see S&P 8:15) lived a poor but faithful samurai called Gyōbu no Jō. Across the street from his residence lived the monk Kōjakubō, who made a profitable living copying sutras. When Gyōbu no Jō would go to the palace, the monk would visit his wife, secretly at first and then openly. At first the samurai ignored the rumors, but finally decided to see for himself. One day he pretended to leave for the palace but stayed in the neighborhood and saw the monk enter his house. Gyōbu no Jō then went home, as though returning suddenly from the palace. There was no way for the monk to escape so he hid in a closet.

Standing next to the closet, Gyōbu no Jō told his wife that he was expecting guests. After refreshments were prepared and several men from the neighborhood invited, Gyōbu no Jō called Kōjakubō from the closet. Then he addressed the guests.

"I had heard that Kōjakubō was visiting my wife, but I was not sure if the rumors were true. Today I found out that they were. As this man is my foe from a previous existence, I ought to shame him; but he is a monk and I hesitate to do so. Moreover, it must be because of some affinities from a former life that he visited my wife. So I shall give her to him. In this world there is no greater treasure than one's wife, so in giving her away I give away my family and all my possessions. And since I would not shame Kōjakubō by putting him at a disadvantage, I will accept in exchange his wife, servants and all of his belongings. What do you think of this?" The guests agreed that this was a reasonable solution to the problem, but Kōjakubō could not utter a word.

"My wife and goods are now forfeit," continued Gyōbu no Jō. "If you do not reciprocate, I shall be considered a fool, unable to face my colleagues or serve my lord. Then I will use my sword on you."

Kōjakubō agreed to the conditions and a detailed contract was drawn up. Thus Gyōbu no Jō exchanged his wife and meager possessions for Kōjakubō's wife and rich property. It is a crime to kill a monk. Gyōbu no Jō did not act for the sake of notoriety and his righteous behavior was recognized for its wisdom.

9:13 Respect for the Teacher

The late Shōgombō (Gyōyū, 1163-1241) of the Jufukuji[342] was noted for his virtue and was respected by the Kamakura Minister (Minamoto Sanetomo, 1192-1219), who took him as his spiritual adviser. People came to him with petitions to present to the shogun, but Sanetomo eventually told him to stop interfering: "In the affairs of the world one man's joy is another's sorrow." Shōgombō agreed, but in time became involved in a serious affair and was reprimanded by the shogun.

The monk respectfully retired and for more than seventy days there was no communication between the two. Then one midnight Sanetomo suddenly came to the Jufukuji with only two or three attendants and apologized to his mentor for having acted contrary to the teacher-disciple relationship. The monk replied that he was the one at fault and begged Sanetomo's forgiveness. I was told this by an old monk belonging to the temple. An old man who had served Sanetomo said that someone had appeared to him in a dream, dressed in white, asking: "Why do you torment the worthy monk?" Sanetomo was frightened and hurried to the temple in the middle of the night.

In Kyoto the monk Zuijōbō (Tan'e, 13th cen.) of Nekoma, who had crossed over to China to study Zen at Ching Shan, was asked by the late Courtly Zen Practitioner (Zenjō Denka, i.e., Fujiwara Michiie, 1191-1252) of the Hosshōji to instruct him. Zuijōbō was seated on a lower level than Michiie and would not proceed until he was given the superior seat, so that the proprieties governing the teacher-disciple relationship might be observed. Michiie became an ardent believer.

In the Latter Days of the Law even the monk who violates the regulations should be respected. The Comentary on the Great Wisdom Sutra *says that just as we would not throw away money enclosed in a smelly bag of dog's skin, so we should have faith in the True Law promulgated even by a worthless monk.*

Long before the Buddha appeared in the world, and before even the word "Buddhism" was heard, there lived a deeply enlightened fox.[343] Running to escape from a lion, he fell into a deep hole from which he was unable to get out. After several days had passed, he assessed his situation and concluded that he should have offered himself to the lion. The sound of his prayer was heard in the Heaven of the Thirty-Three (Tōriten) where it startled Indra (Taishakuten), who set out with countless devas and descended to find the voice of the fox coming from a hole. When Indra asked the fox to discourse on the Law, the fox replied: "You who are lord of the Heaven of the Thirty-Three have no manners. If the teacher is beneath and the disciple above, how can he preach the Law?"

Indra then built a high platform from which the fox expounded the Law. Nowadays, since laymen do not genuinely believe in Buddhism, there are few who respect monks. On the other hand, there are few conscientious monks and most use Buddhism for profit.

"Now in Kyūshū there is a monk called Ennibō, who has returned after receiving the Buddhist Teaching at Ching Shan and who clearly understands both meditation (*zen*) and the doctrinal teachings of Buddhism. He is ten times the teacher I am."

When the monk [Zuijōbō] said this, [Michiie] became interested and sent a messenger to invite him to the capital. Enni first propagated the *zen* teaching at the Tsukinowa Palace.[344] He maintained a meditation hall at the Fumonji. Later on [Michiie] built the Tōfukuji and had a disciple-to-teacher relationship with the priest Shōichi.

Enni was his original name. He was called Shōichi for being the "Foremost Sage"; others say that he was so called by analogy with the Senior First Rank (*shōichii*) among court titles. From this time *zen* prospered in Japan.[345]

10A:1 The Hermit Jōdobō

In the Izu mountains a certain Jōdobō was the second-ranking priest at his temple. He went to visit the head monk once when the old man was sick and reaching the end of his days. The head monk remarked that Jōdobō must be delighted that he was dying because now he would succeed as abbot of the temple. But Jōdobō was a monk with genuine religious aspirations and he was embarrassed by the suggestion. So while the old monk was still alive, he decided to become a hermit (tonsei) to demonstrate the purity of his intentions. Handing over his quarters to his disciples, he went off to live in a small hut.

Once during a heavy rain a landslide buried his hermitage. His disciples dug away the earth fearing the worst, but Jōdobō was alive. The disciples were overjoyed, but the recluse remarked that he had suffered a great loss.

"Since I was a child I have recited the name of Kannon to avoid such calamities as this.[346] I must have recited it during the landslide, so that my life has been spared. But it is a great calamity for me to go on living in this

floating world just as I was about to enter the Pure Land chanting the nembutsu.*"*

In the end Jōdobō is said to have passed away auspiciously.

The Pure Land teachings have been propagated widely in India, China and Japan by many devotees; but the sincere among them have been few, and most have been mediocre men. At Lu Shan (Rozan) in China eighty worthies including Hui-yüan (Eon, 334-416) established the White Lotus Vihāra (Pai Lien She) and devoted themselves to Pure Land practices.[347] But the attainment of birth in the Pure Land is not that easy. The venerable Zōga (917-1003) visited the Komponchūdō on Mount Hiei a thousand times and every night performed a thousand obeisances that he might attain religious understanding (dōshin).

Even Eshin (Genshin, 942-1017) had doubts about his attainment of birth in the Pure Land. While he was standing in the rain in the vicinity of Tsukurimichi and Yotsuzuka in Kyoto to find an omen in the casual conversation of passers-by (michiura), an old man came sliding down the muddy street. Having finally made it safely to where Eshin stood, he remarked: "I have reached paradise." Eshin's doubts were dispelled, for he realized that attaining salvation was most comparable to the old man making his perilous way along the muddy street. Then he compiled the Essentials of Salvation, and his name is known even in China. The Essentials states that although many recite the nembutsu, it is because of their insincerity that few attain birth in the Pure Land.

The Treatise on the Pure Land by Vasubandhu (Tenjin Bosatsu) is the basic commentary of the Pure Land sect. It says that "if one aspires to birth in the Pure Land, he should raise the Desire for Enlightenment;[348] desire for Enlightenment is the intention to save all beings, causing them to be born in a Buddha-land." T'an-luan (Donran, 476-542) in his Commentary on the Treatise on Birth in the Pure Land (Ōjōronchū, T. 1819) says that without the desire to save all beings, there can be no birth in the Pure Land. Diligence is necessary; but people today are fickle.

Someone remarked: " 'Other Power' and 'Original Vow' do not refer to whether or not one has roots of merit (zengon) which depend on one's good or bad attitude, but to the fact that because of our reliance on him, the Buddha will be at our side." The Sutra of Meditation on Amida Buddha (Kammuryō-jukyō T. 365) says that one who has the Three Qualities of Mind (sanshin)[349] for attaining birth in the Pure Land will certainly be born there. The commentary states that with only one of these intentions, he cannot. Shan-tao says that one who keeps Amida in his thoughts from moment to moment should not begrudge the loss of his life, for Amida will come to meet him.[350] Even the Buddha does not interfere with the operation of karma. But when evil takes possession of a man, it first deludes the mind. It is at this time that the Buddha rescues him and encourages him to enter the Way.

Lao Tzu says that a virtuous man travels on the land without having to shun rhinoceros or tiger, and enters a hostile camp without having to fear *armed warriors or sharp weapons. When one is pursuing the Way, there is in him no place of death* (Tao Te Ching 50:4).

It is dangerous to belittle the difficulties of attaining birth in the Pure Land. But the Sutra of Meditation on Amida Buddha *states that even a wicked sinner will attain birth in the Pure Land if he dies in a proper frame of mind reciting the* nembutsu. *If, like Jōdobō, we begrudge the loss of our bodies not even by a single thought and our hearts are not attached to this world, it will not be difficult to reach paradise. I have recorded these matters in detail to encourage the illiterate; this is not intended for scholars.*

10A:2 The Yoshino Temple-bailiffs Who Became Recluses

The office of Temple-bailiff (shugyō [*of the Kimpusenji and Konrinnōji*] *in Yoshino carries great prestige, and it has been a frequent occurrence for the incumbent to be slain and his authority usurped. When the father of the present bailiff held that position, his brother tried to overthrow him. The bailiff reflected that prestige does not last long, and that it would be unfortunate if squabbles between brothers should prevent him from preparing for the afterlife. So he handed over the office to his younger brother, became a recluse* (tonsei), *took the precepts under Shiembō* (Eizon; see S&P 7:17) *of the Saidaiji, and came to a felicitous end. His younger brother, the bailiff, later transferred the office to the son of the elder brother. And it is said that the present bailiff also plans to become a recluse. We might conclude that these men had been destined by affinities in a previous life to lead one another to salvation in this one.*

King Ajātaśatru (Ajase-ō) listened to his wicked friend Devadatta (Chōdatsu) and imprisoned his parents.[351] *Because this caused them to reflect on what evil karma must have caused them to be imprisoned by their wicked child, Devadatta and Ajātaśatru acted as true friends* (zenchishiki) *to King Bimbisāra (Bashara-ō) and Queen Vaidehi (Idaike). During their imprisonment both progressed in the spiritual life. What filial deed can excel leading one's parents to the Way of the Buddha.*

The Sutra on Viewing the Mind-Ground (Shinjikangyō, T. 159) *states that a man may fall into hell because of his children. Thus, a good child may sometimes be an evil influence, and a bad child may be a good influence. In everything, profit and loss are intermingled. We should distinguish profit and loss among things, and the wise and foolish among men. So a poor doctor will make poison of a medicine, a mediocre doctor will use poison as a poison and medicine as a medicine; but a good doctor can use poison as a medicine. Similarly, a person with distorted views has a good child to his own advantage. A mediocre person will be affected adversely by a bad child and well by a good child. But a superior person will turn a bad child into an asset, as did King Bimbisāra and Queen Vaidehi. The child is not the only factor to* be considered. If one is unfortunate in this respect but considers it to be just retribution for past karma, this can be a benefit. The round of transmigration is simply the result of attachment. The Diamond Sutra (Kongōkyō, T. 235) states that we should shun attachment even to the Buddha's Law—how much more so the things of the world.

When others criticize you, pay attention. If you have the fault in question, then what they say is only right. And so it is said: "He who comes to you with censure is your teacher; . . . but he who flatters you is your enemy."[352]

10A:3 Sōshumbō Becomes a Recluse

At the Tōdaiji in Nara lived a compassionate monk called Sōshumbō. A parcel of land which had been bequeathed to him from his teacher was disputed by a fellow-disciple. Sōshumbō felt that the matter was not worth his trouble and took the certificate of ownership to his adversary.

"We have been friends, and I do not wish to have ill feelings over a parcel of land. You may have it."

"I'm talking about the principle of the thing. I won't take it," replied the other.

"Since I intend to become a recluse in any case, I have no use for the land," said Sōshumbō, leaving the certificate and returning home. Immediately thereafter he became a recluse. He was a man of deep compassion and performed many good works.

A famous priest in Nara remarked to the Sage of Kasagi (Jōkei, 1155-1213):[353] "Because I am poor, I look forward for someone to invite me to perform a service, but no one ever does. Although you turn down offers, they come from all directions. I envy you."

"It seems to me that I get the most invitations during those times when I turn down the most," Jōkei replied. "Turn down an offer and people will invite you." Interestingly enough, what he said was true.

In general heaven bestows prosperity as one grows in wisdom, and profit which exceeds one's lot does not last long. Lao Tzu says that (by relying on the Tao) the worn out becomes new and the empty becomes full (Tao Te Ching 22). One should be content with heaven's dispensation.

While the Minamoto were in power after the collapse of the Taira, the elite of Kyoto sent many requests to Kamakura, but they were ignored. Then Yoritomo heard of Yoshida Tsunefusa (1143-1200), who had gone into retirement after the downfall of the Taira. The shogun considered him to be a wise man and consulted with him. Good fortune came to Tsunefusa, the just deserts of an upright heart, and his family was long supported.

It is written that those who win through virtue will prosper, while those who succeed by use of force will fail. Understanding well this principle, we

*should maintain ourselves without immoderate expectations, living our lives
resigned to our destiny.*

10A:4 The Householders Who Became Recluses

*In Tango province lived a householder whose name I heard but do not
recall. His estate was small, but the members of his family were not destitute.
The man had eight sons and several daughters, and when he died he bequeathed the major portion of his estate to the eldest, giving progressively less
to each of the other children. However the eldest was not comfortable with
having inherited the responsibility as head of the family. He proposed that
another be appointed to represent the family, that his share of the estate be
divided among the other children, and that he would build a hermitage and
spend the rest of his life reciting the* nembutsu. *As none of the brothers offered to assume his responsibilities, the eldest appointed his brother Gorō.
The others acquiesced and it is said that they all became recluses.*

*When we examine well what it is that people in the world consider hap-
piness, we find that in their confusion they take what is painful to be
pleasure. Happiness is first of all based on our state of mind. It is nothing to
have status if one is miserable; and a person can be poor, but happy, if his
mind is at ease. Thus the* [Final Admonition] *Sutra says that a contented person will be happy sleeping on the ground, while the discontented will be
unhappy even in heaven.*

*When a deer is captured and held in a fancy cage, it does not stop long-
ing for the mountains, although fed on delicacies. And when it lies down at
ease in the mountains, it grows fat, although it has only grass to eat and water
to drink. Po Chü-i tells us that there is suffering amid riches and happiness
amid poverty, and that it is better to accept things as they come than to pursue what is past or run to meet what lies in the future.*

*In China the sage Hsü Yu (Kyōyu), having received an order [from
Emperor Yao] to become Prime Minister, went to a river and washed his ears.
On his return he was met by Ch'ao Fu (Sōfu) leading a cow to water. Hsü Yu
explained that having heard an order that he was to be Prime Minister, he
reasoned that his ears must have been badly in need of cleaning. So he had
gone to the river to wash them.*

*"The water now must really be dirty!" remarked Ch'ao Fu, and led his
cow back home. This is what is meant by the saying that Hsü Yu washes his
ears and Ch'ao Fu leads away his cow.*

*A great king in antiquity [who was Śākyamuni in an earlier existence]
caste aside his title and worldly goods to learn the Great Law of the Single
Vehicle (as described in the* Lotus Sutra, Chapter 12).

*In Japan the Cloistered Sovereign Kazan (968-1008) became a recluse.
When Lady Kokiden (Fujiwara Yoshiko, d. 985), daughter of Saneyori (actually Tamemitsu, 941-990) died, the sovereign lamented deeply. Seeing the*

Awata Kampaku (Fujiwara Michikane, 961-995) writing on a fan the phrase (from the Great Collection of Sutras)*: "Neither family, jewels, nor kingly rank accompany one at the final hour," the emperor had a religious awakening. He slipped out of the palace on the twenty-third day of the sixth month of Kanna 2 (986), and from that day the door by which he made his escape has been secured. What a felicitous awakening! Even hearing the story at this distance in time we are moved.*

Kakuban (1095-1143) likened even a palace to the Burning House [as discussed, for example, in the Lotus Sutra*] from which the inmates should seek to escape.*

At an Eight Expoundings of the Lotus Sutra *service* (hokke hakkō) *for the late lay priest Shinzei (Fujiwara Michinori, d. 1160; see S&P 2:1) by his descendants in the clergy*[354] *on the thirteenth anniversary of his death, Seal-of-the-Law Shōgaku (1167-1235; see S&P 6:8) and Myōhen (1142-1224; see S&P 1:3) were selected to officiate. Messengers were also sent to Kakuken (1141-1212), Chōken (1126-1203), Jōken and the others. But Myōhen declined to attend on the grounds that he had become a hermit. This offended his clerical brothers, and after some discussion he sent a certain Echibō as his substitute.*

10A:5 The Priest of the Kanshōji

Daiembō (Ryōin, 1212-1291; S&P 7:24) of the Kiyomizu Kanshōji, a disciple of the late Kongō-ō-in Bishop (Jitsugen, 1176-1249), had lived in seclusion for many years and was known for his sanctity. On one occasion the apprentice of some Kiyomizu monk became drunk and broke the sliding doors to the monks' quarters. The monks took their grievances to Daiembō, suggesting that the boy be taken before a Kamakura official at the Rokuhara. But Daiembō rebuked them for their concern over the matter.

"Having met a madman, you yourselves go mad. Why do you do this? Attachment only leads to transmigration," he said. The disciples withdrew grumbling and news of the incident spread. Eventually the apprentice was brought to Daiembō's hut, but the recluse only laughed.

"Boys at mountain temples are all like this. Why should we make an issue of this? Whatever those monks say only shows that they have no understanding of things. This is a good boy. His eyes show that he is sorry for what he did." After this incident the boy behaved exceptionally well.

10A:6 The Robber-Monk with Religious Aspirations

In Nara lived a soldier-monk (akusō, *i.e.,* sōhei) *who from his youth enjoyed the military arts but could not read a single character. In his later years he became reflective and decided to do good. His plan for acquiring merit that he might be born in the Pure Land was to associate with robbers, with the idea of helping people. Whenever the robbers would enter a man's house, the monk would go in first to warn him so that he might escape with his life or hide his valuables. On the surface he looked mean, but he saved the lives of many people. When the time came to divide the spoils, he would take nothing, saying that he would let the other robbers know when he needed something.*

After many years the monk was caught and taken into custody. But as the result of a dream in which the magistrate saw a golden Amida tied to a pillar, he was released and interrogated. When the monk told his story and his reasons for acting as he did, he was released and was not heard from again. He must have realized his desire for birth in the Pure Land.

The good or evil of whatever we do is determined by our state of mind. We would not expect burglary to lead to birth in the Pure Land, but it could be a good act if performed from good motives. Good and evil complement each other: evil can be an influence for good, and good an influence for evil. Thus, a sutra states that the passions may be a cause for liberation.

An ancient has described those who maintain the bodhisattva-precepts in four phrases: (1) Outwardly clean, inwardly dirty. This is the thief of the Law. He gives the semblance of observing the precepts but is inwardly dissolute. Nan-shan (Tao-hsüan, 596–667; cf. S&P 4:9) calls him "a thief without a knife." (2) Inwardly clean, outwardly dirty. Hiding his virtue, this person does not accept support from the faithful. (3) Clean within and without. This is the ideal of the teaching. (4) Dirty within and without. The self-indulgent sinner.

The Sutra of Ten Cakras *says that a monk of genuine understanding who expounds the Law correctly can accomplish good even though he himself does not maintain the precepts. The* Buddha Treasury Sutra *states that a monk who makes a livelihood from Buddhism while leading people astray commits a greater crime than gouging out the eyes of the inhabitants of the three-thousand worlds (cf., S&P 6:17, "Preaching for a Livelihood").*

10A:7 Religious Awakening from an Evil Influence[355]

In the capital lived a couple who passed their lives in poverty.

"I can't stand this miserable existence," the wife told her husband. "People will do anything to improve their condition in life. You can support me by becoming a robber or a highwayman!"

"Lots of people are poor. How could I possible do what you ask?" But his wife cried and whined bitterly.

"If that's the way you feel, then give me a divorce. I'll find a real man to live with."

And so, because of his deep affection for his wife, the man set out in the direction of Uchino,[356] looking for an opportunity.

Around sunset a woman with a young girl attendant passed him. There was no one in sight, so the man killed them both, stripped them of their clothes, and returned home.

"Here it is! I got what you asked for." The man handed the blood-stained garments to his wife, telling her what he had done. He expected her to say something about its being a wretched business even though she had urged him to do it. Instead her face wrinkled with smiles, giving an appearance of utter delight.

The man was repelled, and the love and affection which he had felt for her vanished. He immediately left the house, cut off his locks, and became a monk. Then he went up to Mount Kōya, where he earnestly prepared for the next life. Profoundly aware of his sin of senseless murder, he prayed for his victims happiness in the next world.

One day a fellow lay-priest came to talk with him. "That which has led us to aspire for enlightenment can be an inspiration to others and we should speak of these matters. I should like to know your reasons. As for me, I used to live in the capital. I had a misfortune; and the great city, where I had felt at home, lost its hold on my affections. I came away distraught and climbed this mountain."

"I am also from the capital," said the first monk. "But something unexpected happened and I abandoned the world."

"There must be some karmic reason behind our meeting. Please tell me all about it." His companion was persistent although the monk was reluctant to speak.

"Urged on by one with whom I had exchanged vows, I committed an unthinkable act." When the monk related what he had done, the other inquired when it happened, the color of the woman's robe, her age, and all the details. Suddenly the lay-priest clapped his hands.

"You are my true friend!" he exclaimed. "The woman was my beloved wife. After that day of bereavement I abandoned the world. Had it not been for what happened how should I have considered entering on the difficult path of Buddhist austerities? You were destined to be my true friend; I have no dearer bretheren in the faith. Let us pray for my wife's future happiness and now enter the path of escape from the world of illusion."

Together they strove for salvation. Someone told me he had heard that one of the monks had already met death in a proper state of mind, having been carefully tended by his companion. The other may still be alive.

Bitter bereavements are common in the world of men, but they do not always lead people to the desire for enlightenment. We should bestir ourselves!

10A:8 Shōgatsubō's Abandoning the World

Shōgatsubō (Keishō, d. 1268) of Matsu-no-o belonged to the Mii[dera] school of Tendai and was known to be a conscientious monk. This is the way people say he first became a recluse. Going deep into the Matsu-no-o mountains he took with him provisions for seven days. Setting up a temporary hut, he began his religious exercises. When the seven-day supply of food was exhausted, he was considering eating dried potato stalks softened in water when he was met by a woodcutter who offered him a day's ration of food as alms. The same thing happened on the following and succeeding days, so that Shōgatsubō never had an opportunity to use the dried potato stalks. Eventually a temple (Hokkeyamadera) was built. the monk continued his austerities and came to a felicitous end. This was a curious thing to have happened in these Latter Days. Today those who would strictly practice the religious exercises must not lack food or clothing.

A venerable monk known as Shinchibō of Hira went into the Hira mountains with a twenty-day supply of food to practice [Tendai's] Cessation and Contemplation and was provided for by the mountain folk.

The beasts of the fields and the fish of the sea all have food, clothing, and a place to live. How much more should those who have had the good fortune to be born human be provided with these necessities? Rely on Heaven and pass over this dream world without anxiety; for there is no summit of desire, no limit for the covetous heart. King Mūrdhaja (Chōshō-ō) was king of the Southern Region. Not satisfied, he seized the Four Kingdoms. Still unsatisfied, he stormed the Heaven of the Thirty-Three (Tōriten) when his good fortune ran out and he died. We should know our limitations and act accordingly.

When the late Ichijō-in (1199-1256) was visited in Nara by Bishop Kakuhen (?1172-1258) he remarked that poverty was a state of mind.

"Who would think himself into being poor?" replied the Bishop. "Poverty is in fact the rule, and everyone thinks that he would like to be prosperous."

"No one thinks himself into poverty, but to plan foolishly and to exceed one's capacity is to be poor through one's thinking. If a person knows his capacity and acts within it, he will not be in need. But if a person attempts to do more than falls to his lot, he will be disappointed."

"In that case, when I, Kakuhen, am summoned by the court for an official function, shall I go up on a skinny horse, wearing a sedge hat?"

"If such is your condition, then it will be enough," was the reply.

The late Kongō-ō-in Bishop [of Kyoto's Tōji temple (Jitsugen, 1176-1249; see S&P 10A:5)] was on his way to the palace for an official ceremony when his groom had an argument over precedence with the attendant of Prince Omuro (?Dōjo, 1196-1249; see S&P 6:15) and damaged the Omuro's carriage. The Omuro's valet brought the matter to the Bishop's attention, but was rebuffed. "No monk takes precedence over the head of the Tōji. Although Prince Omuro is of high rank, he has assumed the role of a recluse and is called Omuro, 'August Retreat,' as one who conceals himself in the palace as a hermit. So he has no business going about in a carriage."

The late Courtly Zen Practitioner (?Fujiwara Michiie; see S&P 9:13) of the Hosshōji was told of this incident and remarked that the likes of Jitsugen should not be riding around in carriages. Nowadays people feel that the observance of the old rules is rather strange and so they act according to common custom.

On the contrary, Daigo no Sonshi (Shōbō, 832-909) went to the court to give thanks for his appointment to the rank of Bishop (sōjō) wearing a straw hat, which he hung on a railing at the palace. He came in with Bishop Kangen (835-925) of the Hannyaji carrying his shoes. The sovereign was greatly moved by Kangen's modesty and humility. In olden times people were motivated by virtue rather than by a desire for fame. Today it is otherwise.

Kakuchō (960-1034), Priest of the Tosotsu[in], was a pioneer in promoting esoteric practices within the Tendai sect. Once when the empress (?Fujiwara Takeko, consort of Goichijō) was having difficulty in childbirth (1026?), Kakuchō was summoned to perform a spell but he replied that he did not have time. Orders were sent that if Kakuchō did not come, he should be slain on the spot. He went reluctantly, the spell was performed, and the delivery was successful. As soon as it was over he withdrew, turning his back on the imperial proclamation (semmyō) honoring him.

This may have happened in the days of the Cloistered Sovereign Ichijō (r. 986-1011), but I am not certain. A daughter of Michinaga (966-1027), who was being carefully reared in the hope that someday she might be empress, died suddenly in her second year after a brief illness. The Great Omuro of Kōya (?Shōshin, 1005-1085) was approached for his help, and the child was taken up to Kōya in a brocade bag. Since it was a girl, although only a baby, the spell was performed outside the monastery gate, the child was restored to life and in time became empress. I know her name but I hesitate to mention it.[357]

Prince Omuro [of the Ninnaji] was presented with all kinds of delicacies during the day which disappeared at night. It was discovered that the Prince

himself went outside the palace enclosure to distribute offerings to the poor
and sick. When he performed spells, the sick recovered.

Because there were such eminent priests in antiquity filled with wisdom
and compassion, the world was at peace. In these Latter Days calamities are
many and miraculous manifestations of the Law are rare. People are without
compassion and amuse themselves with Buddhism for the sake of prestige
and profit. If one would abandon the world with the attitude of Shōgatsubō,
truly he would receive help and protection.

10A:9 The Amida Welcome Service[358]

A holy man at Fukō in Tango Province longed for birth in the
Pure Land. Putting all else aside, he strove to maintain the state of
mind proper to the time of death and looked forward to the appearance of the holy assemblage welcoming him to the Pure Land.

"It is customary for people in society to pray for what they want
at the beginning of the year, if only to ease their minds," the monk
thought to himself. "So I too will say my prayers." On New Year's
Eve he wrote something on a piece of paper and handed it to a
young monk who attended him.

"Take this paper. Now tomorrow morning, the first day of the
year, you are to rap on the gate and say, 'I have a message for you.'
Then when I ask where you are from, you say, 'I am a heavenly
messenger from the Buddha Amida. I have a letter for you.' Then
give me this piece of paper."

The attendant was excused, and next morning rapped on the
gate, calling out just as the holy man had instructed him; and the
questions and answers were exchanged as agreed. The holy man
came out in his bare feet and accepted the letter with alacrity and
excitement. Holding it up, he read as follows:

"This world of birth-and-death is a country filled with misery.
Detach yourself from it, and through recitation of the Buddha's
name, good works and chanting, come to My Land. I and the holy
assemblage will welcome you." As the holy man read, his tears
flowed copiously; and he performed the ritual every year without
fail.

When the governor of the province came down from the capital
and people were telling him about the local customs, he came to
hear of this holy man. Rejoicing at his spiritual good fortune, the
governor arranged a meeting with the priest.

"You shall receive whatever you request so that I may establish
a good karmic affinity with you."

"I am a recluse," replied the holy man, "and so I have no special needs."

"Although their circumstances in life may differ," insisted the governor, "All men have necessities." To which the holy man replied:

"I have been thinking that it would be good for us to get used to, and to feel comfortable about, our final moments by instituting our own holy assemblage and calling the ceremony the Amida Welcome Service (*mukaekō*)."

Costumes for the Buddha and Bodhisattvas and other gear were prepared according to the holy man's directions and sent to him. For many years the priest performed the ceremony of the coming of the holy assemblage, a ritual for dying. As might be expected, the ceremony of welcoming was held during his own final moments, and he came to an auspicious end.

This is said to have been the origin of the Amida Welcome Service. Some say that it started in Ama no Hashidate, and others that it began with Priest Eshin [Genshin, 942–1017] spreading pieces of broken chopstick over his armrest and drawing it slowly forward, saying that it was like the Buddha's coming to welcome souls into the Pure Land.

Those who would truly commit themselves to something and enter upon the path toward its realization will immerse themselves in it whether waking or sleeping. "What is the purpose of thought if not to precede practice?" as has been said. We should diligently prepare ourselves for the important matter of right thinking at the moment of death. People in the world seem to desire birth in the Pure Land, but the delusive affairs of birth-and-death are what engage their attention from morning to night. We should make a ritual of right thinking and preparing for the appearance of the holy assemblage.

10A:10 The Man Who Fell into an Evil Path through Attachment

Some time ago a man said to have been a certain Councillor had a reputation for ability and wisdom, but he abandoned the world and secluded himself on Mount Kōya. The nembutsu was his main practice, but he also studied Shingon, and he was known to be a religious man. He prepared for his final recitation of the name of Buddha in the hope that he would chant it peacefully and with a clear mind. And he did indeed die chanting the nembutsu.

But a year or two later his spirit took possession of a lay priest and re-

vealed to his fellow monks that although he had performed the nembutsu *for years, his mind had been obsessed by political concerns. He was constantly thinking how he could do better than those in office, and by virtue of these delusive attachments, he was reborn into one of the evil paths beneath the human world.*

Even if one abandons the world, lives deep in the mountains, and enters upon the True Path, it is difficult to cast off delusive thoughts. This man was known to be wise and serious-minded, and his attachment was for the sake of people and society, attachment which was partly concern to benefit sentient beings. We do not usually think of this as evil. But when a person truly enters the religious life, even love for the Buddha's Law—called "religiosity" (hōshu), is a hindrance. No wonder the lay priest fell into an evil path. It is difficult to know the state of a man in his final moment.

Whenever people remarked that someone's final moment was good or bad, Kyōbutsubō of Makabe in Shinano province, a disciple of Myōhen (1142-1224; see S&P 1:3), would reply that we cannot know what is in a person's mind.

An old priest from Kōya said that if one had disciples, birth in the Pure Land was impossible, and that the afterlife was to be feared. But because people are ashamed to admit that their intimate associates came to a bad end, they usually say something pleasant. In these Latter Days people talk only about birth in the Pure Land. They say that even the wicked are born in the Pure Land, and that we should not worry about bad karma.

Some recluses on Mount Kōya gathered to consider the final moments of their colleagues, and decided that perhaps not a single one was born into the Pure Land. It was proposed that one of the priests who had died with his legs crossed, his palms together, and his voice chanting the nembutsu *had succeeded. But Eshinbō of Kohata (Shinkū, 1205-1269) felt that he had not: "When one is being welcomed into the Pure Land, he ought to have a pleasant expression on his face. This man looked terrible. He must have entered an evil path."*

The Sage of Kōya (Kūkai) said that the recluse (tonsei) *was one who truly entered into the third important stage of abandoning the world. The first stage is to abandon society, and this is easy. To be abandoned by people because one happens to be poor comes to the same thing as abandoning them. There are many in this condition. The second stage is to abandon the body. One becomes an outcast and after bearing hunger and cold has the look of abandonment. But the third stage is to abandon the mind, so that the Five Dusts, the Six Desires, and fame and fortune do not adhere to it. Seeing this floating world as a dream and being lucid to the bottom of one's heart—this is to abandon the mind.*

In one of ten dreams of a king who reigned in the days of the [Kāśyapa][359] *Buddha, a large elephant was seen going out a window. Its body had passed through but the tail became blocked. "This is one of my future disciples who finds it difficult to abandon the world," explained the Buddha. "Although he says he has left it, he still has a desire for fame and profit."*

10B:1 The Spirit Versed in Buddhism Which Possessed a Woman

In Kyoto a woman was possessed by a spirit and all attempts to cure her were in vain. She laughed scornfully at the exorcists and they were unable to help her. Usually when an amulet of the holy man of Kanshōji (Daiembō, 1212-1291; see S&P 7:24) was placed on such a person, his lunacy was cured. But the woman only laughed: "I know this talisman. The good man has mastered the Jewel Box Spell; and, since he is a person with virtue, I respect it."

Several others were tried without effect; and one she even trampled with her feet. "How can this be within the Buddha's Teaching? There are such things as this in Buddhism, but he who employs them for the sake of fame and profit is unclean. I do not trample on the Buddha's Law."

Since she justified herself in terms of Buddhist doctrine, the exorcists asked how it was that although she understood the significance of Buddhism, she still tormented people.

"The aim of Buddhism," replied the spirit speaking through the woman, "is to seriously study the doctrines, perform the practices with wisdom and compassion, leave the round of birth-and-death, and open the mind to Enlightenment. I was present at the establishment of the sect on T'ien T'ai Mountain [by Chih-i in 575]. Although I am versed in all the doctrines, I lacked serious purpose and so have not escaped from the round of birth-and-death. I have become a spirit, but I am not harmful to people."

When she was asked her opinion of the famous teachers of the day, the spirit replied that it was useless to speak of them. Her response concerning Shōichi (Enni Ben'en, 1202-1280; see S&P 3:8, 9:13) of the Hosshōji was that although he was a sage difficult to find in these Latter Days, his meditation practice was lacking. A certain recluse came to interrogate her about Buddhism but she dismissed him out of hand.

A close friend of this woman's husband was a Shingon priest on Mount Kōya. At hearing that a letter was secretly being prepared to invite him to perform a service of exorcism, the woman remarked that he would only make a nuisance of himself but would be unable to effect a cure. The letter was not sent.

At Kitano the woman struck a monk on the head who was reading the sutras. "Is this any way to read the scriptures?" she asked, and then impressed everyone by chanting them herself. This happened ten years ago and the incident was told to me by a person who actually witnessed it. The woman was said to be from Tango province.

What people heard from the spirit accords with the holy teaching.

Learning (tamon) *and wisdom* (chie) *are not the same, and practice is important. The* Sutra of Heroic Deed (Shuryōgonkyō)[360] *states that from the observance of the precepts grows the practice of meditation, and from meditation is born wisdom.*

In the days of the late Courtly Zen Practitioner of the Hosshōji (Fujiwara Kanezane, 1149-1207)[361] a woman within the palace was possessed by a spirit. Shōgatsu (d. 1268; see S&P *4:9) of Matsuo interviewed her, and the woman said that all of the sages and scholars from the time of the Heian period had entered into evil paths. He asked how Gedatsubō (Jōkei, 1155-1213) and Myōe (Kōben, 1173-1232) had fared, but the woman replied that she was unable to see this.*

Once when Shih-te (Jittoku; see S&P *9:10) saw some monks holding a Repentance Assembly (fusatsu) he called out laughing: "How profound you all look with your heads together!" When this angered the monks, Shih-te continued: "Not getting angry is to observe the precepts. Having a pure heart is what is meant by being a monk."*

Once he drove an ox along the road, calling it by the name of an ancient monk. Every time he would call the name, the ox would low in reply. "This monk was reborn as an ox because he did not observe the precepts in a former life," wept Shih-te. "He had the face of a man but the heart of an animal."

When Cunda (see S&P *5A:4) offered the Buddha his last meal (of poisoned mushrooms) he did it in a proper state of mind and was praised for this.*

Although one has a human form, a person's actions throughout life will express the mind of those in the hells, of the hungry demons, of beasts, or whatever. Thus the Net of Brahma Sutra *states that a person who does not practice the precepts with compassion is the same as a beast. Shan-tao (cf.,* S&P *7:25) has a similar remark. The monk of the Kuo-ch'ing temple, even though he lived in antiquity when men were more virtuous than they are now, was lacking in practice and became an ox.*

The ruler of a country is said to be the father and mother of the people because he cherishes them and pacifies the land. But if a king is without benevolence and wisdom, this is like losing the Five Grains through the mischief of a large rat. And bad ministers are like the big hole in the bottom of the sea from which water leaks continually.[362]

When Śākyamuni was living in this world the monk Samgharakkhita (Sōgo Biku) lost his way near the sea and entered a temple for his mid-day meal. He took the food and was about to eat when he saw that it was molten copper. After the monks at the temple ate this, they and the temple burned up without a trace. This happened to Samgharakkhita more than fifty times. When he asked the Buddha about it he was told that these were the hells of priests who had violated the precepts after the extinction of the Buddha Kāśyapa.[363]

When the Great Teacher of Tendai (Chih-i, 538-597) was at Kuo-ch'ing Temple, a monk borrowed salt from the temple stores without returning it, and this became an obstruction to his practice of meditation. After he returned the salt, he was able to meditate. Yung-chia (Yōka, 665-713; see S&P 5A:5) said that he always tried to eat food which was not produced laboriously in the fields, and to wear clothes not made by the toil of silkworms. Tao-hsüan (Dōsen, 596-667; see S&P 4:9) remarked that a bowl of food came from a bowl of sweat, and sweat is blood, So a bowl of food is like a bowl of blood, and food is scarcer than blood. People of sensitivity, lay or cleric, should consider the labor which has gone into a product and not dispose of it wastefully. Nor should we unnecessarily distress man or beast.

Priests at a mountain temple met in a bath house with some laymen and discussed various topics. When a layman argued that monks were the most covetous of people, one of the priests replied that although monks were indeed inexpressibly greedy, the warrior was worse, especially the cowardly soldier. There was no rebuttal. As for monks and laymen who observe the precepts in these Latter Days, Tao-hsüan says that laymen should offer much with faith, but that monks should maintain their integrity and take little. Nowadays it is just the reverse.

I-ching (Gijō, 635-713) notes that although there are 80,000 varieties of the Holy Teaching, only two things are important: inwardly to concentrate on Suchness (shinnyo) and outwardly to observe the ordinary rules of behavior. Chih-i says that the true immortal does not even do good, much less evil. And the Commentary on the Great Wisdom Sutra makes a similar remark about the bodhisattva who abides in the Ultimate (jissō). It is necessary to apply the teachings of Buddhism. Although the spirit (whose story is told at the beginning of this chapter) knew the Law, he did not escape from birth-and-death but became an evil thing.

10B:2 The Man Who Understood the Underlying Purpose
of the Various Sects

After the late Kongō-ō-in Bishop (Jitsugen; see S&P 10A:5) had become advanced in years, he told his disciples that when he was young he had made a pilgrimage to Mount Kōya, and then visited some mountain temples in Yamato. In the vicinity of Kazuraki mountain he sought temporary lodging at the house of a woodcutter, where he met an old priest who revealed that in his youth he had studied at the Kōfukuji. After he became a monk he was numbered among the better scholars and even invited to lecture before the nobility.

"But scholars are only interested in prestige. My father became ill, and when I returned home I became involved with a woman and stayed in the village. After many years my attachment to things weakened and I came to

*understand the meaning of Buddhism. That which was practiced before the
various sects were propagated has been lost from the time their founders
caused them to flourish. The Hossō sect lost its basic purpose from the time
of Dharmapāla (Gohō, 6th cen.), and the same holds for the Sanron, Kegon,
Tendai and Shingon sects. Conceptualization kills the message. In a place
without directions, directions are set up; in a place without words, words are
introduced. From words come thinking and from thinking comes systems of
thought "*

*Jitsugen met the priest on several occasions but had to pledge that he
would not reveal the priest's existence to the outside world. I heard this from
a disciple twice removed from Jitsugen who regarded this as a very confiden-
tial matter.*

The Commentary on the Great Sun Sutra (Dainichikyō)⁴⁷ *says:
"Enlightenment is something bestowed on a person; it is not like giving him a
handful of nuts. It should be possible to obtain wisdom without a teacher,
but it is not given to men to understand the marvel of its operation." Lao
Tzu's Tao [Te] Ching (Ch. 18) says: "When the Great Tao (Way or Method)
ceased to be observed, benevolence and righteousness came into vogue.
(Then) appeared wisdom and shrewdness, and there ensued great
hypocrisy." (Legge's translation).*

*In an age when men are used to the written word, there are many
falsehoods. Even the teachings of the Buddha—all being devices to attract by
that to which people are attached—generate false views for the deluded. So
in the* Lotus Sutra *(Chapter 2) the Buddha says that his words are simply
words and descriptions to guide sentient beings. And in the* Lankāvatāra
Sutra *([Nyū]ryōgakyō, T. 671) he states that from the night when he attained enlightenment until the night of his death, he did not expound a
single word. The [Northern Sung] poet Su Shih (Tōba Koji, 1036–1101)
came to understand the Law of the Buddha on hearing the sound of a mountain stream, and in a verse extolled the sounds of nature as so many gathas.*

How can we understand the wonderful Law of the Buddha
through discriminations? The Lotus Sutra says: "This Dharma is not
a thing that discursive or discriminatory reasoning can
understand."³⁶⁴ We cannot know the substance (*tai*) of the
marvelous Dharma by weighing the matter through discriminative
reasoning (*fumbetsu*). "Discursive and discriminative reasoning"
(*shiryō fumbetsu*) are all provisional workings (*yū*: function) of illusion (*komō*). As for True Mind, mind is identical with the dharmas
[constituting the phenomenal world]; and the dharmas are identical
with mind.³⁶⁵ What discriminates and what is discriminated? It is
like the eye, which does not see itself; or the sword, which does not
cut itself. We call this [Awareness] the dharma of One Mind, the
substance of the marvelous Dharma. Thus, the Buddhas and
Patriarchs are not lacking in mind. Their mind is mind which does

not stagnate in discriminations; that is, it is the mind of no-mind (*mushin*). Moreover, they are not lacking in verbal explanations. It is simply that their explanations do not stagnate as explanations; that is, their words are no-words (*mugon*), [words which do not stagnate in any speciic dogmatic formulation]. Accordingly, whether one empty the mind or let it shine forth, whether one dispenses with words or uses them — what is the difficulty? The accommodations (*hōben*) of the Buddhas and Patriarchs are all devices to instruct madmen.

The Sutra of Heroic Deed *tells the parable of Yajñadattā*[366] *who looked in a mirror one morning and could not see her face because of the way she was holding the mirror. Believing that her head had been taken by a demon, she ran about distractedly until someone showed her how to hold the mirror correctly. Then she thought that her head had been restored. Both her wretchedness and her delight were without foundation. The unenlightened man is like one who looks for his lost head. The original mind of enlighten-ment* (hongaku), *like the man's head, is not lost; the loss comes only from thinking that this is so. Thinking that we have discovered and attained something for the first time is what we feel when we experience enlighten-ment for the first time* (shigaku). *But how can we attain it for the very first time (when it has been there all along from the beginning)? The Sutra of Perfect Enlightenment states that because people have this understanding from the first, they have become Buddhas from the very beginning; birth-and-death and nirvāṇa are both as illusory as yesterday's dream. Sanron's Chi-ts'ang (Kichizō, 643-712; see S&P 6:10) as well as Tendai and Hossō theory support the view that the various doctrinal positions are merely expe-dients.*

We should act reasonably according to circumstances and not be trapped by rules and regulations. *The Lotus Sutra was being copied at a tem-ple in Nara which had been strictly purified for the occasion when one of the banners in the sacred hall caught fire. One of the novices asked an old monk if they should take a bath to purify themselves before going into the sacred enclosure to stamp out the fire. This is an example of inability to transcend the letter of the law. This was also the case of the abbot of a temple in Musashi province who had studied in China. He returned with the obser-vances of a great Ch'an monastery and applied them out of context to a small isolated temple in Japan.*

When Izumi Shikibu (cf., S&P 5B:2) *was out of favor with Yasumasa (958-1036), she arranged for a shrine maiden to perform a Ceremony of Har-monious Relations* (keiai no matsuri) *at Kifune (in Kyoto). Hearing of this, Yasumasa concealed himself behind a tree by the shrine. An old vestal came out beating a drum and walked around the party three times lifting up the front of her dress. When Izumi was told to do likewise, her face reddened and she did not reply. Then, after being scolded by the vestal for not cooperating, she composed a poem expressing her embarrassment. Yasumasa revealed himself and the two were reconciled. This is an example of abridging the letter of the law to arrive at the desired result. Had Izumi behaved as the vestal had asked, Yasumasa would have been disgusted and they would never have been reconciled.*

When prince Hōjo (1237-1284) was being ordained at the Tōdaiji, the stone platform was piled with snow. When Hōjo was asked to remove his sandals, as was customary, a member of the congregation scolded the others for not adapting to circumstance. Hōjo was permitted to wear them. Rules are rules, but to have consideration for the prince walking barefoot in the snow is to transcend the formalities. The monk who spoke out was Chūdōbō, at that time called Taihōbō (1219-1291).

As for those who have no understanding of the proprieties, nothing need be said. They are like those base people who do not understand that we should repudiate birth-and-death and seek enlightenment. Those who know the proprieties and apply them without flexibility are like those who live in the serenity of the two lesser vehicles (śrāvaka and pratyekabuddha), but who do not act for the benefit of sentient beings as the bodhisattva does. And those who understand the proprieties but are not obsessed with them are like the bodhisattvas. Thus, the [Garland] Sutra says of such a man: "Because of his great wisdom, he is not stained by birth-and-death; and because of his great compassion, he does not abide in his status as a bodhisattva."

10B:3 People Who Died Auspiciously

At Yamagami in Kōzuke province lived a Shingon monk called Gyōsen, formerly a disciple of Jōben (1166-1224; see S&P 6:14) but later a devotee of the nembutsu. A year before his death in the first year of Kōan (1278), he wrote down the day when he would get sick, and the year and day of his death. Then he placed the paper at the bottom of a box, unknown to his disciples. After his death the box was opened and the facts found to be just as he had recorded them. Gyōsen dressed eccentrically, and often discussed doctrine with the Elder Myōsen of Serada. When asked what to do when disturbing thoughts arose during the recitation of the nembutsu, he replied with this verse (collected in the Fuboku wakashō 34):

Ato mo naki	Contending against
Kumo ni arasou	Clouds that leave no trace,
Kokoro koso	That very will
Nakanaka tsuki no	Is the real obstacle
Sawari narikere	Between us and the moon!

Gyōsen died auspiciously. A purple cloud appeared before his cell, and there was heavenly music and the smell of incense.

In these Latter Days those who devote themselves to the nembutsu *neglect the cultivation of Mind. Is this because they have little wisdom? The* Amida Recollection Sutra (Midashiyuikyō)[367] *states that with a tranquil mind we should meditate* (zazen) *for a period of time and then for the sake of all sentient beings call to mind the Buddha Amida. When every practice is viewed as* zen, *then they are all* zen. *And when every practice is viewed as* nembutsu, *then they are all* nembutsu. *The* nembutsu *devotee should not neglect mental discipline, nor should those of other sects take lightly the practice of the* nembutsu.

Felicitous Final Moments
Among Followers of the Kenninji

Stories of our predecessors in various sects have come down to us from ancient times. Outstanding in wisdom, practice and virtue, they all died as though entering into meditation (zenjō). *Those who enter the Way of the Buddha, in whatever sect, should earnestly prepare themselves for the moment of death.*

After Eshin (cf., S&P 3:4) aroused the aspiration for enlightenment, he venerated the two characters myō-ri *("fame and profit"). From the desire for prestige he had studied, and from his learning the aspiration for enlightenment arose. Truly it is said that we enter the Way of the Buddha having been caught on the fish-hook of desire.*

The king of Magadha (Magada) in India became a monk, took the name Śubhākarashiṃha (Zemmui Sanzō, 637-735), and brought the esoteric teachings to China. They flourished for barely three generations and were completely lost at the time of the wicked king [Wu Tsung] of the T'ang (during the persecution of 845). Because his writings had been kept secretly in the palace and not widely circulated, they were lost.

The Great Teachers Dengyō [Saichō, 767-822], Kōbō [Kūkai, 774-835], Jikaku [Ennin, 792-862], and Chishō [Enchin, 814-891] brought the teachings of Shingon to our country because we have an affinity for it. Japan is a country which has had an affinity for Tendai, Shingon, and the *nembutsu*. Hossō, Sanron, and Kegon are merely studied in Nara and have not been promulgated throughout the provinces. The Ritsu and Zen sects have not been remiss in propagating their ideas, but until now results have been few. However, perhaps it is the skillful design (*hōben*) of the Great Sage that Ritsu and Zen will be widespread in the world today. In these times they are being established and promoting practice. Perhaps the time has arrived for them to be popular. Although there are many Tendai and Hossō scholars, in these Latter Days people practice *zazen*, those being few who employ the reflective techniques (*kannen*) of Mind Only, or the Perfect and Sudden (*endon*) methods of Tendai. The scholars merely argue points of doctrine, quarrel over what is provisional or absolute in a sect, and decide what is shallow or profound in a teaching.

Among those belonging to the Ritsu sect some practice the nembutsu, *and others practice the methods of Shingon or Zen. Shingon priests likewise practice the death-bed* nembutsu. *Recently among those who practiced Zen methods were some who died auspiciously. An old priest of the Jufukuji in Kamakura whose name I do not recall practiced esoteric methods successfully for many years, and then spent many more doing* zazen *under Lan-ch'i (Rankei, 1213-1278) of the Kenchōji,*[368] *But he left after having a falling-out with Lan-ch'i. He died seated in the Enjōdō, his hands folded, and as though he had gone to sleep. I heard this from a colleague of his.*

The school of Eisai (1141-1215; see S&P 2:5), late founder of the Kenninji, does not discriminate among the various methods. It respects the precepts and accommodates itself to Tendai, Shingon, Zen and the nembutsu. *Eisai used his reputation as a famous monk for the sake of Buddhism instead of self-aggrandizement. The practice of begging, with three garments and a bowl, began with the Buddha and his disciples. As the children of Śākyamuni, can we turn our backs on the ways of our foremost teacher and act like householders? But in these Latter Days, people look down on those who solicit alms as beggar-monks (kotsujiki hōshi).*

Eisai founded the monasteries of Shōfukuji in Chinzei (Kyūshū), Kenninji in Kyoto, and the Jufukuji in the Kantō. He did not oppose the customs of the provinces into which he went but accommodated himself to Ritsu, Tendai, Shingon, and other methods—and without making a fetish of Chinese ways. His Zen was inwardly Zen, but Shingon elements appeared on the surface. He predicted that fifty years after his death the Zen sects would flourish. This is to be found in his Propagation of Zen for the Protection of the Country (Kōzen gokokuron). *Later the Kenninji was built and the Zen procedures were adopted from the Sung. The custom of naming temples after reign names, such as Kennin and Kenchō, is an old one. Various methods of Buddhism flourish according to the times; and with determination, how can one not succeed in his religious objective? Prince Jōgū (i.e., Shōtoku, 574-621), a manifestation of Kannon, instituted the precepts; and Priest Chien-chen (Ganjin, 687-783; see S&P 3:5) built the ordination platforms.*

The Bishop (Eisai) asked the Great Minister of Kamakura (Sanetomo, 1192-1219; see S&P 9:13) for permission to go to Kyoto to prepare for death. He went and died auspiciously.

The Preceptor Eichō (Shakuembō; see S&P 6:9), Elder of the Chōrakuji at Serada in Kōzuke province, was a disciple of Eisai. He was known to be a good and wise man and died on the twenty-sixth day of the ninth month in the first year of Hōji (1247). According to those at the temple, this happened at the end of the Hour of the Dog. A bright light shone all around. Eichō was found seated in the posture of meditation, his hands folded.

Higambō no Ajari, the Elder [Zōsō] Rōyo (1194-1277), succeeded (Eichō at the Chōrakuji) and later became head monk of the Jufukuji (see Appendix B). He died during the Hour of the Tiger on the fifth day of the sixth month in Kenji 2 (1276). He made careful preparations the day before. Burning incense before an image of Kannon and sitting in a chair with his hands clasped, he expired. The gatha which he composed at the time of his death is recorded. Wu-an [P'u-ning (Gottan Funei, 1197-1276)],³⁶⁹ former head of the Kenchōji, remarked that Rōyo was one of the outstanding wise men of Japan.

The Venerable Hosshimbō

Hosshimbō (Thirteenth Century), elder of Matsushima in Mutsu province, became a monk late in life. Although illiterate, he traveled to China, studied under Wu-chun,³⁷⁰ and is said to have had a deep understanding of Buddhism. He developed painful boils on his buttocks from sitting in meditation for many years, but he was not discouraged and refused to give up. When he told his attendants that he would die on a certain day, they did not believe him. When the day came, he seated himself in a chair and recited his death-verse:

> It was bright when I arrived,
> And it is bright as I depart.
> What an experience this has been!

His attendants remarked that the stanza was incomplete, lacking one line. At this he shouted once inarticulately and expired. It is said to have been truly inspiring.

His teacher Wu-chun had given him the character tei enclosed in a circle as his subject for meditation. He applied himself so strenuously that afterwards everything seemed to have the character tei inscribed on it.

It is gratifying that even in these Latter Days the Mahāyāna disciplines are practiced. To practice under a good teacher and to apply oneself assiduously without concern for fame, profit, or learning is to make progress in the Dharma more surely than merely having skill with letters. Without zeal, even the Pure Land devotee will find his practice difficult; with zeal, even those who practice the Mahāyāna disciplines will find them easy.

Cūḍapanthaka (Shurihandoku) was so dull that he forgot his own name.

Under the tutelage of the five hundred arhats he applied himself to one gatha: "One who guards mouth, thought and body can transcend the world of birth-and-death." He attained arhatship.[371] *Practice is essential, not learning. Devadatta (Chōdatsu) knew the 60,000 items of the canon, but he did not escape falling into hell,*[372] *whereas Jidō (Mettākumārī) was born into the Tuṣita heaven through a single thought of compassion.*

Lao Tzu renounces learning (Tao Te Ching 20, 48), and I-hsing (see S&P 2.7) says that discriminative thought must be employed in studying the ways of the world, but not for attaining release from it. The Commentary on the Great Wisdom Sutra says that conceptualization is the net of Māra, and no-thought (munen) is a mark of the Law. Hosshimbō was thus able to understand the Dharma without the use of writings but with deep zeal.

The Elder [Lan-ch'i] Tao-lung (Rankei Dōryū, 1213-1278;) of the Kenchōji died on the twenty-fourth day of the seventh month in the first year of Kōan (1278), leaving behind a death-verse. After the cremation the ashes yielded many precious relics, and some were even found stuck to the leaves of trees. The same thing is said to have happened to Kuei-feng (Keihō, 780-841; see S&P 3:8).

The Elder (*chōrō*) of the Tōfukuji, priest Shōichi, died on the seventeenth day of the tenth month of Kōan 3 (1280). He had been ill for some time since the early summer, and, being unable to carry on his normal routine, was cared for in a detached building on the temple grounds. On the fifteenth day of the tenth month, he announced that he would go up to the Dharma Hall to lecture and then to pass away; but his disciples would not permit it. Then on the seventeenth day he told his attendants to call the monks together and to beat the drum in the Dharma Hall to announce his death. Seated in a chair, he wrote his verse of departure from the world and expired. In the capital, priest and layman and those of high and low station assembled in droves to pray for three days. After this Shōichi was placed in a coffin still seated in his chair. This happened just recently, so I will not record the details. The death verse said:

> Seventy-nine years of Skillful Means
> To benefit sentient beings;
> We desire to know the Ultimate as it is,
> But this is transmitted by no Buddha or Patriarch.
>   Kōan 3, 10/17   The Elder of Tōfuku
>   Take Care.

The Elder [In]gō (Ichiō, 1209-1280) of the Chōrakuji in Serada also left behind a death-verse.

Epilogue

Although I wrote concerning my purpose in setting down these stories in the preface, I am not satisfied that I have made my position clear, so I will express again what is in my heart.

There is an abundance of old stories, but it seems that people do not write about things which have happened recently. As a means, possibly, of encouraging those with foolish aspirations to seek a better life, disregarding my clumsiness with words I have written down what I consider interesting and which otherwise might not be transmitted to later generations.

The *Essentials of Salvation* of priest Genshin says: "The coarse passions make men enlightened; and it is only by meaningless babble that without realizing it we constantly obstruct the way to salvation." People are such that whether they are reciting the name of Amida or practicing meditation, they are forever aware of the time. But when they are engaged in useless talk, they do not know when the sun sets and night has fallen.

Stories written about such a world are for the most part concerned with petty affairs and desires for useless things — the faults of the mouth being many and the desires of the heart deep. Those things which contribute to transmigration in the cycle of birth-and-death are common; those which become instruments for enlightenment in the afterlife are rare.

Consequently, I have written down, just as I have happened to recollect them, various anecdotes from here and there, things which happened in China and Japan, and tales from ancient and modern times. If a person reads these stories instead of those others, he will see people who appreciated the profound intentions of the gods, trusted in the encompassing grace of the Buddhas, respected the exalted virtues of men of religious conviction, learned from the honesty and simplicity of householders, understood the operation of moral causation, discriminated between the wise and the foolish, became aware of the marvelous goal of the various doctrines, and entered the blessed path of the anchorite.

I have been constrained to assemble these stories, although I cannot recommend them to the educated. I am an utter rustic, born and raised in the country, illiterate, unversed in the art of poetry, and without having seriously studied the tenets of a single sect of Buddhism. Imitating the example of others in order to escape the troubles of the world, I became a hermit, inquiring about and practicing only the basic doctrines of release from the round of birth-and-death, and associating with men of sincere conviction.

Although my zeal is weak, I have assembled these stories from a desire for enlightenment. Consequently, among these worldly stories I have interspersed the basic tenets of the various sects, important statements of the sutras and commentaries, and literary allusions which I have picked up here and there, so that they might be the occasion for people to meet the Law of the Buddha.

Living in a thatched mountain hermitage out in the country, I have had only my own heart and mind to rely upon, for I am without books, and I have set down only the simplified essentials of these things as they have happened to occur to me. Although there may be many errors throughout, my main theme does not differ from the aims of Buddhism. And my wish will have been attained if there are those who may learn from this the gist of Buddhist Teaching.

The citations from literary works and the names of men of old are, I think, correct, but there may be many inadvertent errors. I hope that some future scholar will make the necessary corrections and disseminate them.

Both Ching-ch'i's *Diamond Stick*[373] in China and Shikibu's *Tale of Genji* in Japan are fictitious works written in imitation of real life, but their writers bequeathed them to us so that, on the one hand, we would understand the feelings of the human beings, and on the other, that we would come to comprehend the significance of Buddhism. So also in this book have I included worldly matters which one might see or hear about, in order that they might point the way to release from the world.

There are differences between ancient and modern times, but people share the same goals. Perhaps there will be those with sensibility who will support my objectives, correct my mistakes, and continue to add to the collection, acting as intermediaries to lead the foolish to salvation. And perhaps there will be those who, seeing and hearing these things, will rejoice in the good and become future comrades in the faith. That these stories may be a cause of their praising the Buddha's teaching, a condition for their turning the Wheel of the Law, a seed of religious awakening, and food for the genuine practice of the discipline is the fervent hope of this disciple of the Buddha.

Let us praise Śākyamuni and the Three Treasures. Let us praise the Gods who "soften their light," and may they bestow their protection, leading us out of darkness, fortifying the resolution of the children of Buddha, propagating the Law to future generations, and guiding the many who are deluded.

The time is mid-autumn in the sixth year of Kōan (1283). I

started writing this book in the second year of Kōan (1279) and then put it aside for two or three years. This year I took it up again and finished it. As a result, the styles of writing in the earlier and latter parts of the book are not the same. I mention this for the sake of those who in the future may wonder about it.

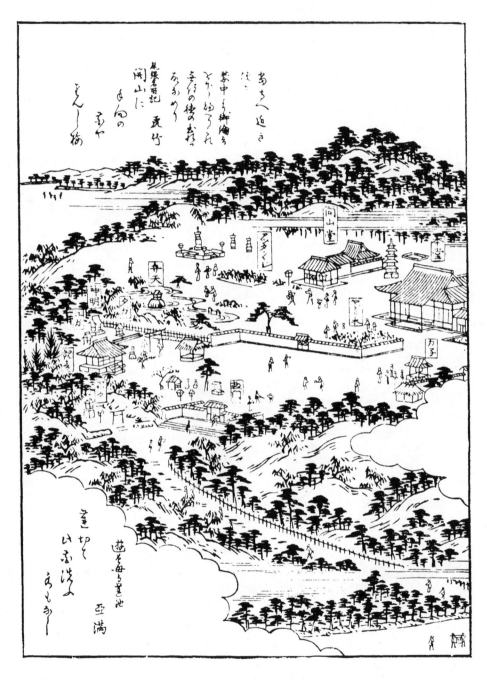

Figure 6. Chōboji and environs. From the *Owari meisho zue* (Illustrated Gazetteer of Owari Province), Latter Series, 1880.

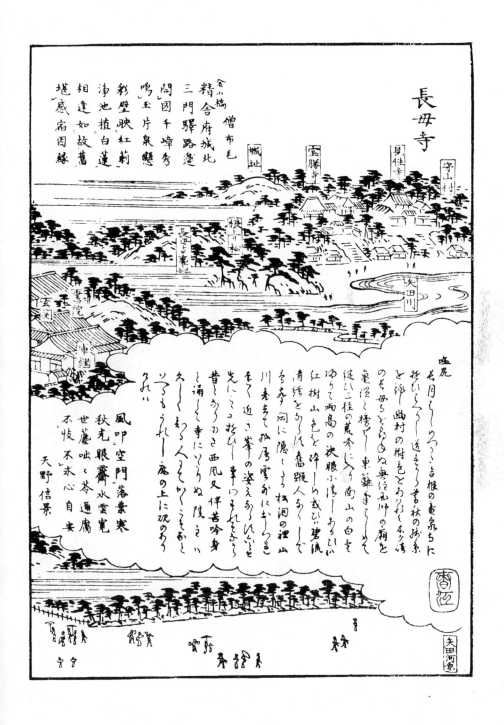

長母寺

守山村
貝佐寺
宝勝寺
城址
根ヶ松
長母寺裏山
玄央院
書写院
東継
矢田川
矢田河原

僧布毛

金糸橋
精舎府城北
三門驛路邊
閣圖千嶂秀
鳴玉片泉懸
彩壁映紅菊
淨池植白蓮
相逢如故舊
堪感宿因縁

風叩空門麥葉寒
秋光眼簷水雲寛
世塵呦々苔通屬
不恢不末心自安

天野信景

Part III.
Casual Digressions
(Zōtanshū)

Selected Translations

Collection of Casual Digressions (Zōtanshū)

2:3 The Monkeys' Religious Service[374]

Long ago in a mountain village lived two neighbors, one industrious and the other shiftless. The industrious man tilled the fields from morning till night, enjoying a harvest of peas, beans and millet. It happened on one occasion that he was taking a nap, being exhausted from his work in the fields, and was seen by some monkeys.

"It's a Buddha," they said. "Let's have a religious service."

So they brought a great quantity of yams, sweet potatoes, chestnuts and sweet acorns, made a great mound of them in front of the man, and then went away. The diligent man was almost bent to the ground as he carried the load of donations to his home.

The old wife of the shiftless man badgered her husband to borrow the other's clothes and go out to do the same. Again the monkeys appeared.

"Well now," they said. "Let's take this Buddha to the other side of the river and hold the religious service there." So placing the man on a seat made of their crossed hands, the monkeys began crossing the swift and deep current of the mountain stream.

"Everyone pull up your skirts," they mimicked, and up went their tails. It was so funny that the man suddenly giggled.

"It's a human," cried the monkeys, tossing him into the river. The man returned home half dead, his clothes soaked and his stomach full of water. His old wife was angry and detested him all the more. It was a senseless thing to do and not to be imitated . . .

2:4 Pickled Eggplants

There was a priest who ate boiled chicken eggs, but tried to

275

conceal his behavior from a young novice by calling them "pickled eggplants." The novice knew what was going on and waited for an occasion to call the priest to account. On hearing the cock crow at dawn he remarked: "You worship, the father of the pickled eggplant is crowing. Can you hear him?"

Another priest who furtively ate dried sweetfish wrapped it in paper and said that it was a straight razor. A novice who was waiting to take the priest to account was crossing a river with his master when some sweetfish appeared in the stream.

"Your worship, I see a fresh straight razor," he cried. "Watch you feet that you don't hurt yourself!"

5:1 Wealth from a Stalk of Straw[375]

Long ago a devout layman made frequent visits to Hasedera. His efforts did not go unrewarded, for he was vouchsafed a divine revelation: "Whatever it is you find in the street, pick it up and carry it with you."

Now in the street on which he was returning from his visit there was a piece of straw; and then he found a horse-fly which he tied with the straw to divert himself. A quite ordinary young gentleman from the capital happened by and begged the layman to give him the straw and the fly, which he did. The gentleman was delighted and presented the layman with a single tangerine. From the capital a group of ladies looking quite ordinary were on their way by foot to Hase, and to them the layman offered the tangerine. They were so pleased that they removed their sweat-soaked underrobes and presented him with them.

An official of the Great Watch, it seems, was making a pilgrimage to the Seven Great Temples of Nara. In the vicinity of Inari [in SE Kyoto] his cermonial horse suddenly became ill and fell to the ground, hovering between life and death. The official entrusted the horse to an attendant and went on his way.

"This horse is already beginning to die," said the layman to the attendant. "I think the chances of his miraculously surviving this crisis are one in a hundred thousand. If I give you these robes, will you let me have him?" Without any ado, the attendant let him take the horse and went on his way.

The attendant had been gone only a short time when the horse revived, to the layman's delight. As he was riding it in the vicinity of the Hosshōji, he was seen by a Senior Assistant Governor-General of Dazaifu on his way down to Tsukushi [Kyūshū].

"Is that horse for sale?" The official indicated that he wished to buy it and asked the price.

"I haven't thought about it," answered the layman. "It is difficult to determine the price of such a splendid horse. Make an offer and you can have it."

"Just at the moment I have no money," replied the official. "So I will entrust to you two plots of rice-field in Toba for four years. Take care of them until I return." The man accepted the position without further ado, maintained the property during the four years, and even turned the rice-straw into mats. When his tour of duty was over and the official returned to the capital, he was delighted by the man's stewardship and commended him.

All this transpired because the man had faith; how could you say that it was all made up? That would be wrong-headed reasoning.

9:10 The Confidence Game

The "beggar monk" (*kotsujiki hōshi*)[376] in Japan makes his way through life by deceiving people. If he succeeds in this deception, he counts that as a gain; and if he bungles it, he is not blamed as an ordinary person would be. He then declares that he is just a poor beggar and is sent packing. This has been going on since antiquity. While those being tricked are usually not aware of the deception, it often happens that people are conned knowing perfectly well what is going on. We learn from the sacred teachings that the Five Dusts and Six Desires which becloud our understanding are all false and unreal, and that they deceive us. And yet we cannot abandon our delusive thinking and discard our attachments to enter upon the Way of Truth. How regrettable!

In the days of the Great Lord General of Kamakura [Yoritomo], he was approached by a beggar monk.

"With your gracious permission, I will outwit even you."

"If I know that you are trying to trick me," replied Yoritomo, "I can surely not be deceived. But if you can trick me, you shall have a reward."

The beggar monk agreed to accept the challenge. "To perform my trick I need a rug. I will take and spread it out and then I shall trick you."

Yoritomo gave him the rug.

"This is itself the con [i.e., getting you to give me a rug under false pretenses]," said the beggar monk, who was given an additional reward.

A lay priest whose name I have forgotten—perhaps it was the same fellow I just spoke of—was very clever. Another individual, who considered himself to be very adept at the con game, felt that if he were to trick this lay priest, he would make a name for himself.

"What is this lay priest most fond of?" he inquired, and was told that the man fancied hawks.

The challenger, feeling that this would be an easy assignment, assumed the pose of a priest taking up a subscription and went to the house of the lay priest with his apprentice playing the part of a young novice.

"I am a priest from Ōyama, where the old temple buildings are in ruin. I have come to take up a subscription for their restoration."

"We don't make any such donations," said the person at the gate. "Leave here at once."

Now there was a hawk at the house, and the man had earlier instructed his young novice to make the following remark to those in the service of the lay priest: "Near this monk's hermitage on Mount Ōyama, a bird looking very much like this one has a nest which seems to have babies in it."

The monk left and was two or three blocks away when the people in the house told the lay priest of his visit, his young novices reporting that when the apprentice had seen the hawk, he had mentioned that there was a similar bird with a nest full of babies near the monk's hermitage.

"Call the monk back!" ordered the lay priest; and out they went in hot pursuit. The monk was delighted.

Then the lay priest questioned him. "I heard what your novice disciple said. Is it true that a hawk has set up its nest near your hermitage, and that it has a litter?"

The monk gave the appearance of trying to hide something. It never occurred to me," he said. "Perhaps my novice is lying. Even if there is a nest there, I have no recollection of it."

"Look, I never make donations to establish good relations with people, but in your case I will give you a little something to promote our relationship." The lay priest, excited by his desire for a baby hawk, forced a bolt of cloth on the monk and fussed about to entertain him, bringing out a tray of food and plying him with drink. "Now tell me about it," he insisted.

"I have noticed some such thing but my duties at the temple keep me so busy that I have no leisure to check it out. Send along a messenger to see if perhaps there is a nest." The lay priest was delighted and dispatched a messenger to accompany the monk.

Along the way the monk prompted his young novice to say: "This bird that built the nest does look like a hawk, but the sound it makes is "Hi-yo-ro — just like a swallow-tailed kite."

At this the messenger decided that the bird was indeed a swallow-tailed kite, and retraced his steps to tell the lay priest that such was the case. But even this was a fabrication!

The will to deceive is deeply rooted and resembles the good expedients through which the bodhisattva benefits sentient beings. However, one kind of deception is a worldly wisdom which drops us into hell; the other is a spiritual strategem in the interest of Liberation.

There was an old lay priest who lived in Hitachi province. Whenever a beggar monk whom he had known in Kamakura traveled to Mutsu province to play the confidence game, the monk would notify the lay priest, who lived conveniently along the route, of his plans. On the return leg of the journey the lay priest would the hear the beggar monk relate all the tricks he had been involved in. One of the incidents which the beggar monk told on one of his return trips was this:

"This time when I went out I performed the Body Lamp Ritual[377] three times and once I almost got killed. The escape tunnel collapsed and I was choked by the smoke, but somehow I got out all right."

The "dead body" had first been placed on the ground and covered with a lot of firewood, which was then set on fire. The beggar monk would slip through the escape tunnel to join the other celebrants in calling on the name of the Buddha and in reciting the sutras. Many spectators would gather and make offerings of money and rice, which the beggar monk would pocket as his fee.

Now after escaping through the tunnel, he again continued on his way. Somewhere in the mountains he crossed paths with a layman on horseback who had been especially devout at the service during which the priest had performed the Body Lamp Ritual. He thought he might trick the man a second time.

"I have the sense of having known you in the world of birth-and-death. Because of the empathy which I feel for you by virtue of the karmic affinities which we established when I performed the Body Lamp Ritual, I would like to help you. Proceding through this intermediate existence between rebirths, I have the vivid sense of being reborn into my former state. Perhaps it will turn out that way."

"That's exactly the way I feel!" added the man.

"It's a sad state of affairs, I do believe, being here in the intermediate existence," sobbed the monk. "However, I know a way to return you to the world of the living. I shall perform some rites to send you back."

Confused by it all, the man could not tell if he were living in a dream or in reality. The beggar monk put on a show of performing various mudras with his hands and reciting mystic formulas.

"Take off your outer garments and your robe, leaving just your tunic and underpants. Then blindfold your eyes with your sash and let your horse lead you back. If you do this you will be able to return to where you lived. Now there will surely seem to be people along the way who, when they see you, will say, "There goes such-and-such a lord," and who will ask what has happened to you. But this is all demonic fabrication and has no reality. By no means are you to respond. If you just apply the whip and spur your horse on, you will be saved. And this will all seem to you as having been a dream."

With deep conviction, the man put the whip to his horse and started off. Later he was seen by an acquaintance: "Hey there! You're Mr. What's-his-name! What in the world is going on?"

"I know all about your tricks," replied the man, and galloped away . . .

Figure 7. Chōboji today. *Photo by Kawabe Ryōsuke.*

Appendix A.

Two Tokugawa Biographers: Kenryō and Tainin

Two decades after Mujū took leave of the world in the earthen sarcophagus ornamented with implements of the Eight Sects, the Kamakura era in which he was born and passed his long life came to an end. In 1333, the military government with its headquarters in the city of Kamakura was overthrown by the Ashikaga, who continued to administer the government in the name of the emperor with ever-decreasing efficiency. The following three centuries were a time of confusion and chaos.

The fourteenth century saw rival claimants to the throne: a Southern court in Yoshino and a Northern court in Kyoto. This problem was resolved peacefully, although inequitably, in 1392; but the country had even more serious prospects ahead. Ashikaga authority waned as social unrest increased. The Ōnin War (1467-74) began a long period of civil strife among the feudal lords which only ended with the decisive reunification of the country under the Tokugawa clan early in the seventeenth century.

During these three centuries, Chōboji's fortunes rose and fell with the vicissitudes of change in Japanese society, the temple being now too centrally located and too close to the major arteries of travel for its own good. The details are unclear, but Chōboji was evidently a pawn in the power games which continued for several centuries. Why, in these worst of times for the quiet, considered evaluation of a man's life and work, did Emperor Gonara in 1546 bestow on Mujū the posthumous title of Daien Kokushi, "National Teacher of Great Perfection"? And might not Chōboji have fared better *without* the generous support of the Odas: Nobunaga (1534-82), Nobutada (1557-87) and Nobuo (1558-1630)? Support by this year's political victor would guarantee destruction by the opposition whose time would come next year or the year after. Finally, during the Bunraku era (1592-96) Chōboji's property was confiscated in a land survey conducted by Toyotomi Hideyoshi (1536-98) and the temple complex was virtually destroyed. Biographer Kenryō tells us that with the death of Priest

Ryōgaku in 1620, the line of succession from Mujū was discontinued and for the next three decades the fortunes of the temple were at an all time low. It is through this bottleneck in time that a few remnants from the founder managed to survive—the wooden statue and a few manuscript fragments. We can only wonder what manuscripts and artifacts must have been lost after having endured for half the span between Mujū's day and our own. Unfortunately, the biographers Kenryō and Tainin lived on our side of the time divide and had little more to work with than the fragments that are available to us today—little more, but still something. Where their information is confirmed by Mujū's own works, it is redundant; when it offers us a new detail, we are prone to question its accuracy.

But accuracy is not the only value of a writing. When sober biography gives way to legend, at the very least we can know how Mujū was generally regarded by generations of his readers. Many details by word of mouth could easily have bridged the gap between Ryōgaku in 1620 (the year the Mayflower reached Plymouth!) and Priest Shōzan who came to live at Chōboji in 1650; and even the far-fetched anecdote probably contains some factual seed. Kenryō tells us that the buildings were restored in 1682, although to only a fraction of their former glory. Continuity has been maintained from that day to the present. The *Biographical Sketch* and the *Religious Traces* are the two major sources of information about Mujū apart from his own writings. The entries in such compilations as *The Empō Era's Record of the Transmission of the Lamp* (1678) and the *Biographies of Eminent Japanese Priests* (1702) are comparatively brief and not necessarily as accurate as their no-nonsense Chinese format suggests. Moreover, the *Biographical Sketch* and the *Religious Traces* complement each other nicely, being products of two quite different temperaments.

A. Kenryō's *Biographical Sketch* [378]

We know very little about the author of the *Biographical Sketch*. Tainin tells us that a priest called Zekan (Kenryō's Shōzan?, circa 1650) restored Chōboji, and that he was succeeded by Sekkei Keikyō, and then Kenryō Keigan. Since the *Biographical Sketch* is dated 1707, the chronology is possible. Toward the end of his biography, Kenryō refers to a six-volume history of the temple which was a mine of information; but "being replete with Chinese characters, one cannot expect women and children to read it." This detailed history was evidently not available to Tainin, and it is not mentioned by subsequent scholars.

The *Biographical Sketch* falls into two parts, the latter half being subtitled *A Short History of Kigasaki*. But only at the end does Kenryō affix his name and date, the two parts being published as a single item. The writing style is unpretentious and the selection of details often imaginative. Kenryō is particularly concerned to establish Mujū's association with

Atsuta Shrine. When he goes on to conclude his story by telling us about
the azaleas, the elm tree in the garden, and the white lilies in the pond, we
sense that our historian has been transformed into a tour guide before our
very eyes. Kenryō's is a friendly voice. If we listen carefully, we can almost
hear him speaking to travelers from the Tōkaidō, who, three centuries ago,
had a few free hours to visit the rustic temple where the author of *Sand and
Pebbles* used to live.[379]

B. Tainin's *Religious Traces* [380]

Unlike Kenryō, Tainin (1705-1786) was a scholar of some preten-
sions. He was abbot of Hachijisan Kōshōji, a Shingon temple established in
1688, several miles south of Chōboji in Nagoya. His interest in Mujū can be
explained partly by geographical circumstance, partly by the fact that
both monks shared a breadth of doctrinal learning, and perhaps by
Tainin's concern for native writers as a thinker with nationalistic leanings.

Tainin's major scholarly effort was *Questions and Answers on the
Syllabary* (Iroha momben, 1763), which proposed that the Japanese had
their own writing system during the Age of the Gods (*shindai moji*), later
replaced by Chinese characters and the subsequent *kana* syllabaries.
["How could Susa-no-wo have composed the first poem of thirty-one letters
(*waka*) if there were no letters?"] The Sun Goddess Amaterasu gave the
writing system to Oho Anamuchi no Mikoto (i.e., Ō-Kuni Nushi, "The
Great Land-Ruler Deity" enshrined at Izumo); much later, Prince Shōtoku
substituted Chinese characters for the original symbols; and eventually
Kūkai simplified these with the *kana* of the "Syllabary Verse" (*I-ro-ha uta*),
deriving the letters from the cursive forms of T'ang writing. The theory anticipated the views of Hirata Atsutane (1776-1843) as argued in his
Japanese Writing in the Divine Script (Shinji hifumi den, 1819). Several
syllabaries were "reconstructed" over the years, often bearing a likeness to
the Korean *han'gŭl* system developed in the fifteenth century. But claims
for a writing system in Japan before the importation of Chinese characters
have now been thoroughly discredited.[381]

Tainin wrote a number of other works, among which is *Legends of the
Nembutsu and the Power of the Gods* (1762),[382] an anthology of seventeen
stories beginning with a selection from *Sand and Pebbles*. His admiration
for Gidō Shūshin (1325-88) of Kyoto's Nanzenji led him to adopt the noted
Zen scholar's pen-name, Kūge.

Religious Traces is largely a composite of extracts from Mujū's
writings and other works relevant to his life, and the dating is sometimes
questionable. It stiffly records a number of specific facts and allusions, in
curious contrast to Kenryō's potpourri of local legends about Mujū.

Appendix B.
Mujū's Doctrinal Affiliations

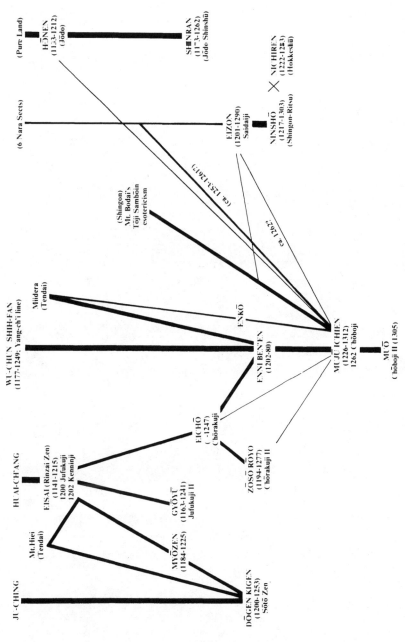

287

Appendix C.
Mujū and the Esotericism of the Sambōin School

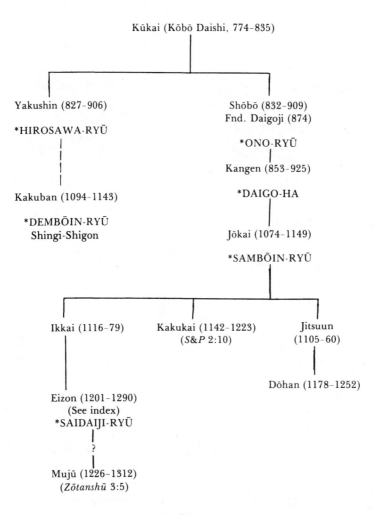

Kūkai (Kōbō Daishi, 774–835)

Yakushin (827–906)

*HIROSAWA-RYŪ

Kakuban (1094–1143)

*DEMBŌIN-RYŪ
Shingi-Shigon

Shōbō (832–909)
Fnd. Daigoji (874)

*ONO-RYŪ

Kangen (853–925)

*DAIGO-HA

Jōkai (1074–1149)

*SAMBŌIN-RYŪ

Ikkai (1116–79)

Kakukai (1142–1223)
(*S&P* 2:10)

Jitsuun
(1105–60)

Dōhan (1178–1252)

Eizon (1201–1290)
(See index)
*SAIDAIJI-RYŪ

?

Mujū (1226–1312)
(*Zōtanshū* 3:5)

Appendix D.
Yamada Family Genealogy

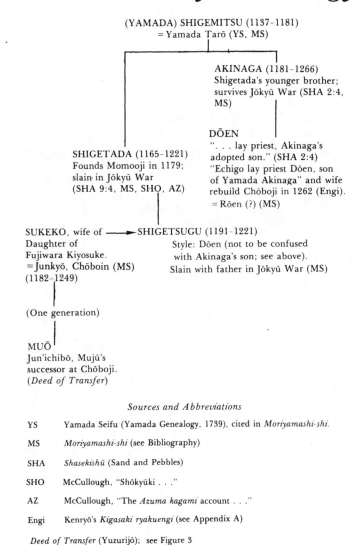

(YAMADA) SHIGEMITSU (1137-1181)
= Yamada Tarō (YS, MS)

AKINAGA (1181-1266)
Shigetada's younger brother;
survives Jōkyū War (SHA 2:4,
MS)

DŌEN
". . . lay priest, Akinaga's
adopted son." (SHA 2:4)
"Echigo lay priest Dōen, son
of Yamada Akinaga" and wife
rebuild Chōboji in 1262 (Engi).
= Rōen (?) (MS)

SHIGETADA (1165-1221)
Founds Momooji in 1179;
slain in Jōkyū War
(SHA 9:4, MS, SHO, AZ)

SUKEKO, wife of ——▶ SHIGETSUGU (1191-1221)
Daughter of   Style: Dōen (not to be confused
Fujiwara Kiyosuke.   with Akinaga's son; see above).
= Junkyō, Chōboin (MS)   Slain with father in Jōkyū War (MS)
(1182-1249)

(One generation)

MUŌ
Jun'ichibō, Mujū's
successor at Chōboji.
(*Deed of Transfer*)

Sources and Abbreviations

YS   Yamada Seifu (Yamada Genealogy, 1739), cited in *Moriyamashi-shi.*

MS   *Moriyamashi-shi* (see Bibliography)

SHA   *Shasekishū* (Sand and Pebbles)

SHO   McCullough, "Shōkyūki . . ."

AZ   McCullough, "The *Azuma kagami* account . . ."

Engi   Kenryō's *Kigasaki ryakuengi* (see Appendix A)

Deed of Transfer (Yuzurijō); see Figure 3

Notes

1. The notion of the three periods of the Law is first clearly stated in China in a work (A.D. 558) by the T'ien T'ai patriarch, Hui-ssu (515-577), followed by the Chinese translation (566) of the influential *Daijikkyō* (T. 397) and the *Daijōdōshōkyō* (T. 673) in 570. Kenneth Ch'en's *Buddhism in China*, pp. 297-300, describes the contemporary Sect of the Three Stages founded by Hsin-hsing (541-594). A useful survey of Latter Day thought, including Indian and Chinese antecedents, is to be found in Matsunaga, *Foundation of Japanese Buddhism I*, pp. 218-223, which is partly based on Yamada Ryūjō's "Mappō shisō ni tsuite," *Indogaku Bukkyōgaku Kenkyū* IV:2, 54-63.

A lucid explanation of Latter Day thought as formulated in Vasubandhu's *Treasury of Analyses of the Law* (Kusharon, T. 1558; translated by Hsüan-tsang A.D. 651-54), correlated with the five periods of the deterioration of human abilities and the constructive influence of ancestral *kami*, appears in Brown and Ishida, *The Future and the Past*, p. 420ff.; also Figure 1. On the influential *Treasury of Analyses*, the basic text of the realistic Kusha sect (registered as an adjunct of the Hossō sect in 793), see Takakusu, *The Essentials of Buddhist Philosophy*, p. 57ff.

Although common belief allotted a thousand years to each of the first two periods of the Law, major variations in the scheme could result from assigning a span of 500 years to either, or both. Thus, if the combined interval for the True Law and Imitation Law were calculated at 1500 years, the commencement of the Latter Days would be A.D. 552, the year of the introduction of Buddhism to Japan according to the *Chronicles of Japan* (Nihon shoki, 720).

The *Mappō tōmyōki* (Record of the Lamp during the Latter Days), a work attributed to Saichō but probably a Heian forgery, was the scriptural authority most widely accepted in Kamakura. This work allowed a thousand years for each of the first two periods, thus placing the beginning of the Latter Days at 1052, a date suitably marked by calamities to reinforce the view that it was a major turning point in history: the burning of Hasedera temple, and the continuing depredations of the military and armed clergy. See Rhodes, "Saichō's *Mappō Tōmyōki*: The Candle of the Latter Dharma." It should be noted that although the theory of the three periods of the Law was widespread during the Heian, and especially the Kamakura, periods, it was not universally accepted. Kūkai and Dōgen were two prominent dissenters. Hakeda, *Kūkai: Major Works*, p. 78;

Nishiyana and Stevens, tr. *Dōgen Zenji's Shōbōgenzō*, Vol. 1, p. 158 (Bendōwa chapter).

2. Brown and Ishida, *The Future and the Past*, p. 199ff.; cf., 348-9. Okami and Akamatsu, *Gukanshō*, p. 319 (Ch. 7); pp. 126-28 (Ch. 2). For the sake of a clearer presentation in English, Brown and Ishida have rearranged the order of the chapters somewhat.

3. Until those who hotly contest the issue come up with a viable alternative, I am persuaded by Ury's arguments in *Tales of Times Now Past*, pp. 9-12, that "tale literature" is still the best translation for *setsuwa bungaku* "if it is kept in mind that they [the *setsuwa*] are tales of a particular sort." Mills also uses the term in *A Collection of Tales from Uji*, but Kyoko Nakamura in her *Miraculous Stories from the Japanese Buddhist Tradition: The Nihon ryōiki of the Monk Kyōkai* prefers "legendary literature" (p. 42). "Anecdotal literature" is another possibility.

In translating *kana hōgo* as "vernacular tract," I should point out that a more literal, but too cumbersome, translation might be "doctrinal tract [whose proportion of] syllabary characters (*kana*) [to Chinese characters is higher than in the formal *hōgo*]." Neither *kana hōgo* nor the later *kanazōshi* were written exclusively with the *kana* syllabary, although both were directed at popular audiences. Hence, "vernacular tract."

4. *Miao-fa lien-hua ching (Myōhōrengekyō*, T. 262). Kumārajīva's translation of the *Saddharma-puṇḍarīka sūtra* made in A.D. 406 which became the most influential scripture in East Asian Buddhism. It is the basic sutra of the Tendai and Nichiren sects. Additional references will be made to the English version of Leon Hurvitz, tr., *Scripture of the Lotus Blossom of the Fine Dharma* (New York: Columbia University Press, 1976).,

5. DeVisser, *Ancient Buddhism in Japan II*, p. 677ff. One of numerous literary references to the *hokke hakkō* is the ceremony on the anniversary of the old emperor's death, at the conclusion of which Fujitsubo announces her intention to become a nun, in Lady Murasaki's *Genji monogatari*; Seidensticker, tr. *The Tale of Genji I*, pp. 204-206.

6. For a translation and commentary on this group of poems see Morrell, "The Buddhist Poetry in the *Goshūishū*," *Monumenta Nipponica* XXVIII:1 (Spring 1973), 87-100; also *Early Kamakura Buddhism: A Minority Report*, Chapter Two.

7. *Daihatsu nehangyō*, T. 374, the "Northern Book" (*Hokuhon*) among several translations into Chinese of the Mahāyānist *Mahāparinirvāṇa-sūtra*, and the version popular in Japan. The Hīnayāna had described the death of Guatama simply as a historical event in the *Mahāparinibbāna sutta* (cf., Warren, *Buddhism in Translations*, p. 95 ff.) of which there are also several translations into Chinese. Complementing the *Lotus Sutra*, the Mahāyānist *Nirvana Sutra* distinguishes the eternal Law Body (*hosshin, dharmakāya*) of the Buddha from its physical manifestation as the historical Gautama.

8. *Ōjōyōshū*, T. 2682. Mujū also cites this noted work in *Sand and*

Pebbles (4:9, 10A:1 and the Epilogue). After describing the torments of hell, it recommends the practice of reciting the name of Amida Buddha. For a recent study see Allen Andrews, *The Teachings Essential for Rebirth: A Study of Genshin's Ōjōyōshū.*

9. *Mo-ho chih-kuan (Maka shikan,* T. 1911). The T'ien T'ai manual on meditation by its great philosopher, Chih-i (538-597), recorded by his disciple Kuan-ting. See Hurvitz, *Chih-I,* pp. 318-31. The work was influential on the poetic practice of Fujiwara Shunzei (1114-1204) and his circle who treated poetry as a quasi-religious exercise. See Brower and Miner, *Japanese Court Poetry,* p. 257; Konishi, "Shunzei no yūgentei to shikan" (Shunzei's style of Mystery and Depth, and the practice of Cessation and Insight), *Bungaku* XX (1952), pp. 108-16.

10. The phrase is frequently found in Zen contexts; but cf. Kūkai's *Memorial Presenting a List of Newly Imported Sutras and Other Items* (Shōrai mokuroku, T. 2161): "Though one may at times err by taking the finger pointing at the moon to be the moon itself, the Buddha's teachings which guide people are limitless" (Hakeda, *Kūkai: Major Works,* p. 145).

11. *Jōjitsuron,* T. 1646, the *Satyasiddhi Śāstra* of Harivarman (250-350); Takakusu, *The Essentials of Buddhist Philosophy,* pp. 74-79.

12. *Kusharon,* T. 1558; see note 1.

13. One of the few articles in English to discuss Eizon and his movement is Inoue Mitsusada's "Eizon, Ninshō and the Saidai-ji Order," *Acta Asiatica* 20 (1971), pp. 77-103.

14. *Kegonkyō,* T. 278, 279, 293, three translations of the *Avataṃsaka Sūtra* in 60, 80, and 40 fascicles, respectively. The title *Avataṃsaka* is applied to all three; but the third version comprises merely the final chapter, Sudhana's pilgrimage, of the two earlier translations, and is also referred to as the *Gaṇḍavyūha.* See D.T. Suzuki, *Essays in Zen Buddhism, Third Series,* p. 49; Cleary, *The Flower Ornament Scripture,* a translation of the 80-fascicle version. Myōe Shōnin, who appears frequently in Mujū's works, was the major patron of the Sudhana theme in Japanese art. And Kakusan Shidō, founder of Kamakura's Tōkeiji convent, made a copy of this sutra to commemorate the death of her husband, Hōjō Tokimune (1251-84). See Kaneko and Morrell, "Sanctuary," p. 205; Fontein, *The Pilgrimage of Sudhana: a Study of Gaṇḍavyūha Illustrations in China, Japan and Java,* pp. 78-115.

15. The prominent role of the "failed hero" in the Japanese literary consciousness is persuasively argued in Morris, *The Nobility of Failure;* see especially Chapter 5, "Victory Through Defeat," the account of Yoshitsune. The legend is to be found in McCullough, tr. *Yoshitsune,* where the villain Kagetoki appears prominently.

16. The 1689 journey which included a visit to Hiraizumi is recorded in Bashō's *Oku no hosomichi* (The Narrow Road Through the Provinces), translated in Earl Miner's *Japanese Poetic Diaries;* see, especially, pp. 176-77.

17. Mujū's citation is a paraphrase. "Misery! — happiness is to be

found by its side! Happiness! — misery lurks beneath it! Who knows what
either will come to in the end?" *Tao Te Ching* 58; Legge, *The Texts of Taoism* I, p. 102.

18. Phrase appearing in Chih-i's *Fa-hua wen-chü* (Words and
Phrases of the Lotus; *Hokke mongu*, T. 1718). It also turns up in Shinkei's
Sasamegoto (1463), a work which cites many items from *Sand and Pebbles*;
see Gidō and Imoto, eds., *Rengaronshū haironshū*, p. 184.

19. Collcutt, *Five Mountains: The Rinzai Zen Monastic Institution in
Medieval Japan* provides valuable background on the Jufukuji and other
temples, the monastic system, and individuals contemporary with Mujū.

20. Kuroita Katsumi, ed. *Azuma kagami I*, p. 646.

21. *tonsei*. In other contexts Mujū uses the word in its original sense
of "one who escapes from the world." Here, however, it has the special
sense of a monk who practices the discipline without any binding temple or
monastic affiliation.

22. Higan Chōro, or Zōsō Rōyo (1194–1277), Rinzai monk attached
to the Jufukuji in Kamakura, succeeded Eichō (d. 1247) at the Chōrakuji
in Serada, where Mujū had heard him discuss the esoteric *Shakuron* in
1252. Rōyo's presence at the Jufukuji in 1260 was evidently a temporary
engagement for him to lecture on his specialty. His last moments are
recorded in *Sand and Pebbles* 10B:3.

23. The *Shakumakaenron* (C. Shih-mo-ho-yen lun, T. 1668) is a
commentary on Aśvaghosa's *Awakening of Faith* by a Nāgārjuna who was
someone other than the famous philosopher of the Mādhyamika School.
The work is highly regarded by the Shingon Sect, whose founder, Kūkai
(Kōbō Daishi, 774–835), used it extensively. See Yoshito S. Hakeda, *The
Awakening of Faith*, pp. 9–10; *Kūkai: Major Works*, p. 151, passim.

24. Influential in the Zen and Kegon sects, the *Engakukyō* (T. 842)
belongs to the doctrinal family of the *Śūrangama Sutra* (J. *Ryōgonkyō*, T.
945; tr. Charles Luk), with ideas incorporated from the *Awakening of
Faith*. It is now thought to have originated in China, rather than being a
translation from a Sanskrit work. The meaning of Perfect Enlightenment
is explained in the format of the Buddha taking a question from each of
twelve bodhisattvas.

25. Chōrakuji in Serada, founded by Eisai's disciple Eichō (d. 1247)
in 1221, was an influential center of Zen practice with a strong esoteric
component; it is not to be confused with another Chōrakuji near the
Jufukuji. Serada, in Kōzuke Province (Gumma Prefecture) is about
halfway between Kamakura and Zenkōji (modern Nagano), Kōzuke being
just west of Hitachi Province in which Mujū's Hōonji was located.

26. *Tsuma kagami*; Morrell, "Mirror for Women," p. 73.

27. For one explanation of this phenomenon, with examples from
Hōnen, Shinran, Nichiren and Dōgen, see Nakamura, *Ways of Thinking
of Eastern Peoples*, pp. 562–73.

28. *Tsuma kagami*; Morrell, "Mirror for Women," p. 59.

29. Kim, *Dōgen Kigen*, p. 56, cites Dōgen's *Shōbōgenzō, Bendōwa* chapter.

30. Petzold, *Buddhist Prophet Nichiren*, Chapter V: "Nichiren's Criticism of Other Buddhist Sects, pp. 94-111.

31. *Tsuma kagami;* Morrell, "Mirror for Women," pp. 73-74.

32. *Kusharon jujo*, T. 1823. A commentary by the T'ang monk Yüan-hui about whom little is known. Vasubandhu's early views, represented by the *Treasury (Abhidharma-kośa*, T. 1558-9), argued for the Sarvāstivādin plurality of ultimate elements, an early moment in the dialectic which arrived at Tendai by way of Nāgārjuna.

33. *Fa-hua hsüan-i (Hokke gengi*, T. 1716). Commentary on the *Lotus Sutra* by T'ien T'ai's great philosopher. See Hurvitz, *Chih-I*, pp. 205-14: "Chih-i's View of the *Lotus.*"

34. Identity uncertain; but possibly a certain Shingon Ritsu monk called Genkai who studied at Eizon's Saidaiji. Yamada and Miki, *Zōtanshū*, p. 111, n. 23.

35. Travel as a metaphor for life in Japanese travel diaries is discussed in the introduction of Plutschow and Fukuda, *Four Japanese Travel Diaries of the Middle Ages*, pp. 1-24.

36. From Gidō's *Kūgeshū*, which might be rendered "Collection of the Flower of Emptiness"; however, Kūge was Gidō's (and Tainin's!) pen name, so perhaps we should settle for "Kūge's Collection". The work is included in Uemura Kankō, ed., *Gozan bungaku zenshū* II, pp. 1771-72.

37. Originally completed in 749, the head and hands of Tōdaiji's Great Buddha were melted during the burning of the enclosure in 1180, for which Kiyomori's son Shigehira paid with his life. The image was repaired in 1186 under the direction of Shunjō (Chōgen, 1121-1206), who is alluded to in *S&P* 4:6, 4:9, and 9:8. The head was again damaged in 1567, and the stodgy restoration is what we know today.

38. The Shōryakuji, which still exists as a temple of the Kogi Branch of the Shingon Sect. Restored by Shin'en of the Hossō sect's Kōfukuji in 1218.

39. Collcutt, *Five Mountains*, pp. 41-48 gives a biographical sketch of Enni with illustrations of Wu-chun's portrait, a Sesshū painting of Tōfukuji, and a woodblock of the *Sugyōroku* (see note 41.) See also Dumoulin, *A History of Zen Buddhism*, pp. 144-50; Tsuji, *Nihon bukkyōshi* III: *Chūseihen* 2, pp. 98-124.

40. The widespread pronunciation, *gozan*, for the characters meaning "Five Mountains" (e.g., Nakamura Hajime's authoritative *Bukkyōgo daijiten*, p. 361) is not supported by Shōgakukan's *Nihon kokugo daijiten*, VIII, p. 129, which prefers the reading *gosan*, following João Rodrigues's *Arte da Lingoa de Iapam (Daibunten)*, 1604-1608; the *Vocabulario da Lingoa de Iapam (Nippo jisho)*, 1603-1604, also has *gosan*.

41. *Tsung Ching Lu (Shukyōroku, Sugyōroku*; T. 2016). In a hundred books divided into three parts, the *Mirror* comprises pp. 415-957 of

Taishō daizōkyō, vol. 48. The work is useful today for its citation of sources whose original has been lost.

42. Dumoulin, *the Development of Chinese Zen*, pp. 36–37 and Table II; *A History of Zen Buddhism*, pp. 125 and 110–111; Ch'en, *Buddhism in China*, pp. 404–05.

43. *Ta-chih-tu-lun (Daichidoron*, T. 1509). An encyclopedic commentary on the *Great Wisdom Sutra* attributed to Nāgārjuna. See Ramanan, *Nāgārjuna's Philosophy as Presented in the Mahā-Prajñāpāramitā-Sāstra*. Tainin says that Mujū studied the work with Eisai's disciple, Eichō of Serada (d. 1247) in 1252, but this is chronologically not possible. In any case, the commentary figures prominently in Mujū's works.

44. In 1260 Mujū was thirty-four, Enni fifty-eight. Both had many years ahead of them.

45. *Tani no gōgyō*. The "Valley School" (Taniryū) a branch of Tendai esotericism inaugurated by Ennin (Jikaku Daishi, 793–864), was established by Kōkei (977–1049). The Dual Ritual was a ceremony utilizing both Diamond and Matrix Mandalas. Enni had been ordained at eighteen at Tendai's Onjōji (Miidera).

46. *Himitsu kanjō*. Ritual symbolizing attainment of the fifth of five levels of esoteric practice, performed on a secret platform. On these anointment ceremonies (*abhiṣeka, kanjō*) see Matsunaga, *Foundation of Japanese Buddhism* I, p. 191ff.

47. *Dainichikyō gishaku* (Commentary on the Mahavairocana Sutra, T. 1796), is an esoteric work recorded by I-hsing (683–727). This version, brought to Japan by Ennin and used in the Tendai Sect, closely parallels the *Dainichikyō sho* introduced by Kūkai and used in Shingon. Mujū cites the work to justify his view of poetry (*waka*) as *dhāraṇī* (*S&P* 5A:12); and also at *S&P* 10B:2: "Enlightenment is something bestowed on a person; it is not like giving him a handful of nuts. It should be possible to obtain wisdom without a teacher; but it is not given to men to understand the marvel of its operation."

48. *Yung chia chi* (J. *Yōkashū*, T. 2013), a work on the theory and practice of Ch'an by Yung-chia Hsüan-chüeh (Yōka Genkaku, 665–713, one of Hui-neng's five major disciples and author of the popular "Song of Enlightenment" (T. 2014) translated in Suzuki's *Manual of Zen Buddhism*, pp. 106–21. See also H. Dumoulin, *The Development of Chinese Zen*, pp. 4–5 and Table I.

49. *P'u t'i hsin lun (Bodaishinron*, T. 1665), a basic scripture in the Shingon sect, is erroneously attributed to Nāgārjuna. It is frequently cited by Kūkai, especially in his *Precious Key to the Secret Treasury* (Hizōhōyaku), a work also known to, and cited by, Mujū (*S&P* 6:18; *Mirror for Women*). See Hakeda, *Kūkai: Major Works*, p. 9.

50. *Kanyō no roku*. Not identified.

51. *Tōfukuji kaizan Shōichi Kokushi nempu*, collected in *Dainihon bukkyō zensho*, vol. 73, p. 151ff. Cited by Tainin.

52. See also Miki Sumito, "Mujū to Tōfukuji," *Bukkyō bungaku kenkyū VI*, pp. 151–180.

53. Translation by Derk Bodde in Fung Yu-lan, *History of Chinese Philosophy* II, pp. 390-91, which cites the version of Hui-neng's *T'an ching* (Platform Sutra) edited by Tsung-pao (preface dated 1290), T. 2008, vol. 48, p. 349. The wording of the *gatha* written by Mujū (see Fig. 1) is identical to the wording in this popular Tsung-pao version, which differs from the Tun-huang text (T. 2007 and later editings) in seven of its twenty-five characters. See Yampolsky, *The Platform Sutra of the Sixth Patriarch*, p. 132 (including footnote 38), also W.T. Chan, *The Platform Scripture*, pp. 40-41, 20-23 — both of which are translations of the Tun-huang text, considered today to be earlier and more authentic, although less popular, than the version used by Mujū.

54. The famous Taoist classic, *Tao Te Ching*, dating from the third century B.C., is well represented in *Sand and Pebbles:* [1:3], [3:2], 4:9, [5A:12], 5B:9, [6:5], 7:25, 8:23, 10A:1, 10A:3, 10B:2, [10B:3].

55. Ascribed to Chuang Chou (ca. 369-286). Although Taoism never flourished as an independent institution in Japan, the *Way and Its Power* and the *Chuang-tzu* were known, especially since Taoist ideas could often be used to reinforce Buddhist arguments. See *Sand and Pebbles* 1:9 (two items), [5A:8, two items], [10B:1].

56. Although the *Lun-yü* only appears once (3:2) in *Sand and Pebbles,* Mujū also cites other Confucian works, although not always by name: *Hsiao Ching, Hsün-tzu, Ch'uan Ch'iao Pen* and the *K'ung-tzu Chia-yü.*

57. The story of Pei Sou is found in the *Huai Nan Tzu* of the second century B.C. *S&P* 7:25 and *Mirror for Women.*

58. The story of Kudokuten and Kokuanten, retold in *Sand and Pebbles* 7:25, originates in Chapter 12 of the *Nirvana Sutra (Daihatsu nehangyō*, T. 374).

59. One of the sub-schools of the Ono branch of Shingon esotericism, i.e., *tōmitsu,* the "esotericism (*mitsu*) of the East (*tō*) Temple" (i.e., Tōji), where Kūkai first performed the esoteric rites in Japan. The Sambōin school was established by Jōkai (1074-1149). See Appendix C.

60. Ninshō is remembered for unsuccessfully accepting Nichiren's challenge to produce rain by prayer during a severe drought in 1271. *Sand and Pebbles* does not record this incident, but it does refer (9:9) to the long droughts of the Bun'ei period (1264-74) in which Mino and Owari provinces were hit by widespread famine so that many people fled to other provinces. The droughts were surely a contributing factor to Chōboji's decline during Mujū's tenure.

61. *Kantō ōgenki,* in *Shiseki zassan* I, pp. 1-2. Eizon's trip is also discussed in Wajima, *Eizon Ninshō,* pp. 40-42.

62. Reischauer, "Izayoi nikki," pp. 60-61. This Moriyama is not to be confused with the present city ward in Nagoya, nor with Moriyama hamlet (visible in the top right of the *Owari meisho zue* illustration, figure 5, across the Yada River from Chōboji) from which the ward takes its name.

63. *Kissa yōjō ki,* partially translated in Tsunoda et al., eds., *Sources of Japanese Tradition I,* pp. 237-40.

64. Reischauer, "Izayoi nikki," pp. 60-66.

65. *Brahmajāla-sūtra* (J. *Bommōkyō*, T. 1484), The major text of the Mahāyāna disciplinary code, detailing ten major and forty-eight minor rules. For a discussion of these in the context of the earlier disciplinary code, see Dutt, *Aspects of Mahāyāna Buddhism and its Relation to Hīnayāna*, pp. 293-95.

66. That is, he performed special rites to "bind the site" (*kekkai*) selected for religious practice — temple grounds or an altar — against evil influences. For instances of this practice see DeVisser, *Ancient Buddhism in Japan* I, pp. 174, 305; II, p. 479. Eizon presumably constructed a cermonial platform in his quarters where he might perform such esoteric rites as the Fire Ceremony (*goma*).

67. *shibun fusatsu*. At Repentance Meetings (*fusatsu*), normally conducted twice a month, monks assembled to recite the regulations and to make public confession of transgressions. On these occasions lay devotees observed the Eight Commandments (*hakkai*), heard the Teaching expounded, and provided vegetarian fare for the clergy. Repentance Meetings based on the Four Groups of Regulations probably refers to an assembly at which was recited the Four-part Vinaya (*shibun ritsu*) introduced to Japan by Ganjin, founder of the Disciplinary Sect which Eizon was attempting to restore.

68. *bosatsukai*. The Ten Principal Commandments expounded in the *Net of Brahma Sutra* (note 65): against killing, stealing, committing adultery, lying, dealing in intoxicating drinks, revealing others' faults, praising oneself and abusing others, giving way to anger, or speaking ill of the Three Treasures of Buddhism. Eizon was noted for conducting such public ceremonies. See Inoue, "Eizon, Ninshō and the Saidai-ji Order," pp. 87-88.

69. Tainin's *Traces* gives 1262 as the date for Mujū's meeting with Enni and 1263 for the year he "came to live" at Chōboji, However, Mujū's own "Deed of Transfer", dated 1305, says that he had lived there for forty-four years, i.e., since 1261. His "Record of a Dream" states that he succeeded to Chōboji the year after he came to live there, i.e., in 1262. These dates are compatible with Eizon's account.

70. R.A.B. Ponsonby-Fane, *Studies in Shintō and Shrines*, Chapter XV, "The History of Atsuta Jingu," pp. 429-53; also p. 14ff. on the Three Imperial Regalia.

71. The story of Susa-no-o finding the Heavenly Grass-Mowing Sword (Ame no Kusanagi no on Tsurugi), the central object of worship at Atsuta Shrine, is recorded in the earliest Japanese history, the *Record of Ancient Matters* (Kojiki, 712). The Sun Goddess, Amaterasu, subsequently gave the sword to her grandson Ninigi as one of the Three Imperial Regalia when he was dispatched from the heavens to rule the Central Land of the Reed Plains, i.e., Japan. See Philippi, tr. *Kojiki*, pp. 88-90. The Story of the "Brave Man of Yamoto" is told in both the *Record of Ancient Matters* and the *Chronicles of Japan* (Nihon Shoki, 720); he is the first important instance of the Japanese "failed hero". See Ivan Morris, *The Nobility of Failure*, Chapter 1, pp. 1-13.

72. The authors of Kaidōki (Sea Route Journal) and Tōkan kikō (Journal of a Trip to the Eastern Barrier) are not known although both works were traditionally ascribed to Kamo no Chōmei (1153-1216), the first having been written in early Kamakura and the latter ca. 1242. Tōkan kikō has been anonymously translated in Katō, Commemoration Volume, pp. 143-201.

73. "The Izayoi Nikki," in Reischauer and Yamagiwa, eds. Translations from Early Japanese Literature, p. 66.

74. According to Moriyamashi shi, p. 565, Shōkai's Kantō ōgenki is the earliest written account in which the temple is called Chōboji.

75. For a loose paraphrase and interpretation see Andō (a), pp. 149-50. The manuscript is reproduced in color in Nihon kōsō iboku (see Selected Bibliography, A.5).

76. Collcutt, Five Mountains, pp. 171-72; on Zen celibacy, pp. 145-46. See also Suzuki's classic, The Training of the Zen Buddhist Monk (1934), which includes much detail on modern practice, but with reference to the earlier tradition.

77. For a representative selection of translations from the thousand-plus anecdotes in Konjaku monogatari shū, see Ury, Tales of Times Now Past: Sixty-Two Stories from a Medieval Japanese Collection. Mills, A Collection of Tales from Uji: A Study and Translation of Uji Shūi Monogatari includes a detailed survey of the setsuwa genre.

78. An elaborate examination of Owari Manzai may be found in Owari manzai tazune tazunete (In Search of Owari Manzai), vol. 49 (zempen) and 53 (chūhen) of the series, Bunkazai sōsho (Nagoya: Nagoyashi Kyōiku Iinkai, 1970-71), 137 and 139 pp., respectively, with additional maps. I have not seen the projected third volume.

79. The chart in Watanabe, Shasekishū, pp. 3-10, is helpful for correlating anecdotes. See Selected Bibliography, A.1.

80. Tainin's Traces cites "a note written in a copy of the work presently held by Chōboji."

81. Recently there has been speculation that Mujū may not, in fact, be the author of Tsuma kagami. Even if this proves to be true, the similarities between the Mirror and S&P are remarkable. For a complete translation of the work see Morrell, "Mirror for Women: Mujū Ichien's Tsuma Kagami," Monumenta Nipponica XXXV, No. 1 (Spring 1980), pp. 45-75.

82. Tao-hsüan (J. Dōsen, 596-667), founder of the Disciplinary Sect (Nan Shan Tsung) in China, is noted for his codifications of monastic rules. Mujū's Japanese rendering of these seven grave vices is from Ching Hsin Chieh Kuan Fa (Rules to Purify Mind and Maintain Insight), J. Jōshinkaikanbō, T. 1893.

83. A translation of Onna daigaku by Kaibara Ekiken (1630-1714) is conveniently available in Chamberlain's Japanese Things (Tuttle, 1971), pp. 502-508, a reprint of the fifth edition of Things Japanese (1905).

84. For a general account of Azuma kagami, see Shinoda, The Founding of the Kamakura Shogunate, 1180-1185. Shigetada and Shiget-

sugu, see below, are also mentioned in this work, although less prominently than in *Shōkyūki.* See McCullough, "The *Azuma kagami* account of the Shōkyū War," pp. 118, 120, 125, and 127.

85. Aston, tr., *Nihongi* I, p. 207; Morris, *Nobility of Failure,* p. 8.

86. The final sentence echoes an old poetic recitation (*rōei*), based on a statement by Po Chü-I (772-846), which is included in the *Wakan rōeishū* (Collection of Poetic Recitations in Chinese and Japanese) of Fujiwara Kintō (944-1041). Kawaguchi, ed., *Wakan rōeishū; Ryōjin hishō,* p. 200, No. 588: "May the error of wild words and specious phrases, the karma of my vulgar writings in this life,/Henceforth be cause instead to praise the Vehicle of Buddha, and condition for turning the Wheel of the Law." See Harper, "Motoori Norinaga's Criticism," p. 57; Waley, *The Life and Times of Po Chü-I,* pp. 193-94. Tainin also picks up the phrase.

87. Source unknown. Yamada and Miki cite a parallel passage from the *Fumbetsu kudokuron* (Comments on Discrimination and Virtuous Behavior, T. 1507), a detailed discussion of the first four articles of the *Zōichiagonkyō* (T. 125; cf., *Aṅguttara nikāya*), apparently known to Mujū since several items from that work appear in *Sand and Pebbles.*

88. *Tennōji no goshuin engi,* a history of the Temple of the Four Heavenly Kings founded by Prince Shōtoku in what is now the city of Ōsaka. The history has traditionally been ascribed to Prince Shōtoku (573-621) but probably dates from the early Heian period.

89. "If eaten raw they are said to cause irritability of temper, and if eaten cooked, to act as an aphrodisiac; moreover, the breath of the eater, if reading the sutras, will drive away the good spirits." (Soothill and Hodous, *A Dictionary of Chinese Buddhist Terms,* p. 128.)

90. Kobayashi Tadao, "Mujū to Rengeji," p. 10.

91. The *Honchō Kōsōden* (Biographies of Eminent Japanese Priests, 1702) and *Empōdentōroku* (The Empō Era's Record of the Transmission of the Lamp, 1678), both by the Rinzai monk Mangen Shiban (1626-1710), state that Mujū died at Rengeji. The claim has been repeated in many modern accounts of his life.

92. Henjō's poem appears in the *Kokinshū* (III:165):

Hachisuba no	The lotus petals
Nigori ni shimanu	Have a heart within unstained
Kokoro mote	By any muddiness:
Nani ka wa tsuyu wo	Why then do they deceive us
Tama to azamuku	That their dewdrops are jewels?

Saeki, *Kokinwakashū,* p. 165. Yamada and Miki refer us further to a phrase in the *Lotus Sutra,* Chaper 15; Sakamoto and Iwamoto, eds., *Hokkekyō* II, p. 318; Hurvitz, *Scripture of the Lotus Blossom,* p. 235; "They have well learned the bodhisattva-path, and / They are untainted by worldly dharmas, / Like the lotus blossom in the water."

93. The document is also reproduced, together with a printed rendering of its Chinese text, in Mainichi Shimbunsha, ed., *Nihon kōsō*

iboku (see Bibliography A.5). Andō (a), pp. 156–57, includes a loose explanatory paraphrase which is a helpful guide through some of its obscurities.

Andō, p. 157, speculates that Muō's grandmother referred to in the deed was the wife (i.e., Sukeko; see Appendix D: Yamada Family Genealogy) of Shigetsugu, son of Yamada Shigetada, founder of Momooji. Both father and son died in the Jōkyū War, and Sukeko had passed away before Mujū arrived on the scene. Given the close association of the Yamadas with Chōboji over several generations, it is not improbable that Muō was a member of the family.

94. Nishikawa Kōtarō, *Chinzō chōkoku*, p. 40.

95. Transliterated from the Chinese verse of four 4-character lines.

96. Strictly speaking, the Kegon, Ritsu, Hossō, Sanron, Jōjitsu, Kusha, Tendai and Shingon; here, however, the meaning is perhaps better rendered as "various sects". The Jōjitsu and Kusha never developed into independent sects in Japan, but remained schools of philosophy; and the Zen sect, to which Mujū belonged, is not included in the enumeration.

97. This carving (Frontispiece) is an Important Cultural Property, 79.4 cm. high, with the main body made of Japanese cypress. The image is colored and crystal is used for the eyes, although the colors have faded and the lacquer worn away. When the statue was dismantled for repair in 1951, nineteen lines of the *Hōkyōin darani* in Sanskrit characters were found within. A colored closeup of the head and a monochrome photograph of the entire carving — less the abbot's hat which he customarily wears — can be seen in Nishikawa Kōtarō, *Chinzō chōkoku*, Plate 8 and pp. 40–41.

98. See, for example, Welbon, *The Buddhist Nirvāṇa and Its Western Interpreters*.

99. Fung, *A History of Chinese Philosophy* II, pp. 240–43; Ch'en, *Buddhism in China*, pp. 68–69.

100. The problem is discussed in Conze, "Buddhist Philosophy and Its European Parallels," and "Spurious Parallels to Buddhist Philosophy"; see also comment by Alex Wayman, "Conze on Buddhism and European Parallels," *Philosophy East and West*, 1963-64.

101. *Tsuma Kagami*; Morrell, "Mirror for Women," p. 51.

102. The philosophy of Japanese estoericism is lucidly outlined in Kiyota, *Shingon Buddhism: Theory and Practice* and in Hakeda, *Kūkai: Major Works*, which also includes translations. The pictorial symbolism of the system is described in Saunders' *Mudrā*, Rambach's *The Secret Message of Tantric Buddhism*, and Sawa's *Art in Japanese Esoteric Buddhism*.

103. For an extensive study of this notion see Matsunaga, *The Buddhist Philosophy of Assimilation: The Historical Development of the Honji-Suijaku Theory*; see also Kiyota, *Shingon Buddhism*, pp. 74-80, for a characterization of *honji-suijaku* as "folk religion" rather than as the logical extension of Buddhist philosophical theory.

104. From Kūkai's *Shōrai mokuroku* (A Memorial Presenting a List

of Newly Imported Sutras and Other Items), translated in Hakeda, *Kūkai: Major Works*, p. 145; cf., n.10.

105. Conze, *Buddhism: Its Essence and Development*, p. 130, commenting on a famous definition of the bodhisattva in the *Diamond Sutra*.

106. Dutt, *Aspects of Mahāyāna Buddhism and its Relation to Hīnayāna*, p. 129ff., especially 151ff. on the views of La Vallee Poussin, Stcherbatsky, and Keith; Murti, *The Central Philosophy of Buddhism*, p. 271ff.

107. *Tsuma kagami*; Morrell, "Mirror for Women," pp. 57, 73.

108. For a discussion of this problem with reference to additional Japanese sources, see Harper, "Motoori Norinaga's Criticism," pp. 56–58.

109. Kobayashi Tadao, *Shimpen Mujū Kokushi kashū*, supplement to *Kyōdo Bunka* V:3 (1950).

110. Brower and Miner, *Japanese Court Poetry*, p. 257.

111. Although Mujū ardently defends the notion of *waka* as *dhāraṇī*, he did not, of course, originate the idea. See Yamada Shōzen, "Chūsei kōki ni okeru waka soku darani no shissen," *Indogaku Bukkyōgaku Kenkyū* XVI:I, pp. 290–292.

112. For an extended discussion on the importance of *Shintōshū* for textual comparisons, see Ruch, *Otogi Bunko and Short Stories of the Muromachi Period*, pp. 148–181.

113. Tsukudo Reikan, *Chūsei geibun no kenkyū*, pp. 285–88, compares a substantial excerpt from *S&P* 1:1 with a parallel passage in *Shintōshū*.

114. See Tsutsumi, "Weird Tales from Tokugawa Times," pp. 32–33.

115. Morrell, "Passage to India Denied," p. 196.

116. *Sasamegoto*. Kidō and Imoto, eds. *Rengaronshū haironshū*, p. 183.

117. *S&P* 5A:12. For a detailed discussion on the influence of *S&P* of *Sasamegoto*, see Kidō, "Sasamegoto ni oyoboshita Shasekishū no eikyō," pp. 265–90.

118. *Muchū mondō shū*, 1344. Three-volume work consisting of 91 items on the principles of Zen in the form of Musō's answers to questions put to him by Ashikaga Tadayoshi (1306–1352), Takauji's brother.

119. Adapted from *Tetsugen zenji kanahōgo* (Vernacular Tract by the Zen Master Tetsugen) as cited in Nakamura, *Ways of Thinking*, p. 686, note 25.

120. Kobayashi, "Shasekishū no hampon ni tsuite," *Kokugakuin zasshi* (1959), pp. 39–50, is the most comprehensive discussion of Tokugawa printed editions of *Sand and Pebbles* . . . "For several centuries after its compilation, *Konjaku* seems not to have been widely known. Its title is not mentioned in any other book until 1451. There is only one premodern printed edition, a curious and corrupt partial one, edited by Izawa Nagahide and printed in Kyoto in 1720." Ury, *Tales of Times Now Past*, p. 22.

121. Kishimoto, *Japanese Religion in the Meiji Era*, pp. 111-24.

122. Phrase from the Mahāyānist *Nirvana Sutra (Daihatsu nehangyō,* T. 374). The "First Principle" is Ultimate Reality: *nirvāṇa, śūnyatā,* the Unconditioned from which all determinate existence proceeds.

123. Mujū uses two pillow-words (*makurakotoba*) in this sentence — conventional epithets used to modify and amplify certain nouns, usually in poetry but also in high-flown formal prose. The association between pillow-word and noun is often tenuous and frequently involves word-play. Here, the pillow-word *Naniwae no* (of Naniwa Bay) associates by word-play with the second element of *yoshi ashi* (good and bad), which also means "reeds". The pillow-word *moshiogusa* (seaweed) associates by word-play with *kakiatsumu* (to compile), from the fact that this seaweed was used to collect (*kakiatsumu*) salt from the sea. Inasmuch as a strained English equivalent would only add unnecessary ambiguity, I have not included these two phrases in the translation.

124. *Wakō (dōjin).* The doctrine that the buddhas and bodhisattvas "moderate the light (of their wisdom) and identify with the dust (of the human world)," i.e., they assume human forms for the sake of benefiting sentient beings. The phrase can be traced to the *Tao Te Ching* IV: ". . . we should attemper our brightness, and bring ourselves into agreement with the obscurity of others." (Legge, tr.) The phrase frequently appears in Book I of *Sand and Pebbles.* Cf., *honji suijaku.*

125. "In this [Takejizai] heaven there is a separate locality called the dwelling place of Māra, the killer or tempter, who, filled with passion and lust, destroys all virtuous principles, as a stone-mill grinds corn. He is called the *Dairokuten maō,* Māra of the sixth heaven." Coates and Ishizuka, *Hōnen the Buddhist Saint,* p. 95.

126. Mujū's list differs somewhat from the words specified in the *Procedures of the Engi Era* (Engishiki, 927) as tabu for the Princess who served at the Ise Shrine. Here the Buddha is referred to as the "Central One" (*nakako*), and death (see below, note 139 and associated text) as "getting well" (*naoru*). Childbirth is not listed among these *imikotoba,* but the act itself was a source of ritual defilement. See Bock, *Engishiki: Procedures of the Engi Era, Books I-V,* p. 152; *Kokushi taikei* XXVI, pp. 99-100. See also the [*Zōise'nisho*] *Hōkihongi* in Ishida Ichirō, *Shintō shisōshi,* p. 127; Ponsonby-Fane, *Studies in Shintō and Shrines,* pp. 32-33.

127. This folk etymology is found in the *Kogo shūi* (807) but not in the *Kojiki* or *Nihon shoki,* which also relate the story of Amaterasu concealing herself in a cave. Katō and Hoshino, tr. *Imbe no Hironari's Kogoshūi or Gleanings from Ancient Stories,* p. 22.

128. The Naikū and Gekū dedicated respectively to the Sun Goddess Amaterasu and to Toyoukehime, an agricultural goddess of fertility.

129. Mahāvairocana (Dainichi Nyorai) is the central Buddha in both the Matrix (*taizōkai*) and Diamond (*kongōkai*) Worlds, together known as the Two-Part (*ryōbu*) Mandala. The Matrix Mandala represents the state

of Buddhahood as preached in the *Mahāvairocana Sūtra* (J. *Dainichikyō*, T. 848); the Diamond Mandala follows the *Vajraśekhara Sūtra* (J. *Kongōchōgyō*, T. 865). Kiyota, *Shingon Buddhism: Theory and Practice*, pp. 81-104 ("The Two Mandalas"); Rambach, *The Secret Message of Tantric Buddhism*, p. 44ff.

130. *Tosotsuten.* The fourth desire heaven where all bodhisattvas are reborn before birth as Buddhas; hence, the present abode of Maitreya, the future Buddha. For a Muromachi map which depicts this region among some twenty-eight heavens above Mount Sumeru in the center of our world, see Rosenfield and Cranston, *The Courtly Tradition in Japanese Art and Literature*, pp. 108-109.

131. *takama ga hara.* The abode of the Shinto gods, described as " a place with mountains and rivers, but . . . clearly a mytho-religious location rather than an actual place in the real world." Philippi, tr. *Kojiki*, p. 597.

132. *naishō no hokkaigū. Naishō* ("inner realization") in contrast to *geyū* ("outward manifestation"), the knower and the known. The World-of-Dharma Palace is Mahāvairocana's abode in the Matrix Assembly; *mitsugonkoku* (or *mitsugon jōdo*), the name of his Pure Land. See Morrell, "Shingon's Kakukai," pp. 204-210.

133. The design of the Four-Enclosure (*shijū*) mandala, described in Book VI of the *Dainichikyō sho* differs from the "iconographic" (*genzu*; see Kiyota, *Shingon Buddhism*, p. 83) version of the Matrix world commonly employed in Japan and introduced from China by Kūkai. The basic pattern of the Four-Enclosure Mandala, also called the Three-Enclosure Mandala when the central constellation is not counted, is a central square within three squares of increasing size. It approximates the layout of the Inner Shrine more closely than the more complicated standard version. Oda Tokunō, *Bukkyō daijiten*, pp. 448-9.

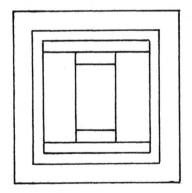
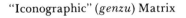
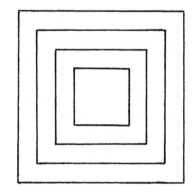

"Iconographic" (*genzu*) Matrix   Four-Enclosure (*shijū*) Matrix

134. The Inner Shrine is surrounded by a series of fences forming rectangular enclosures. Beginning with the innermost fence they comprise a *mizugaki*, then an "inner" and "outer" *tamagaki*, and finally an *aragaki*. The design indeed suggests that of the Four-Enclosure mandala.

135. The central Mahāvairocana surrounded by eight Buddhas and Bodhisattvas on an eight-petalled lotus design is the inner constellation of the Matrix World. Kiyota, *Shingon Buddhism*, p. 88; Rambach, *The Secret Message*, pp. 52, 55.

136. This pattern bears no relationship to the ground plan of the Outer Shrine, unlike the correspondence between the Matrix World and the Inner Shrine. The Diamond World Mandala is sometimes referred to as the Moon Disc (*gachirin*) Mandala, from the design of its central constellation (the "Karma Assembly") consisting of four circles around Mahāvairocana's central circle. The five major Buddhas of the Diamond World, each the focus of a circle, are correlated with various groups of five; wisdoms, elements, *vajras*, etc. The Five Wisdoms and their associated Buddhas are: 1. Wisdom That Perceives the Essential Nature of the World of Dharma (Mahāvairocana); 2. Mirrorlike Wisdom reflecting reality without distortion (Akṣobhya); 3. the Wisdom of Equality which perceives the fundamental identity of all phenomena (Ratnasambhava); 4. the Wisdom of Observation, that observes the objects of mind free from discrimination and subjective calculations (Amitābha); and 5. the Wisdom of Action, that is manifested as actions to help bring all sentient beings to enlightenment (Amoghasiddhi). Hakeda, *Kūkai: Major Works*, pp. 83-84; Kiyota, *Shingon Buddhism*, pp. 97-98; Rambach, *The Secret Message*, pp. 53-54.

137. *yaotome.* A group of eight vestals whose principal duty is the performance of the sacred Shintō *kagura* dance.

138. A coarse "three-pestle rice" (*mikine yone*) has traditionally been used in preparing ceremonial offerings to the gods.

139. Literally, *ubuya* ("parturition hut"), but Watanabe points out that in this context the act of childbirth is indicated. The tabus against childbirth and death were not peculiar to Ise Shrine, although the fifty-day pollution period may have been. See also note 126.

140. Both Bonshun's manuscript and the *rufubon* use the characters, *shiki* (literally, "death-spirit) and the commentators mention no textual variants. *Shiki* may have been what Mujū intended, but it is not much of a euphemism for the word "death." The *Hōkihongi* says that the substitute word is *naoru*, "restoration." Ishida, *Shintō shisōshū*, p. 127.

141. *hosshin. Dharmakāya*, the Buddha as Ultimate Reality, whose diversity is phenomena; the basic aspect of the Three-fold Body of the Buddha.

142. *jōdo.* Any of several regions inhabited by the buddhas and bodhisattvas, the most popular being Amida's Western Paradise, into which one might hope to be born (*ōjō*).

143. Mānava (J. Judō) was Śākyamuni's name while he was still a bodhisattva serving his apprenticeship under Dīpamkara. See Matsunaga, *Buddhist Philosophy of Assimilation*, pp. 101–2, for the origins of this theory to accommodate Confucianism and Taoism under the Buddhist umbrella. Kāśyapa was the sixth of seven Buddhas of the past, Śākyamuni being the seventh; and Dīpamkara was the first of a series of twenty-five Buddhas, Śākyamuni being the twenty-fifth.

144. Gankai, Confucius' favorite disciple.

145. It should be noted that those in the upper four stations (worlds) of being are, strictly speaking, not subject to delusion; and that the "nine worlds" presumably indicate the stations below that of the Buddha. But Mujū is here concerned to emphasize the all-encompassing nature of the Law Body.

146. Mujū perhaps refers to such legends as Susa-no-o and the eight-headed dragon, whose contest can be viewed as an allegory for the triumph of good over evil.

147. See note 136.

148. *sokushin jōbutsu*; also translated "instant Buddhahood." The three categories of "attaining Buddhahood in this very existence" (*rigu, kendoku, kaji* — see the following notes) were defined by Kūkai in his *Ihon sokushin jōbutsu-gi* (Attaining Enlightenment in this Very Existence, Variant Text). Kiyota, *Shingon Buddhism*, pp. 123–27.

149. *rigu-jōbutsu.* The inherent principle is identified as the "mind of enlightenment" (*bodhicitta; bodaishin*), interpreted by Kūkai in two senses: (1) the aspiration to attain enlightenment, and (2) the potentially enlightened mind. (Hakeda, *Kūkai: Major Works*, pp. 96–97). In the first sense, "raising the desire for enlightenment' (*hotsubodaishin*) is an important concept in Kegon and Zen. (See Suzuki, *Essays in Zen Buddhism, Third Series*, pp. 137–85). In the second sense, esotericism speaks of the "mind of enlightenment," i.e., the Buddha-nature (*busshō*) inherent in all sentient beings. See Kiyota, *Shingon Buddhism*, p. 126 and Glossary.

150. *kendoku-jōbutsu.* "Kendoku, the union of principle and practice, is the actualization of Buddhahood . . . (It) is the goal of Shingon practitioners . . . 'ken' meaning 'to reveal,' 'doku', 'to acquire, kendoku-jōbutsu means to acquire (Buddhahood) by revealing its inherent nature in the mind of man." Kiyota, *Shingon Buddhism*, p. 126.

151. *kaji no jōbutsu.* The empirical realization of Buddhahood through the practice of integrating human activities with the activities of Mahāvairocana. *Kaji* is viewed as the integration of the Body, Speech and Thought of the Great Sun Buddha with those of the devotee.See *S&P* 6:1, for a humorous misunderstanding of this concept. Also Hakeda, p. 92; Kiyota, p. 126.

152. A tantric rite performed by five Esoteric Masters (*ajari*) before the Five Vidyārāja (Myō-ō): Fudō (central platform), Gōzanze (east plat-

form), Gundari (south platform), Kongō Yasha (north platform), and Daiitoku (west platform).

153. Passage from the *Kegongyō zuisho engishō*, T. 1736, an influential commentary on the *Garland Sutra* by Ch'eng-kuan (Chōkan, 737–838).

154. Fugen. The idealization of compassion, activity, production. The bodhisattva complements Mañjuśrī (Monju), who symbolizes wisdom.

155. *Fuzōfugengyō*, T. 668.

156. Here the five worlds are those of the heavenly beings, men, animals, hungry ghosts and those in the hells (including asuras).

157. En no Ozunu (634–?), legendary founder of the *shugendō* (mountain ascetic) tradition.

158. Identity uncertain. The anecdote is later reported in *Genkō shakusho* (1322) and *Tōkoku kōsōden* (1687). In any case, this is not the Jōgambō who immediately preceded Mujū at Chōboji.

159. Yoshino is the site of the famous Kimpusenji Temple founded by En no Gyōja. Since Jōgambō is evidently on a pilgrimage to a shrine, Kimpu Shrine is his likely destination.

160. Presumably a reference to the *Profound Meaning of the Lotus*.

161. Death and childbirth are both ritually defiling in Shintō belief. Confucian teaching also holds that it is unfilial for a child to precede his parents in death, but in this context the important fact is that someone died.

162. Kōben (1173–1232). Influential Kegon prelate, author of a tract, *Saijarin* (Smashing the Bad Vehicle), criticizing Hōnen's *Senjakushū*. But Kōben was no bigot. In fact, Mujū's attraction to him was probably his like-minded spirit of eclecticism. See Nakamura, *Ways of Thinking*, pp. 387–8; *S&P* 3:8; Morrell, "Kamakura Accounts of Myōe Shōnin as Popular Religious Hero."

163. Kasuga enshrines four main deities among at least seven with the title *Daimyōjin* ("Great Deity"); but perhaps here the deity of the Ichinomiya shrine, Kashima Takemikazuchi, is indicated. See Matsunaga, *The Buddhist Philosophy of Assimilation*, pp. 231–33, for several lists of Shintō deities (*suijaku*) with their corresponding Buddhas (*honji*). Zeami's *Kasuga ryūjin* (The Dragon God of Kasuga) is a dramatization of the Kasuga deity's refusal to let Myōe travel to India; see Morrell, "Passage to India Denied: Zeami's *Kasuga Ryūjin*," *Monumenta Nipponica* XXXVII: 2 (Summer 1982), pp. 179–200.

164. The verse is included in the *Gyokuyōshū* (Collection of Jeweled Leaves), XX: 2720, with this headnote: "When Jōkei Shōnin moved to the place called Wisdom Heights, he wanted to invite the Great Deity of Kasuga, which caused the god to respond with this poem." *Kōchū kokka taikei*, vol. 6, p. 604.

165. The verse is included in the *Shokukokinshū* (Collection of An-

cient and Modern Times Continued), VII: 691, with a short headnote ascribing the poem to the Great Deity of Kasuga. *Kōchū kokka taikei*, vol. 5, p. 491. See Morrell, "Jōkei and the Kōfukuji Petition," p. 11.

166. An apparent reference to the Confucian philosopher Hsün Tzu (c. 298–c. 238).

167. *Daisan no goten*, i.e., Sannomiya, whose Original Ground is the bodhisattva Jizō.

168. *Daihannya (haramitta) kyō*, T. 220. A collection of sixteen sutras in six hundred fascicles on the doctrine of "Perfect Wisdom" translated by Hsüan-tsang (600–64). Cf. E. Conze, *The Large Sutra on Perfect Wisdom*.

169. *tengu*, a mythical Japanese creature. Cf., *S&P* 7:20: "The goblin (*tengu*) is a Japanese tradition. There is nothing conclusive written about them in the scriptures. I think that perhaps they are what are referred to in the commentaries of the former sages as 'evil demons' (*maki*). Generally speaking, they certainly belong in the class of demons (*ki*) . . ." Watanabe, *Shasekishū*, p. 318. This explanation would seem to place the *tengu* in the world of fighting-spirits, but perhaps among the hungry-ghosts (*pretas*) or in the hells.

170. The Hiyoshi deity, later identified with Sannō Gongen, is the protector of Tendai's Enryakuji; Śākyamuni is considered to be its Original Ground. Jūzenji, deity of one of the seven shrines also protecting the temple, is considered a Manifest Trace of the bodhisattva Jizō. The story also appears in Nakamura, *Miraculous Tales*, Book 8.

171. *Hsin Ti Kuan Ching (Shinjikangyō*, T. 159). However, Watanabe notes that the phrase does not appear in this sutra.

172. *sōjō no ninjin wo uke, udon no buppō ni ai*. . . . Two common but awkward-to-translate metaphors in which the likelihood of being born in human form is compared to the dirt on a toe-nail as against that of the entire world (*Nirvana Sutra*), and the opportunity to encounter the teaching of the Buddha is said to be rarer than the appearance of the flower of the Udumbara tree, which blossoms only once in three thousand years (*Lotus Sutra*).

173. The *Yugaron* (T. 1579) and *Jōyuishikiron* (T. 1585), translations of idealist treatises by Asaṅga (c. 410–500) and Dharmapāla (VI century). Both are basic works of the Hossō school, whose Kōfukuji is the tutelary temple of the Fujiwara clan, just as Kasuga is its shrine.

174. Shinra, the protector god of Miidera, was a Korean deity (the characters may also be pronounced 'Shiragi') who appeared to the temple's founder, Enchin, during his return from study in China.

175. Verse included in the *Shinkokinshū* (New Collection of Ancient and Modern Times), XX: 1966, with this headnote: "On the topic 'Such-like Retributions' (*nyozehō*) while poems on the Ten Categories of the Such-like [condition of the dharmas] were being composed at the residence of the late Regent lay-priest." Hisamatsu, et al., eds, *Shinkokinwakashū*, p. 397. On the Tendai doctrine of the Ten Such-likes (*jūnyoze*), see Hurvitz, *Chih-I*, pp. 280–83.

176. Sannō Daishi, another name for Hiyoshi. *Sannō-ichijitsu shintō* is the Tendai version of Shintō-Buddhist syncretism. See Matsunaga, *Buddhist Philosophy of Assimilation*, pp. 189–92.

177. The shrine, in Fushimi ward in southern Kyoto, is dedicated to the gods Uka no mitama, Saruta hiko, and Ōmiya no me, and is the central shrine of the popular Inari cult.

178. Shrine in Hiroshima prefecture dedicated to three daughters of Susa-no-o, the first two by the sun-goddess Amaterasu: Ichiki shima hime (later identified with Benzaiten), Tagori-hime, and Tagitsu-hime. This was the tutelary shrine of the Taira clan. Katō, *A Study of Shintō*, pp. 158–59, cites *S&P* on this conflict of Shintō and Buddhist practice.

179. The three major shrines at Kumano are the Hongū, Shingū, and Nachi, respectively enshrining the native deities Ketsumi-no-Miko-no-ōkami, Hayatama-no-o, and Izanami. Buddhist syncretic thought identified their Original Ground as Amida, Kannon, and Seishi. Shingū and Nachi came to be referred to as the "Two Manifestations Sites" (*ryōsho gongen*). Cf., *S&P* 1:9.

180. An old manor at the upper reaches of the Yōrō river, in what is now central Chiba prefecture.

181. Or possibly, according to Watanabe, a pilgrimage made to counteract the dangers of certain "unlucky years" (*yakudoshi*) according to Yin Yang beliefs. In general, these were the 25th and 42nd years for men, and the 19th and 33rd years for women.

182. A local adaptation of the famous Hantan (Kantan) theme, which had its origins China and India and a number of variations in Japanese literature, including the nō, *Kantan*, by Zeami (1363–1443), and *Kinkin sensei eiga no yume* (Professor Clink-Clink's Dream of Glory") by Koikawa Harumachi (1744–89).

183. K'uei Chi (632–82), founder of the Fa-hsiang (Hossō) sect of Buddhist idealism in China.

184. See Matsunaga, *Assimilation*, pp. 123–4. In Tantrism Kannon is an emanation of Amida.

185. Mts. Hakusan, Fuji, and Tateyama constitute the "three sacred mountains" of Japan. Hakusan, east of Fukui, enshrines, among others, Shirayama-hime no Mikoto, whose Original Ground is the Eleven-Faced Kannon of our story.

186. *Kammuryōjukyō* (T. 365), the *Amitāyur-dhyāna-sūtra*. This sutra, the *Muyrōjukyō* (see following note), and the *Amidakyō* are the three basic scriptures of Japanese Pure Land Buddhism.

187. *Sōkangyō*, i.e., the *Muryōjukyō* (T. 360).

188. Zendō (613–81), third of the five patriarchs of the Pure Land tradition. The quotation is from his hymn, the *Hanjusan* (T. 1981).

189. The Three Qualities of Mind (sincerity, faith, aspiration) as propounded in the Pure Land sutras are reflections of the single mind of Amida; possession of one presumes the existence of the other two. See Daigan and Alicia Matsunaga, *Foundation of Japanese Buddhism*, II, pp. 98ff.

190. *tade.* The significance of this disrespectful action is not clearly understood.

191. A recitation at which a sutra was parcelled out and chanted by a thousand monks. The recitation could also be performed by a single individual.

192. The *Sesshu fusha mandala* (Mandala Embracing All and Forsaking None), which was attacked both by Jōkei and Kōben early in the century. Because of the criticism it evoked, this early variety of Pure Land picture lost favor and no examples of the genre survive. Mujū paraphrases the second article of the *Kōfukuji sōjō* of 1205. See Morrell, "Jōkei and the Kōfukuji Petition," p. 22.

193. *shiku.* Strictly speaking, "existing, not existing, both, neither." The context suggests that Mujū is saying: "When we examine what is apparently true carefully and critically, we find . . ."

194. Fujiwara Michinori (d. 1160), prominent during the Hōgen and Heiji Disturbances (1156, 1159), was a noted scholar and grandfather of the Hossō monk, Jōkei. See Reischauer and Yamagiwa, eds. *Translations from Early Japanese Literature*, pp. 375-457.

195. *Kanayaki Hotoke*, also called the Hōyake Amida ("Cheek-Burned Amida"), the main object of worship at Kamakura's Kōsokuji, a Ji sect temple founded by Ippen (1239-1289), is variously attributed to the famous Kamakura sculptor Unkei 1151-1223), or possibly his brother, Kaikei (fl. ca. 1185-1220).

196. In the sixth month of 1221 Yamada Jirō Shigetada (founder of Chōboji) attempted to make a stand at the Kuize River which commanded "both the Tōsendō and Tōkaidō routes" with a force of 300 horsemen. Facing an army of Kamakura supporters ten times that size, his band was routed and Shigetada and his son Shigetsugu were slain. McCullough, "Shōkyūki," *MN* XIX 3-4, pp. 201-203.

197. An old temple now in Nagoya's Moriyama Ward, once on the territory of the Yamada manor, and not far from Chōboji.

198. Batō Kannon. A discussion of this curious variant on the Kannon image as it appears in China and Tibet, as well as Japan, may be found in Getty, *The Gods of Northern Buddhism*, pp. 94-95.

199. Chapter 25 (*Fumonbon*) of the *Lotus Sutra* (T. 262), but often treated as an independent sutra.

200. The locale of this story in both the *Companion for a Solitary Retreat* (Kankyō no tomo, 1222) and the *Miraculous Records of the Hasedera [Kannon]* (Hasedera reigenki; probably early Kamakura) is the Hasedera. *S&P* either borrowed the story or shared a common tradition with these two works. See Dykstra, "Tales of the Compassionate Kannon," pp. 121, 132-34 (2:27); Minobe, *Kankyō no tomo*, pp. 134-140 (2:5).

201. See Dykstra, "Jizō, the Most Merciful," pp. 179-182; Getty, *The Gods of Northern Buddhism*, pp. 104-106.

202. *Chifu no ketsu.* Recent research indicates that this is an alternate name for Eisai's *Bodaishin bekki*; see Yamada and Miki, *Zōtanshū*, p. 191, n. 30; cf., Watanabe, *Shasekishū*, p. 105, n. 30.

203. The standard size of Buddhist images was one *jō* six *shaku* (roughly, 10 feet plus 6 feet), although most sculptures were made smaller by using this figure as a multiple of its dimensions. Watanabe also speculates that the site of the building may have been the beach south of Midarebashi in the Zaimokuza ward, today a popular resort area.

204. Kenjō (d. 1295), distinguished for his restoration work on Tōji, the noted Shingon sanctuary in Kyoto. Late in life he traveled to the eastern provinces where he became spiritual adviser to Hōjō Tokimune. It was perhaps at this time that he became involved with moving the Jizō image from Zaimokuza beach to the Nikaidō area, the site of the Shingon Kakuonji, whose "Black Jizō," still extant, is thought to be the Jizō of Mujū's story. Kamahara, "Shasekishū to Kamakura," p. 127.

205. This and the following story appear in *Jizō bosatsu reigenki* (Miraculous Tales of the Bodhissattva Jizō), Book 10. The first three books of the Ryūkoku text may have been compiled in the mid-Heian period by Jitsuei, of Tendai's Miidera; the remaining eleven books (including the *S&P* stories) perhaps no earlier than 1576. See Dykstra, "Jizō the Most Merciful," pp. 179-200, for seven additional translations from the collection and an informative discussion of the Jizō cult in China and Japan, with references to *S&P*.

206. Kade-no-kōji is an east-west lane in northern Kyoto; Karasumaru (now Karasuma), a north-south street east of the original site of the Imperial Palace.

207. That is, the period (1278-1287) during which Mujū was writing *Sand and Pebbles* (1279-1283).

208. Jōkei (Gedatsubō, 1155-1213), who appears elsewhere in *S&P*, was perhaps the age's most prominent Maitreya devotee. See Brock, "Awaiting Maitreya at Kasagi," in *Maitreya the Future Buddha*; Morrell, "Jōkei and the Kōfukuji Petition," pp. 9-10.

209. The conspicuous Indophile of the period was Myōe (Kōben, 1173-1232), who is paired with Jōkei in *S&P* and elsewhere in the literature of the time. See Morrell, "Passage to India Denied" and "Kamakura Accounts of Myōe Shōin as Popular Religious Hero."

210. *bodaishin; bodhicitta.* The nature and importance of the Aspiration for Enlightenment were central issues between the establishment and the new Pure Land movement. Myōe attacked Hōnen for what he believed to be Hōnen's disregard of this precondition for all religious progress. See Bandō, "Myōe's Criticism of Hōnen's Doctrine," pp. 37-54. The issue was complicated because of ambiguities in the interpretation of the term. See Kiyota, *Tantric Concept of Bodhicitta*, pp. 6-7, *passim*; Suzuki, *Essays in Zen Buddhism, Third Series*, pp. 137-185 ['The Desire for Enlightenment (Bodhicittotpāda)'].

211. The connection is doubtless because Amida is also called the Tathāgata of Everlasting Life (Muryōju Nyorai).

212. The *Sukhāvativyūhopadesa* (Jōdoron, T. 1524). For a translation and commentary on this work and its influence on Chinese and Japanese Pure Land Buddhism, see Kiyota, ed. *Mahāyāna Buddhist Meditation*, pp. 249-296.

213. The concept is conspicuous in Kakukai's *Discourse*; see following note.

214. Kakukai (Nanshōbō, 1142-1223), thirty-seventh abbot (*kengō*) of Shingon's Kongōbuji headquarters on Mt. Kōya from 1217 to 1220, left behind a popular doctrinal tract, *Bridge-of-the-Law Kakukai's Discourse on the Dharma* (Kakukai Hōkyō hōgo), which reaffirms the traditional Shingon view that Buddhahood and the Pure Land of every Buddha is to be realized in our present existence. See Morrell, "Shingon's Kakukai on the Immanence of the Pure Land," pp. 206-220. On Mujū's probable connection with Kakukai through Sambōin esotericism, see Appendix C.

215. The incident is related in Book 48 of the *Marvels from the Sutras and the Vinaya* (Kyōritsu isō, T. 2121).

216. The "personal possessions" (*shiyū zaisan*) permitted the monk: an assembly robe, a shirt, an upper garment, and a begging bowl.

217. Chigon (602-668). Second patriarch of the Hua-yen (Kegon) school, succeeded by its leading philosopher, Fa-tsang (643-712).

218. Indian and Chinese thinkers of the idealist school. Takakusu, *The Essentials of Buddhist Philosophy*, pp. 83-4. The life of Hsüan-tsang is treated in Waley, *The Real Tripitaka and Other Pieces*, pp. 9-130, based on three Chinese sources. This anecdote concerning Jayasena is in Hui-li's *Ta Tz'u-en Ssu San-tsang Fa-shih Chuan* (Life of the Master of the Law, Tripitaka, of the Great Monastery of Mother Love), T. 2053, of which a complete translation is San Shih Buddhist Institute, ed., *The Life of Hsüan-tsang*, which refers to Jayasena as Prasenajit, pp. 148-9.

219. Harshavardhana of Kanauj. See Watters, *On Yuan Chwang's Travels in India* I, p. 343ff.

220. Two of Mujū's favorite metaphors, from the *Nirvana* and *Lotus* sutras, respectively, Cf., *S&P* 3:7.

221. Yasutoki (1183-1242), the third Hōjō regent (*shikken*), became the close friend of Kegon's Myōe (*S&P* 1:5, 3:8) after the monk was brought before him for harboring fugitive soldiers during the Jōkyū Disturbance of 1221. The account of their meeting, well-known in Mujū's day, is recorded in the *Biography of the Venerable Myōe of Toga-no-o* (Toga-no-o Myōe Shōnin denki); see Kaneko and Morrell, "Sanctuary: Kamakura's Tōkeiji Convent," pp. 206-209.

222. The widespread notion of the Decline of the Law (*mappō*) was demoralizing for those who hoped for a return to the strict observance of the precepts, but many continued to try: Jippan, Jōkei, Shunjō, Eizon, and those in the new Zen groups, including Mujū himself. At the other pole was the antimonianism of the Pure Land extremists. See Inoue, "Eizon, Ninshō and the Saidaiji Order." It is likely that this attempt by Jōkei to revive the

practice of the early precepts occurred around 1208 and is the subject of the *Gedatsu Shōnin kairitsu saikō gammon* (The Venerable Gedatsu's Written Vow for the Restoration of the Precepts), translated in Morrell, *Early Kamakura Buddhism: A Minority Report*, Chapter 1.

223. Mount Toga-no-o is the site of Kōzanji, a temple in the northern environs of Kyoto ceded to Myōe in 1206 by Retired Emperor Gotoba as a center for the restoration of the Kegon sect. The tea plantation created behind Kōzanji from seeds brought from China by Eisai in 1191 is claimed to be the oldest in Japan.

224. *arubekiyō*. This phrase was Myōe's trademark. The opening statement of the *Final Injunctions of the Venerable Myōe of Toga-no-o* (Toga-no-o Myōe Shōnin ikun), composed by his disciple Kōshin in 1235, is as follows: "People ought to hold fast to this seven-syllable phrase, 'that which is appropriate' (*arubeki yō wa*). There is that which is appropriate for the monk and that which is appropriate for the layman; that which is appropriate for the emperor and that which is appropriate for his subjects. Every evil arises because people turn their backs on what is appropriate for them." The phrase appears in several other works and a "hanging board" in Myōe's calligraphy is preserved at Kōzanji. Miyasaka, ed. *Kana hōgoshū*, p. 59. Morrell, "Kamakura Accounts of Myōe Shōnin as Popular Religious Hero," pp. 182-195, contains a complete translation of the *Ikun*; also Rasmus, "The Sayings of Myōe Shōnin of Togano-o."

225. According to one view expressed in the *Daichidoron*, a short kalpa is the time required to empty a hundred square mile (40 *li*²) city enclosure filled with poppy seeds if one seed were removed every three years.

226. *Lotus Sutra* 12; Hurvitz, *Scripture of the Lotus Blossom of the Fine Dharma*, pp. 199-201. This favorite literary-religious theme frequently appears in the poetry of the time, and in the concluding scene of Zeami's *Kasuga ryūjin*; see Morrell, "Passage to India Denied," pp. 198-199.

227. Wealthy layman in the famous sutra of the same name (*Yuimakitsukyō*, T. 474-5) whose "thundering silence" on being asked to discuss the doctrine of non-duality was highly extolled by the bodhisattva Mañjuśrī. See Suzuki, *Manual of Zen Buddhism*, frontispiece. The sutra also considers the concept of non-abiding (*mujū*), which our monk took as his religious name.

228. "This is what the old text means when it says, 'The ruler is the boat and the common people are the water. It is the water that bears the boat up, and the water that capsizes it.' Therefore if the gentleman desires safety, the best thing for him to do is to govern fairly and to love the people." Burton Watson, tr. *Hsün Tzu: Basic Writings*, p. 37.

229. Tendai's Saichō had vehemently defended the Mahāyānist One Vehicle (*ichijō*), by which *all* sentient beings would be brought to Buddhahood, against Hossō's Tokuichi, who supported the earlier (Hīnayāna) view of Three Vehicles (*sanjō*). Saichō's view generally prevailed.

230. This *Verse of Admonition Handed Down by the Seven Buddhas*

(Shichibutsu tsūkai ge) appears in various earlier sources, including two translations of the *Dharmapada*—the *Hokkukyō* (T. 210) and the *Shutsuyōkyō* (T. 212), Cf., *S&P* 5A:5 and Kakukai's *Discourse* (n. 214).

231. See *S&P* 4:4.

232. Kenshin (1131-1192). Tendai prelate who became a disciple of Hōnen, with whom he is seen in *S&P* 4:9. See also Coates and Ishizuka, *Hōnen, the Buddhist Saint*, pp. 274-88. Since the incident described could have occurred no later than the year of Kenshin's death, Mujū must have heard of it early in life and/or his informant would have witnessed it as a youth.

233. *betsuji nembutsu.* "We ought to arrange special times for the recitation of the *Nembutsu*, and stimulate both mind and body in its practice . . . Where several do it together, you should enter the room by turns, only keeping up the practice without cessation, and this as the circumstances of each severally permit . . . By thus arranging so as to suit everyone's convenience, these special services may always be held for seven days at a time." Hōnen's explanation as cited in Coates and Ishizuka, *Hōnen the Buddhist Saint*, pp. 406-7.

234. See Ramanan, *Nāgārjuna's Philosophy as Presented in the Mahā-Prajñāpāramitā-Śāstra*, pp. 375-376 (note 1).

235. The *Jōshinkaikambō* (T. 1893) of Tao-hsüan (Dōsen, 596-667), founder of the Disciplinary Sect in China, is cited at length in the *Tsuma kagami.* See Morrell, "Mirror for Women," pp. 67-68.

236. Cf., Takakusu, *The Essentials of Buddhist Philosophy*, p. 64.

237. ". . . 'on whatever sphere of being/The mind of a man may be intent/At the time of death'—that is the one action/(And the time of death is every moment)/Which shall fructify in the lives of others . . ." (Eliot's *Four Quartets*).

238. *Ninnōkyō*, T. 245. The *Benevolent Kings, Lotus,* and *Golden Light (Konkōmyōkyō*, T. 663-665) sutras are especially esteemed for their benefit to the country.

239. This and the subsequent questions are first stated in Chinese, parodying the formal debates of the Buddhist scholastics of his time, after which Mujū explains the meaning in Japanese. In the translation I have simply used a single formal statement of each question to cover both phrases, although a better solution might be to render the first into Latin.

240. *ryūgo.* An implement anciently used in theatrical performances and shaped like an hourglass.

241. *shittentei.* A kind of drum, the name derived from its sound, hence "tom-tom."

242. *nozuchi.* A semi-fictitious viper described in *S&P* 5A:3.

243. The *Fa-yüan chu-lin (Hōonjurin*, T. 2122; Forest of Pearls in the Garden of the Law) is the Chinese source for this tale which developed a number of Japanese folk variants. See, for example, Yanagita, *Japanese Folk Tales* (tr. F.H. Mayer), pp. 20-1: "Why the Jellyfish Has No Bones," which closely parallels a version collected in Ichinose, *Nihon mukashibanashi kō*, pp. 214-217. Other variants of the monkey liver story

(with and without the jellyfish) are discussed in Seki, *Nihon mukashibanashi shūsei*, pp. 229–34.

244. Poem by Ki no Tsurayuki (884–946), *Shūishū* (Collection of Gleanings) XX: 1322. It is preceded by the headnote: "I [Tsurayuki] had an unusual sensation while pondering the wretchedness of this world, so I sent the following poem to Lord Kintada's place (Minamoto Kintade, 889–948). Shortly thereafter I became seriously ill." Mujū's version of the poem varies slightly from the original; Yamagishi, ed. *Hachidaishūshō* I, p. 615. The poem is also followed by the note: "Tsurayuki's Personal Collection says that shortly after composing this poem he passed away."

245. The source of this anecdote is *Fukuro sōshi* (1159), Book 3, by the distinguished conservative poet, Fujiwara Kiyosuke (1104–1177).

246. *Shūishū* XX: 1327. A later reworking of the famous *waka* by Priest Mansei (c. 720), *Manyōshū* III: 351.

247. *Shokushūishū* (Collection of Gleanings Continued, ca. 1278) XIX: 1393. It is preceded by the topic: "On Seeing the Moon." *Kōchū kokka taikei* 5, p. 856.

248. Variant on *Shokugosenshū* (Later Collection Continued, 1251) XVII: 1117. The headnote says: "The late Tokudaiji Minister of the Left went to Ōhara with Priest Saigyō and others. At the Raigōin this verse was composed on Personal Grievance as perceived by an old man. It is by the Venerable Ennin."

249. *kokoronaki/ mi ni mo aware ni*. Mujū incorporates the first two lines of Saigyō's famous *waka* (SKKS IV: 362):

Kokoro naki	A sense of wonder
Mi ni mo aware wa	Touches even one whose heart
Shirarekeri	Has renounced the world:
Shigi tatsu sawa no	From a marsh in autumn twilight
Aki no yūgure	Sandpipers take to the sky.

250. *sōji*. The "completely sustaining" mystic syllables which support the religious life of the reciter. This is a translation of *dhāraṇī*, of which the Japanese *darani* is simply a transliteration; both terms are equivalent to *shingon*, "true words." Short mystic verses, simplifications of *dhāraṇī*, are called *mantra*.

251. The thirty-one syllable *waka*, the basic verse form in the Japanese poetic tradition, is said to have first been composed when the Wind God built a palace at Suga on the occasion of his marriage to Kushinada Hime, as recorded in the early histories. Mujū cites the second line:

Yakumo tatsu	A many-layered fence
Izumo yaegaki	At Izumo, where clouds billow—
Tsumagome ni	A fence I build
Yaegaki tsukuru	To live therein with my wife.
Sono yaegaki (w)e	Ah, that many layered fence!

Sakamoto, et al., *Nihon shoki* I, p. 123. Cf. Aston, *Nihongi* I, pp. 53–54; Philippi, tr. *Kojiki*, p. 91.

252. From a verse in Kūkai's *The Meanings of Sound, Word, and Reality (Shōji jissō gi)*; Hakeda, *Kūkai: Major Works*, p. 240. Mujū omits the second and fourth lines.

253. goin. The "five tones" in any of several pentatonic modes employed in the ancient musical systems of China and Japan.

254. *A-ji.* The Sanskrit letter "A", seen in esoteric Buddhism as the foundation of all vowels and consonants, and, by extension, as the origin of all elements of the world. Kiyota, *Shingon Buddhism*, pp. 71–74, "A-ji Meditation."

255. The *Mahāvairocana Sūtra (Dainichikyō*, T. 848), one of the basic esoteric scriptures and the focus of I-hsing's commentary. See Kiyota, *Shingon Buddhism*, pp. 19–20.

256. *ō*. Response. Both *ō* and *kan* refer to the response of the gods and buddhas to human needs, and they frequently appear as the compound, *kannō*. *Ō* is also the first component of *ōjin (nirmāṇakāya)*, The Buddha's Transformation Body.

257. *Shinkokinshū* XX: 1917, the first of the "Poems on Śākyamuni's Teachings" *(shakkyōka)* in the collection; cf., Brower and Miner, *Fujiwara Teika's Superior Poems of Our Time*, p. 124. Mujū begins the verse with *tada* rather than *nao*, but the meaning is not significantly changed.

258. Mujū here echoes the opening statement of his Preface.

259. The circumstances of Michizane's exile, with a translation of his poem, may be found in Morris's *Nobility of Failure*, p. 56.

260. Possibly Tō no Taneyuki (1194–1273), who contributed some twenty-two *waka* to the *Shokugosenshū* (Later Collection Continued, 1251) and later Imperial Anthologies of poetry.

261. *warinashi.* Mujū uses this as a term of approval five times in this short chapter seeming to imply that a verse is appropriate or suitable to an occasion; hence, apposite. What makes Lady Wakasa's platitude interesting, for example, is that it usually appears when one is discussing a short life. Taneyuki was seventy-nine.

262. Or perhaps (since one bad pun deserves another): "In all ewer world." *Nabe* (pot, ewer; cf., kettle) associates with *nabete* (all).

263. The place name, Toki, associates with the verb *toku* ("to untie a knot, to loosen"): "I came here to Toki thinking that should I be depressed *(musuboru*, "all tied up"), then I should be relieved *(toku*, "loosen up"); but since these are all real and not artificial flowers *(musubi-hana)* there is no knotting *(musubi-me)*, no depression." Yoshiyuki's answer takes up the knotty imagery: the wind blows the blossoms into nodes, clusters, knots *(fukimusubu)*. Watanabe also sees a contrast between *ito* (lit., "thread") *-zakura* and *musubi-me*, "knot," etc.

264. Tonamiyama. Battle site during the Gempei war where Kiso no Yoshinaka defeated Taira no Koremori. Kitagawa and Tsuchida, tr., *The Tale of the Heike*, II. p. 402ff. (Book 7:4). As in Motomasa's quiver-

blossom verse, the interest lies in the tension between the rough warrior images and the softness of the natural images.

265. *areku*; in later works, *kōku*. Stanzas using words considered inappropriate for serious *renga* according to the standards borrowed from the imperial anthologies of *waka*.

266. *hana no moto*, "under the blossoms." A term originally applied to the non-aristocratic practitioners of linked verse, in later centuries becoming a designation of the highest accomplishment.

267. The poem is ambiguous. Perhaps, in his intensity, the painter as well as the old doll becomes a child again.

268. Our natural propensity is to read *fune* as "boat": cf., Bashō's "Sailors whose lives float away as they labor on boats" (Miner, *Japanese Poetic Diaries*, p. 157). The response is a pleasant surprise by taking *fune* as "vat, basin": "The new leaves flow into the basin where they will stagnate and grow old." A similar switch is to be found in Takasuke's subsequent "belly" poem.

269. Work-play similar to that in 5A:8, "The Discussion of the Ant and Tick Scholars."

270. Bishamon, another name for Tamonten among the Four Heavenly Kings, is popularly known as the God of Wealth and is included among the Seven Gods of Good Fortune.

271. ca. 1252. Son of the famous poet Fujiwara no Ietaka (1158-1237), Takasuke, whose dates are uncertain, has his own private poetic collection, *Fujiwara Takasuke Ason shū*, numbered in *Zoku kokka taikan*.

272. *ushin*, serious or standard, linked verse followed the rules of decorum inherited from the courtly *waka* tradition; *mushin*, "comic" or non-standard, linked verse was merely freer in form and not necessarily amusing. See Miner, *Japanese Linked Poetry*, pp. 16-18; also, Keene, "The Comic Tradition in Renga," p. 249, which mentions the poems in this chapter.

273. The poem does not appear in Takasuke's collection.

274. The official title appears to refer to Minamoto Sanetomo (1192-1219), but Professor Watanabe notes that the poem is not in fact by him.

275. Ueda Akinari (1734-1809) elaborates Saigyō's visit to Sutoku's tomb in the "Shiramine" story of his *Ugetsu monogatari*. Both poems are included, for translations of which see Zolbrod, tr. *Ugetsu Monogatari: Tales of Moonlight and Rain*, pp. 105, 107.

276. Kūkai (774-835). Mujū translates the phrase as "*Kokoro wo motte kokoro wo tsutau. . . ,*" better known in its Chinese reading, *isshin denshin*, and generally associated with the Zen teaching. Professor Watanabe locates the Chinese phrase in the *Seireishū* (or *Shōryōshū*, The Collected Works of Prose and Poetry of Kūkai). We are reminded of another "Zen" metaphor, the "finger pointing at the moon," also used by Kūkai; see note 104.

277. *Nihon ryōiki* 3:19 has a similar theme; see Nakamura, *Miraculous Stories from the Japanese Buddhist Tradition*, p. 246ff., "On a Girl Born of a Flesh Ball Who Practiced Good and Enlightened People."

278. *Daibutchō darani.* A spell from one of two works known as the *Śūrangama Sūtra*, the *Daibutchō-shuryōgonkyō* (T. 945), translated by Pāramiti in 705.

279. This was the original construction of Tōdaiji in 749. The Hossō priest Gyōgi (668-749), one of the leaders of Nara Buddhism, is even today something of a folk hero.

280. *wasan.* A "Japanese hymn" in the *imayō* style of alternating phrases of seven and five syllables.

281. *Shokugosenshū* X:575, in a slightly variant form, is the first of that collection's Poems on Śākyamuni's Teachings (*shakkyōka*). The head-note states that it was a poem of final admonition as Gyōgi was dying at the foot of Mount Ikoma in Tempyō 21 (749).

282. A variant of this poem is also to be found in *Casual Digressions* IV; see Yamada and Miki, *Zōtanshū*, p. 149.

283. Mujū frequently refers to events as happening in the Bandō, literally "East of the Slope": also known as the Eastern Provinces. The "slope" comprised the boundary between Suruga and Sagami provinces, i.e., the Hakone range. The eight Bandō provinces consisted of Sagami (Kanagawa prefecture), Musashi (Saitama; Tokyo), Kazusa (part of Chiba Pref.), Shimōsa (part of Chiba), Hitachi (Ibaraki), Kōzuke (Gumma), Shimotsuke (Tochigi), and Mutsu (Aomori). With the addition of Awa (part of Chiba Prefecture) and Dewa (Yamagata; Akita) this brought the total to the "Ten Bandō Provinces." Bandō is thus a wider designation than the current Kantō, which excludes the northern provinces.

284. *zenni.* A nun who assumed the robe but continued to live in a secular household.

285. *kaji.* One of the three aspects of "attaining Buddhahood in this very existence" (*sokushin jōbutsu*).

286. *Tao Te Ching* 49. Waley, *The Way and Its Power*, p. 202.

287. Chapter XIV; Hurvitz, *Lotus Blossom*, p. 216: "By being in perfect accord with Dharma, to all living beings he is to preach Dharma consistently, neither exceeding it nor falling short of it. Even to a person who deeply loves Dharma he is not to preach overmuch."

288. Lake Biwa is just to the east, of course, of the great Tendai temple complex on Mt. Hiei. Mujū is here taken by the preacher's accommodating remarks, but elsewhere (e.g., *S&P* 1:8) he has a more difficult time rationalizing the killing of fish.

289. The Rokkakudō of Chōbōji in Kyoto, said to have been founded by Prince Shōtoku in 587, and with associations to Shinran (1173-1262) and later the Ikenobo school of flower arranging. Centrally located in the Kyoto of Mujū's day, its structures were frequently destroyed by fire.

290. Also Seikaku or Shōkaku (1167–1235), son of Chōgen (Chōken, ca. 1125–1205), founder of the school of popular preachers associated with the Agui Temple in Kyoto. Shōgaku became one of Hōnen's leading disciples; see Coates and Ishizuka, *Hōnen the Buddhist Saint*, p. 326–339. Also Mills', "The Taketori Legend," p. 44.

291. Shōgaku is quoting a ten-character phrase from the second chapter of the *Lotus Sutra*. Sakamoto and Iwamoto, *Hokkekyō* I, p. 116; Hurvitz, *Scripture of the Lotus Blossom*, p. 40.

292. *Tachibana no Uji*. The flowers of the mandarin orange (*tachibana*) are noted for their fragrance.

293. Cited in Part I, "No Fixed Abode."

294. The famous account of Hsüan-tsang's pilgrimage to India is his *Record of a Journey from the Great T'ang to the* Western Regions (Ta T'ang Hsi Yü Chi; Daitō saiiki ki, T. 2087), the inspiration of the popular fantasy, *Journey to the West* (Hsi Yu Chi); Waley's *Monkey*) by Wu Ch'eng-en (ca. 1506–1582).Hsüan-tsang's example was a powerful influence in Myōe's attempts to visit India (see *S&P* 1:5 and note 163).

295. The source of this anecdote is the *Shih-shuo Hsin-yü (Sesetsu shingo*, New Specimens of Contemporary Talk) of Liu I-ch'ing (403–444).

296. Lines from the *Verse of Admonition Handed Down by the Seven Buddhas*. See *S&P* 4:1 and note 230.

297. *Ōjōraisange*, T. 1980. In his *Kōfukuji sōjō* (Article 3) of 1205 Jōkei also appeals to this work as evidence of Shan-tao's recognition of other practices. See Morrell, "Jōkei and the Kōfukuji Petition," p. 23.

298. *Oki no gosho*; that is, the residence of Gotoba (1180–1239) on the island of Oki, to which he was exiled in 1221 after his abortive attempt to recapture political power from the Hōjōs during the Jōkyū Disturbance.

299. Anecdote traced to the *Requital for Kindness Sūtra* (Hōonkyō, T. 156).

300. *Daichidoron* III.

301. Kūkai (774–835), in his *Precious Key to the Secret Treasury (Hizō hōyaku*, T. 2426); see Hakeda, *Kūkai: Major Works*, p. 186.

302. *seijō*, i.e. *kishōmon*. Written documents, occasionally binding legally, but deriving their force mainly by calling the gods and buddhas to witness. The courtesan is presumably pledging to remain faithful to the man if he takes his wife back. For discussions of this and other Kamakura legalities, see Ackroyd, "Women in Feudal Japan," pp. 36–37; Mass, *The Development of Kamakura Rule, 1180–1250*, p. 137ff.

303. Maxim based on a statement in the *Mirror of Sectarian Differences*, Ch. 34.

304. *Kaki*, "fence, hedge, railing"; cf., *Yamato monogatari* 158: kabe, "a wall."

305. Variations on the poem and the story appear in *Yamato monogatari* 158 and *Konjaku monogatari* 30:12, the poem alone in

Shinkokinshū XV:1372. Cf., Tahara, tr. *Tales of Yamoto: a Tenth-Century Poem-Tale*, pp. 158-59. *Shika* pivots the meanings "thus" and "deer."

306. *Temmon hakase.* An official in the bureau of Astrology and Divination, established by the Taihō Code (702) and traditionally held by members of the Abe family.

307. This final anecdote about the Pure Land preacher follows the Ajari of Asahi in the *Yonezawabon* (but not in our *bonshunbon*), and has been included to augment the sequence. See Watanabe, *Kōhon shasekishū*, p. 277; Watanabe, *Shasekishū*, p. 493 (appendix).

308. This story appears later in the Tokugawa cycle of stories about Ikkyū. See note 114 and associated text.

309. In abbreviated texts this and the following anecdote (*rufubon* 7B:6) follow the story of the lady with the straw mat, but both are missing from the *bonshunbon*, the basis of Watanabe's *Shasekishū*. The original appears in Fujii, *Kōchū shasekishū*, pp. 289-90; Tsukudo, *Shasekishū* II, 37-38; Watanabe, *Shasekishū*, pp. 493-94 (addendum of textual variants). In Bonshun's manuscript the Jizō of Yada story follows the lady with the straw mat.

310. Fashioned by the monk Mammai and enshrined in 796 at Yadadera (Yatadera, or Kongōsenji) in the present city of Yamatokoriyama in Nara prefecture. The Fukuchiin, Jūrin'in and Chisokuin are all temples in the Nara area.

311. [*Butchō*] *sonshō darani*, the Spell of the Holy and Virtuous [Head Bump], a personification of one of the 32 marks of Śākyamuni (as Butchōson) represented in the Matrix maṇḍala. The scriptural source is the *Buddha Head Sutra* (Butchō sonshō daranikyō, and associated writings, T. 967-974).

312. [*Bussetsu*] *mokkuremmon kairitsuchū gohyaku kyōjūji* [*kyō*], the [Sutra Taught by the Buddha Concerning] Maudgalyāyana's Questions on the Five Hundred Light and Serious Items of the Regulations, T. 1483. The questions discussed the observance of the regulations in the latter periods of the Law.

313. The four-line verse from the *Nirvana Sutra* whose teaching is said to be paraphrased in the famous *i-ro-ha uta* by which the *kana* syllabary was organized before the adoption of the Fifty-syllable Table (*go-jū onzu*). The first phrase is also conspicuous in the opening lines of the *Heike monogatari*.

Shogyō mujō	All conditioned things are impermanent;
Zeshō metsubō	It is their nature to be born and die.

Shōmetsu metsui	When birth-and-death itself disappears,
Jakumetsu iraku	Nirvana is our lasting bliss.

314. *Hōkyōin darani.* A mystic formula described in the sutra of the same name, T. 1022b. In Shingon and Tendai monasteries it is chanted daily. Mujū is said to have inserted a hand-written copy of this spell into the statue which he made of himself before he died. See Part I, "Chōbuji, 1262-1312."

315. *Senju darani.* A mystic formula in eighty-two lines addressed to the Thousand-Armed Kannon. It is described in the *Senjukyō*, T. 1060.

316. *Jikuju*, the second of three major spells addressed to Fudō Myō-ō, the *Kakaiju* (Fireworld), *Jikuju*, and *Shinshu* (Heart) being known respectively as the great, middle and lesser spells.

317. The source of this anecdote is the *Huai Nan Tzu (Enanji)*, a compilation of various schools of thought made at the court of Liu An, Prince of Huai-nan (d. 122 B.C.). Mujū has more to say about Pei Sou in the *Tsuma kagami* (see Morrell, "Mirror for Women," pp. 65-66), and was intrigued by the paradox that fortune and misfortune are inseparable aspects of the same phenomenon. See the selections from *Casual Digressions* 1:1 and 3:5 translated above in Part I, "No Fixed Abode: 1226-1261".

318. Anecdote traced to the *Various Items from the Sutras and Regulations* (Kyōritsu isō, T. 2121), a sixth century collection of Buddhist items from the southern Buddhist (Hīnayāna) canon.

319. As we have seen in Part I, Mujū may have visited the Shōryakuji for instruction in 1254 and 1261 (*CD* 3:5). See also note 38.

320. Guatama's younger half-brother, Sundarananda; not to be confused with the Buddha's cousin, Ānanda (Anan).

321. Watanabe is uncertain about the meaning of Chiumbō's reply: "*Ara bō* ['stick'] *ka to omoite.*" Perhaps it is a pun on *doro-bō*, "robber."

322. *Amida no daiju*, or *Muryōju nyorai kompon darani* (The Basic Spell of the Tathāgata Everlasting Life), is described in the *Amida Ritual Manual* (Muyrōju giki, T. 930).

323. This anecdote is thought to be the inspiration for the *kyōgen* farce "Busu", in which the monk and his apprentice are replaced by a master and two servants, Tarōkaja and Jirōkaja. See Keene, *Anthology of Japanese Literature*, pp. 305-11; McKinnon, *Selected Plays of Kyōgen*, pp. 51-62. A variant is also to be found in *Ikkyū kantō banashi* (1672); see Kokusho Kankōkai, ed. *Kinsei bungei sōsho* VI, pp. 144-5.

324. *ame.* A viscous confection prepared from malted rice and wheat. In *Busu* this becomes *kurozato*, "black (unrefined) sugar".

325. In the abbreviated versions of *Sand and Pebbles* this anecdote follows the Jizō of Yada, translated above. Its theme may have suggested the famous *rakugo* story, Jugemu (Mr. Eternal Life), which tells of a man who sought advice at the neighborhood temple for an auspicious name for his son, arriving at a lengthy composite of allusions to longevity.

326. This story is sometimes mentioned as the prototype of the wiseacre with an answer for everything, a familiar character in *rakugo* and other popular genres.

327. Japanese rendering of four phrases of a regulated verse (*lü shih*), the second of "Ten Poems in the Old Style." See Yang Chia-lo, ed. *Pai hsiang-shan shih chi*, vol. 3, p. 165; Takagi Masakuzu, ed. *Haku Kyoi* II. p. 149. *Tsuma kagami* repeats a variation of this poem. See Miyasaka Yūshō, ed. *Kana hōgoshū*, p. 173; Morrell, "Mirror for Women," p. 64.

328. The source of this comparison may be the *Sūtra of Meditation on the True Law* (Shōbōnenjokyō, T. 721).

329. Source undetermined.

330. As noted in Part I, Japanese Buddhists of Mujū's day generally calculated the death of Gautama to a date corresponding to the Western 949 B.C.; and evidently Aśoka's period was viewed as similarly remote. A southern (Singhalese) tradition places the date at 544 B.C.; but some recent Japanese scholars opt for 383 B.C. (Nakamura Hajime) and 386 (Ui Hakuju)—which would still place Aśoka's reign within about a century of the Buddha's death. See Yamazaki and Kasahara, eds. *Bukkyōshi nempyō*, p. 1.

331. Anecdote recorded in the *Sūtra of King Aśoka* (Aikuōkyō, T. 2043), Chapter 3.

332. The poem reminds us that Prince Takaoka, son of Emperor Heizei and grandson of Kammu, anticipated Myōe in his desire to travel to India. His *Zuda shinnō nittō ryakki* (A Brief Journal of the Trip to China by the Imperial Prince Trainee in Buddhism) is translated in Shimizu, "Takaoka, Priest Imperial Prince Shinnyo," pp. 1–35.

333. In 1052, the initial year of the Latter Days of the Law, Fujiwara Yorimichi (992-1074), son of the powerful Michinaga (966-1027), converted his villa at Uji into a Buddhist temple, Byōdōin, with a Pure land emphasis within Tendai. The main temple structure, popularly called the Phoenix Hall, still enshrines a magnificent statue of the Buddha Amida. The hall was consecrated in 1053.

334. The temple had survived a little more than two centuries when Mujū wrote; but the original Amida Hall still stands today, an additional seven centuries later! Mosher, *Kyoto: A Contemplative Guide*, pp. 62–70 provides an imaginative visit to the Phoenix Hall, with several illustrations.

335. Possibly in 1246, 1256, 1258, and 1268, according to Watanabe. However, Kenninji was especially vulnerable to fire, being situated within

developed areas on all sides, just south of the Gion district in Kyoto. Only a gate from the original complex has survived several fires.

336. This and the next two anecdotes appear in the *Various Items from the Sutras and the Regulations* (Kyōritsu isō, T. 2121).

337. Jimyō. Posthumous title for Shih-shuang Ch'u-yüan (Sekisō-Soen, 986-1040), in the seventh generation after Lin-chi (Rinzai). Dumoulin, *Development*, pp. 37-38 and Table III.

338. *Zōbōhotsugikyō*, T. 2870. Believed to be a pre-Sui forgery, the sutra was especially favored by the Tendai sect. It advocates the cultivation of compassion and almsgiving during the millennium beginning a thousand years after Śākyamuni's death.

339. Founder of the Momooji (later the Chōboji) in 1179. See Appendix D: Yamada Family Geneology.

340. Chōgen. Kegon monk and follower of Hōnen; see note 37. A splendid wooden statue of Chōgen, believed to have been carved shortly after his death in 1206 is preserved at the Tōdaiji. See Nishikawa, *Kamakura chōkoku*, color plate 4; Mōri, *Shōzō chōkoku*, color plate 10 (detail).

341. Areas now incorporated into Hiroshima and Yamaguchi prefectures in Western Honshū along the western edges of the Inland Sea. The hauling of timber from such great distances reflects the difficulty and expense of the reconstruction. *Nihon no bunka chiri 14: Hiroshima, Yamaguchi, Shimane*, p. 114.

342. After Eisai's death in 1215, Gyōyū succeeded him as abbot of the Jufukuji, where Mujū is said to have served as a page from his thirteenth year (1238; *Traces*). If Mujū was too young at the time to have known the venerable monk well, he would certainly have had the opportunity to meet those who did.

343. Anecdote appearing in the *Extraordinary Operations of Cause and Effect* (Mizuoinnengyō, T. 754).

344. The Higashiyama (Kyoto) villa of Fujiwara Kanezane (1147-1207), statesman, brother of Tendai's Jien, and disciple of Hōnen.

345. This brief section is translated in its entirety because it is one of the few references to Mujū's Zen mentor, Enni Ben'en.

346. As guaranteed in Chapter 25 of the *Lotus Sutra*.

347. Tradition sees this as the founding of the Pure Land movement in China in 402, with Hui-yüan as the first Chinese patriarch. But there are anomalies. See Ch'en, *Buddhism in China*, pp. 106-108.

348. *bodaishin wo okosu*. A Japanese rendering of *hotsu bodaishin*. See note 210.

349. Sincerity, faith, and aspiration. Cf., *S&P* 1:10. Mujū also discusses these central Pure Land concepts in his *Tsuma kagami*. See Morrell, "Mirror for Women," pp. 70-71.

350. In his [*Kangyō*] *Sanzengi* (Many Good Principles [Expressed in the Meditation Sutra], T. 1753); cf., *S&P* 1:10.

351. According to the *Sutra of Meditation on Amida Buddha*.

352. According to the *Hsün Tzu*, a didactic work in thirty-two chapters, a large part probably by the Confucian, Hsün Ch'ing (ca. 298-ca. 238); Watson, tr. *Hsün Tzu: Basic Writings*, p. 24. Mujū also cites this work in *S&P* 1:5 and 4:1.

353. Hossō's Jōkei had a reputation for being a skillful preacher and came to the attention of the influential Fujiwara Kanezane (1149-1207) around the time the restored Kōfukuji was dedicated in 1193. See Morrell, "Jōkei and the Kōfukuji Petition," p. 9. Myōe's friend Jōkei is also mentioned in *S&P* 1:2 and 1:5.

354. Shinzei, a prominent figure in the Heiji Disturbance of 1159, had twelve sons who were sent into exile. See Reischauer and Yamagiwa, *Translations from Early Japanese Literature*, pp. 428-429. Subsequently, several of these sons and their descendants became prominent clerics. Jōkei (n. 353, above), for example, was Shinzei's grandson.

355. The famous *otogizōshi*, *Sannin hōshi*, is a more elaborate version of this story. See Keene, *Anthology of Japanese Literature*, pp. 322-331.

356. Area in the western part of Kamigyō-ku ward in Kyoto. It is said to have been the site of the Great Palace Enclosure (*Daidairi*) of Heian times, and in Mujū's day was a wasteland. The present site of the Imperial Palace was established in the Tokugawa era, well to the east of its earlier location.

357. Several abbreviated texts of the *Shasekishū* give the empress's name as Jōtōmon'in but there is a discrepancy between her dates and Shōshin's.

358. Mujū's version of this story is considered to be the inspiration for the opening chapter of Kobayashi Issa's *Oraga haru* (1819). Teruoka and Kawashima, eds. *Busonshū Issashū*, pp. 433-434; Yuasa, tr. *The Year of My Life*, pp. 37-38.

359. According to several abbreviated texts.

360. The [*Daibutchō*] *Shuryōgonkyō*, T. 945. See note 278. This sutra is to be distinguished from another *Sūrangama*, [*Shu*] *ryōgon zammaikyō* (T. 642), translated by Kumārajīva.

361. Watanabe notes that although Kanezane appears to be the person indicated by this title, there is a chronological discrepancy. The incident would have to have occurred after Myōe's death in 1232, a quarter of a century after Kanezane's.

362. *Chuang Tzu* 17 refers to the big hole in the bottom of the sea, but does not make the comparison. See Watson, *The Complete Works of Chuang Tzu*, p. 176.

363. As related in the *Sutra of [the Buddha Explaining] Cause and Effect to Samgharakkhita* ([Bussetsu] Innen sōgokyō, T. 749).

364. From Chapter 2, "Expedient Devices." Sakamoto and Iwamoto, eds. *Hokkekyō, jō*, p. 88; translation from Hurvitz, *Scripture of the Lotus Blossom of the Fine Dharma*, p. 29.

365. Watanabe (NKBT *Shasekishū*, p. 444, note 1) cites the *Awakening of Faith (Kishinron*, T. 1666) for a parallel notion expressed somewhat differently: ". . . therefore all things from the beginning transcend all forms of verbalization, description, and conceptualization and are, in the final analysis, undifferentiated, free from alteration, and indestructable. They are only of the One Mind; hence the name Suchness." Hakeda, *The Awakening of Faith*, p. 33.

366. Ennyadatta, i.e., Yajñadattā, sometimes referred to as a man (Yajñadatta), although the anecdote is similar. See, for example, Suzuki Daisetz's summary of the *Śūrangama Sūtra* (see note 360): "Yajñadatta, a citizen of Srāvasti, one morning looked into the mirror and found there a face with the most charming features. He thought his own head had disappeared and thereby went crazy." *Manual of Zen Buddhism*, p. 78. Mujū also refers to this story about Yajñadattā in *Tsuma kagami*; see Morrell, "Mirror for Women," p. 68.

367. The *Sutra of Collected Dharanis* (Darani jikkyō, T. 901) includes a fragment from an otherwise obscure, or lost, *Sutra of Great Recollection on Amida Buddha* (Amidabutsu daishiyuikyō), in which the original of Mujū's paraphrase appears. See *Taishō shinshū daizōkyō*, vol. 18, p. 800.

368. Concerning Lan-ch'i and the Kenchōji, see Collcutt, *Five Mountains: The Rinzai Zen Monastic Institution in Medieval Japan*, pp. 65-68, passim.

369. On the relationship between Wu-an Hōjō Tokiyori and the Kenchōji, see Collcutt, op. cit., pp. 68-70.

370. Wu-chun Shih-fan (Mujun Shiban, 1177-1249), also Enni Ben'en's mentor. See Appendix B: Mujū's Doctrinal Affiliations.

371. As related in the *Dharmapada (Hokkuhiyukyō*, T. 211).

372. The *Commentary on the Great Wisdom Sutra*, Book 14, is indicated as the source of this comment.

373. *Chin Pei Lun (Konbeiron*; here *Kinhiron*. T. 1932). Work in question-and-answer form explaining how non-sentient beings will ultimately attain Buddhahood. Its author was Ching-ch'i Chan-jan (Keikei Tannen, 711-782), ninth patriarch of Chinese T'ien T'ai. Selected translation and commentary in Fung Yu-lan, *A History of Chinese Philosophy* II, pp. 384-6.

374. Yanagita, *Mukashibanashi to bungaku*, pp. 104-106, cites this tale as an early recounting of the "Monkey-Jizō" theme prevalent in Owari province as well as in the Eastern Provinces.

375. Variant on the *Warashibe chōja* ("Wealth from a Stalk of Straw") folk theme which is finely elaborated in *Ujishūi monogatari* 7:5, a work composed ca. 1190-1242. Mills, *A Collection of Tales from Uji*, pp.

276-281; Yanagita, *Mukashibanashi to bungaku*, p. 135. Mujū's rendering of these stories of folk origin (cf., *CD* 2:3, 2:4) is very terse. See also Dykstra, "Tales of the Compassionate Kannon," p. 114.

376. The "beggar monk" theme is discussed in Kintō, "Minken bungei to setsuwasha: Zōtanshū ni tsuite no ikkōsai," pp. 136-153 (*Ōwaku hōshi no keifu*).

377. *shintō*. A rare practice of self-immolation in which the body was transformed into a burning lamp as an offering to the Buddha, based on the story of the Bodhisattva Medicine King (Yakuō bosatsu) related in the *Lotus Sutra*, Ch. 23; see Hurvitz, *Scripture of the Lotus Blossom*, pp. 294-95. In Mujū's incident it appears to have been a stylized ritual in which the performer was expected to escape, except by the most naive in the audience.

378. *Ōshū Kigasaki Ryōjusen Chōbozenji kaisan Mujū Kokushi ryakuengi*. A photocopy of this printed edition, dated Hōei 4 (1707) but without other publishing information, may be obtained through the National Diet Library, Tokyo. Since its cursive script can be deciphered only by calligraphy specialists, we are fortunate in having available a rendering into clear modern script based on a copy held at Chōboji, from which stencil copies may be obtained. The modern version was made in 1968 by Mr. Okada Hiroshi, 8-7 Yadamachi, Higashi-ku, Nagoya.

379. Under its present abbot, Kawabe Ryōsuke, the temple prospers. Address: Kigasaki Chōboji, 2-chōme, Yadamachi, Higashi-ku, Nagoya 461. During the closing decades of the last century, Minomushi Sanjin (Toki Gengo, 1836-1900), a skillful but still little-known painter in the "literary" (*bunjinga*) tradition, frequented the Chōboji, where he died and is buried. His *Minomushi Sanjin enikki* (Pictorial Diary of the Bagworm Hermit): *Tōkaihen* (see Yokoi and Yamamoto, eds.) includes some thirteen delighful sketches of Chōboji and environs.

380. *Mujū Kokushi dōshakukō*. A photocopy of this printed edition, dated Meiwa 7 (1770) and published by Zeniya Shichihei, et al, may also be obtained through the National Diet Library (cf. note 378) since it does not appear in any modern collection.

381. Discussion and charts of several proposed syllabaries (*hifumi, anaichi, ahiru*, etc.) may be found under the entries, "*shindai moji*" and "*iroha momben*" in Fujimura, *Zōho kaitei nihon bungaku daijiten* (Hall #331), vols. 4 and 1.

382. *Nembutsu jinriki den*, 2 vols. The excerpt is from *rufubon* 9A:4; cf., *bonshunbon* 10A:6. A catalogue of Tainin's works may be found in Kawaguchi Kōfū, "Tainin risshi no chosaku no seiri," *Indogaku Bukkyōgaku Kenkyū* XXVII:1, pp. 368-371.

383. It is appropriate in this glossary to focus on the *Japanese* reading of the term since this is what Mujū himself used. These terms are integral to a specific cultural interpretation of Buddhism, the Sanskrit and English

"equivalents" being at best only approximations since they too are parts of their own unique universes of discourse. For the most part it is helpful to our understanding to stress the parallel features of Buddhist developments in various societies, but the differences can also be revealing. On the cultural adaptations of Buddhism, see Nakamura, *Ways of Thinking of Eastern Peoples: India-China-Tibet-Japan* (1964), which argues the differences in thought patterns by considering the ways in which Buddhism was shaped as it adapted to the peculiarities of these four societies.

Glossary of Selected Terms

This list of definitions provides a ready reference to some of the major themes in Mujū's world of ideas. The words are defined under their Japanese readings, with cross-references from their Sanskrit and English counterparts.[383] Specialized terms can be found in the body of the work and in the notes by checking the Index.

accommodation. See *hōben.*

aspiration for enlightenment. See under *bodaishin* entry.

birth-and-death. See under *rokudō* (Six Paths) entry.

bodaishin. The Mind of Enlightenment; *bodhicitta.* (1) The initial aspiration toward enlightenment (*hotsubodaishin*), propounded in the Garland Sutra and other scriptures, had been assumed to be a requirement for spiritual progress until challenged by the sole-practice (*senju*) *nembutsu* movements of Hōnen and Shinran as tainted by "self-power" (*jiriki*). This became a central issue between the new Pure Land movements and the established sects, especially with Kegon's Myōe. (2) Shingon emphasizes that such aspiration is possible because the Mind of Enlightenment, the Buddha-nature, is inherent in all sentient beings. See notes 149, 210.

bodhicitta. See *bodaishin.*

bodhisattva. See *bosatsu.*

bosatsu. "Enlightened-being"; *bodhisattva.* One who has earned the reward of Buddhahood but who selflessly postpones it in order to work for the salvation of others; the Mahāyānist (*daijō,* q.v.) ideal embodying wisdom and compassion. See *honji-suijaku;* also Conze 1951, 125–130.

causality, moral. See *gō.*

chie (wisdom, *prajña*). See under *daijō* and *bosatsu* entries.

chūdō (Middle Way). See under *kū* entry.

daijō. The "Great Vehicle"; Mahāyāna. In contrast to the earlier Southern Buddhism of Gautama's India, Sri Lanka, Burma, Thailand, Laos, etc., characterized as the "Lesser Vehicle" (*shōjō; Hīnayāna*) by proponents of the later Northern Buddhism of China, Tibet, Korea and Japan, the Mahāyāna defines itself as a way to enlightenment for *all* sentient beings rather than for a select few capable of observing the strict regulations of the Buddhist Order. (Southern Buddhists today prefer to be called by the name of their most prominent contemporary

tradition, Theravāda, the "Doctrine of the Elders.") For the earlier
ideal of arhat (*arakan, rakan*), perceived as self-centered, the
Mahāyāna substitutes the ideal of the boshisattva (*bosatsu*, q.v.), a
"being" who in his wisdom (*chie, prajñā*) recognizes the existence of
no beings (*muga;* see *mujō* entry), and yet, contradictorily, in his
compassion (*jihi, karuṇā*) is resolved to save them (e.g., as taught in
the *Diamond Sutra*). The Mahāyānist generally sees the Hīnayānist
Tripiṭaka ("Three Baskets"; *sanzō*) merely as concessions (*hōben*,
q.v.) to human lack of understanding, and it developed its own
Tripiṭaka with an elaborate body of scriptures and new systems of
philosophy. Among Japanese sects of Buddhism, all are counted as
Mahāyānist except the Kusha, Jōjitsu, Ritsu, and (sometimes) Hossō
among the Six Nara sects; but see also *mikkyō* entry.

darani, or *sōji.* That which "completely sustains" the power of good;
    dhāraṇī. Mystic phrases and verses employed in the esoteric schools
    (*mikkyō*, q.v.; cf., *shingon, mantra*). Mujū refers to the Hōkyōin
    darani (Jewel-Box Spell) and the Sonshō darani (Holy and Virtuous
    Spell); he also states that Japanese poetry (*waka*) is *dhāraṇī* when it
    embodies the spirit of the Buddha's Law (*S&P* 5A:12).

decline of the Law. See *mappō.*

dependent origination (*engi*). See under *kū* entry.

dhāraṇī. See *darani.*

emptiness. See *kū.*

engi (dependent origination). See under *kū* entry.

esotericism. See *mikkyō.*

exoteric teaching (overt, *kengyō*). See under *mikkyō* entry.

gō. Action; *karma;* see also *sangō.* Generally speaking, the law of moral
    causality by virtue of which there is retribution for every action: good
    effects from good acts, bad effects from bad, especially re-birth in the
    Three Evil Paths (*san'akudō;* see under *rokudō*). A more subtle argu-
    ment proposes that even "good" action, to the extent that we are
    aware of and attached to it as such, must ultimately be avoided as well
    as obviously bad action. Note, for example, *S&P* 5A:5, as well as
    Shinran's famous axiom: "Even a good person is born in the Pure
    Land, how much more so is an evil person" (*Tannishō* 3).

gokuraku jōdo. See under *hongan* entry.

Hīnayāna. See under *daijō* (Mahāyāna) entry.

hō. Dharma. A word with a variety of meanings (see Takakusu 1956, p.
    57), the two most common of which are sometimes confused: (1)
    Dharma as the teachings of Buddhism, the Law; and (2) dharmas as
    ultimate psychophysical elements whose successive combining and dis-
    junction constitutes the gross forms of the entire phenomenal world,
    which are thus without any persisting self or substance (*shohō muga;*
    see *mujō* and *kū* entries).

hōben. Skillful Means, Accommodation, Expedient Means, etc.;
    upāyakauśalya. The varying methods used by buddhas and bodhisatt-
    vas to apply the Dharma (*hō*, q.v.) to the specific needs and biases of

the individual in his search for enlightenment, rather than prescribing the same remedy for different spiritual ailments. The Absolute ("Law Body," *hosshin;* see *sanshin* entry) ultimately cannot be defined by any conceptual formulation or symbolic representation; yet such provisional signs, forms, myths, and mental constructs can serve as Skillful Means to direct our attention to the Unconditioned, as a finger may point to the moon. The doctrine is conspicuous in the arguments and parables of the Lotus Sutra, and is the basis for Buddhism's (and Mujū's) tolerance of logically conflicting systems. See also *honji suijaku* and *kyōgen kigo* entries.

hōjin (Reward Body). See under *sanshin* entry.

hongan. Original Vow(s); *praṇidhāna.* In a broad sense, the commitment of various buddhas and bodhisattvas made in earlier existences to save all sentient beings. Specifically, the forty-eight vows of the Buddha Amida who, as the Bodhisattva Dharmākara (Hōzō), promised birth (*ōjō,* q.v.) in his Pure Land of Supreme Bliss (gokuraku jōdo) to those who call upon his name (*nembutsu,* q.v.). These vows, recorded in the *Muryōjukyō* (Amitayus Sūtra; the "Larger Pure land Sutra", T. 360) are the basis for faith in the saving Other Power (*tariki,* q.v.) of Amida.

honji suijaku. Original Ground/Manifest Trace. The theory that in order to save sentient beings, the various buddhas and bodhisattvas (as "Original Ground," Essence) assume the forms of (or, "manifest their traces as") native divinities: as Chinese and Taoist sages in China, and as Shintō deities (*kami*) in Japan; see *sanshin.* A rather late attempt to explain the "unification of the Gods and Buddha" (*shimbutsu shūgō*), the theory takes its cue from the Tendai view that in the first 14 chapters of the Lotus Sutra (*shakumon,* "trace teaching"), Śākyamuni employs the Skillful Means (*hōben,* q.v.) of describing himself merely as a mortal; and that in the final 14 chapters (*hommon,* basic teaching"), he reveals his eternal nature.

This "folklore" tradition is adapted less successfully to the Shingon distinction between *honji* (essential body without attributes, the *dharmakāya*; see *sanshin*) and *kaji* (the manifested body as practitioner). See also *wakō dōjin;* also Kiyota 1978, 74–80, and Matsunaga 1969.

hotsubodaishin (aspiration for enlightenment). See under *bodaishin* entry.

impermanence. See *mujō.*

jihi (compassion, *karuṇā*). See under *daijō* and *bosatsu* entries.

jiriki. Self Power. Attaining enlightenment through one's own efforts, in contrast to reliance on the Other Power (*tariki,* q.v.) of Amida's Original Vow (*hongan,* q.v.). The Kamakura Amidist movements frequently criticized, for example, the traditional requirement to "raise the desire for enlightenment" (*hotsubodaishin,* q.v.) taught by the followers of the Holy Path (*shōdō:* Tendai, Shingon, Kengon, Zen, etc.) as a useless assertion of egotism during the period of the Latter Days (*mappō,* q.v.)

jōken (eternalism); *śāśvata-dṛṣṭi.* See under *kū* entry.

karma. See *gō.*

kengyō. See under *mikkyō* entry.

kū. Emptiness, the Void, Interdependence, Relativity, Nothingness, etc.; *śūnya, śūnyatā.* In order to explain the fact of impermanence (*mujō,* q.v.) in the phenomenal world, early Buddhism postulated the existence of ultimate psychophysical elements called *dharma (hō,* q.v.) which coalesced and dispersed according to the principle of Dependent Origination (*engi, pratītyasamutpāda*). Since all persons and things were mere congeries of dharmas, they were without permanent self or substance (*muga,* q.v.); but at the same time, Buddhism as the Middle Way (*chūdō, madhyamā pratipad*) sought to steer a course between the denial of continuity (and hence of the possibility of the operation of *karma;* see *gō*), and the assertion of a permanent substance or soul. The first was the error of viewing things as total nothingness, the error of Annihilationism (*kūken*); the latter was the error of viewing things as substantial and continuous, the error of Eternalism (*jōken*). See *nitai.*

The Mahāyāna, however, viewed Dependent Origination not as the principle of temporal sequence, but as the essential dependence of things in each other, as their ultimate Emptiness. This Emptiness is not an entity apart from this world but, rather, it is the same reality as phenomenal appearance: the world of transmigration (*rinne, samsāra*), when viewed by the enlightened mind, is itself *nirvāṇa (nehan*). Thus. Buddhism's negative terminology does not argue for nihilism but merely that its Ultimate (see under *sanshin*) is empty, devoid of all determinate characteristics. Its *via negativa* would lead us to the *positive* Ground of all things.

kūken (nihilism, annihilationism); *śūnyatādṛṣṭi.* See under *kū* entry.

kyōgen kigo (or *kigyo*). Wild words and specious phrases. The precepts normally condemned "wild words" (*kyōgen* — the term appeared centuries before the theatrical genre of the same name) and "specious phrases" as impediments to enlightenment. *Kigo* (frivolous, flattering, scatterbrained talk) is enumerated among Ten Evils (*jūaku, daśakuśala*) to be avoided. However, writers of the medieval period frequently seized on the four-character phrase made famous by the influential Chinese poet, Po Chü-i (772–846); see note 86) to justify literary activity as a kind of Skillful Means (*hōben,* q.v.) by which to reach the unenlightened. Murasaki Shikibu uses a similar argument in her defense of the novel in the *Tale of Genji,* Book 25.

Latter Days of the Law. See *mappō.*

Law Body (*hosshin*). See under *sanshin* entry.

Mahāyāna. See *daijō.*

mandara. "Cosmogram"; *maṇḍala.* A symbolic representation of religious beings or attributes, usually portrayed in a geometrical pattern and used as a focus for meditation and ritual in esoteric (*mikkyō* q.v.) traditions. In Japan the term usually refers to two complementary paintings, representing knower and known, by whose integration the devotee realizes his identity with the Buddha Mahāvairocana (Dainichi Nyorai), thus "attaining Buddhahood in this very body" (*sokushin jōbutsu*). These two basic *maṇḍalas* are the Diamond (*kongōkai*) and Matrix (*taizōkai*) Assemblies. See also *mikkyō*.

Mujū also refers to several other paintings by this term: the Four-Enclosure (*shijū*) *maṇḍala* (*S&P* 1:1), the Mandala Embracing All and Forsaking None (*sesshu fusha mandara*; *S&P* 1:10) and the *Chihō mandara* (the story of Chikō and Raikō is retold in *Tsuma kagami*).

mappō. The Decline of the Law, the Latter Days of the Law; *saddharma-vipralopa*. The final, degenerative period of the Buddhist teaching during which time both the practice and attainment of the Dharma (*hō*, q.v.) will be forgotten. See *sanji* entry; also note 1.

middle way (*chūdō*). See under *kū* entry.

mikkyō. Esotericism, the "Secret Teaching." Every variety of Buddhism would agree with Kūkai that "the Dharma is beyond speech, but without speech it cannot be revealed. Suchness transcends forms, but without depending on forms it cannot be realized" (Hakeda 1972, 145). Those methods of the Mahāyāna which emphasize "speech" (concepts, discursive reasoning, etc.) as Skillful Means (*hōben*, q.v.) are classified as exoteric, overt teachings (*kengyō*), as opposed to those which employ "signs" (*shingon, mandara*, q.v.; *mudra*, etc.) in order to integrate the Three Actions (*sangō*, q.v.) of sentient beings with the Three Mysteries ("Teaching-practices"; *sammitsu, tri-guhya*) of Mahāvairocana (Dainichi Nyorai). Shingon's Tōmitsu is that sect's central practice; Tendai's Taimitsu is complemented by an exoteric component based on the teachings of the Lotus Sutra; and other sects frequently adapt rituals from these two major systems. Although esotericism is part of the Mahāyāna, Mujū sometimes speaks as if it were a separate tradition: "The Hīnayāna (*shōjō*) had only the first three [of the five groups of the Buddha's teachings], the fourth is common to the Mahāyāna, and the fifth to the esoteric traditions (*misshū*)" (*S&P* 2:8; Watanabe 1966, p. 120).

moral causality (*karma*). See *gō* and *sangō*.

muga (anātman). See under *daijō* and *mujō* entries.

mujō. The transience, inconstancy, impermanence of the phenomenal world; *anitya*. The Three Characteristic Marks (*sambōin*) of the Buddhist teaching are (1) that all conditioned things are impermanent (*shogyō mujō*); (2) that all phenomena are without persisting self or substance (*shohō muga*); and (3) that the goal of religious practice is the peace of *nirvāṇa (nehan jakujō)*. Buddhism proposes a *solution* to the problem of suffering, but its emphasis on the need to escape the inadequacies of the unenlightened state and the dangers of attachment to what is transient often give it an unwarranted reputation for pessimism. See *kū* entry.

nehan. See *nirvāṇa*.

nembutsu. Thinking/calling on the Name [of Amida]; *buddha-anusmṛti.* As the parts of the word suggest, *nembutsu* originally referred to thinking (*nen*) on the Buddha as an adjunct to meditation. This interpretation of the term, based on such scriptures as the *Hanjusammaikyō* (Visualization [of Amida] Sutra, T. 418, was gradually replaced by the view of the practice as *calling* on the holy name (*shōmyō nembutsu*). For the extreme followers of Hōnen and Shinran, "solely uttering the Name" (*senju nembutsu*) was the only religious practice necessary, or even possible, as human ability to attain the Dharma deteriorated during the Latter Days of the Law (*mappō*; see also *sanji*).

nirvāṇa; nehan. The extinction of all karma (*gō*, q.v.), which is the cause of transmigration (*rinne*) through the Six Paths (*rokudō*, q.v.), conceived either literally or metaphorically. Release from illusion; enlightenment. See also *mujō* entry (3).

nitai. The Two Truths; *satya-dvaya.* The multiplicity of the world viewed as arising interdependently is Empty (*kū*, q.v.) of any permanent self or substance (*muga*; see under *mujō* entry); this is the Ultimate or Absolute Truth (*shintai, paramārtha satya*). The same world viewed empirically, however, has an undeniable provisional existence (*ke*); this is the complementary Conventional Truth (*zokutai, saṁvṛti satya*). (See Murti 1960, 243–255.) Hence the famous statement of the *Hannya shingyō*: "Form is no other than emptiness, Emptiness is no other than Form" (*shiki soku ze kū, kū soku ze shiki*). To these Tendai thought adds a Truth of the Middle (*chūtai*) between these two extremes, to create a doctrine of Three Truths (*santai*).

ōjin (Transformation Body). See under *sanshin.*

ōjō. Birth ("going and being born") into Amida's Pure Land of Supreme Bliss (*gokuraku jōdo*); *upapatsyante.* Originally the term referred to birth or rebirth into any other world, including various hells and heavens (see *rokudō*), but it is now used almost exclusively for birth in the Western Paradise. See also *hongan* entry.

original ground/manifest trace. See *honji suijaku.*

rakan (arhat). See under *daijō* (Mahāyāna) entry.

rinne (saṁsāra). See under *rokudō* (Six Paths) entry.

rokudō, also *rokushu.* The Six Paths (or Destinies) of beings within the round of transmigration (*rinne, saṁsāra*) in the Realm of Desire (*yokkai, kāmadhātu*): (1) the heavens of desire (*ten, deva*); (2) the human world (*ningen, manusya*); (3) the world of fighting spirits (*shura, asura*); (4) the animal world (*chikushō tiryagyoni*); (5) the world of hungry-ghosts (*gaki, preta*); and (6) the hells (*jigoku, naraka*). We are reborn into the three Good Paths (*sanzendō*, or *sanzenshu*: 1–3) as the result of good actions (*gō*, q.v.) in previous lives; and into the Three Evil Paths (*san'akudō*) as retribution for bad action. But we regress even from the so-called "good paths," and the proper goal for the religious life is release from all six, either to realize *nirvāṇa (nehan)* or birth (*ōjō*, q.v.) in, say, Amida's Pure Land of Supreme Bliss (*gokuraku jōdo*), from which there is no backsliding.

roots of merit (*zengon*). See under *sandoku* entry.

sambōin (Three Characteristic Marks). See under *mujō* entry.

saṃsāra. See under *rokudō* (Six Paths) entry.

san'akudō (Three Evil Paths). See under *rokudō* entry.

sandoku. The Three Poisons which destroy the Roots of Merit (*zengon*, *kusala mūla*): (1) covetousness (*ton*, *rāga*; note Mujū's poem on this item in *S&P* 3:8); (2) anger, ill will, envy (*shin*, *dveṣa*, *pratigha*); and (3) delusion, ignorance (*chi*, *moha*).

sangō. The Three Actions of sentient beings; *tri-karma*; cf., *gō*. These are (1) deeds of the body (*shingō*, *kāya-karma*); (2) of words, sound, voice (*kugō*, *vāk-karma*); and (3) of thought (*igō*, *manaḥ-karma*). These parallel the Three Mysteries, or "Teaching-practices" (*sammitsu*, *triguhya*) of Mahāvairocana (Dainichi Nyorai), and when the identity of the two is realized experientially, the practitioner "attains Buddhahood in his very body" (*sokushin jobutsu*). See *mikkyō*; also Kiyota 1978.

sanji, also *shōzōmatsu*. The Three Periods of the Law. (1) *shōbō*, *sad-dharma*. The age of the first thousand (sometimes 500) years after the historical Buddha's demise when doctrine, practice and attainment were prevalent. (2) *zōbō*, *saddharma-pratirūpaka*. The age of the Imitation [Image] of the Law, the next thousand years when doctrine and practice prevailed, but no attainment. (3) *mappō* (q.v.), *saddharma-vipralopa*. The age of the Decline of the Law, the final period when only the doctrine is known, but practice and attainment are no longer possible, as Nichiren, Hōnen and others had admonished. See also note 1.

sanshin. The Three Bodies [of the Buddha]; *tri-kāya*. That is, (1) *hosshin*, *dharmakāya*: the "Law Body," the Buddha as Absolute, Unconditioned, Ineffable, Empty (*kū*, q.v.), as "Godhead." (2) *hōjin*, *sambhogakāya*: the "Reward Body" of the Buddha represented in a glorified state as "reward" for his vows and spiritual accomplishments; e.g., Amida in his Pure Land of Supreme Bliss. (3) *ōjin*, *nirmāṇakāya*: the "Transformation Body" of the Buddha as provisional manifestation, as incarnation, to guide sentient beings to enlightenment; e.g., Śākyamuni. "The gods (*kami*) of Japan are Manifest Traces (*suijaku*), unexcelled Transformation Bodies (*ōjin*) of Buddhas and Bodhisattvas" (*S&P* 5A:12).

senju nembutsu See under *nembutsu* entry.

shiki soku ze kū soku ze shiki. See under *nitai* entry.

shimbutsu shūgō (the unification of the gods and buddhas). See under *honji suijaku* entry.

shingon, also *shu*. "True Words"; *mantra*. Syllables, words or short phrases valued in esoteric (*mikkyō*, q.v.) practices for their inherent spiritual power rather than for their conceptual profundity. They are similar to, but usually shorter than, *darani* (q.v.). Mujū often refers to the Jiku no shu (Spell of Compassionate Help), the Kakai no ju (Fire-World Spell), and the Kōmyō shingon (Mantra of Light). The Shingon (Mantrayāna) is named for its emphasis on such mystic spells and related esoteric rites.

shintai (Ultimate Truth). See under *nitai* entry.

shōbō (Period of the True Law). See under *sanji* entry.

shōdō (Holy Path). See under *jiriki* entry.

shōjō (Hīnayāna). See under *daijō* entry.

shōzōmatsu (True-Imitation-Decline). See *sanji.*

skillful means. See *hōben.*

sōji. See *darani.*

solushin jōbutsu. See under *mandara* and *sangō* entries.

suijaku. See under *honji sujaku* and *sanshin* entries.

śūnyatā. See *kū.*

tariki. Other Power. Reliance on the efficacy of Amida's Original Vow (*hongan*, q.v.) to bring to his Pure Land those who invoke his name (*nembutsu*, q.v.).

ten evils (*jūaku*). See under *kyōgen kigo* entry.

three actions [of sentient beings]. See *sangō.*

three evil paths (*san'akudō*). See under *rokudō* (Six Paths) entry.

three poisons. See *sandoku.*

three truths. See under *nitai* entry.

three mysteries (*sammitsu*). See under *sangō* entry.

two truths. See *nitai.*

upāyakauśalya. See *hōben.*

wakō dōjin. "Soften the Light and Identify with the Dust." This phrase, which expresses the notion that the buddhas, bodhisattvas (*bosatsu*, q.v.) and the Gods (*kami*) who are their local manifestations (cf., *honji suijaku*) "soften the light" of their wisdom and "identify with the dust" of human passions in order to save sentient beings, is borrowed from the Taoist *Way and Its Power* (Tao Te Ching, Dōtokukyō) 4. See note 124.

zōbō (period of the Imitation of the Law). See under *sanji.*

zokutai (Conventional Truth). See under *nitai.*

Glossary of Selected Characters

This short glossary includes basically the terms defined in the Glossary of Selected Terms with the addition of a few names and titles specifically associated with Mujū.

Azuma kagami	吾妻鏡 (東鑑)	*gaki*	餓鬼
bodaishin	菩提心	*gedatsu*	解脱
Bommō fusatsu	梵網布薩	*gō* (karma)	業
Bonshun	梵舜	*gokuraku jōdo*	極楽浄土
bosatsu	菩薩	*hō* (dharma)	法
Busu	附子	*hōjin*	報身
chi (delusion)	癡	*hommon*	本門
chie (wisdom)	智慧	*hongaku*	本覺
Chōboji	長母寺	*hongan*	本願
chūdō	中道	*honji suijaku*	本地垂迹
chūtai	中諦	Hōonji	法音寺
daijō	大乗	*hosshin*	法身
darani	陀羅尼	*hotsubodaishin*	發菩提心
Dōen	道円	Ichien	一円
Dōgyō	道暁	*igō*	意業
Dōshakukō	道跡考	*in'en*	因縁
Eichō	榮朝	*jigoku*	地獄
Eizon	叡尊	*jihi*	慈悲
engi	縁起	*jiriki*	自力
Enni Ben'en	円爾弁円	Jōken	常見

339

jōsai	清齋	*muga*	無我
jūaku	十悪	*mujō*	無常
Kajiwara Kagetoki	梶原景時	Mujū	無住
Kakai no ju	火界の呪	Muō	無翁
kami	神	*nehan*	涅槃
kana hōgo	假名法語	*nehan jakujō*	涅槃寂静
kannō	感應	Nehankō	涅槃講
Kano	鹿野	*nembutsu*	念仏
Kantō ōgenki	関東往還記	*ningen*	人門
kengyō	顯教	*nitai*	二諦
Kenryō	乾嶺	*ōjin*	應身
Kigasaki	木賀崎	*ōjō*	往生
Kōmyō shingon	光明真言	Owari Manzai	尾張萬歳
kongōkai	金剛界	*rakan*	羅漢
Konsenshū	金撰集	Rengeji	蓮華寺
kū	空	*rinne*	輪廻
Kūgeshū	空華集	Rōen	良円
kugō	口業	*rokudō*	六道
kūken	空見	*rokushu*	六趣
kyōgen kigo	狂言綺語	*Ryakuengi*	略縁起
mandara	曼荼羅	*sambōin*	三宝印
Mantokuji	万徳寺	*sammitsu*	三密
mappō	末法	*san'akudō*	三悪道
mikkyō	密教	*sandoku*	三毒
Minomushi Sanjin	蓑虫山人	*sangō*	三業
		sanji	三時
misshū	密宗	*sanshin*	三身
Momooji	桃尾寺	*sanzendō*	三善道

sanzō	三藏	shōzōmatsu	正像末
senju nembutsu	専修念仏	shu (= shingon)	呪
sesshu fusha mandara	攝取 不捨曼陀羅	shura	修羅
		sōji (= darani)	總持
setsuwa	説話	sokushin jōbutsu	即身成仏
shakumon	迹門	Sonshō darani	尊勝陀羅尼
Sharikō	舎利講	suijaku. See honji suijaku.	垂迹
Shasekishū	沙石集	Sukeko	資子
shigaku	始覺	Tainin	諦忍
shijū mandara	四重曼陀羅	taizōkai	胎藏界
shiki soku ze kū	色即是空	tariki	他力
shin (anger)	瞋	ten	天
shinbutsu shūgō	神仏習合	Toki Gengo	土岐源吾
shingō	身業	ton (covetousness)	貪
shingon (mantra)	真言	Tsuma kagami	妻鏡
shintai	真諦	wakō dōjin	和光同塵
shōbō	正法	Watanabe Tsunaya	渡辺網也
shōdō	聖道	Yamada Shigetada	山田重忠
shogyō mujō	諸行無常	yokkai	欲界
shohō muga	諸法無我	zazen	坐禅
shōji	生死	zengon	善根
shōjō	小乘	zōbō	像法
shōmyō nembutsu	稱名念仏	zokutai	俗諦
		Zōsō Rōyo	藏叟朗譽
Shōzaishū	聖財集	Zōtanshū	雜談集

Selected Bibliography

Texts of Mujū's Works

1. Collection of Sand and Pebbles (Shasekishū, 1279-83)

Unabbreviated Versions (kōhon)

Watanabe Tsunaya, ed., *Shasekishū*, volume 85 of eds. Takagi
Ichinosuke, et al., *Nihon koten bungaku taikei.* Tokyo: Iwanami
Shoten, 1966.

The well-annotated, standard modern edition of *Shasekishū*. It comprises Books 1-10A of a manuscript copied by monk Bonshun in 1597,
supplemented with Book 10B of a manuscript, ca. 1550-1650, held by
the Yonezawa Municipal Library. The reader who wishes to track down
a citation in one text or another will appreciate the chart comparing the
tables of contents of these two manuscripts with that of the "twelve-
column text of the Keichō Period," a woodblock edition published in
1605 which is the basis for the most widely circulated version of
Shasekishū, the abbreviated "Jōkyō 3 text" of 1686, and other printed
editions. See Fukai, ed. *Keichō jūnen kokatsujibon shasekishū sōsakuin*,
below.

Watanabe Tsunaya, ed., *Kōhon shasekishū*. Tokyo: Nihon Shobō, 1943.

An unannotated edition of the Yonezawa manuscript with doubtful
readings checked against Bonshun's. Largely superseded by the above,
this book is now a rare item but is sometimes cited, e.g., in Joyce
Ackroyd's "Women in Feudal Japan."

Abbreviated Versions (ryakuhon)

Tsukudo Reikan, ed., *Shasekishū*, Tokyo: Iwanami Shoten, 1943, 2 vols.

These Iwanami Bunko paperbacks are based on the popular 1686 woodblock edition, but the editor's alterations make it unreliable as an accurate copy. Frequently cited.

Fujii Otoo, ed., *Kōchū shasekishū*, volume 5 of *Kokubungaku meichoshū*. Tokyo: Bunken Shoin, 1928.

A sparsely annotated edition of the 1686 text with reference to other abbreviated editions. Editing considered generally good.

Fukai Ichirō, ed. *Keichō jūnen kokatsujibon shasekishū sōsakuin.* Tokyo: Benseisha, 1980, 2 vols. Pp. 498, 1226.

This *Complete Index to the Old Movable Type Editions of the Shasekishū Published in Keichō 10* (1605) is based on that year's ten-and twelve-column editions, which are almost identical except for format (see Watanabe, *Shasekishū*, above). The *eiinhen* (facsimile volume) photographically reproduces Professor Watanabe's copy of the ten-column text correlated page by page with a twelve-column version held by Tokyo University. The *sakuinhen* (index volume) includes separate indices on words and phrases, suffixes, Buddhist texts and poetry collections cited, and its *waka* and *renga.*

There have been two modern reprintings of the *Shasekishū* from the original woodblocks (see Figure 7), still preserved at the Chōboji, of the Jōkyō 3 (1686) edition. The first, encased and in five volumes, was prepared by the temple in 1911 to commemorate the six-hundredth anniversary of Mujū's death. The second, boxed and in ten volumes, was prepared by the Nihon Bunka Shiryō Sentā [Nagoya?] in 1981 (to commemorate the seven-hundredth anniversary of the completion of the *Shasekishū* in 1283?).

For a survey of some fifteen manuscripts, eleven woodblock, and thirteen modern printed editions, see my "Representative Translations," pp. 20–39.

2. Collection of Sacred Assets (Shōzaishū, 1299)

Unkyō Chidō, ed., *Shōzaishū*. Kyoto: Issaikyō Imbō, 1893.

This unannotated edition with less than a page of commentary also includes *Tsuma kagami.*

3. Mirror for Women (Tsuma kagami, 1300)

Miyasaka Yūshō, ed., *Kana hōgoshū* (Collection of Vernacular Tracts), volume 83 of eds. Takagi Ichinosuke, et al., *Nihon koten bungaku taikei.* Tokyo: Iwanami Shoten, 1964, pp. 158–94.

Based on a 1641 woodblock edition owned by Kōyasan University Library, this well-annotated text is the best of as many as seven modern printings of the work.

4. Collection of Casual Digressions (Zōtanshū, 1305)

Yamada Shōzen and Miki Sumito, eds., *Zōtanshū.* Tokyo: Miyai Shoten, 1973.

This well-annotated standard edition of the work is based on a woodblock text of 1644.

Matsuura Sadatoshi, ed., *Zōtanshū.* Tokyo: Koten Bunko, 1950. Two volumes.

A reduced facsimile edition of the 1644 woodblock text, with introduction.

5. Deed of Transfer (Yuzurijō, 1305); Record of a Dream (Musō no koto, 1305?)

Mainichi Shimbunsha, ed., *Nihon kōsō iboku* (Calligraphic Legacy of Eminent Japanese Priests). Tokyo, 1970.

Includes beautiful reproductions of both items with a rendering of the texts into modern printed characters.

General Bibliography

Ackroyd, Joyce. "Women in Feudal Japan," vol. VII of *TASJ* Third Series (November, 1959), 33-36. References to Watanabe, *Kōhon shasekishū*.

Aichi-ken Moriyamashi Yakusho, ed. *Moriyamashi shi.* Moriyama, 1963. A "History of Moriyama City," containing detailed information (pp. 554-72) about the Yamada family and its relation to Mujū and the founding of Chōboji. In 1963 Moriyama City was incorporated as a ward (*ku*) in the northeast section of Nagoya. Chōboji is located at the northeast extremity of Higashi-ku, overlooking the Yada River, which roughly serves as the boundary between the ward and Moriyama-ku.

Andō Naotarō. *Setsuwa to haikai no kenkyū.* Tokyo: Kasama Shoin, 1979. This useful book with many concrete biographical items concerning Mujū and *Shasekishū* includes four articles and papers published earlier:

   (a) pp. 131-64, "Mujū Daien Kokushiden kō" (Thoughts on Biographical Accounts of Mujū Daien Kokushi), "Mujū Kokushi no shōgai" (The Career of Mujū Kokushi) in *Setsuwa to haikai* (1962; rev. 1978).

   (b) pp. 165-84, "Shasekishū maki ichi: Jingi setsuwa no kōsatsu" (Collection of Sand and Pebbles, Book One: An Inquiry into Tale Literature concerning the Gods), originally published in *Sugiyama Jogakuen Daigaku Kenkyū Ronshū* III (1972).

   (c) pp. 185-201, "Mujū no kyōkan to hōwa bungaku no sekai" (Mujū's View of the Buddhist Teaching and the World of Didactic Literature), originally published in *Sugiyama Jogakuen Daigaku Kenkyū Ronshū* IX (1978).

   (d) pp. 202-209, "Mujū no Chōboji nyūzan no keii to musōdan" (Details about Mujū's Taking up Residence at Chōboji and His Dream Account). Revision of a paper delivered in 1971 at the Setsuwa Bungakkai in Nagoya titled "Mujū no shutsuji wo megutte" (About Mujū's Family Lineage).

347

Andrews, Allan A. *The Teachings Essential for Rebirth: A Study of Genshin's Ōjōyōshū.* Tokyo: Sophia University Press, 1973.

Aston, W. G. *Nihongi: Chronicles of Japan from the Earliest Times to A.D. 697.* London: Kegan Paul, Trench, Trubner & Co., 1924.

Bandō Shōjun, "Myōe's Criticism of Hōnen's Doctrine," *The Eastern Buddhist,* New Series, Vol. VII, No. 1 (1974), pp. 37-54.

Bock, Felicia Gressitt. *Engi-Shiki: Procedures of the Engi Era, Books I-V.* Tokyo: Sophia University, 1970.

Brock, Karen. *Maitreya the Future Buddha.* Princeton: Princeton University Press (in press).

Brower, Robert H. *The Konzyaku Monogatarisyū: An Historical and Critical Introduction, with Annotated Translations of Seventy-Eight Tales.* Ph.D. dissertation, University of Michigan, 1952.

Brower, Robert H. and Earl Miner, *Fujiwara Teika's Superior Poems of Our Times: A Thirteenth-Century Poetic Treatise and Sequence.* Stanford: Stanford University Press, 1967.

————. *Japanese Court Poetry.* Stanford: Stanford University Press, 1961.

Brown, Delmer M. and Ishida, Ichirō. *The Future and the Past: A Translation and Study of the Gukanshō, an interpretative History of Japan written in 1219.* University of California Press, 1979.

Chamberlain, Basil Hall. *Japanese Things.* Rutland, Vt. and Tokyo: Charles Tuttle, 1971. A reprinting of Chamberlain's *Things Japanese* (Fifth Edition, 1905). Includes a translation of *Onna daigaku* (Greater Learning for Women) by Kaibara Ekiken (1630-1714), pp. 502-508.

Chan, Wing-tsit. *The Platform Sutra.* New York: St. John's University Press, 1963.

Ch'en, Kenneth. *Buddhism in China: A Historical Survey.* Princeton: Princeton University Press, 1964.

Cleary, Thomas, tr. *The Flower Ornament Scripture: A Translation of the Avatamasaka Sutra, Volume 1.* Boulder and London: Shambala, 1984.

Coates, Harper Havelock and Ishizuka Ryūgaku. *Hōnen the Buddhist Saint: His Life and Teaching.* Kyoto: Chionin, 1925.

Collcutt, Martin. *Five Mountains: The Rinzai Zen Monastic Institution in Medieval Japan.* Cambridge: Harvard University Press, 1981.

Conze, Edward. *Buddhism: Its Essence and Development.* New York: Philosophical Library, 1951.

————. "Buddhist Philosophy and Its European parallels," *Philosophy East and West* XIII, No. 1 (April 1963), pp. 9-23.

————. *Buddhist Wisdom Books: The Diamond Sutra and the Heart Sutra.* London: Allen and Unwin, 1958.

————. *The Large Sutra of Perfect Wisdom.* Berkeley: University of California Press, 1975.

————. *The Prajñāpāramitā Literature.* The Hague: 'S-Gravenhage, 1960.

————. "Spurious Parallels to Buddhist Philosophy," *Philosophy East and West* XIII, No. 2 (July 1963), pp. 105-115.

Cowell, E. B., et al., eds. *Buddhist Mahāyāna Texts,* Sacred Books of the East XLIX. Delhi: Motilal Banarsidass, 1965. Reprint of Oxford University Press 1894 edition.

Daihonzan Tōfukuzenji, ed. *Tōfukuji shi.* Kyoto, 1930.

Dainihon bukkyō zensho, ed. Bussho Kankōkai. Tokyo. Dainihon Bukkyō Zensho Hakkōjo, 1913-1922; Suzuki Gakujutsu Zaidan reprint, 1971-72.

Demieville, Paul, et al., eds. *Hōbōgirin: Fascicule Annexe.* Tokyo: Maison Franco-Japonaise, 1931.

De Visser, M. W. *Ancient Buddhism in Japan.* Leiden: E. J. Brill, 1935. 2 vols.

Dōshakukō. See Tainin.

Dumoulin, Heinrich. *The Development of Chinese Zen after the Sixth Patriarch in the Light of the Mumonkan.* Tr. Ruth Sasaki. New York: The First Zen Institute of America, 1953.

————. *A History of Zen Buddhism.* New York: Random House, 1963.

Dutt, Nalinaksha. *Aspects of Mahāyāna Buddhism in its Relation to Hīnayāna.* London: Luzac and Co., 1930.

Dykstra, Yoshiko Kurata, "Jizō, the Most Merciful: Tales from *Jizō Bosatsu Reigenki,*" *Monumenta Nipponica* XXXIII:2 (Summer 1978), pp. 179-200.

————. "Tales of the Compassionate Buddha: *The Hasedera Kannon Genki,*" *Monumenta Nipponica* XXXI:2 (Summer 1976), pp. 113-143.

Fontein, Jan. *The Pilgrimage of Sudhana: A Study of Gaṇḍavyūha illustrations in China, Japan and Java.* The Hague: Mouton & Co., 1967.

Frederic, Louis. *Daily Life in Japan at the Time of the Samurai, 1185-1603.* Tr. by Eileen M. Lowe. New York/Washington: Praeger Publishers, 1972.

Fujimura Saku. *Zōho kaitei nihon bungaku daijiten.* Tokyo: Shinchōsha, 1950-52.

Fukada Masaki. *Owari shi II.* Tokyo: Rekishi Toshosha, 1969.

Fung Yu-lan. *A History of Chinese Philosophy, Vol. II.* Tr. by Derk Bodde. Princeton: Princeton University Press, 1953.

Getty, Alice. *The Gods of Northern Buddhism: Their History, Iconography and Progressive Evolution through the Northern Buddhist Countries.* Rutland, Vt. and Tokyo: Charles E. Tuttle, 1962, Reprint of 1928 second edition.

Gidō Shūshin (1325-1388), *Kūgeshū;* in Uemura Kankō, ed. *Gozan bungaku zenshū.* Kyoto: Shibunkaku, 1973 reprint.

Golay, Jacqueline. *Le Shasekishū, miroir d'une personnalité, miroir d'une époque.* Ph.D. dissertation, U. of British Columbia, 1975.

Hakeda, Yoshita S., tr. *The Awakening of Faith.* New York and London: Columbia University Press, 1967.

————. *Kūkai: Major Works.* New York: Columbia University Press, 1972.

Harper, Thomas J. "Motoori Norinaga's Criticism of the *Genji Monogatari:* A Study of the Background and Critical Content of his *Genji Monogatari Tama no Ogushi,*" Doctoral Dissertation, The University of Michigan, 1971.

————. "A Twelfth Century Critique of the *Tale of Genji,*" *Criticism in Translation,* Vol 1, No. 1 (Sept. 1976), pp. 1-5. Discussion of *kyōgen kigo* ("wild words and specious phrases") including a selected translation from the *Mirror of the Present (Imakagami,* ca. 1170).

Hinotani Akihiko, Kobaysahi Yasuharu, and Takahashi Mitsugu, eds. *Setsuwa bungaku hikkei.* Tokyo: Tokyo Bijutsu, 1976.

Hirabayashi Harunori, et al., eds. *Nihon setsuwa bungaku sakuin.* Osaka: Nihon Shuppansha, 1943. Osaka: Seibundō Shuppan Kabushiki Kaisha, 1964 (reprint). References are to the abbreviated version (*ryakuhon*) of *Shasekishū.*

Hisamatsu Senichi, et al., eds. *Shinkokinwakashū.* NKBT 28. Tokyo: Iwanami Shoten, 1958.

Hurvitz, Leon. *Chih-I (538-597): An Introduction to the Life and Ideas of a Chinese Buddhist Monk.* Melanges Chinois et Bouddhiques 12. Bruges, 1963.

————, tr. *Scripture of the Lotus Blossom of the Fine Dharma.* New York: Columbia University Press, 1976.

Ichinose Naoyuki. *Nihon mukashibanashi kō.* Tokyo: Sagi no Miya Shobō, 1966.

Inoue Mitsusada. "Eizon, Ninshō and the Saidai-ji Order," *Acta Asiatica* 20 (1971), pp. 77-103.

Ishida Ichirō. ed. *Shintō shisōshū.* Tokyo: Chikuma Shobō, 1970.

Kageyama Haruki. *Shintō no bijutsu.* Tokyo: Hanawa Shobō, 1965.

Kaneko Sachiko and Robert E. Morrell. "Sanctuary: Kamakura's Tōkeiji Convent," *Japanese Journal of Religious Studies* 10:2-3 (June-September 1983), pp. 195-228.

Kantō ōgenki, in Kokusho Kankōkai, ed. *Shiseki zassan* (Miscellaneous Collection of Historical Works), Tokyo: Zoku Gunsho Ruijū Kanseikai, 1974; reprint of 1911-12 edition. Vol. 1, pp. 1-2.

Kato Genchi. *Commemoration Volume: The Twenty-fifth Anniversary of the Foundation of the Zaidan Hojin Meiji Seitoku Kinen Gakkai or Meiji Japan Society.* Tokyo, 1937. Includes a translation of *Tōkan kikō,* pp. 143-201.

————. *A Study of Shinto: The Religion of the Japanese Nation.* New York: Barnes & Noble, 1971. Reprint of 1926 edition.

Kato Genchi and Hoshino Hikoshiro, tr. *Imbe-no Hironari's Kogoshūi or Gleanings from Ancient Stories*. Tokyo: Sanseidō, 1924.

Kawaguchi Hisao and Shida Nobuyoshi, eds. *Wakanrōeishū Ryōjinhishō*. Tokyo: Iwanami Shoten, 1965. NKBT 73.

Kawaguchi Kōfū. "Tainin risshi no chosaku no seiri," *Indogaku Bukkyō-gaku Kenkyū* XXVII: 1 (December 1978), pp. 368-371.

Keene, Donald. *Anthology of Japanese Literature*. New York: Grove Press, 1955.

―――. "The Comic Tradition in Renga," in John W. Hall and Toyoda Takeshi, eds., *Japan in the Muromachi Age*. Berkeley: University of California Press, 1977.

Kenryō Keigen (18th century) *Mujū kokushi ryakuengi* (Biographical Sketch of Mujū Kokushi) including the *Kigasaki ryakuengi* (Short History of Kigasaki). Published 1707.

Kidō Saizō and Imoto Nōichi, eds. *Rengaronshū haironshū*. Tokyo: Iwanami Shoten, 1961. NKBT 66.

Kidō Saizō. "Sasamegoto ni oyoboshita Shasekishū no eikyō," in Bukkyō Bungaku Kenkyū Kai, ed. *Bukkyō bungaku* V. Kyoto: Hōzōkan, 1967.

Kim, Hee-Jin *Dōgen Kigen—Mystical Realist*. Tucson: University of Arizona Press, 1975.

Kintō Fujiko. "Minken bungei to setsuwasha: Zōtanshū ni tsuite no ik-kōsai," Bukkyō Bungaku Kenkyūkai, ed. *Bukkyō Bungaku Kenkyū* 10. Kyoto: Hōzōkan, 1971.

Kishimoto, Hideo. *Japanese Religion in the Meiji Era*. Tokyo: Ōbunsha, 1956.

Kitagawa Hiroshi and Tsuchida, Bruce T., trs. *The Tale of the Heike*. Tokyo: University of Tokyo Press, 1975. Complete translation in two volumes.

Kitagawa, Joseph M. *Religion in Japanese History*. New York: Columbia University Press, 1966.

Kiyota, Minoru. *Shingon Buddhism: Theory and Practice*. Los Angeles and Tokyo: Buddhist Books International, 1978.

―――. *Tantric Concept of Bodhicitta: A Buddhist Experiential Philosophy*. University of Wisconsin-Madison: South Asian Area Center, 1982.

Kobayashi Tadao. "Mujū to Rengeji," *Kaishaku* (June 1959).

―――. "Shasekishū no hampon ni tsuite," *Kokugakuin zasshi* (June 1959), pp. 39-50. The major source of information on printed editions of *Shasekishū* from the early Tokugawa period to the present.

―――. *Shimpen Mujū Kokushi kashū*, supplement to *Kyōdo Bunka* V:3 (1950).

Kōchiyama Kiyohiko. "Setsuwa bungaku kenkyū bunken bunrui mokur-oku," *Kokugo to kokubungaku* XXXIX: 10 (Oct. 1962), 119-158. Of 1161 numbered books and articles on *setsuwa*, the *Shasekishū* is treated in items 887–942, the *Zōtanshu* in items 1015–1020.

Kokumin Tosho K. K. *Kōchū kokka taikei*, Volume 5. Tokyo: Kokumin Tosho K. K., 1976 reprint.

Kokusho Kankōkai, ed. *Ikkyū kantō banashi*, Vol. VI of *Kinsei bungei sōsho*. Tokyo, 1911.

Konishi Jinichi. "Shunzei no yūgentei to shikan," *Bungaku* XX (1952), pp. 108–116.

Kumahara Masao. "Shasekishū to Kamakura," *Ihō kanazawa bunko* XXVI–XXVIII (July-September, 1957).

Kuroita Katsumi. *Shintei zōho kokushi taikei*, volume 32: *Azuma kagami* 1. Tokyo: Yoshikawa Kōbunkan, 1964 reprint.

Legge, James. *The Four Books*. Shanghai: The Chinese Book Company, 1930.

———. *The Sacred Books of China: The Texts of Confucianism, II: The Yi King*. Oxford University Press, 1899.

———. *The Texts of Taoism I*. New York: Dover Publications, 1962 reprint.

Luk, Charles, tr. *The Śūraṅgama Sūtra*. London: Rider and Co., 1966.

———, tr. *The Vimalakīrti Nirdeśa Sūtra*. Berkeley: Shambala, 1972.

Mainichi Shimbunsha, ed. *Nihon kōsō iboku*. See Selected Bibliography #5.

Makara, Mary Lelia, tr. *The Hsiao Ching*. New York: St. John's University Press, 1961.

Mass, Jeffrey P. *the Development of Kamakura Rule, 1180–1250*. Stanford University Press, 1979.

Matsunaga, Alicia. *the Buddhist Philosophy of Assimilation: The Historical Development of the Honji-Suijaku Theory*. Tokyo and Rutland, Vt.: Charles E. Tuttle, 1969. *Monumenta Nipponica* Monograph.

Matsunaga, Daigan and Alicia. *Foundation of Japanese Buddhism, Vol. I: The Aristocratic Age*. Los Angeles/Tokyo: Buddhist Books International, 1974.

———. *Foundation of Japanese Buddhism, Vol. 2: The Mass Movement* (Kamakura and Muromachi Periods). Los Angeles/Tokyo: Buddhist Books International, 1976.

Matsushita Daizaburō and Watanabe Fumio. *Kokka taikan*. Tokyo: Kyōbunsha, 1903.

Matsushita Daizaburō. *Zoku kokka taikan*. Tokyo: Kigensha, 1925–26.

McCullough, Helen C. *Yoshitsune: A Fifteenth-Century Japanese Chronicle*. Stanford: Stanford University Press, 1966.

McCullough, William. "The *Azuma kagami* Account of the Shōkyū War," *Monumenta Nipponica* XXIII:1–2 (1968).

———. "*Shōkyūki*: An Account of the Shōkyū War of 1221," *Monumenta Nipponica* XIX:1–2 (1964); 3–4 (1964).

McCullough, William H. and Helen Craig. *A Tale of Flowering For-*

tunes: Annals of Japanese Aristocratic Life in the Heian Period. 2 vols. Stanford: Stanford University Press, 1980.

McKinnon, Richard N. *Selected Plays of Kyōgen*. Tokyo: Uniprint, Inc., 1968. Pp. 51-68 is a translation of *Busu* ("Sweet Poison").

Miki Sumito, "Mujū to Tōfukuji," *Bukkyō bungaku kenkyū* VI. Kyoto: Hōzōkan, 1968.

Mills, D. E. *A Collection of Tales from Uji: A Study and Translation of Uji Shūi Monogatari*. Cambridge: Cambridge University Press, 1970. Professor Mills' introduction includes a survey of the *setsuwa* genre, with references to *Shasekishū* and *Zōtanshū*, pp. 16-17.

————. "*Soga Monogatari, Shintōshū* and the Taketori Legend," *Monumenta Nipponica* XXX:1 (Spring 1975), pp. 37-68.

Miner, Earl. *Japanese Linked Poetry*. Princeton: Princeton University Press, 1979.

————. *Japanese Poetic Diaries*. Berkeley and Los Angeles: University of California Press, 1969.

————. *An Introduction to Japanese Court Poetry*. Stanford: Stanford University Press, 1968.

Minobe Shigekatsu. *Kankyō no tomo*. Tokyo: Miyai Shoten, 1974.

Miyasaka Yūshō, ed. *Kana hōgoshū*, Volume 83 of eds. Takagi Ichinosuke, et al., *Nihon koten bungaku taikei*. Tokyo: Iwanami Shoten, 1964.

Mori Hisashi. *Shōzō chōkoku*. Nihon no bijutsu 10. Tokyo: Shibundō, 1967.

Moriyamashi shi. See Aichi-ken.

Morrell, Robert E. "The Buddhist Poetry in the *Goshūishū*," *Monumenta Nipponica* XXVIII: 1 (Spring 1973), pp. 87-100.

Early Kamakura Buddhism: A Minority Report (in press).

————. "Jōkei and the Kōfukuji Petition," *Japanese Journal of Religious Studies* 10: 1 (Spring 1983), pp. 6-38.

————. "Kamakura Accounts of Myōe Shōnin as Popular Religious Hero," *Japanese Journal of Religious Studies* 9:2-3 (June-September 1982), pp. 171-198.

————. "Mirror for Women: Mujū Ichien's *Tsuma Kagami*," *Monumenta Nipponica* XXXV: 1 (Spring 1980), pp. 45-75.

————. Mujū Ichien's Shintō-Buddhist Syncretism: *Shasekishu* Book 1," *Monumenta Nipponica* XXVIII: 4 (Winter 1973), pp. 447-88.

————. "Tales from the Collection of Sand and Pebbles," *Literature East and West* XIV: 2 (1970), pp. 251-63.

————. "Passage to India Denied: Zeami's *Kasuga Ryūjin*," *Monumenta Nipponica* XXXVII: 2 (Summer 1982), pp. 179-200.

————. "Representative Translations and Summaries from the Shasekishū with Commentary and Critical Introduction," Ph.D. dissertation, Stanford University, 1968.

————. "Shingon's Kakukai on the Immanence of the Pure Land," *Japanese Journal of Religious Studies* 11:2-3 (June-September 1984), pp. 195-220.

Morris, Ivan, tr. *Modern Japanese Stories: An Anthology.* Tokyo and Rutland, Vt.: Charles E. Tuttle, 1962.

————. *The Nobility of Failure: Tragic Heroes in the History of Japan.* New York: Holt, Rinehart and Winston, 1975.

Mosher, Gouverneur. *Kyoto: A Contemplative Guide.* Rutland, Vt. and Tokyo: Charles E. Tuttle, 1980.

Murti, T. R. V. *The Central Philosophy of Buddhism: A Study of the Mādhyamika System.* London: Allen and Unwin, 1955.

Nagai Yoshimori. *Nihon bukkyō bungaku.* Tokyo: Hanawa Shobō, 1963. A lengthy bibliography of articles on Buddhist-influenced literature, 229-280, includes a page and a half on Mujū and his writings.

Nakamura Hajime. *Ways of Thinking of Eastern Peoples: India-China-Tibet-Japan.* Honolulu: East-West Center, 1964.

Nakamura, Kyoto Motomochi. *Miraculous Stories from the Japanese Buddhist Tradition: The Nihon ryōiki of the Monk Kyōkai.* Cambridge: Harvard University Press, 1973. Harvard-Yenching Monograph 20.

Nihon no bunka chiri 14: Hiroshima, Yamaguchi, Shimane. Tokyo: Kōdansha, 1968.

Nishida Masayoshi. *Bukkyō to bungaku: Chūsei nihon no shisō to koten.* Tokyo: Ōfūsha, 1967. Chapter 7 is a lengthy essay on Mujū.

Nishikawa Kōtarō, ed. *Chinzō chōkoku* (Sculptures of Zen Priests), vol. 123 in the magazine series, *Nihon no bijutsu* (Arts of Japan). Tokyo: Shibundō, 1976. Pages 40-41 and Plate 8 (color). The Chōboji statue of Mujū (Figure 1) without his hat.

Nishikawa Shinji. *Kamakura chōkoku.* Nihon no bijutsu 40. Tokyo: Shibundō, 1969.

Nishio Kōichi and Minobe Shigekatsu, eds. *Konsenshū* (Collection of Golden Extracts. Tokyo: Koten Bunko, 1973. Koten Bunko series vol. 308.

Modern printing, with explanatory appendix of a *Shasekishū*-related manuscript discovered only a few decades ago at Jingū Bunko in Kuradayama, a library based on collections held by the Ise Shrine. The title suggests a further refinement of Mujū's "extracting gold and jewels from the sand pebbles of everyday life," although the selection includes seven stories and 112 *waka* not found in *Shasekishū.* The manuscript appears to be a late Muromachi copy of a 1470 (Bummei 2) original, with Book 3 of four books missing, and is not to be confused with the *Shasekishū Nukigaki* (Extracts from Sand and Pebbles), dated 1602 and also held by Jingū Bunko. The editors have included a table comparing the contents of this work with the Bonshun and Yonezawa manuscripts and the Jōkyō printed edition of *Shasekishū.* (See Selected Bibliography, Part A.)

Nomura Hachirō. *Kinko jidai setsuwa bungakuron.* Tokyo: Meiji Shōin, 1935.

————. *Zōho kamakura jidai bungaku shinron.* Tokyo: Meiji Shōin, 1942.

Oda Tokunō. *Bukkyō daijiten.* Tokyo: Ōkura Shoten, 1927.

Okami Masao and Akamatsu Toshihide, eds. *Gukanshō*, Volume 85 of eds. Takagi Ichinosuke, et al., *Nihon Koten bungaku taikei.* Tokyo: Iwanami Shoten, 1967.

Owari Manzai tazune tazunete (In Search of Owari Manzai), Vol. 49 and 53 of the series, *Bunkazai sōsho.* Nagoya: Nagoyashi Kyōiku Iinkai, 1970, 1971.

Owari shi. See Fukada.

Owari meisho zue (Illustrated Gazeteer of Owari Province), Latter Series (1880), in Harada Miki, *Dainihon meisho zue* (Illustrated Gazeteers of Japan's Famous Sites). Tokyo: Dai Nihon Meishozue Kankōkai, 1918–22. Vol. 8.

Pandey, Rajyashree. "Paradox in the Thought of Mujū Ichien," M.A. thesis, Washington University (St. Louis), 1980.

Petzold, Bruno. *Buddhist Prophet Nichiren—a Lotus in the Sun.* Shotaro Iida and Wendy Simmonds, eds. Tokyo: Hokke Jānaru, 1978.

Philippi, Donald L., tr. *Kojiki.* Princeton: Princeton University Press, 1968.

Plutschow Herbert and Fukuda Hideichi. *Four Japanese Travel Diaries of the Middle Ages.* Ithaca: Cornell China-Japan Program, 1981. Cornell University East Asia Papers Number 25.

Plutschow, Herbert Eugene. "Is Poetry a Sin?—*Honjisuijaku* and Buddhism versus Poetry," *Oriens Extremus* 25:2 (1978), pp. 206–218.

Ponsonby-Fane, R.A.B. *Studies in Shintō and Shrines.* Kyoto: Pomsonby Memorial Society, 1942; printed by Kenkyūsha in Tokyo.

Radhakrishnan, Sarvepalli and Moore, Charles A. *A Source Book of Indian Philosophy.* Princeton: Princeton University Press, 1957.

Ramanan, K. Venkata. *Nāgārjuna's Philosophy as Presented in the Mahā-Prajñāpāramitā-Śāstra.* Tokyo and Rutland, Vt.: Charles E. Tuttle, 1966.

Rambach, Pierre. *The Secret Message of Tantric Buddhism.* New York: Skira/Rizzoli, 1979.

Rasmus, Rebecca, tr. "The Sayings of Myōe Shōnin of Togano-o," *The Eastern Buddhist, New Series* 15:1 (Spring 1982), pp. 89–105.

Reischauer, Edwin O. and Yamagiwa, Joseph K. *Translations from Early Japanese Literature.* Cambridge: Harvard University Press, 1951.

Rhodes, Robert F., tr. "Saichō's *Mappō Tōmyōki*: The Candle of the Latter Dharma," *The Eastern Buddhist, New Series* 13:1 (Spring 1980), pp. 79–103.

Rosenfield, John M., and Cranston, F. E. and E. A. *The Courtly Tradition in Japanese Art and Literature: Selections from the Hofer and Hyde Collections.* Cambridge: Fogg Art Museum, 1973.

Rotermund, Hartmut O. *Collection de sable et de pierres: Shasekishū par Ichien Mujū*. Paris: Gallimard, 1979. A translation of the major part of *Shasekishū* (NKBT edition, see Selected Bibliography) with extensive introduction and notes. Reviewed by R. E. Morrell in *Monumenta Nipponica* XXXVI:2 (Summer, 1981), pp. 201-202.

————. "La conception des kami japonais à l'époque de Kamakura — Notes sur le premier chapitre du Shasekishū," *Revue de l'Histoire des Religions*, CLXXXII, 1 (July 1972), pp. 3-28.

————. "Materiaux ayant trait à la predication bouddhique au 13e siecle. Un extrait du Shasekishū de Mujū," *Cahiere D'Etudes et de Documents sur les Religions du Japon II* (1980), pp. 89-118.

Ruch, Barbara Ann. *Otogi Bunko and Short Stories of the Muromachi Period*. Ph.D. dissertation, Columbia University, 1965.

Saeki Umetomo, ed. *Kokinwakashū*. Tokyo: Iwanami Shoten, 1958. *NKBT* 8.

Sakamoto Yukio and Iwamoto Yutaka, eds. *Hokkekyō (jō, chū, ge)*. Tokyo: Iwanami Shoten, 1962-67. Iwanami Bunko edition, 3 volumes.

San Shih Buddhist Institute, ed. *The Life of Hsuan-Tsang*. Peking: The Chinese Buddhist Association, 1959.

Sawa Takaaki. *Art in Japanese Esoteric Buddhism*. Tr. by Richard L. Gage. New York/Tokyo: Weatherhill/Heibonsha, 1976.

Seidensticker, Edward, tr. *The Tale of Genji*. New York: Alfred A. Knopf, 1976. 2 volumes.

Seki Keigo. *Nihon mukashibanashi shūsei*, Vol. 1. Tokyo: Kadokawa Shoten, 1950.

Sekiguchi Shindai, ed. *Maka shikan (jō, ge)*. Tokyo: Iwanami Shoten, 1966. Iwanami Bunko edition, 2 volumes.

Senzaki, Nyogen and Reps, Paul. *101 Zen Stories*. London: Rider and Co., 1939. Reprinted in Reps, Paul, comp. *Zen Flesh, Zen Bones: A Collection of Zen and Pre-Zen Writings*. Tokyo and Rutland, Vt.: Charles Tuttle, 1957. *Sand and Pebbles* stories 24, 28, 46, 49 and 71.

Shidehara Michitarō and Whitehouse, Wilfrid, "Seami's Sixteen Treatises," *Monumenta Nipponica* IV:2 (1941), V:2 (1942). Translation of only *Kadensho (Fūshi Kaden*, "The Book of the Transmission of the Flower").

Shinoda, Minoru. *The Founding of the Kamakura Shogunate, 1180-1185*. New York: Columbia University Press, 1960.

Shimizu Isamu, "Takaoka, Priest Imperial Prince Shinnyo, with a Translation of the *Zuda shinnō nittō ryakki*," *The Transactions of the Asiatic Society of Japan*, Third Series, Vol. 5 (December 1957), pp. 1-35.

Shimizu Yūshō. "Aguiryū no shōdōsho ni tsuite," *Bukkyō bungaku kenkyū* X. Kyoto: Hōzōkan, 1971, pp. 107-128.

Soothill, William E. and Hodous, Lewis. *A Dictionary of Chinese Buddhist Terms*. London: Kegan Paul, Trench, Trubner & Co., 1937.

Stcherbatsky, Theodore. *The Conception of Buddhist Nirvana.* The Hague: Mouton, 1965.

Suzuki, Daisetz Teitaro. *Essays in Zen Buddhism (Third Series).* Kyoto: The Eastern Buddhist Society, 1934.

———. *Manual of Zen Buddhism.* Kyoto: The Eastern Buddhist Society, 1935.

———. *The Training of The Zen Buddhist Monk.* Kyoto: the Eastern Buddhist Society, 1934.

Tahara, Mildred M., tr. *Tales of Yamato: A Tenth-Century Poem-Tale.* Honolulu: The University Press of Hawaii, 1980.

Tainin (1705-1786). *Mujū kokushi dōshakukō* (Religious Traces of National Teacher Mujū). Published 1770.

Takagi Masakazu, ed. *Haku Kyoi (ge)*, Vol. 13 in the series *Chūgoku shijin senshū.* Tokyo: Iwanami Shoten, 1968.

Takakusu Junichirō. *The Essentials of Buddhist Philosophy.* Honolulu: Office Supply Co., 1956.

Takakusu Junjirō et al., eds. *Taishō shinshū daizōkyō.* Tokyo: Taishō Shinshū Daizōkyō Kankōkai, 1962; reprint of 1924-32 edition. 100 volumes. Numbering through vol. 55 in Paul Demieville, et al., eds. *Hōbōgirin: Fascicule Annexe.* Tokyo: Maison Franco-Japonaise, 1931.

Teruoka Yasutaka and Kawashima Tsuyu, eds. *Busonshū Issashū*, Volume 58 of eds. Takagi Ichinosuke, et al., *Nihon koten bungaku taikei.* Tokyo: Iwanami Shoten, 1959.

Tōfukuji Kaizan Shōichi Kokushi nempu (Chronological Record of Shōichi Kokushi, Founder of Tōfukuji Temple), collected in Bussho Kankōkai, ed. *Dainihon bukkyō zensho* (Complete Collection of Japanese Buddhism). Tokyo: Kōdansha, 1972 reprint. Volume 73, p. 151.

Tsuchihashi, Paul Yachita. *Japanese Chronological Tables from 601 to 1872 A.D.* Tokyo: Sophia University Press, 1952.

Tsuji Zennosuke. *Nihon bukkyōshi III: Chūseihen 2.* Tokyo: Iwanami Shoten, 1949; reprint 1970.

Tsukudo Reikan. *Chūsei geibun no kenkyū.* Tokyo: Yūseido, 1966.

Tsunoda, Ryūsaku, Wm Theodore deBary, and Donald Keene, comps. *Sources of Japanese Tradition 1.* New York: Columbia University Press, 1964.

Tsutsumi, Kunihiko. "Weird Tales from Tokugawa Times: Connections with Buddhist Fable," *Undercurrent: The Japan Scene, Past and Present.* No. 1 (March 1983), pp. 31-41.

Ueda Akinari (1734-1809). *Ugetsu Monogatari: Tales of Moonlight and Rain.* Translated and edited by Leon M. Zolbrod. Tokyo: Charles E. Tuttle, 1977.

Uemura Kankō, ed. *Gozan bungaku zenshū.* See Gidō.

Ury, Marian. *Tales of Times Now Past: Sixty-Two Stories from a Medieval*

Japanese Collection. Berkeley: University of California Press, 1979.

Varley, H. Paul. *Imperial Restoration in Medieval Japan.* New York: Columbia University Press, 1971.

Wajima Yoshio. *Eizon Nishō.* Tokyo: Yoshikawa Kōbunkan, 1959. Jimbutsu sōsho series, v. 30.

Waley, Arthur. *The Life and Times of Po Chü-i.* New York: Macmillan, 1949.

———. *The Real Tripitaka and Other Pieces.* London: George Allen and Unwin, 1952.

———. *The Way and Its Power: A Study of the Tao Te Ching and Its Place in Chinese Thought.* New York: Grove Press, 1958.

Warren, Henry Clarke. *Buddhism in Translations.* Cambridge: Harvard University Press, 1909.

Watanabe Tsunaya. "Shasekishū shohon no oboegaki," *Kokugo to kokubungaku* XVIII:10 (1941). A study of the manuscripts and early printed editions of the *Shasekishū.* Much, but not all, of this material has been revised and incorporated into the introduction of the NKBT *Shasekishū.*

Watson, Burton, tr. *The Complete Works of Chuang Tzu.* New York: Columbia University Press, 1968.

———. *Hsün Tzu: Basic Writings.* New York and London: Columbia University Press, 1963.

Watters, Thomas. *On Yuan Chwang's Travels in India.* London: Royal Asiatic Society, 1904-1904, 2 vols.; reprinted in one volume, 1961.

Wayman, Alex. "Conze on Buddhism and European Parallels," *Philosophy East and West* XIII, No. 3 (Jan. 1964), pp. 361-64.

Welbon, Guy Richard. *The Buddhist Nirvāṇa and Its Western Interpreters.* Chicago and London: University of Chicago Press, 1968.

Yamada Ryūjō, "Mappō shisō ni tsuite," *Indogaku bukkyōgaku kenkyū* IV:2 (March 1956).

Yamada Shōzen. "Chūsei kōki ni okeru waka soku darani no shissen," *Indogaku bukkyōgaku kenkyū* XVI:1 (December 1967), pp. 290-292.

Yamagishi Tokuhei, ed. *Hachidaishūshō* I. Tokyo: Yūseidō, 1968.

Yamamoto, Kōshō, tr. *The Kyogyoshinsho or The 'Teaching, Practice, Faith, and Attainment'.* Tokyo: Karinbunko, 1958.

Yamazaki Hiroshi and Kasahara Kazuo. *Bukkyōshi nempyō.* Kyoto: Hōzōkan, 1979.

Nihonshi nempyō. Rekishigaku Kenkyūkai, ed. Tokyo: Iwanami Shoten, 1966.

Yampolsky, Philip B., tr. *The Platform Sutra of the Sixth Patriarch.* New York: Columbia University Press, 1967.

Yanagita Kunio. *Japanese Folk Tales: A Revised Selection*, tr. Fanny Hagin Mayer. Tokyo: Tokyo News Service, 1966.

———. *Mukashibanashi to bungaku.* Tokyo: Hakuhōsha, 1971.

Yang Chia-lo, ed. *Pai hsiang shan shih chi*, Vol. 3 in the series Chung *Kuo wen hsüeh ming chu.* Taipei, 1968.

Yokoi Yoshisuke and Yamamoto Hitoshi, eds. *Minomushi Sanjin enikki: Tōkaihen.* Nagoya: "Minomushi Sanjin Enikki" Hozonkai, 1980.

Yuasa, Nobuyuki, tra. *The Year of My Life: A Translation of Issa's Oraga Haru.* Berkeley: University of California Press, 1972 (Second edition).

Index

Numbers in bold type indicate major items.

abbreviations, xvii
abhidharma (commentaries), 118, 120
Abhidharma kośa. See *Kusharon.*
Abutsu, nun, xxi, 30, 35
accommodation. See Skillful Means
   (*hōben*).
Agui school, 65
Ai, Duke, 132
Aikuōkyō (Sutra of King Aśoka), n331
Aizen Myō-ō, 211
Ajātasatru (Ajase-ō), 245
Akazome Emon (ca. 957–ca. 1041), 166
akusō ("bad monks"). See *sōhei.*
A-ji meditation, 164, 179, n254
Akinaga. See Yamada family.
Amaterasu (Sun goddess), 35, 73,
   285, n127
ami (nets)
Amida (see also Muryōju), xix, 7, 19,
   23, 64, 74, 98, 100, 105, 117, 142
   143, 182, 220, 249; identity with
   Jizō 110
Amidabutsu daishiyuikyō (Sutra of
   Great Recollection on Amida
   Buddha), n367
Amida no daiju (Great Spell of Amida),
   or *Muryōju nyorai kompon darani,*
   n322
Aida Recollection Sutra. See
   Midashuikyō.
Amidakyō (Amida Sutra), 192, 212
Amida's Welcome Service (*mukaekō*),
   66, 188, **253**
Amoghavajra (Fukū, 705–774), 103
Analects (*Lun-yü*), 26, 126, n56
analogy,method of, 57
Ānanda (Anan), 128, 141, 217
Anātman. See *muga.*
Aniruddha (Zenshi Bosatsu), 128

ango (retreat), 130
animals, 203, 204, 205, 206, 207, 216,
   232, 240
Anrakuji, 171
Anyō, nun (ca. 947–1010), 111
ant and tick scholars, 158–59
apposite. See *warinashi.*
Aragaki, 74
areku (harsh stanzas), 175, n265
Ariwara Motokata (883–953), 161
arhat, 332
arubekiyō wa ("that which is appropriate"), 133, n224
Asahi, Ajari of, 198, 199
Asoka, King (Aiku Daiō, ca. 269–ca.
   232), 228
aspiration for enlightenment. See
   hotsubodaishin.
Aspiration to Enlightenment. See
   Bodaishinron.
asura, 58
ateji, 46
Atsuta Deity, 29, 49. See also Kitayū.
Atsuta Shrine, 25, **35**, 36, 46, 67
   (Fig. 1), 83, 84, 105, 107, 221,
   285 n71.
attachment, dangers of, 146, 147, 148,
   149, 150, 151, 152, 157, 163, 171,
   200, 209, 212, 216, 217, 227, 230,
   255, **332**
Autograph History of the Tennōji.
   See *Tennōji no goshuin engi.*
Awakening of Faith. See *Kishinron.*
"Awaken the mind without fixing it
   anywhere" (Diamond Sutra), 20
azaleas, 235
Azuma kagami (Mirror of the East),
   xxi, 46

Back and Forth to the Kantō Region.
See *Kantō ōgenki.*
Bandō ("East of the Slope"), 182,
214, 219, 220, n283
Bashō, Matsuo (1664-1694), 14, 20
"bat-monks," 141
Batō Kannon, 108, n198
bees, 176
beggar-monk. See *kotsujiki hōshi.*
begging, 232, 263
bekkyō (Special Teaching), 157
Ben'a, 140
benevolence (*jin*), 154
Ben'en. See Enni.
Ben no Ajari, 172
Benevolent Kings Sutra. See *Ninnōkyō.*
berry, Nawashiro, 188
Bhāvaviveka (Shōben, ca. 490-570),
140
Bimbisāra (Bashara-ō), 245
Biographical Sketch of Mujū Kokushi.
See *Ryakuengi.*
*Biographies of Eminent Japanese
Priests.* See *Honchō kōsōden.*
Biographies of Filial Sons. See
Hsiao Tzu Ch'uan.
"Bird-nest monk," 156
birth-and-death. See *shōji.*
Bishamon, 174, n270
boats, 227
Bodai, Mount, 21, 29, 217
bodaishin, **331**
Bodaishin bekki. See *Chifu no ketsu.*
Bodaishinron (Aspiration to Enlighten-
ment), n49
Bodhidharma (d. 528), 125, 180
bodhisattva (*bosatsu*), 23, 25, 58, 60,
61, 80, 93, 111, 118, 125, 130,
136, 154, 186, 261 **331**
Bodhisattva Vows (*bosatsukai*), 32, 130,
249, n68
Bodhisena (704-760), 180
Body-lamp Ritual. See *shintō.*
Bommō fusatsu, 32
Bommōkyō (Net of Brahma Sutra),
31, 74, 97, 104, 141, 152, 158,
216, 235, 240, **n65**, n68
Bonshun (1553-1632), xxii, 257
bosatsu. See *bodhisattva.*
Brahmajala Sutra. See *Bommōkyō.*

bridge, 185
Buddha-Head Spell. See *Daibutchō
darani.*
bukkyo setsuwa, 3, 6. See also
setsuwa.
bugaku, 186
Burachi ("turnip stalk"), 222
burdock (*gobō*), 186
Busu, 85, 222, n323
Butchō [*sonshō darani*] *kyō* (Buddha
Head Sutra), 194, n311
Butsuzōkyō (Buddha Treasury Sutra),
141, 194, 249
butterfly, Chuang Chou as, 95, 96
Byōdōin, 191, 230, n333

Casual Digressions. See *Zōtanshū;*
abbreviations (CD).
CD. See *Zōtanshū.*
Cessation and Insight. See *Maka
shikan.*
chaconne, 2
Ch'an Amidism, 24. See also Zen.
Chan-jan. See Ching-ch'i. Chan-jan.
Ch'ao Fu (Sōfu), 247
Ch'eng-kuan (Chōkan, 737-838), n153
chi (delusion), 337
chie (wisdom), 128, 152, 154, 257,
332
Chieh and Chou, 132
Chien-chen. See Ganjin.
Chifu no ketsu (The Mystery of Jizō
and Fudō), 111, n202
chigo (pages), 130, 167, 171, 200,
222
Chih-i, (Chigi, 538-597), 79, 103,
139, 141, 142, 152, 156, 157, 187,
190, 256, 258, n18
Chih-yen (Chigon, 602-668), 123
Chikō, 22, 61
children of monks, 143, 144
Chin Pei Lun (Konbeiron; Diamond
Stick), 79, 267, n373
Ching-ch'i Chan-jan (Keikei Tannen,
711-782), 79, 141, 142, 267, n373
Chishō. See Enchin.
Chita peninsula, 43
Chi Ts'ang (Kichizō, 643-712), 190,
260
Chiumbō, 218

Chōboji, 6, 21, 24, 30, 31, 32, 35 ff., 50, 67, 270-71, 281 (photo), 283 ff.; current address 37

Chōgen (Shunjō, 1121-1206), 22, 65, 147, 150, 237, n37, n290, n340

Chōken (1126-1203), 248

Chōrakuji (in Serada), 17, 264, 265, n25

Chronicles of Japan. See Nihon shoki.

Chronological Record of Shōichi Kokushi, Founder of Tofukuji. See Tōfukuji kaizan Shōichi Kokushi nempu.

Chuang Tzu, 28, 95, 96, 97, 161, n55, n362

chūdo, 142, 334

Chūdōbō (Taihōbō. 1219-1291), 261

Chūgun, 105

chūin (memorial period), 202

Chūkan (Shōshimbō), 217

Chūrembō, 145

chūtai, 336

Chu Tao-sheng (ca. 360-434), 144

Ciñcā, 46

Citta (Shitta Koji), 128

clam, 120

Classic of Documents. See Shu Ching.

Collected Sayings on Zen Principles. See Zengenshosenshū.

Collected Tales of Pious Resolution. See Hosshinshū.

Collection of Ancient and Modern Times. See Kokinshū.

Collection of Ancient and Modern Times Continued. See Shokukokinshū.

Collection of Casual Digressions. See Zōtanshū; abbreviation, CD.

Collection of Gleanings. See Shūishū.

Collection of Gleanings Continued. See Shokushuishū.

Collection of Golden Extracts. See Konsenshū.

Collection of Golden Leaves. See Kin'yōshū.

Collection of Jeweled Leaves. See Gyokuyōshū.

Collection of Passages. See Senjakushū.

Collection of Sacred Assets. See Shōzaishū.

Collection of Sand and Pebbles. See Shasekishū; abbreviation, S&P.

Collection of Tales from Uji. See Ujishūi monogatari.

Collection of a Thousand Years. See Senzaishū.

Collection of Verbal Flowers. See Shikashū.

Collection of Verbal Flowers Continued. See Shokushikashū.

Commentary on the Great Sun Sutra. See Dainichikyō gishaku, -sho.

Commentary on the Great Wisdom Sutra. See Daichidoron.

Commentary on the Treasury of Analyses of the Law. See Kusharon jujo.

Comments on Discrimination and Virtuous Behavior. See Fumbetsu kudokuron.

compassion. See jihi (vs. wisdom, q.v.).

Compassion Flower Sutra. See Hikekyo.

Completion of Mere Ideation. See Jōyuishikiron.

Completion of Truth. See Jōjitsuron.

Confucianism, 28, 45, 64, 93, 99, 131, 132

Confucius (551-479 B.C.), 75, 132, 135, 156

criticism of other's beliefs. See dogmatism.

"crow-chicken", 129

Cūdapanthaka (Shurihantoku), 104, 264

Cunda (Junda), 155, 257

Daianji (temple), 21

Daibongyō (Perfection of Wisdom in 25,000 Lines), 141

Daibutchō darani (Buddha-Head Spell), 181, n278

Daichidoron (Commentary on the Great Wisdom Sutra), 24, 104, 112, 141, 150, 159, 164, 182, 190, 216, 242, 258, 265, n43, n300, n372

Daiembō (Ryōin, 1212-1291), 214, 248, 256

Daien Kokushi (Mujū), xxii, 55, 283; see also Mujū.

Daigo, Emperor (885-930), 229

Daihannyaharamittakyō (Great Wisdom Sutra), 86, 120, 207, 213, 214, n168

Daihatsunehangyō (Nirvana Sutra), 7, 120, 133, 144, 152, 165, 215, n7, n58, n122, n172, n313

Daihikyō (Sutra of Great Compassion), 195

Daijikkyō (Great Collection of Sutras), 120, 195, n1

daijō, 331. See also Mahāyāna.

Daijōdōshōkyō (The Immediate Insight of the Mahāyāna), n1

daijuku. See vicarious suffering.

daimoku, xxi

Dainichikyō (Great Sun Sutra), 164, n255

Dainichikyō gishaku, or -sho (Commentary on the Great Sun Sūtra), 25, 164, 259, n47

Dainichi Nyorai. See Mahāvairocana.

Daisan no gotan, n167

Daishimbō, 167

Dandaloka, Mount, 124

darani, 332

Darani jikkyō (Sutra of Collected Dhāranīs), n367

death, 228, 229, 261 ff.

Decline of the Law. See mappō.

Deed of Transfer. See Yuzarijō.

deer-king, 154

Dengyō Daishi. See Saichō.

Devadatta (Chōdatsu), 112, 154, 245, 265

Dhāranī (darani), 8, 60, 62, 63, 66, 118, 164, 165, 214, 332

Dharmamitra (Ren Oshō, 356-442), 234

Dharmapada. See Hokkukyō and Hokkuhiyukyō.

Dharmapala (Gohō), 259

Dialogue in a Dream. See Muchū mondō.

Diamond Head Sutra. See Kongōchōgyō.

Diamond Stick. See Chin Pei Lun.

Diamond Sutra. See Kongōkyō.

Diary of the Waning Moon. See Isayoi nikki.

Discourse on Doctrine in Phonetic Writing by Zen Master Tetsugen. See Tetsugen zenji kanahōgo.

Dīpamkara Buddha (Jōkō), 75, 125, n143

Disciplinary (Ritsu) sect, 9, 17, 45

divorce, 197, 198, 205

Dōe, 51

Dōen (Akinaga's son), 37, 46, 52, Appendix D; cf. Rōen.

Dōen (Shigetsugu), Appendix D.

Dōgen Kigen (1200-1253), xx, xxi, 7, 18, 19, 23, 27, Appendix B.

dogmatism, 6-7, 18-19, 54, 99, 100, 139, 142, 181, 190, 260

Dōgyō, 32. See Mujū.

dogs, 50, 97, 203

Dōin, 163

Dōjo (1196-1249), 192, 252

Dōkei, 178

Dōkyō, (d. 772), 9

Dōkyō (Eizon's disciple), 30

Dōshakukō (Religious Traces), xvii, xxii, 52, 285, n380

dōshin (religious understanding), 244

Dragon girl (Lotus Sūtra 12), 136

Drink Tea and Prolong Life. See Kissa yōjōki

duck, Mandarin, 206

ears, 120, 212

Echibo, 248

eggplant, 275

Eichō (1014-1095), 87, 264

Eichō (Shakuembō, d. 1247), 17, 23, 26, 189, 264, Appendix B

Eiheiji, xxi, 27

Eisai (1141-1215), ix, xx, 7, 15, 22, 23, 26, 30, 111, 230, 263

Eizon (Shiembō, 1201-1290), xxi, 2, 9, 17, 21, 29, 30, 32, 65, 108, 245, n13, n68, n222, n308

Eliot, T.S., 57, n237

Emma (Yama), 79, 110, 114

Empōdentōroku (Empō Era's Record of the Transmission of the Lamp), 284, n91

Empō Era's Record of the Transmission of the Lamp. See *Empōdentō-roku*.
Empty Flower Collection. See *Kūgeshū*.
Emptiness, eighteen kinds of, 150. See also *Kū*.
en (causality), 125
Enchin (Chisho Daishi, 814–891), 22, 262, n174
endon (perfect and sudden) teaching, 152
endon (meditation), 22, 152, 263
engaku. See *pratyekabuddha*.
Engakukyō (Sutra of Perfect Enlightenment), 17, 96, 139, 260, n24
engi, 334
enjō (ultimate existence), 125
Enjōbo, 212
Enkō Kyōōbō, 16, 20, 158
enkyō (Perfect Teaching), 157
Enni Ben'en (Shōichi, 1202–1280), ix, xx, 7, 9, 20, **22**, 23, 24, 25, 26, 27, 40, 52, 135, 136, **243**; death, 26, **265**, n39.
Ennin (Jikaku Daishi, 794–864), 22, 104, 262, n45, n47
Ennin Shōnin (12th cen.), 163
Ennyadatta. See Yajñadattā.
En no Gyōja (634–?), 80, n157, n159
Enryakuji, xix, 6, 86, 87, 88, 90, 143. See also Mount Hiei.
epilepsy (*kutsuchi*), 121
Eshin. See Genshin.
Esoteric Disciplinary (Shingon Ritsu) sect, 2, 9, 17, 39
esotericism, **8**, 24, 59, 78, 79, 110, 117, 118, 164, 262, 332, n102. See also Shingon.
Essentials of Salvation. See *Ōjōyōshū*.
eta (dependent existence), 125
Evil Path. See Three Evil Destinies.
Explanation of Mahāyāna. See *Shakumakaenron*.
exemplum, 63
Exotericism (the Overt Teaching), vs. esotericism, q.v. 118, 332, 335
Explanatory Notes to the Lotus Sutra. See *Hokke no godaidai*.

Expounding-on-Birth-in-the-Pure Land. See *ōjōkō*.

Fa-hua hsüan-i (Hokke gengi; Profound Meaning of the Lotus), 20, 136, n33, n160
Fa-hua wen-chü (Hokke mongu; Words and Phrases of the Lotus), n18
"failed hero," n15, n71
faith, 110, 114, 116, 119, 277
farting, 187, 188, 222
fast, post-noon (*jōsai*), 17, **30**, 31, 40, 114, 130, 134
Fa-tsang (Hōzō, 643–712), 151
Fa-yen (Hōgen) school of Ch'an, 24
Fa-yüan chu-lin (Hōon jurin; Forest of Pearls in the Garden of the Law), n243
fences, shrine, n134
Feng-kan (Bukan, 8th cen.), 240
filial devotion, 145, 236, 237, 238, 239, n161
finger pointing at the moon, **8**, 60, 61
Fire World Spell. See *kakai no ju*.
fish-hook of desire, 130, 262
fishing, 89, 92, 239, n288
Five Aggregates. See *goshu*.
five commandments (*gokai*), 134
Five Constant virtues (of Confucianism), 132
Five Desires, 134, 228
Five Hundred Arhats, 104
Five Hundred Questions Sutra. See *Gohyaku monron*.
five mountains (*gosan*), 20, 22
Five-Pedestal Ceremony, 80, n152
Five Tones, 164, n253
five wisdoms (*gochi*), 74, 79
Forest of Pearls in the Garden of the Law. See *Fa-yuan chü-lin*.
four great elements, 182
"Four Heavenly Kings" (poets), 176
fox, 242
Fubokuwakashō, 261
Fudō Myō-ō, 64, 80, **116**
Fugen. See Samantabhadra.
Fuji, Mount, 173
Fujiwara family:
Akisuke (1090–1155), 168

Ietaka (1158-1237), 166, n271
Kanezane (1149-1207), 257, n344, n353, n361
Kintō (966-1041), 171
Kiyosuke (1104-1177), 166, n245
Michiie (1193-1252), 22, 242, 252
Michikane (961-995), 248
Michinori. See Shinzei.
Morozane (1042-1101), 168
Nagatō (fl. ca. 980), 171
Sadakuni (867-906), 229
Shunzei (1114-1204), 63, 178, n9
Takasuke (ca. 1252), n271
Takatō (949-1013(, 171
Takeko, 252
Tameie (1198-1275), 178
Teika (1162-1241), xx, 63
Toshitsuna (1028-1094), 168
Yasumasa (958-1036), 260-61
Yorimichi (992-1074), 191, 230, n333
Yoritsune (1218-1256), 127
Yoshiko (d. 985), 247
Fukan zazengi (General Teaching for Meditation, xx
Fukūkensakukyō (Full Rope of Salvation Sutra), 118
Fukuro Sōshi, 171, n245
Full Rope of Salvation Sutra. See Fukūkensakukyō.
fumbetsu (discriminative reasoning), 259
Fumbetsu kudokuron (Comments on Discrimination and Virtuous Behavior), n87
fusatsu (repentance meetings), 257, n67
fusego (drying cage), 217
futai (backsliding), 117
Fuzōfugengyō (Sutra of Neither Increase Nor Decrease), 80, n155

gaki, 336
Gangōji, 8, 9, 21
Gangyō (Kenjō, d. 1295), 112, n204
Ganjin (Chien-chen, 687-763), 9, 17, 130, 263, n67
Garland Sutra. See Kegonkyō.
Gautama. See Śākyamuni.
gedatsu (liberation), 58, 142

Gedatsubō. See Jōkei.
General Teaching for Meditation. See Fukan zazengi.
Genji monogatari (Tale of Genji), 5, 63, 267, 334
Genjirō (of Yamato), 170
Genjōbō, 221
Genkō shakusho (The Genkō Era's History of Buddhism), xxi, n158
Genshin (Eshin, 942-1017), xix, 7, 82, 111, 130, 161, 244, 254, 262, 266
Gidō Shūshin (1325-1388), 20, 285
Gleanings from Ancient Stories. See Kogoshūi.
go (game), 137
gō (karma), 332
goblins. See tengu.
gochi. See Five Wisdoms.
gods. See kami.
Gohyaku monron (Five Hundred Questions Sutra), 210, n312
Gokurakuji, 29, 172
gokuraku jōdo, 117, 118, 33, 336
goma (fire ceremony), 214
Gonara, Emperor (1496-1557), xxii, 55, 283
Gon'yūbō, 127ff.
Gosaga, Emperor (1220-1272, 168
gosan. See five mountains.
Gosenshū (Later Collection), 178
Goshirakawa, Emperor (1127-1192), 193
goshu (more commonly, goun; The Five Aggregates, skandhas), 133
Goshūishū (Later Collection of Gleanings), 182, n6
Gotakakura, Emperor (1179-1223), 192
Gotoba, Emperor (1180-1239), 5, 6, 36, 178, 192, 235, n223, n298
Gouda, Emperor (1267-1324), 25
Gōzanze, 80
grasshopper, 168
Great Spell of Amida. See Amida no daiju.
Great Cessation and Insight. See Maka shikan.
Great Collection of Sutras. See Daijikkyō.
Great Sun Buddha. See Mahāvairocana (Dainichi Nyorai).

Great Sun Sutra. See *Dainichikyō.*
Great Wisdom Sutra. See *Daihannya-haramittakyō.*
Greater Learning for Women. See *Onna daigaku.*
Gukanshō (Miscellany of Ignorant Views), xx, 2, n2
Gunavarman (Gunabatsuma, 367-431), 140
gussokukai, 232
gyakushu (pre-death rite), 191, 213
Gyōbu no Jō, 241
Gyōgi Bosatsu (668-749), 9, 180, **181**
Gyokuyōshū (Collection of Jeweled Leaves), xxi, n164
Gyōsen, 261
Gyōyū (1163-1241), n342, Appendix B.

Hachiman, 37, 39, 76, 182
haibutsu kishaku ("expel the Buddha and destroy the scriptures"), 68
ha'itsudai (lesser offense), 130
Hakusan Gogen, 99
Hakushi monjū (Po's Collected Writings), 216. See also Po Chü-i.
hana no moto (poets), 175, n266
Hanjusan Hymn, 118, 124, 142, 190, n188
Hannyadai ("Wisdom Heights"), 84, 85
Hanjusammaikyō, 336
Hannya shingyō (Heart of Wisdom Sutra), 77, 336
Han Shan (Kanzan), 216, 240
harai (major offense), 130
Hasedera reigenki (Miraculous Records of the Hasedera), n200
Hatakeyama Shigetada (1164-1205), 144
Hatta Tomoie, 127
hawks, 278
Heart of Wisdom Sutra. See *Hannya shingyō.*
hehirimushi (fart-bug), 188
Heigo, Lady, 169
Heike monogatari (Tale of the Heike), 13, n313
Heishi Biography of the Crown Prince (Heishi ga taishi den). See *Shōtoku Taishi denryaku* (Bio-

graphical Account of Prince Shōtoku).
henge ("false existence"), 124
Henjō (816-890), 51, 178, n92
Hideyoshi, 283
Hiei, Mount, 6, 7, 21, 41, 104, 108, 153, 167, 230, 244. See also Enryakuji.
Higan Choro. See Zoso Royo.
hihirihitsu, 225
Hikekyō (Compassion Flower Sutra), 120, 195
Hīnayāna (*shōjō;* "Lesser Vehicle") 118, 123, 130, 141, **331,** 335
Hirosawa school, 117, Appendix C
Hirata Atsutane (1776-1843), 285
Historical Records. See *Shih Chi.*
History of the Later Han Dynasty. See *Hou Han Shou.*
Hiyoshi (Hiei) Shrine, 86, 88, 90, 151, n170
Hizō Hōyaku (Precious Key to the Secret Treasury), n49, n301
hō (dharma), 332, 334
Hōben. See Skillful Means.
Hōchibō no Shōshin. See Shōshin (12th cen.)
hōgo (doctrinal tract), 3. See also *kana hōgo.*
hōjin, 333 **337**
Hōjo, Prince (1237-1284), 261
hōjō ("Law stick"), 104
Hōjō family:
  Regents, 5
  Tokimune (regent, 1268-1284), n204
  Tokiyori (regent 1246-1256), 6, 26, 37, 50, 237
  Yasutoki (regent, 1224-1242), 5, 125, 126, 127, n221
  Yoshitoki (regent, 1205-1224), 5, 107
hōki hongi, n126, n140
hokkai engi (interdependent origination), 9
Hokke gengi. See *Fa-hua hsüan-i.*
Hokke hakkō (Eight Expoundings of the Lotus Sutra), 7, 187, 248, n5
Hokkedō (Kamakura), 15
Hokke mongu. See *Fa-hua wen-chü.*

Hokke sammaikyō (Lotus Meditation Sutra), 141
Hokke no gokaidai (Explanatory Notes to the Lotus Sutra), 143
Hokkeshū (Lotus Sect), xxi
Hokkeyamadera, 251
Hokkuhiyukyō (Dharmapada), n371, cf., *Hokkukyō*.
Kohhukyō (Dharmapada), 104, 141
Hōkyōin darani (Jewel-box Spell), 54 118, 214, 256, n96, n314
Holy and Virtuous Spell. See *Sonshō darani*.
hommon, 333
Honcho kōsōden (Biographies of Eminent Japanese Priests), 284, n91
Hōnen (Genkū, 1133-1212), xix, 7, 18, 23, 118, 150
honesty, 233, 234, 235, 236
hongaku, 96, 260
hongan, 333
Hongan Sōjō. See Eisai.
honji suijaku (Original Ground/Manifest Trace) 59, 60, 63 74-75, 78, 86, 92, 163, 182, 333, 337, n103, n163, n170, n179
Hōonji, xxi, 16, 20, 21
Hōonkyō (Requital for Kindness Sūtra), n299
horses, 31, 206, 207, 218, 219, 240
Hōryūji (temple), 21
Hosshimbō, 20, 264
Hosshimbō (of Matsushima), 264
hosshin (Law Body; Dharmakāya), 78, 79, 80, 110, 333, 337
Hosshinshū (Collected Tales of Pious Resolution), 200
Hossō sect, 2, 8, 21, 22, 124, 139, 140, 259, 260, 262, n173
hossu, 55
hotsubodaishin (aspiration for enlightenment), 88, 117, 124, 130, 152, 163, 187, 244, 331, 333, n149, n210, n348
Hou Han Shu (History of the Later Han Dynasty), 126
Hōzō (Amida as Dharmākara), 143, 333
Hsi Shih, 197
Hsin-hsing (Shingyō, 540-549), n1

Hsiao Ching (Classic of Filial Piety), 132
Hsiao Tzu Ch'uan (Biographies of Filial Sons), 131, 132
Hsüan-tsang (Genjō, 600-664), 8, 123, 189, n218, n294
Hsün Tzu (Junshi, ca. 298-238), 85, n166, n228, n352
Huai Nan Tzu (Enanji), n317
Hsü Yu (Kyōyu), 247
Huang-lung, xix
Hui-kuo (Keika, 746-805), 118
Hui-neng (Enō, 638-713), xix, 27, 28 (Fig. 1), 103, n53
Hui-ssu (Eshi, 514-577), 190
Hui-yüan (Eon, 334-416), n347, 244 n347
Hundred Parable Sutra. See *Hyaku-yukyō*.
hunting, 92, 119, 154, 204
Hyakuyukyō (Hundred parable Sutra), 126, 141
Hyegwan (Ekan, 7th cen.), 8

Ichien. See Mujū.
Ichihijiri Kyōju, 83
Ichijō, Emperor (980-1011), 252
Ichijō-in (1199-1256), 251
I-ching (Gijō, 635-713), 258
Ietaka. See Fujiwara Ietaka.
igo, 337
Igyō songai, 144
Ihon sokushin jōbutsu-gi (Attaining Enlightenment in this Very Existence, Variant Text), n148
I-hsing (Ichigyō, 683-727), 116, 151, 156, 164, 265
Ikkyū kantō banashi (Stories of Ikkyū in the Eastern Regions), n323
Ikkyū shokoku monogatari (Ikkyū's Travels All Over), 65
imayō, 227
Imikotoba. See tabu words.
Imitation Law. See *zōbō*.
Inari, 90, 168, 276, 177
incense, 207, 208
India, 78, 84, 117, 123, 127, 155, 189, 212, 216, 262
Indra (Taishakuten), 242

ineffability, 333, 337, n365. See also *musō munen.*

in'en, 47

Ingō Ichiō (1209-1280), 265

inner realization/outer function (*naishō geyū*), 78, 79

Innen sōgokyō (Sutra of Cause and Effect Explained to Samgharakkhita), n363

intolerance. See dogmatism.

Ippen (1239-1289), xxi, n195

Iroha momben (Questions and Answers on the Syllabary), 285

Iroha uta (Syllabary verse), 285, n313

Isayoi nikki (Dairy of the Waning Moon), xxi, 35

Ise Shrine, 40, 60, 64, 73, 76, n134

Ishihijiri Kyōjū, 83

Issa (1763-1827), 66, n358

isshin denshin (transmission from mind to mind), 179, 180, 190

Itenshōgun, 195

Itsukushima Shrine, 76, 91

Iwamigata divers, 168

Iwashimizu Hachiman Shrine, 166

Iyobō, 218

Izayoi nikki. See *Isayoi nikki.*

Izumi Shakibu (b. 976), 168, 178, 182, 260

Jakujō, 104

Jakunen (fl. ca. 1170), 163

jamyō seppō (improper livelihood through preaching), 194

Japanese Writing in the Divine Script. See *Shinji hifumi den.*

Jayasena (Shōgun Ronji), 123, 124, 216, n218

Jen Tso (Jinza), 127

Jewel-box Spell. See *Hōkyōin darani.*

Ji sect (Ippen), xxi

Jichin. See Jien.

Jidō, 265

Jie (Ryōgen, 912-985), 80

Jien (Jichin, 1155-1225), xx, 2, 5, 179

jigyōja, 218

jihi (compassion; vs. wisdom), 154, 155, 332, 333

Jijū, 153

Jiju Ajari. Yamada Jirō, i.e., Akinaga. See Appendix D.

Jigen (Mujū's disciple), 51

jigoku, 336

Jikaku. See Ennin.

Jikishi ninshin, 125, 180

Jikkinshō (Tales to Illustrate Ten Maxims), xxi

Jiku no shu (Spell of Compassionate Help), 111, 116, 215, n316; also *jikuju.*

Jimyō. See *Shih-shuang Ch'u-yüan.*

jingūji, 105

jippōkai (Ten Stations), 58

jissō, 258

jiriki, 142, 244, 331, 333

Jissōbo (1001-1084), 214

Jitsudōbō, 20

Jitsugen (1176-1249), 248, 252, 258

Jīva (Giba), 112

Jizō, 62, 64, 85, 86, 101, 110, 111, 113, 116, 143, 210, 223

jō (meditation), 141, 142, 152

Jōben (1166-1224), 261

Jōdo (Pure Land) sect, xix, 118

Jōdobō, 243, 245

Jōdoron (Treatise on the Pure Land), 117, 244, n212

Jōdo sambukyō (Three Pure Land Sutras), n186

Jōen, 52

Jōgan (Jōgambō of Chōboji), 32, 37, 39, 52, 54

Jōgamō (of Miwa), 81ff.

Jōgambō (of Takedani), 118

jōgyō sammai (perpetually-moving *samādhi*), 142

Jōhen (1166-1224), 192

Jōjitsuron (The Completion of Truth), 8, 165

Jōjitsu sect, 8

Jōkai (1075-1149), n59, Appendix C

Jōkei (Gedatsubō, 1155-1213), 2, 9, 65, 75, 84, 130, 246, 257, n194, n208, n297, n353

Jōken, 248

jōken, 333, 334

Jōkyū Disturbance, xx, 5, 36, 46, 84, 85, 106, 235

jorō ("old man's helper"), 104

jōsai. See fast, post-noon.

Jōshinkaikambō (Rules to Purify Mind and Maintain Insight), 151, n82, n235

Jōshōkyō (Sutra of the Bodhisattva Maitreya's Birth in the Tuṣita Heaven), 117

Jōshun, 31

Jōtōmon'in (Shōshi, 988-1074), 236

Journal of a Trip to the Eastern Barrier. See *Tōkan kikō.*

Jōyuishikiron (completion of Mere Ideation), 87, 97, n173

jūaku, 334

Jufukuji, xx, 14, 15, 16, 17, 23, 24, 26, 184, 242, 263, 264

Jugemu (rakugo), 66, n325

jukkai (personal grievance), 163, 216, n248

Jūnembō, 175

Jun'ichibō. See Muō.

Juringyō (Sūtra of Ten Cakras), 111, 120, 194, 195, 249

Jūzenji, 86, 91

Kade-no-kōji, 62, 113

kafuro, 144

Kagetoki. See Kajiwara Kagetoki.

kai (morality), 140, 141, 142, 152

Kaibara Ekiken (1630-1714), 45, n83

Kaidōki (Sea Route Journal), 35, n72

kaji (spiritual integration), 183, 333, n285

Kajiwara Kagesue, xx

Kajiwara Kagetoki (d. 1200), xx, **14, 15**, 230

Kakai no ju (Fire-world Spell), 111

kaku (enlightenment), 125

Kakuban (1095-1143), 248, Appendix C

Kakuchō (960-1034), 252

Kakuhen (ca. 1172-1258), 251

Kakukai (Nanshōbō 1142-1223), 119, 120, n214, Appendix C

Kukuken (1141-1212), 248

Kakuonji, n204

kalpa, 134, n225

Kamadoyama (in Kyūshū), 173

Kama no Kuchi ("Kettle Mouth"), 173

kami (gods), 1, 73, 75, 87, 92, 97, 165, 333, 338, n1

kaminaga ("longhairs"), 73

Kammuryōjukyō (Sutra of Meditation on Amida), 99, 154, 244, 245, n186, n351

Kamo no Chōmei (1153-1216), xx, n72

kan ("insight," meditation), 104; cf. *kannen.*

kana hōgo (vernacular tract), ix, 2, 3, 41, 44, 61, 64 n3

Kanayaki hotoke ("Coin-burned Buddha"), 105, n195

Kanchi, Ajari, 185

Kanchō (Hirosawa no Daisōjō, 918-998), 80

Kanemori (d. 990), 163

Kangen (835-925), 252

Kan'in Kubu, 143

kanjin (mind concentration), 136, 139

Kanjizai-ō, 143

kanjō (abhiṣeka), 110, 118, 211, n46

Kankyō no tomo (Companion for a Solitary Retreat), n200

kannen (meditation), 22, 263

kannō, 164

Kannon, 64, 83, 98, 106, 108, 110, 143, 164, 180, 188, 233, 243, 263

Kannon Sutra (Lotus Sutra, Chapter 25, 108, n199

Kannonji (in Kyushu), 130

Kano, nun, 15, 16, 230

Kanshō (Chōboji abbot), 37, 39

Kanshōji, 248

Kanshun (978-1057), 90

Kantan, n182

Kantō ōgenki (Back and Forth to the Kantō Region), 29ff., n61

Kanyō no roku (Record of Essentials), 25

karma. See *gō.*

Kasagi, 75, 112

Kasai Kiyoshige (13th cen.), 235

Kasuga ryūjin (The Dragon God of Kasuga), 65

Kasuga Shrine, 84, 86, 87, **n163**

Kāśyapa Buddha (Kashō), 75, 255, 257, n143

Kāśyapa (Śākyamuni's disciple), 141, 180

katsuogi (logs), 74
Kazan, Emperor, 247
ke (provisional existence), 336
kechien (establish auspicious relationships), 81, 119, 121
Kegonkyō (Garland Sutra), 9, 104, 140, 196, 215, 261, **n14, n153**
Kegon sect, xix, **9**, 22, 259, 262
Kegongyō zuisho engishō (commentary), n153
keiai no matsuri (Ceremony of Harmonious Relations), 260
Keihōkyō (Chōboji abbot), 52
Keiso (955-1019), 143
kekkai ("binding site"), 32, n66
Kenchōji, 23, 263, 264, 265
Kenjō (d. 1295), n204
Kenninji, 15, 23, 26, 230, 262, 263, n335
Kenryō, xxii, 25, 29, 40, **283ff.**
Kensei (lion), 195
Kenshin (1131-1192), 143, 148, 150, n232
Kenshō, 168
kesa (surplice), 194, 195, 196
Keshiki (nun), 195
ki (expedients), 139
Kigasaki, 36
Kigasaki ryakuengi (Short History of Kigasaki), xvii, 37, 284
Kikyō, Mount, 54
kiku (mythical snake), 160
Kimpusenji, 245, n159
Ki no Tsurayuki (884-926), 162, n244
Kin'yōshū (Collection of Golden Leaves), 178
[*Daijō*] *Kishinron* (Awakening of Faith [in the Mahāyāna]), 25, n365
Kissa Yōjōki (Drink Tea and Prolong Life), 30, n63
Kitayu, 29
Kiyomizu Temple, 108, 164, 189, 239
Kōben. See Myōe.
Kōbō Daishi. See Kūkai.
Kodaijin, 165, 166
Kōfukuji (temple), 8, 21, 146, 217, 218, 236, 258
Kōfukuji sōjō (Kōfukuji Petition), n192
Kogoshūi (Gleanings from Ancient Stories), n127

Koikawa Harumachi (1744-1789), n182
Kōjakubō, 241
Kojiki (Record of Ancient Matters), 164, n131
koka (seal of approval), 25˙
Kōkambō, 169
Kokan Shiren (1278-1346), xxi
Kokawa Temple, 171
Kōkei (977-1049), n45
Kōken (Hongakubō, 1110-1193), 76ff.
Kokinshū (Collection of Ancient and Modern Times), 161, 178, n92
Kokonchomonjū (Things Heard from Past and Present), xxi
Koluanten. See Kudokuten.
Komachi. See Ono no Komachi.
komō (illusion), 259
Kōmyō, Empress (702-760), 151
Kōmyō shingon (Mantra of Light), 110, 118, n195
Konbeiron. See *Chin Pei Lun.*
Kongōbuji, xix
Kongōchōgyō (Diamond Head Sutra), 143
kongōkai. See *mandala/mandara.*
Kongōkyō (Diamond Sutra), 20, 125, 246, n105
Konjaku monogatari (Tales of Times Now Past), 42, 66, n77, n305
Konsenshū (Collection of Golden Extracts), 354
koritaki ("incense burners"), 73
Koshikibu Naishi (d. 1025), 166, 178
Kōshin, n224
Kōshōji, 67 (Fig. 4), 285
Kōsokuji (in Kamakura), n195
Kotoku no kuden (Oral Instructions of the Ancient Sages), 143
kotsujiki hōshi (beggar-monks), 263, 277, 279, n376
Kōzen gokokuron (Propagation of Zen for the Protection of the Country), 263
Kōya, Mount, xix, 21, 40, 77, 83, 118, 119, 133, 252, 254, 255
Kōzanji, n223
ku (Emptiness), 96, 97, 142, 150, 156, **333**, 336
Kudokuten and Kokuanten, 28, 215, **n58**

K'uei Chi (Kiki, 632-682), 97, n183
Kuei-feng Tsung-mi (Keihō Shūmitsu, 780-841), 135, 140, 141, 265
Kūen, 52
Kūge, 285
Kūgeshū (Empty Flower Collection), n36
kugō, 337
kugurugutsu, 225
Kujō Michiie. See Fujiwara Michiie.
Kūkai (Kōbō Daishi, 774-835), 8, 21, 22, 80, 91, 120, 143, 164, 179, 182, 190, 196, 255, 262, 335, n23, n276
Kukai's Collected Works of Prose and Poetry. See Shōryōshū.
kūken, 334
Kukkutārāma, 228
Kumano, 169, 226, n179
Kumārajīva (Kumarajū, 344-413(, xix, 144, 194
Kumārāyana (Kumaraen), 143
K'ung-tzu Chia-yü (Sayings of the Confucian School), 132, 151
Kurama, monk of, 114
Kuro (Black) Jizō, n204
Kusaladhamma (Zembō (Bikku), 128
Kusha sect, 8, 22, 155
Kusharon (Treasury of Analyses of the Law), 8, n1, n12, n32
Kusharon jujo (Commentary on the Treasury of Analyses of the Law), 20, n32
kutsuchi. See epilepsy.
Kuwana, 67
Kyōbutsubō, 255
kyōgen (farce), 65
kyōgen kigo (or kigyō), 43, 47, 60, 62, 66, 68, 71, 162, 163, 165, 178, 266, 334, n86
Kyōgoku Tamekane, xxi
Kyōgetsubō, 161
Kyōgyōshinshō (Teaching, Practice, Faith, Attainment), xx
Kyōritsu isō (Marvels from the Sutras and the Vinaya), n215, n318, n336

Lan-chi Tao-lung (Rankei Dōryū, 1213-1278), 23, 26, 263, 265, n368
Lankāvatāra Sutra. See Nyūryōgakyō.

Lao Tzu (Rōshi), 15, 75, 215, 233, 244, 246, 259, 265
Lao Tzu. See Tao Te Ching.
Larger Pure Land Sutra. See Muryōjukyō.
Later Collection. See Gosenshū.
Later Collection Continued. See Shokugosenshū.
Later Collection of Gleanings. See Goshūishū.
Latter days. See mappō.
Law Body (dharmakāya). See hosshin.
lawsuit, 125
learning (tamon)
Lin-chi school of Ch'an. See Rinzai.
linked verse. See renga.
Lotus Meditation Sutra. See Hokke sammaikyō.
Lotus Sutra. See Myōhōrengekyō.
Legends of the Nembutsu and the Power of the Gods. See Nembutsu jinriki den.
liver, 160
Lotus Sect (Nichiren's Hokkeshū), 2
Luy-yü (Rongo). See analects.
Machi no Tsubone, 105
Lü shih (regulated verse), n327

Mādhyamike (Chūgan-ha), 8
Mahāvairocana (Dainichi Nyorai), 59, 73, 74, 75, 77, 79, 111, 116, 180, 183, 335, n129, n132
Mahāyāna (Daijō; Greater Vehicle), 8, 9, 23, 48, 58, 60, 61, 99, 100, 103, 118, 123, 130, 140, 141, 142, 165, 265
Maka shikan (Great Cessation and Insight), 7, 20, 24, 79, 103, 140, 152, 165, 190, 9, n33
Maitreya (Miroku), i, 64, 81, 86, 111, 112, 117, 140, 189, n208
maki (evil spirit), 212. See also Tengu.
Makurakotoba (pillow word), n123
Mallikā (matsuri), Lady, 61
Māṇava (Jūdo), 75, 132, n143
Maṇḍala (mandara)
In general, 8, 117, 118, 165, 334, n129, n361

Diamond (*kongōkai; vajradhātu*), 74, 335

Four-enclosure (*shijū*), 74, 78, 79, 335 **n133**

Matrix (*taizōkai; garbhakośadhātu*), 74, 335

Sesshu fusha mandara (Maṇḍala Embracing All and Forsaking None), 102, 335, **n192**

Mangen Shiban (1626-1710), n91

Mañjuśrī (Monju), 108, 172, 180

Mansei (ca. 720), 162, n246

mantra (*shingon*), 8

Mantra of Light. See *Kōmyō shingon.*

Mantokuji, 51

Man'yōshū (Collection of Ten Thousand Leaves), 169, 170, n246

manzaigaku, 43. See also Owari Manzai.

mappō (Decline of the Law; Latter Days), xix, 1, 17, 22, 52, 83, 91, 108, 117, 118, 124, 133, 144, 189, 194, 234, 235, 242, 251, 252, 262, 265, **335, 337, n1**, n222, n333

Mappō tōmyōki (Record of the Lamp during the Latter Days), n1

Māra (Mara), 73, 265, n125

married clergy, 40, 131, 145, 146

Masakado (d. 940), 144

Masako, 15

Ma-tsu (Baso, 707-786), 129, 140

Matsura, 94

Maudgalyāyana (Mokuren), 232, n312

The Meanings of Sound, Word, and Reality. See *Shōji jissō gi.*

meditation. See *endon, kannen, shikan, zazen, zenjō.*

Memorial Presenting a List of Newly Imported Sūtras and Other Items. See *Shōrai mokuroku.*

Mettākumārī (Jidō), 265

Mibu no Tadami (fl. ca. 960), 171

Michiie. See Fujiwara Michiie.

michiura (street divination), 244

Michizane. See Sugawara Michizane.

Midarebashi (in Kamakura), 107

Middle Way, 62, 334

Miidera (Onjōji), 7, 16, 22, 77, 87, 143, 155, 158, 161, 167, 251, n174

mikkyō, 335. See esotericism.

Mimbu, Ajari, 190

Mimuraji, 29, 30

Minamoto family:
Kintada (889-948), n244
Sanetomo (1192-1219), 15, 178, 242, 263, n274
Yoritomo (1147-1199), xx, 14, 15, 127, 231, 235, 246, 277
Yoshitsune (1159-1189), xx, 14

Minomushi Sanjin, n379

Min Tsu-ch'ien (Bin Shiken), 131

Miraculous Stories from the Japanese Buddhist Tradition. See *Nihon ryōiki.*

Miraculous Tales of the Bodhisattva Jizō. See *Jizō bosatsu reigenki.*

Miroku. See Maitreya.

mirror, 197, 260

Mirror (Mirror for Women). See abbreviations, *Tsuma kagami.*

Mirror for Women. See *Tsuma kagami.*

Mirror of the East. See *Azuma kagami.*

Mirror of Sectarian Differences. See *Sugyōroku.*

Miscellany of Ignorant Views. See *Gukanshō.*

misshū

mitsugon kezō, 117

mitsugonkoku, 74

Miya, 35, 67

Miyasu, Princess, 35

mizagaki, 74

Mizuoinnengyō (Extraordinary Operations of Cause and Effect), n343

mochi (rice cakes), 138

Mokuren. See Maudgalyāyana.

Momooji (later Chōboji), xx, 29, **36**, 37, 39, 54, n339

Momu, 197

monchū (trial by confrontation), 147

Mongol invasions (Mōko Shūrai, 1274, 1281), xxi, 5, 42

monkeys, 160, 182, 275, n374

moral causality. See *gō* (karma).

morality, **62**, 93, 140

Moriyama, 30

Moroie no Ben, 130

Motomasa (1214-1267), 174

Mountain Hut Collection. See *Sankashū.*

Muchu mondō (Dialogue in a Dream), 66, n118

Mūdra, 8, 211, n102

muga (anātman, selflessness), 60, 61 157, 182, 227, 332, 334, 335, 336

mogon (no-words), 260; see also *mushin, musō munen*, ineffability.

mujō (impermanence), 60, 334, 335

Mujin Dōshō (Mujū's disciple), 41, 51

mujū. See "non-abiding."

Mujū Ichien (Dōgyō; Daien Kokushi, 1226-1312). Birth xx, 13; beriberi, xxi, 17, 26, 40, 42, 47; death, xxi, 51, 55; discipline, monastic 17; doctrinal affiliations, Appendix B; Kajiwara family, 14, 15, 16; at Chōboji (see separate entry), with Enni, 24, 25, 26, 27; humor, 46; last years, 50, 51; at Momooji, 54-55; statue, 54, 55, n97, Frontispiece; *sake*, 47-48; syncretism, 16, 59; and women, 45-46: worldview, 57ff.

Mujū Kokushi dōshakukō (Religious Traces of National Teacher Mujū). See *Dōshakukō*; abbreviations.

Mujū Kokushi ryakuengi (Biographical Sketch of National Teacher Mujū). See *Ryakuengi*; abbreviations.

mukaekō. See Amida's Welcome Service.

Mukan Fumon (1212-1291), 33

munen. See *musō munen*.

Muō (jun'ichibō), xxi, 27, 37, 46, 52

Murakami, Emperor (926-967), 80, 163

Murasaki Shikibu (d. ?1014), xix, 63, 267, 334

Mūrdhaja (Chōshō-ō), 251

Muryōju (= Amida), 142, 143, n211

Muryōjukyō (Amitāyus Sutra; The "Larger Pure Land Sūtra"), 99, 333, n186

Muryōju nyorai kompon darani (The Basic Spell of the Tathāgata Everlasting Life); also called *Amida no daiju* (Great Spell of Amida), 220, n322

mushin ("comic" linked verse), n272. See also no-mind.

musō munen (formless and ineffable), 116, 194, 265

Musō no koto (Record of a Dream), 32, 37, Fig. 2

Musō Sōseki (1275-1351), 66

Mutsura, 94

Myōan Eisai. See Eisai.

Myōe (Kōben, 1173-1232), xix, 2, 9, 22, 65, 84, 133 ff, 150, 257, n14, n162, n209, n221

Myōhen (Rengedani Sōzu, 1142-1224), 77, 79, 248, 255

Myōhōrengekyō (Lotus Sutra), xi, xix, 6, 7, 19, 20, 37, 38, 39, 43, 100, 101, 102, 104, 114, 133, 143, 144, 150, 153, 178, 186, 188, 233, 234, 247, 248, 259, 260, n4, n92, n172, n226, n287, n291, n364, n377

myōri (fame and profit), 130, 135, 194, 256, 262

Myōsen, 261

Myōzen (1184-1225), 27, Appendix B, 151

Mystery of Jizō and Fudō. See *Chifu no ketsu*.

mystic boundaries. See *kekkai*.

Nāgārjuna (Ryūju), 8, 190, 216, n43

Nagoya, 35, 37, 67. See Miya.

Nakanuma no Awaji no Kami, 190

Nakashima (in Owari), 195

Nanda (Nanda), 217

Nan-shan. See Tao-hsüan.

Nanshōbō, 119

Nan-yüeh (Nangaku Eshi, 515-577), 152

Nanzenji, 31

Nara Sects. See Six Nara Sects.

Narrow Road Through the Provinces. See *Oku no hosomichi*.

nehan. See Nirvāna.

nehan jakujō, 335

nehanko, 32

nembutsu, 19, 22, 23, 59, 98, 99, 102, 105, 115, 118, 142, 143, 146, 148, 175, 187, 188, 190, 196, 202, 244, 247, 254, 261, 262, 263, 336, n233

Nembutsu jinriki den (Legends of the Nembutsu and the Power of the Gods), 285, n382
nenge mishō, 141
Net of Brahma Sutra. See *Bommōkyō*.
New Collection of Ancient and Modern Times. See *Shinkokinshū*.
New Collection of Gleanings. See *Shinshūishū*.
Nichira, 180
Nichiren (1222-1282), xxi, 2, 7, 18, 19
Nichizō Shōnin (d. 985), 229
nightingale, princess acting like a, 223
Nihon ryōiki (Miraculous Stories from the Japanese Buddhist Tradition), n276
Nihon shoki (or *Nihongi*; Chronicles of Japan), xix, 164, n1, n251
Nijō no In no Sanuki, 90
Nikaidō (in Kamakura), 112
Nimmyō, Emperor (810-850), 178
ningen, 336
Ninnōkyō (Benevolent Kings Sutra), n238
Ninshō (1217-1303), 29, n60
Nirvāṇa, 57, 58, 61, 96, 182, 260, 334, **336**
Nirvana Sutra. See *Daihatsunehangyō*.
nitai, **336**. See Two Truths.
Nitta Yoshisada (1301-1338), xxii
Nobunaga (1534-1582), 6, 283
"non-abiding" (*mujū*), 20
no-mind (*mushin*), 157, 260
Nōsetsubō, 193
novices
nozuchi ("field-hammer" viper), **153**, n242
nuns, 98, 147, 193, 207, 219, 223, 230
Nyomu, 229
Nyūryōgakyō (Lankāvatāra Sutra), 259

Obasute theme, 131
Ōe no Takachika (d. 1046), 166
Ōe Sadamoto (Jakashō, 962-1034), 130, 168
ōjin (Transformation Body), 110, 116, 163, 336, **337**
ōjō (birth in a Pure Land), **59**, 61, 101, 149, 244, 255, 333, **336**

ōjōkō (Expounding-on-Birth-in-the-Pure-Land), 148
Ōjōronchū (Commentary on the Treatise on the Pure Land), 117, 244
Ōjōraisange (Praise of Birth in the Pure Land), 190, n297
Ōjōyōshū (Essentials of Salvation), xix, 7, 150, 244, 266, **n8**
Oku no hosomichi (Narrow Road Through the Provinces), n16
Oku no In (on Mt. Kōya), 120
Omoiyorazu, 143
omoshiroshi, 73
Onikurō, 224
Onna daigaku (Greater Learning for Women), 45, n83
Ono no Komachi, 170
Oraga haru (Year of My Life), 66, n358
Oral Instructions of the Ancient Sages. See *Kotoku no kuden*.
ordination platforms, 130
Original Ground/Manifest Trace. See *honji suijaku*.
otogizōshi, 65
Owari Manzai, 43, 226 (figure), n78
Owari meisho zue (Illustrated Gazetteer of Owari Province), 270-271, (Fig. 6)
ox, 210, 257

paradox, 13-15, 19, 28-29, 61, 64, 121ff., 125ff., 132, 137, 143, 156, 215
Pei Sou (Hokusō), 28, 215, n57
Perfection of Wisdom in 25,000 Lines. See Daibongyō.
periods of the Law. See *senji*.
Perry, Commodore, 4
pestle, 158
pheasant, 204, 206
"Philosopher," 224-225
Platform Sutra of the Sixth Patriarch. See *Rokuso dangyō*.
Po Chü-i (Hakukyoi; Hakurakuten, 772-846), 62, 96, 137, 140, 151, 156, 216, 227, 247, 334, n86
poetry, 62. See also Way of Poetry.
pollution, ritual, 74, 75, 82, 83

Polo, Marco (ca. 1254–1324), 42
pot, 94
poverty, 212, 213, 251
Po Yang (Hakuyō), 218
Praise of Birth in the Pure Land.
See *Ōjōraisange.*
pratyekabuddha (*engaku*), 58, 261
Precious Key to the Sacred Treasury.
See *Hizō hōyaku.*
pre-death rite. See *gyakushu.*
preta, 58
Profound Meaning of the Lotus. See
Fa-hua hsüan-i.
*Propagation of Zen for the Protection
of the Country.* See *Kōzen goko-
kuron.*
Pure Land sect. See Jōdo.
Pure Land Buddhism, 19, 97, 101,
118, 190, 199 **244–245**, 331. See
also Ji, Jōdo, Jōdo Shinshū sects.

*Questions and Answers on the Sylla-
bary.* See *Iroha momben.*

Raikō, 22, 61
rakugo, 66 n325, n326
Rankei. See Lan-chi.
Record of Ancient Matters. See
Kojiki.
Record of a Dream. See *Musō no koto.*
Record of Essentials. See *Kanyō no
roku.*
*Record of the Lamp during the Latter
Days.* See *Mappō tōmyōki.*
recluse. See *tonsei.*
relics, 103
Relic Venerating Ceremony. See
sharikō.
relationships, spiritual. See *kechien.*
renga (linked verse), 63, 65, **171**,
199
Rengeji, 47, **48–49**, 51, 67, N91
repentance meetings. See *fusatsu.*
rice-jelly (*ame*), 222
Rigunshi, 89
rinne, 58, 334, 336
Rinzai (Lin-chi) school, xx, 22, 24
Ritsu (Disciplinary) sect, **9**, 16, 17,
22, 23, 130, 131, 151, 262, 263
ritsugaku (study of the vinaya), 21

Rōben (689–773), 179
Rōen. 31, **32**. See also Dōen.
Rokkakudō (Hexagonal Hall), 187,
n289
rokudō, 58, 336
Rokuharamitsukyō (Sutra of the Six
Virtues), 118
rokushu, 58, 336
Rokuso dangyō (Platform Sutra of the
Sixth Patriarch), 27, n53, Fig. 1
rongi (argument), 161
Ronshikibō, 114
rope/snake illustration, 125
*Rules to Purify Mind and Maintain
Insight.* See *Jōshinkaikambō.*
Ryakuengi (Biographical Sketch), xvii,
xxii, 40, 43, 55, **284–85**, n378
Ryōgaku, 284
Ryōin. See Daiembō.
Ryōjusen, **37**
Ryūsenji, 107, 108
Ryūson, 166

Saburō, Father, 208
Saddharmapundarīka. See *Myōhōren-
kyō.*
Saemon jo Jō, 184
Saichō (Dengyō Daishi, 767–822), xix,
6, 17, 22, 262, n229
Saidaiji, 21, 29, 31, 32, 37, 245
Saigyō (1118–1190), 20, 163, 166, 169,
170, 178, n248, n249
Saigyoku, Ajari, 227
Saihōji, 41, 51
Saijarin (Smashing the Bad Vehicle),
n162
Saion, priest, 178
Saionji Kinsuke (1223–1267), 224, 241
Sakuradō (Cherry Hall), 174
Śākyamuni (Gautama), xix, 1, 17, 18,
85, 86, 89, 111, 112, 119, 124,
125, 128, 133, 154, 192, 195, 217,
218, 247, 257, 267, n143; dating
n330
salt, 258
salt-vendor, 157
Samantabhadra (Fugen), 80, n154
sambōin, 335, 337
Sambōin school, 29, (Appendix C)
Samegai, 30

Samoaruran, 143
Samgharakkhita (Sōgo Bikku), 257
sammitsu. See Three Mysteries.
san'akushu. See Three Evil Destinies.
S&P (Sand and Pebbles). See abbreviations.
Sand and Pebbles. See *Shasekishū.*
sandoku, 337. See Three Poisons.
sangō, 335, 337. See Three Actions.
Sanikubō, 114
sanji, 118, 337
Sankashū (Mountain Hut Collection), 178
Sannin hōshi (Three Priests), 65, n355
Sannō Gongen, 90, n170, n176
Sanron (Three Treatise) school, 8, 22, 139, 140, 259, 260, 262
sanshin, 337
sanzendō, 336
Sanzengi (The Many Good Principles Expressed in the Meditation Sutra), 100, n350
sanzō. See Three Baskets.
Śāriputra (Sharihotsu), 89, 217, 232
Sravāstivādin school (Setsu-issaiu-bu), 8
Sasamegoto (Whisperings), xxii, 65, 127, n18, n116, n117
satori, 96

Sayings of the Confucian School. See *K'ung-tzu Chia Yü.*
scholasticism, sterile, 22, 152, 153, 154, 161, 263

Sea Route Journal. See *Kaidōki.*
seijō (legal documents), n302
Seikaku. See Shōgaku.
Seiryōji, 144, 192
Seishi, 188
Seizan branch (Jōdo sect), 118
sekensha (worldling), 153
Sekkei Keikyō, 284
selflessness. See *muga.*
Seng-chao (Sōjō, 374-414), 144
Seng-jui (Sōei, 378-444?), 144
Senjakushū (Collection of Passages), 118
Senju darani (Spell of the Thousand-Armed), 214, n315
senju nembutsu, 331, **336**

Senzaishū (Collection of a Thousand Years), 163
seshubun (donor eulogy), 230
Sesshu fusha mandara. See *mandala.*
setsuwa bungaku (tale literature), ix, 3, 41, 42, 47, 65, n3
Seven Great Temples (Nara), 21, 276
shabadō (human world), 188
shakkyōka (Poems on the Teachings of Śākyamuni), 7, n257
shakujō (staff), 111
Shakamakaenron (Explanation of Mahāyāna), 17, n23
shakumon, 333
Shan-tao (Zendō, 613-681), 100, 118, 124, 142, 190, 216, 257, n188
shariko (Relic Venerating Ceremony), 32, 217
Sharisanden (Hymn in Praise of Relics), 120
Shasekishū (Collection of Sand and Pebbles), ix, xvii, xxi, 3, 24, 25, 26, 28, **40ff.**, 62; abbreviated and unabbreviated texts 41, 43-44, 64, 66; associated techniques 63-64; chapter contents 64-65; colophon 3; influence 65ff.; modern texts 66, 343-344; name 72.
Shasekishū Nukigaki (Extracts from Sand and Pebbles), 354
Shen-hsui (Jinshū, 605?-706), 27
shi (stopping delusion; "cessation"), 104; cf. *kannen, shikan.*
Schichibutsu tsūkai ge (Verse of Admonition Handed Down by the Seven Buddhas), 142, 156, n296
Shiban. See Mangen Shiban.
Shiembō. See Eizon.
shigaku, 96, 260. See *hongaku.*
Shigetada. See Yamada Shigetada.
Shih Chi (Historical Records), 131
Shih-shuang Ch'u-yüan (Sekisō Soen, 986-1040), 233, n337
Shih-shuo Hsin-yü (Sesetsu shingo; New Specimens of Contemporary Talk), n295
Shih-te (Jittoku), 240, 257
shijū mandara. See *mandala.*
shikan (meditation), 151, 251

Shikashū (Collection of Verbal Flowers, 166, 167, 168
shikigo (notations), 51
Shikishima (servant), 166
shiki soku ze kū, 336
shikizō ("store consciousness"), 25
Shikubu (monk), 153
shimbutsu bunri, 67, n121
shimutsu shūgō, 333, 337
shin (anger), 337
Shinchibō, 251
shindai moji (writing system, 285
Shin'en (1153-1224), 217, n38
shingō, 337
Shingon (sect), 8, 22, 23, 29, 59, 81, 110, 117, 118, 120, 165, 190, 211, 259, 262, 331
shingon (*mantra*), 179, 214, 337
Shingon Ritsu. See Esoteric Disciplinary sect.
Shinji hifumi den (Japanese Writing in the Divine Script), 285
Shinjikangyō (Sutra on Viewing the Mind-Ground), 86, 103, 126, 194, 195, 245, n171
shinjin (True Body), 110, 116; cf. *hosshin*.
Shinkan, 129
Shinkei (1406-1475), xxii, 65-66
Shinkō, 168
Shinkokinshū (Collection of Ancient and Modern Times Continued), xx, 165, 171, 178, n175, n257, n305
Shinkū (Eshinbō, 1205-1269), 255
shinnyo (the Real, Suchness), 78, 258
Shinra Myōjin, 88, 153, n174
Shinran (1173-1262), xx, 7, 18, 23, 33, n289
Shinshūishū (New Collection of Gleanings), 178
shintai, 336, 338. See also Two Truths.
Shintō, 28, 38, 59, 60, 62, 67, 77, 84, 87, 93, 98, 151
shintō (Body Lamp Ritual), 279, **n377**
Shintōshū (Collection of the Way of the Gods), 65, n112, n113
Shinzei (Fujiwara Michinori, d. 1160), 104, 248, **n194**, n354
Shirakawa, Emperor (1053-1129), 239

shiryō fumbetsu, 259. See also *fumbetsu*.
Shisainashi, 143
Shitennōji (temple), 21
Shōbō (832-909), 252
shōbō, 118, 228, **337**
shōbōgenzō (eye of the True Dharma), 141, 180
Shōbōnenshokyō (Sutra of Meditation on the True Law), 194, 202, n328
shōdō, 142, **333**
Shōdōka (Song of Enlightenment), 156
Shōfukuji, 15, 23, 263
Shōen, 85
Shōgaku (or Seikaku, 1167-1235), 65, 188, 189, 192, 248
Shōgatsubō (also Shogetsubō; Keishō, d. 1268), 151, 251, 257
Shōgombō (Gyōyū, 1163-1241), 242
shogyō mujō, 335
Shōhen, 32
shohō muga, 332, 335
Shōichi, **243, 265**. See Enni Ben'en.
Shōichiha, 9, 22
shoji (birth-and-death), 58, 61, 72, 73, 75, 76, 86, 87, 96, 99,104, 123, 135, 182, 254, 256, 258
Shōji jissō gi (The Meanings of Sound, Word, and Reality), n252
shōjō. See Hīnayāna.
Shōkai, 29, 32
Shōkambō, 221
shōki ("bearing spirit"), 74
Shokukokinshū (Collection of Ancient and Modern Times Continued), n165
Shokugosenshū (Later Collection Continued), 163, n248, n260, n281
Shokusenzaishū (Collection of a Thousand Years Continued), 178
Shokushikashū (Collection of Verbal Flowers Continued), 166
Shokushūishū (Collection of Gleanings Continued), 162, N247
Shōkyū War. See Jōkyū War.
shōmon. See *śrāvaka*.
Shōmu, Emperor (701-756), 9, 130, 180
shōmyō nembutsu, 336
Shō no Iwaya, 229

Shorai mokuroku (Memorial Presenting a List of Newly Imported Sutras and Other *Items*, n10, n104

Shōrembō (of Owari), 83

Shorembō (of Kawachi), 103

Shōryakuji, 217, n38, n319

Shōryōshū (or *Seireishū*; The Collected Works of Prose and Poetry of Kūkai), 118, 190, n276

Shōshin (1005–1085), 252

Shōshin (12th cen.), 91

Shōtoku, Prince (573–621), xix, 21, 48, 61, 103, 108, 180, 263, 285, n88, n289

Shōtoku Taishi denryaku (Biographical Account of Prince Shōtoku; cf., *Heishi ga taishi den*), 180

Shōzaishū (Collection of Sacred Assets), xxi, 3, 44

Shōzan (939–1011), 111

Shōzan (of Chōboji), 284

Shozenjutenshishomongyō, 120

shōzōmatsu. See *sanji*.

shu. See *shingon*.

Shu Ching (Classic of Documents), 128

shūin shūka, 217, 218

Shūishū (Collection of Gleanings), 162, 163, 168, 171, 180, n244, n246

Shunjōbō. See Chōgen.

shura, 336

Shuryōgonkyō (Śūrangama Sūtra; Sutra of Heroic Deed), 108, 125, 136, 165, 257, 260, n278, n360

shussesha (world-transcender), 153

Śīlabhadra (Kaiken), 123, 233

Śīlāditya, King, 123

Six Nara sects, 8–9, 22, 332

Six Paths (Destinies), 86, 332, 336; see also Three Evil Destinies.

Śīlāditya (Kainichi Daiō), n219

Sketch. See *Ryakuengi*; also, abbreviations.

Skillful Means (*hōben*), ix, 6, 9, 18, 19, 20, 22, 23, 24, 40, 59, 60, 67, 68, 71, 75, 77, 78, 81, 85, 86, 91, 92, 95, 101, 110, 116, 132, 138–39, 142, 178, 179, 180, 260, 262, 265, 279, 332–333, 335

snake, serpent, 119, 120, 200, 201, 211, 214, 228, 232

Sochi Sōzu, 110

Soften the Light and Identify with the Dust (*wakō dōjin*), 71, 75, 76, 79, 80, 81, 83, 85ff., 91, 92, 94, 95, 267, 338, n124

Sōfutsuzan Rengeji, 49

sōhei (monk-soldiers; *ukusō*), 248

sōji (dhāraṇī), n250

sokushin jōbutsu (attain Buddhahood in the Very Existence), 59, 79, 335, 337, n148, n151

somegami ("colored paper"), 73

sōmoku jōbutsu (The Grasses and Trees Attain Buddhahood), 129

Song of Enlightenment. See *Shōdōka*.

Sonshō darani (Holy and Virtuous Spell), 210, 211, n311

Sōshumbō, 246

sotoba, 185

Spell of Compassionate Help. See *Jiku no shu*.

Spell of the Thousand-Armed. See *senju darani*.

Śrāvaka (*shōmon*), 58, 261

Śubhākarashiṃha (Zemmui, 637–735), 262

Sthiramati (An'e), 123

straw, 276

Sugawara Michizane (845–903), 171, 229

sugoroku (backgammon), 195

Sugyōroku (Mirror of Sectarian Differences), 23–24, 25, 141, 156, n41, n303

suijaku. See *honji suijaku*.

Sukeko, 46, 52, 54, n93

Sumiyoshi deity, 166

śūnyatā. See *kū*.

Śūrangama Sūtra. See *Shuryōgonkyō*.

surplice. See *kesa*.

Susa-no-o, 35, 73, 163, 285, n71, n251, n146

SuShih (Tōba Koji, 1036–1101), 259

Sutoku, Emperor (1119–1164), 178

sutra chanter (*jigyōja*), 102

Sutra of Meditation on Amida Buddha. See *Kammuryōjukyō*.

Sutra of Meditation on the True Law.
See *Shōbōnenshokyō.*
*Sutra of the Bodhisattva Maitreya's
Birth in the Tuṣita Heaven.* See
Jōshōkyō.
*Sutra of Neither Increase Nor De-
crease.* See *Fuzōfugengyō.*
Sutra of Perfect Enlightenment. See
Engakukyō.
Sutra of the Six Virtues. See
Rokuharamitsukyō.
Sutra of Ten Cakras. See *Jūringyō.*
Sutra on Viewing the Mind-Ground.
See *Shinjikangyō.*
*Sutra to Resolve Doubts About the
Imitative Law.* See *Zōbōketsugikyō.*
Suwa, 92
sweetfish, 276

T. (*Taishō shinshū daizōkyō*). See
xi, xvii.
tabus against childbirth and death,
74, 75, 83, 84, n139
tabu words (*imikotoba*), 73, n126
Ta-chu (Daiju, 8th cen.), 129
Tachibana Narisue, xxi
Tachibanadera, 21
Tachibana no Uji (Lady Orange Blos-
som), 188, n292
Tachikawa Sect, 194
tachisukumi ("The Cramped-Legged
One"), 73
tai (substance), 78, 259
Taihōbō, 261
Taikenmon'in, 165
Tainin (1705-1786), 16, 20, 21, 48,
51, **283ff.**, n381
Taira Kanemori (d. 990), 171
Tai Yüan (Taien), 189
taizōkai. See maṇḍala.
Tajikara-no-o, 73
Takakura, Emperor (1161-1181), 192
Takaoka, Prince (799-845), 229, n332
Takataki, 94
tale literature. See *setsuwa bungaku.*
Tale of Genji. See *Genji monagatari.*
Tale of the Heike. See *Heike mono-
gatari.*
Tales Gleaned at Uji. See *Ujishūi
monogatari.*

Tales of Times Now Past. See
Konjaku monogatari.
Tales to Illustrate Ten Maxims.
See *Jikkinshō.*
tamagaki, 74
tamon (learning; vs. *chie,* wisdom),
128, **154,** 257
Tanabata festival, 167
Tani no gōgyō (Valley School's Dual
Ritual, 25, n45
T'an-luan (Donran, 476-542), 117, 244
Tao-hsüan (Dōsen, 596-667), 45,
141, 151, 195, 249, 258, n82, n235
Taoism, 28, 57, 93
Tao-jung (Dōyū 4-5th cen.), 144
Tao-lin (Dōrin, 741-824), 156
Tao Te Ching (The Way and its
Power), 28, 77, 127, 151, 165,
179, 186, 215, 233, 245, 246, 259,
265, 338, n17, **n54**
tariki, 244, **333, 338**
taro stalks (*imo no kuki*), 185
tea, 30, n223
Teaching, Practice, Faith, Attainment.
See *Kyōgyōshinshō.*
teeth, 229
tei (the character), 264
Tendai sect, **6, 7,** 17, 22, 23, 58,
63, 129, 139, 151, 252, 259, n175;
opposition to new sects 6-7
tengu (goblins), 86, 211, **212,** n169
Ten Major Commandments/Offenses,
31, 48, 74
Tennōji, 120, 224
Tennōji no goshuin engi (Autograph
History of the Tennoji), 48, n88
ten stations of being (*jippōkai*), 58,
77, 158
Teraato, 48
Te-shan Hsüan-chien (Tokusan
Senkan), 135
Tetsugen Dōkō (1630-1682), 66
Tetsugen zenji kanahōgo (Vernacular
Tract by Zen Master Tetsugen)
Theravāda, 332
Things Heard from Past and Present.
See *Kokonchomonjū.*
Thirty Stanzas on Mere Ideation.
See *Yuishiki sanjūju.*

Three Actions (*sangō*), **59**, 80, 335, **337**
Three Baskets (Tripiṭaka, *sanzō*), 120, 141, 332
Three Bodies of the Buddha. See *sanshin.*
"Three En's," 52
Three Evil Destinies (*san'akushu*), **58**, 59, 85, 86, 124, 142, 152, 188, 240, 254, 332. See also Six Paths.
Three Modes of Consciousness, 124–125
Three Mysteries (*sammitsu*), **59**, 80, 120, 335, 337
Three Periods (of the Law). See *sanji.* also *shōbō, zōbō, mappō.*
Three Poisons (*sandoku*), 59, 128, 134, 220, **337**
Three Qualities of Mind (*sanshin*), 101, 244, n189, n349
Three Realms, 96, 97, 123
"Three Priests". See *Sannin hōshi.*
Three Teachings (morality, wisdom, meditation), 134
Three Treasures, 72, 138, 155, 267
Three Truths (Tendai), 142, 157, 336
Ti Huang, 127
time, perspective on, 3, 4, 10
Tō (priest), 175
Toba, Emperor (1103–1156), 104, 165, 169
Tōbō, 130
tochō (curtain opening), 220
Tōdaiji, 8, 21, 83, 130, 147, 169, 179, **180**, 181, 238, 246, n37
Tōfukuji, 9, 22, 24, 25, 26, 243, 265
Tōfukuji kaizan Shōichi Kokushi nempu (Chronological Record of Shōichi Kokushi, Founder of Tōfukuji), 25, n51
Toga-no-o, 133
Tōhyōe, 236
Tōjōji (Hitachi Province), 158
Tōkan Kikō (Journal of a Trip to the Eastern Barrier), 35, n72
Toki Gengo, n379
Tōkoku kōsōden (Eminent Priests of the Eastern Country), n158
Tokusan Senkan. See Te-shan Hsüan-chien.

ton (covetousness), 337
Tonamiyama, n264
Tō no Taneyuki (1194–1273), 171, n260
tonsei (recluse), 16, 21, **134–35**, 179, 220, 243, 245, 246, 247, 251, **255**, n21
Tōriten (Heaven of the Thirty-Three), 120, 242, 252
Tosa no Jishu, 228
Tōshōdaiji, 9
Tosotsuten (Tuṣita Heaven), n130, 74, 117, 189, 265
Tōtsui, 169
travel, 20, 21, n35
Treatise on the Pure Land. See *Jōdoron.* For *Commentary* see *Ōjōronchū.*
Treasury of Analyses of the Law. See *Kusharon.*
Tripiṭaka. See Three Baskets.
True Law (*shōbō*) period of 1; see also *mappō.*
"Truth", religious, 6–7
Tsukamu, 224
Tsukuba, 115
Tsuma kagami (Mirror for Women), xvii, xxi, 3, **44–46**, 50, 59
Tsunemoto, 76
Tsung ching Lu. See *Sugyōroku.*
Tuṣita Heaven. See Tosotsuten.
Two-Part (*ryōbu*) Mandala, 74. See *maṇḍala*, Diamond and Matrix.
Two Truths (*shinzoku no nitai*), 157, 158
Tz'u-en. See K'uei Chi.
Tz'u Ming. See Shih-shuang Ch'u-yüan.

udumbara flower, 124, 133, n172
Udyāna, King (Uden-ō), 143
Ueda Akinari (1734–1809), n275
Ujishūi monogatari (Tales Gleaned at Uji), xx, 42, n375
Uma no Shiro, 184
Upāli (Ubari), 141
Urabon service, 220
Ureshisa, 168
urinating, 221
ushin, n272

Utsonomiya, 92

Vaidehī (Idaike), Queen, 245
Valley School's Dual Ritual. See Tani
    no gōgyō.
Vasubandhu (Tenjin, ca. 320-400),
    8, 125, 244
Vasumitrā (Washumitta), 61
vernacular tract. See kana hōgo.
Verse of Admonition Handed Down by
    the Seven Buddhas. See Shichibutsu
    tsūkai ge.
vestals, eight (yaotome), n137
vicarious suffering (daijuku), 118
Vimalakīrti (Yuima), 136
Vimalakīrti Sūtra. See Yuimakitsukyō.
vinaya (ritsu; discipline), 120, 130,
    141
Virūdhaka (Ruri Taishi), 89
Vītāśoka (Ashuka-ō), 228

Wada Yoshimori (1147-1213), 235
waka, 62-63, 163ff., 164
Wakan rōeishū (Collection of Poetic
    Recitations in Chinese and Japanese),
    n86
Wakasa, Lady, 172
wakō dōjin. 338. See Soften the Light
    and Identify with the Dust.
Walking Stick Forest Vihara, 123
warashibe chōja ("Wealth from a Stalk
    of Straw"), n375
warinashi (apposite), 172, 173, 261
wasan (Japanese hymn), n280
Watarai Yukitada (1236-1305), n126
The Way and Its Power. See Tao
    Te Ching.
Way of Poetry, 63, 66, 161, 163ff.,
    169, 171, 179
Wen, King (186-226), 127
Wei K'uan (Ikan, 755-817?), 140
wet-nurse, 101
Whisperings. See Sasamegoto.
"wild words and specious phrases."
    See kyōgen kigo.
wisdom (chie, as opposed to tamon,
    learning) and compassion (jihi), 60,
    79, 85, 116, 128, 130, 154, 180,
    331, 332
wisteria nodes, 104

Words and Phrases of the Lotus.
    See Fa-hua wen-chü.
women, 45, 46, 130, 146, 151, 192,
    198, 200, 201, 202, 233
woodpecker, 170
worm, 216
Wu-an P'u-ning (Gottan Funei, 1197-
    1276), 264, n369
Wu-chun Shih-fan (Bujun Shiban,
    1177-1249), 22, 24, 264, n39, n370
Wu Tsung, Emperor, 262

Yadadera, n310
Yajñadattā (Ennyadatta), 46, 260, n366
yakigome (parched rice), 221
yakudoshi (unlucky years), n181
Yakushi (Physician Buddha), 37, 64,
    104, 106, 108
Yakushi Gozen, 181
Yakushiji (in Nara), 21
Yakushiji (in Shimotsuke), 130
Yamada family, 5, 31, 46, 49, n93
Yamada Akinaga (1181-1266), 5, 31,
    32, 37, 106ff.
Yamada Jirō. See Yamada Akinaga.
Yamada Shigetada (1165-1221), xx,
    6, 36, 46, 52, 235, n196, Appendix
    D
Yamato monogatari (Tales of Yamato),
    n305
Yamato Takeru, 35, 46, n71
Yanagita Kunio (875-1962), n243, n374
Yang-ch'i transmission, xx, 22
Yang Chieh (Yoketsu, 11th cen.), 142
yaotome (Eight Maidens), 74
Yasumasa (958-1036), 260
Yatarō (boatman), 227
The Year of My Life. See Oraga haru.
Yen Hui (Gankai, 513-482), 75, 156
yin-yang (onyō), 74, n181
yokkai, 58, 336
Yokokura, 106, 108
Yoshida Tsunefusa (1143-1200), 246
Yōmyō. See Yung-ming.
Yoritsune. See Fujiwara Yoritsune.
Yoshiyuki, 174
yū (function), 78, 259
Yüan Ch'i (Genkei), 131
Yugaron (Treatise on Yoga), 87, 154,
    n173

Yuigahama (in Kamakura), 107
Yuikyōgyō (Final Admonition Sutra), 129, 151, 152, 163, 247
Yuimakitsukyō (Vimalakīrti Sūtra), 130, 157, n227
yuishiki (consciousness only), 140
Yuishiki sanjūju (Thirty Stanzas on Mere Ideation), 125
Yuishimbō (of Iwashimizu), 117
Yung-chia (Yōka, 665–713), 156, 258, n48
Yung Chia Chi (Yōkashū), 25, n48
Yung-ming Yen-shou (Yōmyō Enju, 904–975), 24, n42, 143
Yūsuke, 43
Yuzurijō (Deed of Transfer), 27; translation 52–54; Fig. 3.

Zao Gongen, 81
zazen, 22, 25, 182, 263
Zeami (1363–1443), 65, n182
Zekan, 284
Zemmui. See Śubhākarasimha.
Zen sect, 7, 15, 22, 24, 65, 94, 125, 129, 140, 141, 179, 180, 190, 233, 262; Chinese models, 23, 39, 260, 263; syncretism, 22–23

Zen'amidabutsu, 77, 79
zenchishiki (good friends in the faith), 245
zenjō (meditation), 262
zenkiku (meditation ball), 104
Zengenshosenshū (Collected Sayings on Zen Principles), 141
zengon, 116, 119, 244, 337
Zenkōji, 21, 36, 200
Zentōin, 104
Zenzebō, 215
zōbō, 118, 233, 337
Zōbōketsugikyō (Sutra to Resolve Doubts About the Imitative Law), 141, 233, n338
Zōga (917–1003), 244
Zōichiagonkyō (Sutra of Grouped Records), n87
zōjōen (incidental cause), 119
zokutai, 336; See also Two Truths.
Zōsō Rōyo (1193–1276), 17, 26, 264, n22
Zōtanshū (Collection of Casual Digressions), x, xvii, xxi, 3, 13, 25, 47–48, 51, 275–280
Zuijōbō (Tan'e, 13th cen.), 242, 243
zuiki (taro stalks/gratitude), 185